HINTS FOR SELF-CULTURE

HINTS FOR
SELF-CULTURE

BY

HAR DAYAL, M.A., Ph.D.

GYAN

Published by

Gyan Publishing House
5, Ansari Road
Daryaganj, New Delhi-110002
Phone: 011-47034999, 9811692060
E-mail: books@gyanbooks.com

Distribution Network
gyanbooks.com
India, USA, Canada, UK, Australia, France

ISBN : 978-81-212-2101-6 (HB)
First Published, 1934

2nd Impression 2021

Printed at: Gyan Press, Delhi.

Hints for Self-Culture
Author: Har Dayal

HINTS FOR SELF-CULTURE

BY

HAR DAYAL, M.A., Ph.D.

Author of

"THE BODHISATTVA DOCTRINE," *etc.*

LONDON:

WATTS & CO.,

5 & 6 JOHNSON'S COURT, FLEET STREET, E.C.4

TO

SANKTA AGDA

IN TOKEN OF

FRIENDSHIP AND ESTEEM

PREFACE

In this little book, I have tried to indicate and explain some aspects of the message of Rationalism for the young men and women of all countries. If it helps them in their efforts for self-improvement in the least degree, I shall be amply rewarded.

I shall be grateful for criticism and suggestions from fellow-Rationalists.

For the choice of books in English, I may recommend J. M. Robertson's excellent and indispensable book, *Courses of Study*.

HAR DAYAL.

London.
April, 6934 A.H. (1934 A.D.).

TO A YOUNG FELLOW-RATIONALIST

These short hints on Self-Culture are addressed to you in the hope that you will try to make the best use of your life according to the philosophy of Rationalism.

Life is a wonderful privilege. It imposes great duties. It demands the fulfilment of great tasks and the realization of noble ideals. As our revered philosopher-poet Lucretius has taught us, Life is a racial heritage that you receive for use and development, and not as a personal possession. You stand between the past and the future: the world is yours to enjoy, to organize, and to reconstruct. Your lot is cast in these sad times of turmoil and tribulation. Mankind anxiously asks if there is a way out of the gloom and horror of to-day into light and life. It is for you to blaze the trail for great movements that will build up a happier world.

If you wish to develop your personality as a free and cultured citizen, these hints and notes may help you in your struggles and strivings. They are not exhaustive, but only suggestive.

Man's personality needs growth and development in its four different aspects: Intellectual, Physical, Æsthetic, and Ethical. These are the four facets of a complete life. I shall discuss how you may successfully pursue this fourfold Self-Culture, as far as your opportunities permit.

CONTENTS

CHAPTER I

INTELLECTUAL CULTURE

SECTION I. SCIENCE.
II. HISTORY.
III. PSYCHOLOGY.
IV. ECONOMICS.
V. PHILOSOPHY.
VI. SOCIOLOGY.
VII. LANGUAGES.
VIII. COMPARATIVE RELIGION.

CHAPTER I

INTELLECTUAL CULTURE

It is your duty to train and develop your Mind and acquire Knowledge, as much Knowledge as you possibly can obtain. Knowledge is like a deep well, fed by perennial springs, and your Mind is the little bucket that you drop into it: you will get as much as you can assimilate. The Brain, which is the physical organ of the Mind, is one of the two precious products of the æons of Evolution: the other is the imponderable "social instinct." This wonderful Brain, whose every convolution represents millions of years of Time, really distinguishes you from the animals. Many animals have very powerful sense-organs: the eagle, the ant, and the dog have keener senses than Man. But no animal has a more evolved Brain and a higher Intelligence. If you do not develop and use this Brain to the utmost of your power, you are more akin to the beasts than to *Homo sapiens*.

Knowledge and mental self-culture will confer untold blessings upon you. You will not be the victim of superstition and demagogy in religion and politics. You will know your duty and do it. To be wise and independent in your religion and your politics, not to be doped and duped by the selfish priests and the scheming politicians of Capitalism and so-called Socialism: is this not a noble aim worth striving for? Most men and women to-day are not free and wise: they are like kites flown by the priests and politicians who hold the string. They are fleeced and fooled on account of their ignorance of Science, History, Economics, and other subjects. Half the ills of Mankind are due to Ignorance; the other half arise from Egotism. Knowledge is fully as important as Ethics: they are really interdependent. As Lessing says: "The aim of Knowledge is Truth, and Truth is a need of the soul." The Persian poet Saadi exhorts all to acquire Knowledge with unremitting zeal: "Like a taper, one should melt in pursuit of Knowledge. This is thy duty, even if thou hast to travel over the whole earth."

In the never-ending struggle for Knowledge, you should work

regularly and methodically. Devote a certain portion of your time daily to study or experiment. You feed the body several times a day: don't starve the Mind. Keep a diary, in which you should note the titles of new books. Get new and second-hand catalogues from the booksellers. Hunt for cheap second-hand books in the shops. Own a private library, however small. Take pride in the books that adorn your home. With every book you buy, you add a millimetre to your mental stature. Borrow books from the public libraries and from your friends: don't forget to return them punctually. Keep notes and summaries of what you read, otherwise your studies will be like rainfall on a sloping roof. Revise much and refresh your memory frequently; like Macaulay, have all your knowledge instantly available. Know exactly what you know, as you know how much money you have at the bank, and as a housewife knows what she has in the pantry. Make plans for your studies a few years in advance, as the statesmen plan an economic or military campaign. Set apart a fixed proportion of your income for the purchase of books and journals; call it "The Book Fund," and don't draw upon it for any other purpose. Thus you will find it easy to spend money on books. Join scientific and literary societies and study-circles; don't grudge the small subscriptions. It is a good plan to form a small group, in which each member reads a new book and then offers a paper on it, with copious quotations from the original. Such co-operative study is necessary, as your spare time is unfortunately limited. Life itself is short, far too short, for the lover of Knowledge. If you had the gift of immortality like Tithonus, and also unfading youth, then you would surely devote a hundred years to the study of Astronomy, a hundred years to Biology, a hundred years to History, and so on, until you could call yourself a well-educated man or woman. But alas! our life is reckoned in months and years, not in centuries and millennia. We are old before we have discovered that we know very little indeed. Make haste to learn. J. R. Green, the famous historian, wrote: "I know what men will say of me, 'He died learning.'" Let men say the same of you, and it may be, it may be, that you will perhaps get the chance of continuing to learn even after your farewell to this short life. Resolve, like Odysseus,

> "To follow Knowledge, like a sinking star,
> Beyond the utmost bound of human thought."

Perhaps, beyond that utmost bound, is more Knowledge, and more, and more, and more!

There are two obstacles and obstructions to mental self-culture. You should overcome them first.

(1) Many men and women are so money-minded that they do not undertake any serious work that does not pay. They believe that it is foolish to exert themselves for such study and brain-work as cannot be converted into cash. Hard work only for money, and then plenty of play and pleasure: this seems to be their rule of life. They value intellect only as the key to material prosperity, and regard personal mental development as a foolish fad. This miserable materialistic psychology is very deep-rooted in all classes of society. Rich and poor, all suffer from it. An old working-woman complained to me of her son's habit of occasionally buying some cheap books, and said: "He wastes his money on books. What good are they to him? He is a carpenter, not a school-master." We meet many people whose lives are spent in a monotonous see-saw between their trade (whatever it may be) and their frivolous amusements. They may be successful and distinguished in their business or profession, in law, theology, medicine, or art; but they know only golf and chess and mountain-climbing, when they leave their bread-and-butter studies behind them.

To such one-sided, over-worldly people, I would say: "Take heed lest you grasp the shadow and miss the substance. You may coin your Brain into money, but then you are abusing and misusing this rare gift of Nature. Intellect should be employed chiefly as an instrument of growth and social service. It must not be a tool for exploiting your fellow-citizens. If you look upon all brain-work as a money-making device, you are a degraded and pitiable prostitute. Such prostitution is so rampant in our capitalistic world that you take it as a matter of course. You are not repelled by it or astonished at it. Nature has given you a Brain to know, to think, to understand, to reflect, to discover, to invent, and to feel the deep joy that comes to all who fulfil Nature's great law. No words can describe the happiness and beatitude that the pursuit of Knowledge confers on its votaries. The French speak of 'la joie de vivre' (the joy of living); let us enrich their beautiful language with another phrase: 'la joie de savoir' (the joy of knowing). If you shirk the duty of all-round mental development, you rob yourself of ineffable bliss, such bliss as far transcends all that money can buy. Therefore, be not content with living as intellectual dwarfs, bent under the burden of heavy money-bags. Strive rather to grow to your full mental stature, as Nature commands you to do. Be not your own worst enemies. Despoil not yourselves."

(2) Certain false theories and dogmas have diverted millions of men and women from the pursuit of intellectual culture, and persuaded them even to take pride in their ignorance and stupidity. This may seem strange and incredible: but it is only too true.

Some religious teachers have taught that Man is made up of a body and a soul: but they have been silent about the Intellect. Their followers try to feed the body on earth and to save the soul from perdition after death: but they neglect the claims of the Mind. Bread for the body and Virtue for the soul: these are regarded as the indispensable requisites of human welfare here and hereafter. Nothing is said about Knowledge and Education. Thus Jesus Christ spoke much of feeding the hungry, healing the sick, and converting the sinners: but he never taught the duty of teaching the ignorant and increasing scientific knowledge. He himself was not a well-educated man, and intellectual pursuits were beyond his horizon. Gautama Buddha also laid stress on morality, meditation, and monkery, but he did not attach great importance to history, science, art, or literature. St. Ambrose deprecated scientific studies, and wrote: "To discuss the nature and position of the earth does not help us in our hope of the life to come." St. Basil said very frankly and very foolishly, "It is a matter of no interest to us whether the earth is a sphere or a cylinder or a disc." Thomas Carlyle also followed the Christian tradition, when he declared that he honoured only two men and no third: the manual labourer and the religious preacher. He forgot the scientist, the scholar, and the artist. The Cynics of Greece despised education and intellectual pursuits, and declared that Virtue was the only Good. Such an incomplete ideal has led many earnest men and women to neglect intellectual pursuits as unnecessary and superfluous. You should not allow your mind to be enslaved by such unsound theories of life, which would convert the best men and women into virtuous and holy animals. Ignorance is brutish; Knowledge is a peculiarly human prerogative.

Having got rid of frivolity, cupidity, and superstition, you should apply yourself diligently and earnestly to mental self-culture. The field is vast. You will feel like a boy wandering in some tropical orchard, where many varieties of luscious fruits tempt the eye and the palate, mango and lichi and avocado, guava and papiya and mangosteen. Infinitely more delicious and wholesome are the fruits of Knowledge. Let us now glance at the different subjects that you should study as far as your means and opportunities permit.

Section I.—SCIENCE

The study of Natural Science is an essential part of education. You should not become lop-sided in your pursuit of Science, like Herbert Spencer and Charles Darwin. Herbert Spencer thought that Natural Science was the only valuable subject of study, and Darwin almost lost his capacity for enjoying Art on account of his excessive devotion to Science. But you should give Science its due, and a little more. At present it is often neglected in favour of literature, history, politics, and economics.

You may think that Science is dull and difficult, and some treatises on Science do bristle with technical terms and formidable formulæ. But you need not master all the details of all the branches of Natural Science; that is the task of the specialists in each branch. In fact, you have already been a scientist in a general way ever since you were born. You may be surprised at this compliment, as M. Jourdain was astonished when he was told that he had spoken prose for forty years. But you know that Science means only observation of the phenomena of Nature, experiments under controlled conditions, classification and verification, deduction and speculation, formulation of laws and hypotheses, discovery, invention, application of knowledge to the practical purposes of life, etc. When you were a child, you observed the habits of birds and insects, and drew certain inferences about them: you then acted as an amateur scientist. Science only asks you to keep your eyes and ears open; your alert and well-trained mind will apprehend the sequence and significance of the facts observed.

Science studies all the phenomena of Nature (and Nature includes Man). Your inborn curiosity prompts you to know something about the things and happenings around you. You see the sun and the stars, the plants and the animals, and your wonder and interest are aroused. You want to find out the how and the why of this external world. So you cannot really help being a scientist. As T. H. Huxley said: "Science is trained and organized common sense." You should not allow this natural curiosity to be dulled and blunted by disuse or by lack of opportunities for scientific study and research. When you cease to wonder at the marvellous and mysterious phenomena of Nature, you will be intellectually inert, quite dead though not buried. It is an excellent plan to keep a regular Nature-Diary, in which you note the interesting natural phenomena that you happen to observe. A beautiful sunset, a double rainbow, a bed of wild flowers, a flight of birds, the hooting of an owl, the life in an ant-hill, flying-fishes, the Aurora Borealis, and many other sights and sounds of Nature will then find a place in your diary. You will thus develop the habit of quick and intelligent observation. The diary will also help you to revive such memories for " the inward eye, which is the bliss of solitude." Further, Science will free you from superstition. This is one of the greatest blessings that Science confers on its votaries. Primitive man was engendered and cradled in superstition, as he was compelled to attribute all natural phenomena to personal beings like himself, whom he called gods, goddesses, demons, fairies, and what not. Superstition was the ubiquitous enemy of Man in the infancy of civilization. But Science, and Science alone, can liberate and enfranchise your mind from the corroding and demoralizing influence of Superstition in all its ghastly shapes and disguises. Superstition means belief in the reality of that which does not exist; it assumes a thousand forms and enslaves humanity with a thousand fetters. It has led to cruel exploitation and infamous barbarities in the history of the race. All falsehood is dangerous, and Superstition is a particularly perilous, persistent, and pestilential lie which only Science can expose and destroy. As the great Roman poet-philosopher Lucretius sang long ago: " Superstition is put underfoot and trampled upon in turn. . . . This terror and darkness of mind must be dispelled not by the rays of the sun and glittering shafts of day, but by the aspect and the law of Nature."

I shall now indicate the advantages that you will derive from the study of each branch of Science.

Mathematics

Mathematics should be cultivated for the sake of mental culture and also on account of its connection with the exact sciences. You may believe that mathematics is a dull subject, but it is you who are dull, not the mathematics. You should not forget and bury all your mathematics on leaving school and college. You should keep up this enthralling hobby throughout your life. You will then agree with Descartes, who wrote: " I was especially delighted with the mathematics, on account of the certitude and evidence of their reasonings." Mathematics will teach you the habits of clear thinking and sound reasoning. It will cure your mind of slovenliness and sloth. It will train you to deal with abstractions and generalities. It will help you to understand in a general way how the marvels of astronomy and physics have been achieved. You cannot have a clear idea of the solar system, if you know nothing about an ellipse. You should try to acquire some knowledge of the calculus and its beautiful applications in practice. Every one need not and cannot climb to the higher regions of non-Euclidean geometry and relativity, which are accessible only to the specialists and professors; but you should try to have more than a mere smattering of elementary mathematics. It may or may not be true that the entire Universe is comprehensible only with the aid of certain abstruse mathematical formulæ (I hope it is not so); but a substantial amount of mathematics is indispensable for your personal education.

Logic

Logic is also a formal science, which deals with the laws of Thought, the conditions of correct thinking, and the necessary forms of thought. It may also be said to be the art of thinking and reasoning correctly. It is thus akin to mathematics. It will save you from many fallacies and errors. Both logic and mathematics have for their subject-matter certain generalized forms of inference, through which the human mind acquires and applies its knowledge of the environment. You should read a text-book of Logic, which will tell you about inductive, deductive, and mathematical logic. But don't spend much time on this subject.

Physics and Chemistry

Physics and Chemistry will teach you the value of accurate measurement, and also reveal to you the warp and woof of Nature. They will teach you that Energy (and not "God") is the ultimate Substance or Reality, which also assumes the form of Matter with its atoms, electrons, and protons. Nature is an immense machine for changing Energy into Matter and Matter into Energy. The Universe is uniform and homogeneous: there is no essential difference between "heaven" and "earth," between "supralunar" and "sublunar" phenomena. Physics and Chemistry have bestowed on us the welcome gifts of machinery, steam, electricity, wireless, and other inventions which have ushered in a new era in the history of mankind. They will release the human race from deadening drudgery and exhausting toil. They will yet give us much more than all that we have got from them, if we only search and search. Physics and Chemistry will enrich, emancipate, and equip us beyond our wildest dreams. An educated man or woman should follow the march of these sciences with unflagging zest.

Physics and Chemistry will also train your mind to understand the basic concepts of natural law, cause and effect, regularity in the sequence of phenomena, necessary antecedents, etc. You will then cease to believe in the "miracles," which are related in many religious scriptures. You will realize that no holy man, Christian, Moslem, or Buddhist, could create fishes or loaves of bread out of nothing, or walk on water, or fly through the air, or break the moon into pieces, or change a corpse into a sweet pudding, or drink up a river, or cause storms and rainfall, or change his sex, or make himself invisible, or lengthen beams of wood, or produce fertility in the soil, or talk immediately after his birth, or walk through walls, or open a lock with his fingers without a key, or hang his cloak upon a sunbeam, or cure women of barrenness by his word, or restore the dead to life. It was considered a special mark of holiness to possess this power of abrogating the physico-chemical laws of Nature and performing such miracles. Nowadays, if a preacher or his disciples were to make such claims, you would despise them as fools or liars. You would not honour and acclaim a *soi-disant* "miracle-worker" as a prophet, but tell him to seek a job as a juggler and mountebank at a circus. Physics and Chemistry have exploded for ever the old notion that a virtuous saint must be able to play some silly tricks with Nature. Physics and Chemistry teach us that the orderly sequence of phenomena cannot be suddenly and arbitrarily modified by priests and prophets, however holy they may be.

Astronomy

Astronomy introduces you to a realm of mystery and magnificence, which is inexhaustible in its perennial fascination and its never-ending challenge to the human intellect. You should read many popular and semi-scientific treatises on astronomy, and also try to look at the planets and the stars through a telescope. You will get the thrill of your life, when you see additional stars in the Pleiades or find that the Pole Star is really double. Join a scientific Society that owns a telescope. You can also take advantage of the demonstrations held for the benefit of the public at certain Observatories. If you can afford to buy a telescope, you should work as an amateur, and promote astronomical research in a humble way. Lie awake sometimes on warm and clear nights, and gaze at the star-lit heavens in a passive and imaginative mood. Let the glory of Infinity sink deep into your soul. Just gaze and gaze, and do nothing more until you cry out in rapture with Shelley:

> "Spirit of Nature! here!
> In this interminable wilderness
> Of Worlds, at whose immensity
> Even soaring fancy staggers,
> Here is thy fitting temple!
>
> . . . . .
>
> Spirit of Nature! thou!
> Imperishable as this scene,
> Here is thy fitting temple!"

Always try to observe eclipses, and also to follow the movements of the planets as they are reported in the newspapers. Purchase a celestial globe and study it, until the different constellations from Cepheus and Ursa Minor to Octans and Apus are as familiar to you as the countries on a map of the Earth. Thus you will feel that you are in close touch with the entire Universe, which will cease to be something remote and indefinite for you. This exercise of globe-contemplation is very useful and important. Travel much, so that you may observe the stars and the astronomical phenomena that are not visible in your part of the world. Try to feast your eyes on the Aurora Borealis in the north and rejoice in the expanse of the heavens at the Equator. Memorize the chief data of astronomy, so that your mind may move with a sense of security and freedom among all the planets, stars, and nebulæ of the Universe (*e.g.* the distances and other figures relating to the solar system; the distances of the nearest star, of the principal stars, and of the nearest and the remotest extra-galactic nebulæ; the magnitudes of the brighter stars, etc.). In these and other ways, you should make the data of astronomy at least as real and interesting for yourself as the facts of geography. Then you can voyage through Space alone and unafraid. You will not there find the imaginary "love" which was supposed by Dante "to move the sun and other stars"; but you will discover something far more wonderful. You will stand face to face with Law and Evolution, the twin fiery cherubim that guard the Holy of Holies of eternal Nature.

Various and manifold are the benefits that you will derive from the systematic pursuit of astronomical studies. You will of course not prepare the nautical almanac or predict eclipses: that task is left to the professors. But your mind and soul will be lifted into the ethereal regions of Infinity and Mystery. Man's craving for these two elusive gleams is as insistent as his demand for the finite and comprehensible facts of terrestrial Nature. Man is born not only to think, but also to dream. Intellectual reverie is a tonic and a stimulant, without which man's soul would pine and dwindle. Astronomy is the sure cure for mental and spiritual anæmia. When you gaze into Space, you cannot fathom it (in spite of the formulæ of Einstein and Lorentz); your mind is strengthened by the strenuous gymnastics, and is then forced to take a rest. You long to fly to the moon, or to Venus, Mars, Jupiter, and Pluto, or to Proxima Centauri, Sirius, and Procyon: you cannot do it to-day. But you know that the time must surely come when men will fly in Space and take a holiday trip to Vega, Aldebaran, or Betelgeuse. You may laugh at this foolish flight of fancy; but wait. He laughs best who laughs last. These things shall be, as Victor Hugo and Walt Whitman have sung.

You must ask these questions about the stars and nebulæ: " How vast? How old? How many? " If you are up-to-date in your knowledge of contemporary science, you are thrilled at a fleeting glimpse of the remote nebulæ, and then ask, " What next? " The Universe really deserves all the epithets that the theologians have applied to the " Deity ": it is infinite, incomprehensible, indescribable, inscrutable, self-existent, without beginning or end.

Astronomy thus elevates and inspires your soul, and gives you the purest poetry of Science. Thus it develops your imagination and ennobles your emotional life. But it does much more. It provides you with a true Cosmogony. Now, it is of the first importance for a civilized man or woman to have some sound and scientific ideas about Cosmogony. False Cosmogony has been the basis of false religions, and a false religion is as dangerous for you as a pet snake. It is your duty to understand the scientific theories of the origin, evolution, and destiny of the Universe. All religions, from the crudest African fetishism to the most advanced modern cults, have taught some sort of Cosmogony. Their peculiar superstitions are always derived from their doctrines about the origin and destiny of the Universe. There lies the root of the evil. If you wish to choose a religion that will lead you to Truth and Life, and not to Error and Death, then you must first have the right notions about Cosmogony. If your Cosmogony is wrong, your religion will also be all wrong, and then yours will be a wasted life.

Astronomy will free your mind from your inherited superstitions in this respect. It will make a clean sweep of all the old tangled cobwebs spun by ignorant priests and metaphysicians in the past. It will give you a general idea of the contents and structure of the Universe. You will then find it impossible to believe in the existence of such imaginary regions as the "heaven," "purgatory," and "hell" of Christian theology, the "svarga" and "naraka" of the Hindus, the "jannat" and "dozakh" of the Moslems, the cold and hot hells and the Western Paradise of the Mahayanists, the Hades of the Greeks, the "sheol" of the Jews, and the "arali" of the Babylonians. The big telescopes now peer and penetrate into every cranny and corner of the Universe, as you can observe the stage at the theatre with an opera-glass. What the astronomer cannot see he can photograph. Nothing can escape his piercing eyes and his sensitive plates.

Millions of men and women to-day think that "heaven" and "hell" exist somewhere in the sky, which is the symbol of mystery for them. Astronomy will shatter such superstition more speedily than mere polemical discussion, as the student of astronomy asks: "Where are these places? Where?" Astronomy will also rescue you from the superstitious notions about eclipses, comets, fireballs, bolides, meteors, and falling stars that have prevailed among the ignorant populace during so many centuries. Eclipses and comets have spread terror and consternation among whole nations. Halley's comet was a dire portent for all Europe in the sixty-first century A.H. (eleventh A.D.). The Bayeux tapestry depicts the general panic of the time. Virgil attributed prophetic powers to the sun: "Who would dare to call the sun a deceiver? He often gives tokens that even concealed uprisings are at hand, and that treason and secret wars are swelling to a head. He also showed his pity for Rome at Cæsar's death." Shakespeare speaks of "Comets importing change of times and states." Aytoun, in his poem "Edinburgh after Flodden," connected the Aurora Borealis with the defeat of the Scots at Flodden.

> "All night long the northern streamers
> Shot across the trembling sky:
> Fearful lights that never beckon
> Save when kings or heroes die"

A Chinese Ode thus speaks of an eclipse of the sun of the year 4226 A.H. (775 B.C.): "The sun was eclipsed—a thing of very evil omen. Henceforth the people will be pitiable indeed. The sun and moon presage evil by not keeping to their proper paths."

In some countries, marriages are still arranged by comparing the horoscopes of men and women. Many "astrologers" exploit half-educated persons even in Europe by pretending to foretell the future. The study of astronomy will rid European and American society of such quacks. Once I spent some evenings with a few friends on the top of a hill near Salsomaggiore in Italy in the pleasant pastime of looking at the stars with the aid of a star-map. A few days later, I was agreeably surprised by the visit of a charming middle-aged lady, who asked me to draw a horoscope for her. She had seen our party on the hill and found out our address! I had to explain to her that I was not versed in astrology.

The "heavenly" bodies have indeed been responsible for a tremendous amount of superstition, priestcraft, and exploitation in the past. Now you can enjoy even a total eclipse of the sun as a curious phenomenon; but in former times it was a frightful catastrophe, which magic and prayer alone could terminate. The sky has long crushed and fettered our minds with fear and anguish; but now we are free, and the astronomers are our liberators. No longer do we bow down before the suns and the stars as cringing slaves and suppliants! No longer is the blue vault of heaven an incubus on the soul of man! Man now boldly faces the entire Universe, and counts the vast fiery furnaces of the remotest regions of space as a fruiterer deals with the fruits in his shop. Study astronomy and free your mind and heart and soul from the craven terror and ignoble slavery in which the victims of false cosmogonies still languish. At no great price you can purchase this freedom to-day.

Astronomy will teach you that the Universe is eternal and uncreated. The process of the conversion of energy into matter and of matter into energy is also eternal. The Universe was never created by the fiat of Marduk, Yahweh, Elohim, Brahmā, Allah, Shang-ti, T'ien, Ahura Mazda, or Dimmera. Democritus, Aristotle, Epicurus, and some Indian thinkers conceived this great idea, but modern astronomy explains and substantiates it. As you think of the past, your mind will at last be lost in what Robert Bridges has called "that darkness where all origins are." Thus you must reject all the legends of Creation that are related in the Vedas, the Koran, the Puranas, the Bible, the Zend-Avesta, and other ancient religious scriptures. The authors of those valuable books were great and good men, but they were ignorant of modern Mathematics, Physics, and Chemistry. In Cosmogony, our teachers are the living scientists, and not the old prophets. You need not also pay much attention to the queer and absurd notion of Plato, Augustine, and J. Jeans, that Time had a beginning. The idea of eternity, both in the past and the future, is implicit in the very definition of Time. "Time with a beginning" is a meaningless phrase, like "cold fire" or "hot ice." Al-Farabi has well defined Time as "the movement that holds things together." If Creation is an impossible figment of the unenlightened theologian's imagination, then a Creator is also a fictitious, non-existent person altogether. Astronomy will teach you that the Universe is all that is: we cannot conceive of a "spiritual" invisible Being who should stand outside this Universe and create it. The telescope reveals part of the Universe to us (and much more of the same kind is beyond), but we cannot discern a "Creator" moulding it and meddling with it. Thus you will learn this supreme truth: Nature is automatic and autonomous. It moves itself from within; it changes itself from within; it is not moved or changed by any external "God" or gods or goddesses. Its phenomena obey invariable laws that no "deity" can modify or abrogate. I once asked a pious Christian lady if "God" could change the time of the next eclipse of the sun or the moon. She replied, "Why not? God is almighty." Astronomy will abolish such intellectual infantilism for ever. Such an answer is a scandal and a shame in this century.

Astronomy also teaches that the Universe is indestructible and everlasting. It is continually changing, but it can never disappear altogether. The ideas of a "Day of Judgment," a "pralaya," a "universal conflagration," are thus seen to be absurd. You can confidently reject the old myths about "the end of the world" that are found in religious scriptures. In the Middle Ages, writers like Gregory of Tours and Ekkehard thought that the destruction of the world was impending, because they were ignorant of astronomy. You need not be alarmed by the modern doleful prophecies about the ultimate destruction of human life on a frozen earth. Long before that time comes (if it ever does), we shall be able to migrate to other planets of our own or some other solar system. We can live and work in the faith that Humanity, in its highly evolved types of the future, is imperishable. As Ovid sings: "Thus do all things suffer change, but nothing ever shall perish."

Astronomy will thus teach you these essential general principles of scientific cosmogony.

As regards the stages of evolution of the stars, the nature of curved space, the four-dimensional "space-time," the five-dimensional world of space-time-matter, the "expanding universe," the "cosmic rays," and other such details, you can accept the most recent theory propounded by the specialists, and you can also abandon it when they do so. Your Cosmogony will always be free from superstition, if you hold fast to these fundamental truths, viz.

(1) Nature is automatic and autonomous.
(2) The Universe is without beginning or end.
(3) There is no Creator and no Creation.

Lucretius has proclaimed in immortal verse this first principle: "Nothing is ever produced out of nothing by divine power."

Meteorology

Coming down from the heavens to the earth, you should learn the elements of Meteorology and understand the causes of such common phenomena as rain, thunder, and lightning. False Meteorology has also been a foster-mother of gross superstition in the past. Almost all nations have worshipped the gods of rain and thunder, and we must confess with shame that some "educated" priests still pray to "God" for rain, as if rainfall depended on the will of some god or goddess. St. Chad, an English Christian saint of the fifty-seventh century A.H. (seventh A.D.), behaved as a foolish child on account of his ignorance of Meteorology, as the Venerable Beda relates: "If it happened that there blew a strong gust of wind when he was reading or doing any other thing, he immediately called upon God for mercy; and if the wind grew stronger, he closed his book, and prostrating himself on the ground, prayed still more earnestly. But, if it proved a violent storm of wind or rain, or else that the earth and the air were filled with thunder and lightning, he would repair into the church and devote himself to prayers and repeating of psalms till the weather became calm. Being asked by his followers why he did so, he answered: 'The Lord raises the winds and darts lightning and thunders from heaven to excite the people of the earth to fear Him, and put them in mind of the future judgment. . . . Wherefore it behoves us to answer his heavenly admonition with due fear and love.'" Meteorology would have taught St. Chad that all atmospheric phenomena were due to natural causes, and that an umbrella and a mackintosh were more valuable in rain than prayers and psalms. Aristophanes relates in "The Clouds" that Socrates explained to Strepsiades how "the clouds were borne along by the natural æthereal vortex" and not by Zeus, as the superstitious Greeks believed. You may start a movement for the scientific control of the weather, but you will never pray to "God" or to any god or goddess for rain or sunshine. Zeus, Indra, Uiracocha, and Thor are dead: we appeal now to Science for protection against wind and storm.

Geology

Descending from the sky through the atmosphere, you at last stand on solid earth. Geology, with its sub-divisions of Mineralogy and Palæontology, now claims your attention. Read some treatises on this science, and also buy or collect some minerals and fossils. Visit the Geological Museum and see the fossils and the minerals, with their beautiful geometric patterns and their curious names in -ite. When you travel, always try to learn something about the geology of the region that you visit. Don't content yourself merely with the beautiful mountain-scenery; put some science into your æsthetics. Like all branches of Science, Geology will destroy certain superstitious notions. It will teach you that volcanoes and earthquakes are not due to demonic or divine agency, and that the "feng-shui" (geomancy) of the Chinese is not to be taken seriously. This latter superstition has produced a host of charlatans and swindlers in China, and often hinders the development of public enterprises.

Geology will also provide excellent gymnastics for the mind, as you must try to think of vast periods of time, reckoned in hundreds of millions of years. You must also imagine that almost incredible changes have taken place on the surface of the globe.

> "There rolls the deep where grew the tree.
> O earth, what changes hast thou seen!
> There where the long street roars, hath been
> The stillness of the central sea.
> The hills are shadows, and they flow
> From form to form, and nothing stands;
> They melt like mist, the solid lands,
> Like clouds they shape themselves and go."
> (*Tennyson.*)

Geology enables us to accustom our minds to the idea of extremely slow but continual and incessant change, which is destroying the old and creating the new, every moment, everywhere, around us. Thus you follow the story of the earth until Life first appears on this planet.

Botany

Now you must tackle Biology, with its sub-divisions of Bacteriology, Botany, and Zoology. Botany is of the greatest importance for educational, utilitarian, and æsthetic purposes. It will teach you the meaning and method of Classification. You will struggle with the numerous species, genera, natural orders, etc., and wonder why such a beautiful flower should have such an ugly and unwieldy name! You will be amazed and thrilled, when you see some of the marvels described in the treatises on Bacteriology and Botany: the coccus, which has a diameter of about 1/1000 millimetre; the twenty-minute generations of bacilli; the invisible viruses, photographed by ultra-violet light; the spores found in hailstones; the giant redwoods of California; the amygdalina of Australia; the macrocystis of the Antarctic Seas; the Kauri pines of New Zealand; the talipot palms and the giant bamboos of Ceylon; the cruel carnivorous *Apocynum andrasoemifolium*; the sensitive *Mimosa pudica*; the telegraph-plant (*Desmodium gyrans*) of Bengal; the luminous *Rhizomorpha subterranea* and *Agaricus gardneri*; the "mummy wheat" of Mohenjo Daro; the curious giant-dwarf *Welwitschia mirabilis*; the umbrageous banyan; the long-lived baobab; the enormous parasitic *Rafflesia arnoldi*; the Victoria regia water-lily; the beans of the *Dimorphandra oleifera*; and other interesting botanical products found in different parts of the world.

You will be introduced to the wonders of the microscope. Your eyes will be privileged to observe and discern what is hidden from the uninitiated. Buy a microscope if you can afford it; or borrow one from a friend. Microscopy is a most delightful hobby. You can join a Microscopical Club, and work with other amateurs. Collect rare wild flowers, ferns, and other botanical curiosities. Perform simple experiments on plants at home. Visit the local Botanical Gardens and learn what you can. Without some knowledge of Botany, you cannot understand many similes employed by the great poets. Your walks in the country will become doubly interesting and instructive, if you can greet each plant and flower with its name and know something of its life-history. The meadows and hedges will then be alive with old friends, and you will cease to regard them as a mere mass of verdure. You will learn to refrain from plucking flowers or uprooting plants without real necessity. Remember that a flower often looks prettier and lives longer in its free plant-home than in a vase indoors. You may perhaps even feel sympathy with a sick rose, as William Blake did, or begin to say with Wordsworth:

> " And 'tis my faith that every flower
> Enjoys the air it breathes."

Zoology

From Botany, you should pass on to Zoology, which deals with the morphology, physiology, and other aspects of the animal world. It is advisable to study the biological facts and problems of the human body in connection with a complete Science of Man (which should be constituted and elucidated in the near future), and not just as the culminating point of Zoology. Man, *Homo sapiens*, occupies a special privileged position in the realm of Life, and is not merely "*primus inter pares*" (" first among equals "). Zoology should include all that appertains to the sub-human species, from the protozoa to the anthropoid apes and the " missing links," the " Pithecanthropus erectus," the " Homo Heidelbergensis," the " Eoanthropus," the Neanderthal man, the Rhodesian man, the " Sinanthropus," etc.

Even those physiological activities which Man shares with the animals should be studied in close relation to human psychology. They do not properly belong to Zoology. Even when Man only breathes, digests food, or mates, he does so as a Personality, not as a mere animal. It is an entirely wrong idea that Man's biology can be separated from his psychology for purposes of investigation. Normal human personality is one and indivisible, and even the processes of respiration and digestion in a human being are both biological and psychological. Understand and appreciate this important doctrine of the Unity of Human Personality. Avoid the grave error of blurring the line of demarcation between Man and the animal world. It is necessary to regard Man as a being apart. He has certainly evolved from the primates, but has now developed into that marvellous species, *Homo sapiens*. Cultivate the habit of terminating your Zoology, even the sections on anatomy and physiology, with the anthropoid apes, and never think of Man as just another similar link in the same chain, the highest of the mammals. The synthetic Science of Man (what name?) must take the human species as a new starting point, and not as the top storey of a building, whose lower floors are tenanted by cows and pigs, like a poor farmer's cottage in the mountains.

Having thus boldly rescued Man from the crippling clutches of

Zoology, let us examine this great science and its place in your personal education. Most children are fond of some animals, and this early interest should lead you on to the study of Zoology. Zoology will impress on your mind the meaning and method of Classification even more effectively than Botany. No other branch of Science can give you this necessary training. You must go through the important varieties, species, genera, families, sub-orders, orders, classes, and phyla, carefully noting the distinctive characteristics of each group. Devote special attention to the Phylum "Arthropoda," and its Classes, "Arachnida" and "Insecta," with the many interesting Orders of the latter Class, the collembola, orthoptera, plectoptera, neuroptera, diptera, thysanoptera, lepidoptera, platyptera, hemiptera, coleoptera, hymenoptera, etc. Living insects may be a nuisance in the summer, but they can be most useful mind-trainers as dead specimens under the microscope during the long winter evenings. You will be amazed at the vast and varied scheme of Classification unfolded by Zoology, and the habit of close observation will stand you in good stead throughout your life. You will be constantly amused and interested on account of many remarkable zoological phenomena, such as the self-regenerating starfishes, newts, and sea-squirts; the free wandering cells of the oyster and the earthworm; the huge eyes of the crustacean Cystosoma; the luminous Noctiluca and Aulastomatomorpha; the walking, climbing, and flying fishes; the blind termites and their sky-scrapers; the highly developed civilizations of the ants and the bees; the hydraulic cement of the caddis-worm; the self-lengthening Nemertine worms; the courtship of the birds; the egg-laying mammals like the Australian duck-bill; the curious nests of the African umbre and the weaver-birds; the migrations of the eels; the lovely Rotifera; the colonies of Obelia; the sewed nests of the Indian tailor-bird; the impossible giraffe and the enormous sulphur-bottom whale; the generations of the liver-flukes; the never-caged okapi; the 14-oz. eggs of the kiwi; the waltzing mice of Japan; the egg-eating snakes and the snake-eating giant cobras; the grotesque Moloch-horridus of Australia and the aye-aye of Madagascar; the ugly wart-hog, and the fossils of the extinct animals like the diplodocus, the tyrannosaurus, the iguanodon, and the archæopteryx.

Zoology will prepare you for the study of human anatomy and physiology, which is necessary for the preservation of your health and physical efficiency. It will cure you of morbid pruriency, and teach you to talk about sexual matters in a natural and rational manner. You will learn much about cells, tissues, organs, organisms, heredity, variation, mutations, mimicry, symbiosis, chromosomes, genes, etc. Finally, you will be called upon to tackle such fundamental problems as the Origin of Life, Evolution, Teleology, and Vitalism. Zoology leads you from the lowliest worms to the loftiest wisdom.

Zoology will also provide you with a scientific theory of the Origin of Life, which excludes the dogma of Creation by a Deity. Man and the animals have been evolved from the protozoa, and the latter are either eternal or were evolved out of inorganic Matter at a remote period in the history of the earth. Arrhenius has suggested that spores were brought by radiation-pressure to the earth from some other planet; or, according to Kelvin, they may have been carried by meteorites. But this explanation does not solve the problem at all. How did Life originate? The question is, "Is living Matter an ultimate category by itself, like Energy and inorganic Matter, or is it derived from the latter?" There is no theoretical difficulty in admitting that there is a difference of kind, and not merely of degree, between living and inert Matter. Philosophy must recognize one or more basic realities beyond which it is impossible to penetrate. It must stop somewhere at some Ultimates. Thus you may reasonably hold that living Matter has not been evolved from inert Matter, but has existed eternally as an independent factor in the Universe and has propagated itself on this earth and in other worlds according to its own laws of Evolution. As far as we know, all life comes from pre-existing life. It is not absolutely necessary to assume that this universally valid law was not operative at a certain period in the past. Spontaneous generation has been shown to be impossible through the researches of Redi, Spallanzani, and Pasteur. You need not create such an avoidable difficulty for your own mind, if you find that it is impossible for you to conceive of Life as developing spontaneously out of lifeless Matter. Philosophy is under no obligation to refer all things to the one category of Energy-Matter: such a factitious Monism is unscientific. So if you are inclined to believe that living and non-living Matter cannot be reduced to a common denominator, you are free to postulate that Life is *sui generis* and has existed eternally, like Energy and Matter. Then you need not worry about the problem of the Origin of Life. The chief point is that you must not believe in the creation of Life by a Deity.

There is, however, another side to this thorny question. T. H.

Huxley wrote: "If it were given to me to look beyond the abyss of geologically recorded time to the still more remote period when the earth was passing through physical and chemical conditions, which it can no more see again than a man can recall his infancy, I should expect to be a witness of the evolution of living protoplasm from not-living Matter." Professor J. C. Bose's researches have demonstrated that inert and living bodies have much in common: even metals suffer from fatigue and can be poisoned. He says: "Living response in all its diverse manifestations is found to be only a repetition of responses seen in the inorganic." Several organic compounds have been built up in chemical laboratories since Wohler first produced urea in 6828. The chemical composition of living protoplasm has been ascertained; it consists of a few well-known elements. The ultra-microscopic units called "bacteriophages" may be an intermediate form between living and non-living Matter (if they exist at all). It is conceivable that the simplest forms of Life, like the invisible viruses or even the micro-organisms, may have appeared on earth spontaneously about 1300 million years ago, when the temperature and the atmospheric conditions were favourable for such a radically new development. Of course, the process of the transformation of chemical matter into the first living cells will ever remain a mystery. But Science and Philosophy must at least attempt to unify and simplify Nature. The mind of Man loves the logic of Monism, and must ever strive to arrive at one ultimate category, if it is at all possible. The assumption of more than one ultimate category seems to be unsatisfactory and transitional. There was a time when the scientists postulated two independent categories, Energy and Matter, and even Matter was supposed to consist of more than ninety irreducible "elements." But now we know that Matter and Energy are mutually convertible, one gramme of Matter yielding 9×10^{20} ergs of Energy. It is indeed an amazing achievement that such apparently diverse categories as Energy and Matter have thus been proved to be identical. How can we then be so sure that a living cell can never be produced from inert Matter under certain circumstances? Such dogmatism would be unworthy of a modern philosopher. If a monistic interpretation of Nature can be achieved without doing violence to facts, it must be appreciated and acclaimed as the crowning glory of Science and Philosophy. But the time is not yet ripe for such a conquest. At present, you may hold either of the two alternative theories without any danger of slipping into superstition, so long as you do not believe in a Creator. You may even take refuge in *hylozoism* (without slipping into Theism).

Superstition is indeed the enemy to be faced and foiled. The Egyptians and the Hindus worshipped many animals, instead of dissecting and studying them. Zoology will help you to battle successfully against many false dogmas that are now inculcated by the priests of almost all the religions in the world. Thus the Biblical and Miltonic narrative of the creation of man, woman, and the animals must be regarded as an ancient legend. Slow evolution precludes the idea of Creation. Such mythical beings as fairies, fravashis, pretas, ghosts, jinns, devas, centaurs, unicorns, phoenixes, hydras, sphinxes, mermaids, asuras, demons, nats, dakkinis, satyrs, houris, angels, amesaspentas, dhyani-buddhas, apsaras, nymphs, shojos, sennins, and "mahatmas" can be shown to be non-existent. They have not been discovered and classified by any zoologist, and their anatomy and physiology are unknown. All nations have attributed several diseases to demons and evil spirits, and resorted to exorcism instead of hygiene. How much superstition would be destroyed, if all men and women were to learn the simple truth that there can be no living sentient beings other than those catalogued and described by the zoologists! From the bacteria and the protozoa to the anthropoid ape and *Homo sapiens*—this is the entire gamut of animal and human Life on this earth. Zoology will also enable you to demonstrate the absurdity of the popular legends of virgin-mothers, resuscitated corpses, and the metamorphosis of men into animals. A student of Zoology is convinced that parthenogenesis is simply impossible in a human being, who can never be generated without the union of an ovum and a spermatozoon. A dead organism can also never be restored to life under any circumstances whatsoever. You need not then waste your time in arguing about the "historical evidence" for such imaginary incidents. You dismiss them as inherently impossible and incredible, whatever the deluded or fraudulent chroniclers may say. As a Zoologist, you know what is possible and what is not possible.

Zoology will also teach you compassion towards animals. Study always evokes interest and sympathy. To a Zoologist, a sheep is not merely mutton and wool, a lobster is something more than a "delicacy," and a spider is not just a horrid ugly creature. He has learned to look upon all worms and birds and beasts as struggling, scheming, suffering, food-hunting, mate-seeking, death-fearing individuals, born without their consent and compelled to complete their short life-cycles in an infinite Universe that they do not understand. Zoology reveals the beauty and diversity of the myriad forms of Life on earth, but it also lays bare the deep pathos and poignant tragedy of it all. A course in Zoology will leave you a sadder and a wiser man. It will also help you to realize the essential unity of living beings, so that you will begin to feel that you owe a duty to them all. You will then understand the joys and cares of a mouse, as interpreted by Robert Burns. You may even feel that tender sympathy with "our dumb friends," which breathes so softly in the Chinese poet Han-yu's gentle verse:—

> "Oh, spare the busy morning fly, spare the mosquitos of the night.
> And if their wicked trade they ply, let a partition stop their flight.
> Their span is brief from birth to death. Like you, they bite their little day,
> And then, with autumn's earliest breath, like you, too, they are swept away"

History of Science

You should also study the history of Science in order to understand how Humanity has acquired the immense stores of scientific knowledge through the centuries from Ahmes to Einstein. The biographies of the great scientists must be read; their struggles and adventures will show you that Science is the fruit of noble sacrifice. You will learn to love Truth and Fact more than gold and silver. You will acquire that stern intellectual integrity and incorruptible spiritual veracity which no amount of merely ethical and religious training can ever bestow upon you. For a scientist, a fact is sacred, and an experiment is a sacrament. He can never accept or advance alluring theories and agreeable hypotheses in order to subserve any noble or ignoble political or religious movement; he is incapable of committing "pious frauds." The study of the history of Science will instil this unfailing love of Truth into your soul, and thus counteract the "will to believe" what you know to be false. You should make yourself familiar with the details of the lives and achievements of such intellectual giants as Aristotle, Hipparchus, Archimedes, Eratosthenes, Aristarchus, Hippocrates, Copernicus, Kepler, Newton, Cuvier, Lamarck, Darwin, Pasteur, Aryabhata, Al-Haitham, who have patiently devoted their lives to Science and thus paved the way for the advent of

> ". . . the crowning race
> Of those that, eye to eye, shall look
> On knowledge, under whose command
> Is Earth and Earth's, and in their hand
> Is Nature like an open book."

First Principles

The study of Physics, Chemistry, Botany, and Zoology will suggest certain general ideas about the Universe as a whole. These fundamental philosophical principles may now be considered very briefly. The Universe, or Nature, consists in the last analysis of Energy. What is called Matter is only a form of Energy. As Sir J. Jeans puts it, "All the life of the Universe may be regarded as manifestations of energy masquerading in various forms." Nature is fundamentally homogeneous and unitary. All phenomena are manifestations of Energy, and they are essentially of the same kind. The reality, which we sometimes call "Matter" and sometimes "Energy," has been named "Material-energy-tensor" by A. Eddington. If you are in a poetical mood, you may personify this eternal and everlasting Energy, and imagine it saying, as Swinburne's "Hertha":—

> "I am that which began,
> Out of me the years roll,
> . . . .
> Before ever land was,
> Before ever the sea,
> Or soft hair of the grass,
> Or fair limbs of the tree,
> Or the flesh-coloured fruit of my branches, I was, and thy soul was in me.
> First life on my sources
> First drifted and swam,
> Out of me are the forces
> That save it or damn,
> Out of me man and woman, and wild-beast and bird; before God was, I am
> Beside or above me
> Nought is there to go,
> . . . .
> I the mark that is missed,
> And the arrows that miss,
> I the mouth that is kissed,
> And the breath in the kiss,
> The search and the sought, and the seeker, the soul and the body that is."

All phenomena exhibit three characteristics:

(1) They happen in Space and Time. The various objects or things in the Universe bear to one another certain relations of size, shape, distance, and direction of motion. These relations of the quantitative features of the constituents of matter are designated as "Space."

The phenomena of Nature are also related in another way. They co-exist, or they precede or follow one another. These relations of simultaneity or succession are denoted by the word "Time." Change or movement is the measure of Time.

Space and Time are not absolute, as has been definitely demonstrated by Minkowski and Einstein. They are also not independent of each other; there is a spatio-temporal order. These constituents of the physical world, which are limited in time and space, are "events." According to Bertrand Russell, the Universe "is something occupying a small finite amount of space-time." Space-time is a four-dimensional continuum of "events," and four measurements fix the position of an event in space-time. Space, Time, and Matter must be treated together and inseparably as a single system. (But you must try to understand the whole theory of Relativity, if you can. If you can't, I shall be the last to blame you, as I don't understand it myself. I was brought up on the old Euclidean geometry.)

(2) All phenomena are subject to the law of Causality, which may be interpreted in different ways. The Universe is not a haphazard conglomeration of objects and events: the golden chain of Cause-and-Effect links them all together. Every change and every event must have a cause. This relation converts chaos into a cosmos and makes knowledge possible. Without the idea and fact of Causality, Science would not exist; indeed, life and action would be rendered impossible. Causation is the Ariadne's thread that guides Man in this mighty maze of Nature. There may be some phenomena of discontinuous change in atoms, whose causal relations have not been discovered; but we assume that these must exist. There is nothing absolute and uncaused: all things and beings are enveloped and enmeshed in Causality. The Universe is one interdependent whole. An efficient Cause is that antecedent which can be shown to lead to the Effect by a demonstrable process. The notion of Cause is not derived from the mere association of two events in regular sequence. The Chinese philosopher Chuang-tzu quaintly explains Causality thus: "The Penumbra said to the Umbra, 'At one moment you move; at another you are at rest. At one moment you sit down; at another you get up. Why this instability of purpose?' The Umbra replied: 'I depend upon something which causes me to do as I do; and that something depends upon something else which causes it to do as it does. My dependence is like that of a snake's scales or a cicada's wings (which do not move of their own accord).'"

(3) Nature is in constant flux. The entire Universe changes every moment. It does not remain the same even while you wink. Plato wrote: "Herakleitos says somewhere that all things pass and naught abides; and, comparing things to the current of a

river, he says that you cannot step twice into the same stream." Aristotle also teaches that "all things are in motion, and nothing steadfastly is." Nothing is immutable. Nature is dynamic, and not static or stagnant. As Goethe says: "Nature is eternally changing; she does not stand still for a moment. Of rest she knows nothing."

These general ideas about Nature and the Universe should be thoroughly comprehended and inwardly digested. Your personal religion should be based on them; otherwise you will fall headlong into the bottomless pit of superstition. You may study the details of the most recent theories of space-time, Euclidean and non-Euclidean space, physical and perceptual space and space-time, events and intervals, geodesics, causal routes and units, etc., in the treatises of modern scientists; but the fundamental ideas of Space-Time, Causality, and Flux are sufficient for your general philosophy of life. These are absolutely indispensable. Without them, you will stray from the highway of Science and flounder helplessly in the quagmire of Error.

Five Groups

All natural phenomena arise in the universe of Energy, but they may be divided into five groups or orders: Physical, Chemical, Botanical, Zoological, and Human (or Anthropological). The fundamental unity of Nature does not mean dull uniformity, but variety-in-unity. Each group includes the phenomena of all the preceding groups. Some universal laws are common to all the groups; but there are also special laws that are valid only within a particular group. The phenomena of each group merge by gradations into those of the next group: there are thus often border-line cases between two groups. The phenomena of each group are distinguished by certain marked characteristics.

(1) *Physical Phenomena*, or all the phenomena of Energy in its different forms, and Matter (which is also a mode of Energy). Motion is the principal phenomenon in this group; and Physics is the science that investigates it.

(2) *Chemical Phenomena*. Chemistry deals with the phenomena of Matter, its structure, transformations, and combinations. These phenomena are marked by Chemical Affinity, which distinguishes them from purely physical phenomena.

(3) *Botanical Phenomena*, or all the phenomena of plant-life. Here begins Life in its simplest form, with living cells and their phenomena of respiration, nutrition, growth, reproduction, and

death. Simple inorganic matter is built up into living protoplasm by the plants. Plants have Life, but neither Sentiency nor Consciousness.

(4) *Zoological Phenomena.* Zoology inquires into the phenomena of animal life. Animals depend on plants for food, as they cannot live on simple inorganic substances. They have not only Life (like the plants), but also Sentiency, as they possess a nervous system. They lack Consciousness, with its twin attributes of Reason and Emotion. Physiology is the principal science for this group. The border-line cases between the fourth and fifth groups exhibit the dawn of Consciousness.

(5) *Human or Anthropological Phenomena.* These phenomena of human life are studied by the sciences of Anatomy, Physiology, Psychology, History, Politics, Ethics, Economics, Sociology, etc. Psychology is the principal science for this group. Human beings have not only Life and Sentiency, but also Consciousness, with its double aspect of Reason and Emotion.

Some writers do not distinguish clearly between botanical and zoological phenomena, and group them together as "biological." Others transfer some human phenomena to the fourth group as merely "biological"; but I believe that all human phenomena (including respiration, nutrition, and reproduction) are bio-psychological. It is advisable not to mix up the five Orders of phenomena, as each Order reveals certain special laws that do not apply to the others.

Some Errors

Now I must warn you against some serious errors, which are due to inadequate knowledge or confusion of thought.

(1) You should get rid once for all of the notion that the Universe exhibits phenomena of two kinds, "material" or "phenomenal," and "spiritual" or "noumenal." Nature is one and indivisible: there are not two worlds, one of which is sometimes despised as "material and mutable," and the other is often glorified as "spiritual and supra-sensible." Most people who talk glibly of the "spiritual" world have no clear idea of what is meant by "spirit." They perhaps think of something gaseous or smoky; or they really wish to assert that there is a region where Space-time, Causality, and Flux do not exist. Such notions are found in the Upanishads, and in the writings of Plato, the religious mystics, the classical German philosophers of the Absolute, Rudolf Steiner, and others. They postulate that the "spiritual" world

is free from change, as it is beyond time and space and matter. It is immutable, uncaused, deathless, painless, and undifferentiated. This seems to be their vague conception of "spirit." But such a "spiritual" or "noumenal" world is a sheer impossibility. Remember the wise words of Ssu-ma Chien: "Educated people mostly deny the existence of a spiritual world." Whenever you hear the high-falutin' sounds, "unchanging," "undecaying," "absolute," "spiritual," you may be sure that the speaker is talking nonsense, like Dean W. R. Inge, who says: "Our citizenship is in heaven, that is to say, in a spaceless and timeless world." Can you imagine anything that is "timeless" and "spaceless"? Everything and every being exist only in time and space, as the fish live in water. Time passes, and we pass with Time, which is indeed another name for Flux. There is Nothing, there can be Nothing, that does not change. "Immutability" and "spirituality" are mere words; they correspond to no fact or reality in the Universe. Do not trouble about the antithesis of "matter" and "spirit," as you emphatically deny the existence of "spirit." At the same time, you should not be careless in using the terms "matter" and "material" in philosophy. Bertrand Russell has pointed out that "the notion of matter, in modern physics, has become absorbed into the notion of energy. . . . Matter has become no more than a convenient shorthand for stating certain causal laws concerning events. . . . Relativity demands the abandonment of the old conception of matter, which is infected by the metaphysics associated with 'substance.' . . . One unit of matter is a series of events, or a series of sets of events." In view of the new concepts introduced into modern physics, it is best to discard both these terms, "material" and "spiritual," in philosophical discussion. You should speak only of "natural" phenomena. Don't be drawn into the meaningless controversy about the "material" and "spiritual" worlds. Both these terms are mere metaphysical abstractions. You should be interested in natural phenomena, not in abstract terms. Remember Pasteur's remarkable dictum, which should be memorized by all students of Philosophy: "When I am in my laboratory, I begin by shutting the door on materialism and on spiritualism; I observe facts alone; I seek but the scientific conditions under which life manifests itself."

So you can declare, on Pasteur's authority, that you are neither a materialist nor a spiritualist, but a *scientist*. Dismiss the metaphysicians of both materialism and spiritualism with the curt and contemptuous farewell: "A plague o' both your houses!" Dreamy metaphysics, which deals with "the Absolute," "Spirit," "Reality," and "Noumenon," is really a pretentious abracadabra, an acoustic edifice of words, which have no intelligible sense or meaning whatsoever. It has been thus described by Mephistopheles in Goethe's "Faust":—

> "And after—first and foremost duty,
> Of metaphysics learn the use and beauty!
> See that you most profoundly gain
> What does not suit the human brain!
> A splendid word to serve, you'll find
> For what goes in—or won't go in—your mind.
>
> . . . .
>
> With words 'tis excellent disputing,
> Systems to words 'tis easy suiting,
> On words, 'tis excellent believing;
> No word can ever lose a jot from thieving."

Such metaphysics is like the pretty but poisonous berries that children sometimes eat in the woods. Beware!

(2) You should not apply all the special laws and concepts, which are derived solely from Physics and Chemistry, to the botanical, zoological, and human orders of phenomena. There are some laws that apply to all phenomena (*e.g.* the conservation of energy). But there are other laws that are valid only for a particular order of phenomena. Thus Physics cannot explain the mystery of chemical affinity or the process of reproduction in plants and animals. Chemical laws are not wholly applicable even to the simple process of digestion, if an animal or a human being is exposed to sudden fear or danger. Psychology investigates the mental phenomena of human beings. Physics and Chemistry cannot usurp the place of Psychology, though they may explain certain subsidiary processes. Ethical and Sociological phenomena again are governed by their own laws, and they cannot be tackled by a botanist or a zoologist. It is foolish to apply all the physical and chemical laws to the other three orders of phenomena, when the facts protest loudly against such an arbitrary procedure. We must agree with Lowell that

> "Life's bases rest
> Beyond the probe of chemic test."

Let each science reign in its own domain, and let no relevant facts be neglected, perverted, or misinterpreted. Thus you should not be misled by the sweeping generalizations advanced by J. Loeb and other philosophers, who seem to recognize only the physical and chemical orders of phenomena in Nature and ignore the purely biological and psychological concepts and laws. J. Loeb says: "All life-phenomena are determined by chemical processes." E. A. Schäfer thinks that "living beings are governed by laws identical with those which govern inanimate matter." Sir Ray Lankester makes Physics the predominant science, when he says: "To me the conclusion has for many years commended itself, that the materialist and mechanical scheme of Nature (including man's nature), elaborated by physical science, is true and trustworthy." Bertrand Russell also assumes, "as a working hypothesis, that the human body acts according to the same laws of physics and chemistry as those which govern dead matter, and that it differs from dead matter, not by its laws, but by the extraordinary complexity of its structure." Herbert Spencer applied the physical concept of "persistence of force" and the biological concepts of "organism" and "embryonic evolution" to the human phenomena of History and Sociology, and the result was disastrous. Such methods lead only to confusion and error. Sound philosophy demands that the special laws governing each of the five orders of phenomena should be formulated on the basis of the observed and ascertained facts. The attempt to foist all the physical and chemical laws upon Zoology or zoological laws upon Psychology and Sociology must be abandoned. Each branch of Science deals with its own phenomena and discovers its special laws, besides those universal laws that apply to all phenomena.

(3) You should also beware of the fallacy of "Vitalism." You should admit that the phenomena of plant-life, animal-life, and human life are not always physico-chemical processes; but it is not necessary to go further and postulate a "life-force" in order to "explain" them. Henri Bergson's *élan vital*, H. A. E. Driesch's "entelechy," William McDougall's "soul," and other such terms are really meaningless and superfluous. They are merely metaphysical abstractions. Science deals with phenomena and their laws; it shuns vague and mystical abstractions that only confuse the mind. It is true that biological phenomena are not merely physico-chemical processes. The activity of an organism serves the welfare of the individual or the species in its environment; all its reactions to stimuli are not predetermined and predictable in the same sense as an eclipse or the behaviour of an engine. In J. A. Thomson's words, a living organism is a "self-stoking, self-repairing, self-preserving, self-adjusting, self-increasing, self-reproducing engine." An animal is not a mere machine: a flying bird is something more than a mechanical apparatus like

an aeroplane, as it is a sentient creature with a nervous system. An ant or a worm crawling down a hill presents a phenomenon of a different order from a stone rolling over the same surface, and even the amœba does not grow in the same way as a crystal. That is why I have divided natural phenomena into five distinct groups, each of which has certain special laws that do not apply to the others. *Botany* and *Zoology* are independent sciences in their own right; they are not merely sub-divisions of Physics and Chemistry, though plants and animals are also subject to physical and chemical laws. Professor F. G. Hopkins, the famous bio-chemist, says: "To claim, as I am to claim, that a description of its active chemical aspects must contribute to any adequate description of life, is not to imply that a living organism is no more than a physico-chemical system. It implies that, at a definite and recognizable level of its dynamic organization, an organism can be logically described in physico-chemical terms alone. . . . There may be yet higher levels calling for discussion in quite different terms."

You should thus recognize the existence of fundamentally diverse orders of phenomena, with their special laws; but you need not take refuge in the obscure and misleading terminology of "Vitalism." Like most words in -ism, "Vitalism" is simply a philological trap for the unwary; it is only a metaphysical label. H. Bergson is the victim of self-deception, if he imagines that he makes us wiser by such a sentence as this: "So we come back to the idea we started from, that of an original impetus of life. . . . This impetus, sustained right along the lines of evolution, among which it gets divided, is the fundamental cause of variations." Such a dictum is of no scientific value at all. "Vitalism" discovers no laws and explains no phenomena. What can be gained by asserting that there is "Life-Force" in a living organism? It is mere tautology. It amounts to the highly illuminating statement that a frog is really a living organism, and not a stone or a piece of sulphur. About such verbal jugglers, the witty Samuel Butler has said:

> "He knew what's what, and that's as high
> As metaphysic wit can fly."

A prominent "Vitalist" says: "A time will come when there will be no living beings, but only Life." Can you beat that precious medieval and metaphysical statement for sheer nonsense? Molière has told us of the doctor who "explained" the soporific effects of opium by its "virtus dormitivus." If you name and personify the principle of life and activity in an organism, and endow it with a capital letter of the alphabet, you run the risk of losing your way in the dark labyrinth of metaphysics. This trick of personifying abstractions may be legitimate in poetry, but it is fatal to scientific philosophy. The anatomy and physiology of a crab should be studied; but you need not inquire into the "crab-force" that makes it a crab. Botanical research is not helped by theories of the "oak-force" in an oak and the "banyan-force" in a banyan-tree. Zoology also does not stand in need of the *élan bovin* of oxen, and the *élan poissoneux* of fishes. The "vital force" of organisms possessing vitality or life is a similar abstract term, which only denotes the sum-total of the phenomena exhibited by an organism. It is not an entity by itself. Let us not worship a word coined by ourselves; let us not bow down before the creation of our own minds. Free yourself from the subtle tyranny of abstract terms, which do not represent any objective reality. Do not stir up the mud of metaphysics in the limpid waters of Science. Science must reject and repudiate such superficial thinkers, who take her name in vain (*e.g.* Bergson, Grandjean, Le Roy, Wilbois, Bazaillas, Inge, Rudolf Steiner, and others). They only borrow the goodly garments of Science in order to deck the old hag Metaphysics in her dotage. They wear the leonine skin of modern Science, but their speech betrays the asinine futility within. They have learned to repeat the terms and formulæ of Science, but they are not conversant with her method and spirit. Science must never make a compromise with Metaphysics, modern or medieval. Metaphysics is a life-weakening, mind-perverting, soul-besmirching force, that must be counteracted and suppressed wherever you meet it. It has killed many societies and civilizations by its slow arsenical poisoning, which is often described as "transcendental spirituality." You should also avoid the futile controversy with regard to "repetitive" or "emergent" Evolution. Our plan of dividing all phenomena into five separate groups and investigating their various laws absolves us from the tedious task of arbitrating between rival teams of muddled metaphysicians. In one sense, nothing new emerges when inert matter evolves into living protoplasm; there is only a more complex ordering and arrangement of the same elements. Physically and chemically, an animal and a human being cannot add to or subtract from the sum-total of energy and matter in the universe. Evolution is simply repetitive on the physico-chemical plane. When mighty Cæsar is dead, he is turned to mere clay; and Tennyson consoled himself with the fancy that

Arthur Hallam's dead body would be converted into English flowers:

> "'Tis well, 'tis something, we may stand
> Where he in English earth is laid,
> And from his ashes may be made
> The violet of his native land."

When Shelley's brain and body were cremated, the Universe lost nothing in a chemical sense; it was only a process of oxidation. But what a difference Death made to the realm of Poetry! The physico-chemical cycle is indeed a closed circuit. But a plant exhibits phenomena of Life; an animal adds Sentiency to Life, and Man crowns both Life and Sentiency with Consciousness. In this bio-psychological sense, Evolution is creative and emergent, and not simply repetitive. There is something more in a man's brain and body than the hydrogen, carbon, sulphur, and other chemical elements; this "something" is imponderable; it will not tip the beam of the balance by a millionth part of a millimetre, but it is there as Life, Sentiency, and Consciousness, three qualities and attributes of Man. This controversy need not be taken seriously, as we should walk in the straight and narrow path of Science, and never stray into the blind alleys of the metaphysics of Vitalism. What is the possible use of affixing the labels "emergent" or "repetitive" to Evolution? It is a War of Words that can never end even after a hundred years. We shall not understand the phenomena and their laws a whit better through such fruitless debate about abstract notions. We are so busy with concrete and interesting facts that we have no time for these subtle and unintelligible metaphysical problems.

Rabelais has already told us that nothing can be gained by travelling to the Kingdom of Quintessence or Entelechy, whose Queen eats nothing but abstractions and categories, and where the people make great things out of nothing, cut fire into steaks with a knife, and draw water with a fish-net. That wonderful kingdom is also the fitting home of the philosophers of "Vitalism"!

(4) You should not dogmatically deny the possibility of Life on other planets in the Universe. Reasoning by analogy only, one would be inclined to believe that living beings may exist on other planets circling round other suns, and also on some planets of our own solar system. Of course, planets are very rare. According to the tidal theory, they cannot be born except when two stars pass within about three diameters of one another. Sir J. Jeans says: "As we know how the stars are scattered in space, we can

estimate fairly closely how often two stars will approach within this distance of one another. The calculation shows that even after a star has lived its life of millions of millions of years, the chance is still about a hundred thousand to one against its being a sun surrounded by planets." Even so, the odds are in favour of the supposition that there may be other inhabited planets, as the number of stars photographically visible in the 100-inch telescope is about 1,500 millions. Even if such planets are extremely rare, there may be a few of them somewhere. It is probable that the right temperature, oxygen, and other pre-requisites of organic Evolution are also found elsewhere than on this tiny Earth. As Giordano Bruno says in his poetical and unscientific language: " Everywhere is one soul, one spirit of the world, wholly in the whole and every part of it. This soul . . . produces all things everywhere." In some worlds, only the sub-human species may exist; but other planets may be the homes of Supermen, who are much more highly evolved than *Homo sapiens* and have reached a stage that Man on earth shall attain in a million million years. Evolution has not ceased, because Darwin discovered it and died. It is an eternal process. Man on earth need not claim that he stands at the apex of Life; perhaps he occupies only an inferior position. There may be Beings who are as superior to Man as Man is above the microbes. We cannot even conceive what they are like and how they live; but an oyster and an earthworm too have no idea of the Salzburg Music Festival or the League of Nations. Some day we shall be able to communicate with these denizens of distant worlds. It will be glorious to live (or live again?) in that epoch!

Section II.—HISTORY

"Histories make men wise," said Bacon. History (with Archæology) is certainly one of the many sources of Wisdom.

Advantages of History

(1) You should study History in order to learn the relevant facts about the past experiences and activities of the human race, and also attempt a philosophical interpretation of them. As an individual, you are extremely limited and circumscribed. Your personal life commenced only a few years ago. Compared with the long centuries of human History and pre-History behind you, you are an ephemeral insect that lives and dies in a day. You observe your environment and learn something from the objects and persons that surround you; but there is an immense storehouse of experience that is accessible only through History. This wonderful Aladdin's cave is replete with the precious treasures that Humanity has amassed during five hundred centuries or more. They are all yours. You are the "heir of all the ages," so constituted only by your birth, and not by any legal will or testament. You claim your heritage by commencing the study of History and Archæology. As an individual, you are indeed puny and feeble; but when you have enlarged your experience through History, you are like a dwarf standing on the head of a giant. In your short life, you can see a little, very little indeed. But if you prolong your mental existence backward through the ages, you extend the range of your vision beyond the wildest dreams of clairvoyance. The Rigveda mentions the mythical Purusha, who had a thousand heads and a thousand feet; but the student of History has billions and trillions of eyes and ears, as he has incorporated into himself all the men and women that have ever lived on this earth. Left to yourself, you would be like a tiny mountain stream all the days of your life; but when your mind and heart have been nourished and enriched by the thoughts and feelings of the numberless hosts of the dead, you resemble the mighty Ganga or Amazon, high-swollen with the spoils of a hundred tributaries. Thus History magnifies and expands your personality. Like kings and editors (and with more reason

than they), you can speak of yourself as "We," if you love History. When you speak, you are the mouthpiece of Humanity.

(2) Further, you cannot understand your own life without a knowledge of History. The present has its roots in the past. Each generation has borrowed freely from its predecessors and lent generously to its successors. As you are indebted for your body to your parents and grandparents, and finally to your remote ancestors of the Ice-Age, even so all the customs and institutions, which envelope you like the air you breathe, have arisen and grown in the invisible past. There is no break in the continuity of biological descent or of social evolution.

Matthew Arnold makes Empedocles say:—

> "Born into life—man grows
> Forth from his parents' stem,
> And blends their bloods, as those
> Of theirs are blent in them,
> So each new man strikes root into a far fore-time"

Civilization, as you see it to-day, is like the stem and branches and leaves of an umbrageous oak; but the wide-branching roots are hidden underground. History shows you the roots without uprooting the tree; it sends mind-rays through the solid earth. Without History, you would be like a wayfarer who did not remember the route by which he had travelled; you would know just where you stood, but not whence you came. History prevents such a loss of racial memory. You belong to a Church and a State; you have been educated at a school and perhaps at a college; you have admired the works of the poets and the painters. How and when did the Church, the State, the school, the college, the poets, and the painters first make their appearance? When you eat your bread, or drink milk, or ride a horse, or write a letter, or look at your watch, or talk of a week of seven days, or lie in bed on Sunday mornings, you perhaps forget that you owe these blessings and amenities to unknown unnamed people, who lived and died long ago in different regions of the earth. Your Neolithic forbears still provide you with your breakfast. Egypt, Babylonia, and Phœnicia teach you how to make an appointment by letter with your sweetheart. You cannot be an intelligent citizen without knowing something about the origin and development of the different phases of contemporary civilization. History is the basis of true Citizenship, without which true Ethics is impossible.

(3) History also throws light on human nature, and is an esteemed ally of Psychology. In History, truth is often stranger than fiction.

If you are unacquainted with the vast and wondrous panorama unfolded by History, you can have no idea of the potentialities of human nature, of the Empyrean heights to which it can soar and the Tartarean depths to which it can sink. Dante and Shakespeare dived deep into human nature, but a thousand Dantes and Shakespeares cannot interpret and compass Man's spirit as revealed in History. Love and hate, mercy and cruelty, greed and unworldliness, ambition and humility, cowardice and heroism, these and other qualities are disclosed on their curves of maxima and minima in the far-ranging calculus of History. You feel that Man is in truth fearfully and wonderfully made,

"The glory, jest and riddle of the world."

(4) In your personal life, your past experience helps you to act wisely in different situations. You rely on some friends, keep your promises, abstain from buying on credit, distrust and despise the politicians and the priests, insure your house, guard against falling in love, etc. In the same way, the experience of the race may sometimes help and guide us in discovering the solution of some perplexing problems of to-day. Mankind has probably acquired a small stock of permanently valid principles and precepts by the method of trial and error. But beware of the fallacy of always turning to the past for wisdom. Nature has not placed your eyes in the back of your head. Some say: "There is nothing new under the sun," and "History repeats itself." As a matter of fact, every day, every hour, nay every minute creates something new under the sun, and History never repeats itself. As Lowell sings:

"New occasions teach new duties: Time makes ancient good uncouth.
They must upward still, and onward, who would keep abreast of Truth.
Lo, before us gleam her camp-fires! We ourselves must Pilgrims be,
Nor attempt the Future's portal with the Past's blood-rusted key."

You should learn much from History, but never forget that all men and women must also make new History out of their own creative minds and hearts. Accept Bolingbroke's definition of History as "philosophy teaching by examples," but remember that it is an incomplete and truncated philosophy, which has to be supplemented by our own thought in the living present. Auguste Comte said: "The dead rule the living." If this were true, life would be a grim tragedy. Fortunately, the dead only help us, their children; they do not rule us. You cannot garner a sheaf of cut-and-dried rules and infallible precepts from the past: you can only glean a few general ideas and principles. I cannot agree with Lamartine's dictum: "History teaches everything, even the future." History cannot supply the data for prevision and prediction like Physics and Chemistry. Beware of those plausible orators who try to dissuade you from embarking upon new adventures in religion or politics, because something happened or did not happen in Peru, Rome, or Mesopotamia long ago. No such arguments can be derived from History, as all the facts and circumstances are never the same. We are also ignorant of the whole of History. We depend on inadequate documents, biased and untrustworthy historians, rumour and hearsay, myths and legends, lies and half-truths. But we must admit that History may be useful for our guidance within certain limits. Let us cultivate "historical-mindedness," as Professor J. H. Robinson advises us to do; but let us be careful not to overdo it.

(5) History is supremely valuable for providing one indispensable requisite of social health and vitality, viz. Moral Inspiration. The records of the past, interpreted in practical life by noble men and women, supply the moral tonic, which must be administered to each generation, lest it perish of ethical inanition and debility. History sounds the pæan of triumph of great movements in religion, politics, art, and science. The self-sacrifice of earnest lovers of Humanity was the price always paid for the victory. It seems to be a mysterious law that no Progress can be made without Sacrifice. Some men and women must be prepared to die as martyrs or face death as heroes; to risk their lives as daring pioneers or bold heretics; to practise abnormal abstinence; to drill and discipline the body like merciless martinets; to scorn rank and honour; to suffer hunger and thirst, cold and fatigue; to despise contumely and calumny; to renounce money and marriage; to forgo fame, fortune, and family life; to endure torture and imprisonment, exile and loneliness,—thus to master Sense and conquer Self, and thereby to raise the mass of mankind to ever higher levels of Wisdom and Virtue. History preserves the names and words and deeds of the most remarkable representatives of this small élite of martyrs, apostles, and heroes, as the mountains keep and conceal ruby, jade, and amethyst. These three types, and no others, lead mankind forward: Apostle, Martyr, Hero. They pass away, but the good they do lives after them. The historian's pen introduces us into their living presence, and we are at once spurred and stimulated as by strong wine or Alpine air. Truly does Goethe say: "The best that History has to give us is the enthusiasm that it arouses." Self-sacrifice is contagious. It mocks at time and space. It leaps

over barriers of race and colour. Jesus was a Jew, who taught and died two thousand years ago; but hundreds of martyrs and missionaries in Europe, Asia, Africa, America, and Australasia have chosen a glorious death or the simple life of daily self-denial in his name. Gautama Buddha was a wandering preacher of ancient India; but thousands of monks and laymen in China, Japan, and Tibet have been initiated into the secret of the higher life through the magic of his personality. Petrarch in Italy lit a torch that soon illumined all Europe, and devoted scholars in many lands toiled without reward or recompense to dispel the Stygian darkness of medievalism. The Holy Trinity of Apostle–Martyr–Hero is indeed the adorable Divinity revealed by History to our reverent and dazzled eyes. We bow down in wonder and worship, like those awe-struck pilgrims in the golden pagodas of Cambodia or Ceylon. The historians are the high-priests of this immemorial and everlasting cult. The Egyptian mummies preserve only the body, the husk and shell of Personality: but History keeps alive the Mind and Soul of every great benefactor of the human race. Some Christians were thrown to the lions long ago, but Eusebius has told their story, which we finish with tears in our eyes. Under Shaman Hwui Li's guidance, we travel with Yuan Chwang, who won the prize of Buddhist lore by defying the obstructive and malignant Himalayas and living laborious days in self-imposed exile. The philosophers and statesmen of Greece and Rome live again for us in the pages of Diogenes Laertius and Plutarch. The Sufi saints still teach us through the edifying memoirs of Fariduddin Attar. Valmiki, Asser, Joinville, and Confucius have described the deeds of virtuous rulers like Rama, Alfred, St. Louis, Yao, and Wen. Al-Jazari and Ibn-Khallikan record the achievements of the makers of Islamic culture. Vasari delineates the artists of the Italian Renaissance, and J. Prelooker describes the heroism of the Russian democrats and socialists.

In this fascinating quest of "the footprints" left by great men and women "on the sands of Time," historical Biography is our guide and leader. These footprints are not fleeting, but as imperishable as platinum letters imprinted on gold leaf. We need not accept Carlyle's well-known dictum: "Universal history, the history of what man has accomplished in this world, is at bottom the history of the great men who have worked here." R. W. Emerson was also misled by excessive hero-worship, when he wrote: "There is properly no history, only biography." V. Cousin went so far as to teach that the faults of the great men should not be mentioned, as their virtues and achievements atoned for their sins! E. Renan held the preposterous anti-democratic view that the purpose of History is the production of men of genius, while L. Kossuth identified society only with its great men, when he said: "Nationality is the aggregated individuality of the greatest men of the nation." But I say that History is made by *all* the ordinary men and women working and striving in their environment, as the coral reef is created by the silent labours of numberless tiny polyps. William Morris sings truly:

> "Some had name and fame and honour, learn'd they were, and wise, and strong,
> Some were nameless, poor, unlettered, weak in all but grief and wrong.
> Named and nameless all live in us, one and all they lead us yet,
> Every pain to count for nothing, every sorrow to forget."

Progress is thus the gift bestowed on us by all the eager, active, forward-looking men and women, who have lived and died during five hundred centuries or more. But Biography picks out the famous leaders, who sacrificed more than the others. They guided and organized the people by the force of their superior character and intellect. Organization implies leadership, and the true leader may be regarded as the representative of the masses, as Mickiewicz could say: "I am a million." As the traveller is impressed by Everest, Kanchenchunga, and Aconcagua, and not by all the small peaks and hills, even so the Biographer finds his material in the eventful and interesting careers of the leaders, who worked for and with the "rank and file" of the different movements. An ambassador represents a nation, and a delegate speaks for a society; in the same way, an apostle, hero, or martyr is considered to be the worthy representative of all the members of a historic Church or Party. We honour them by honouring him or her; we admire their energy and sacrifice in admiring him or her. In this sense, Biography is the perennial Fountain of the Moral Elixir for us. We learn Virtue by spontaneous inspiration, not through dull exhortation. Biography offers for our contemplation the noblest thoughts, words, and deeds of the leaders of all the progressive movements that have gradually transformed the Kanjera man into the modern civilized citizen. History thus puts us into direct touch with the true Zoroastrian Succession of saints and sages, who have kept the fire of Enthusiasm burning on the altar of the Temple of Humanity through the ages. Warmed by that eternal fire, we too may save our souls from perishing in the icy hell of cynicism and egotism. Therefore, as you read History, say with Mary Ann Evans (alias "George Eliot"):—

"O may I join the choir invisible
Of those immortal dead, who live again
In minds made better by their presence."

Right Methods of Study

The right method of studying History is very important. History is like a sharp razor: if you handle it skilfully, it helps you to look clean and attractive; but you may also cut your skin, or even your throat, with it. All Churches, political parties, and national States abuse and maltreat History by teaching it in the wrong way in order to turn the children into fanatical bigots or ferocious patriots. History has such tremendous power to make or mar personality and character, that it may be a blessing or a curse, according to the method of presentation. Beware of purblind or mercenary history-mongers! Upon them rests the blame for much of the world's misery.

(1) History should be regarded as the record of the origin and development of Civilization as a whole. Start with the entire human race as the unit in historical studies. The whole of mankind, and nothing less, should be envisaged as the theme of History. History is a universal epic, or it is nothing. If it is written and interpreted by narrow-minded patriots or sectarians, it is changed into "a tale told by an idiot, full of sound and fury, signifying nothing." You must clearly understand that Humanity, one and indivisible, is the only proper subject of History. Humanity and History are the Siamese twins that must never be separated.

(2) You should never follow the dangerous guides, who suppose that "History" means only the history of Europe, and nothing more. It is a strange and saddening experience to discover how some well-educated scholars even now confine themselves to the history of Europe and publish instructive treatises on "the Western mind," "the heroes of the West," etc. European history may be divided into "ancient," "medieval," and "modern": but what about World-history? Some authors claim to write "the history of the world," but they devote only a few pages to ancient China, Japan, Persia, and India, and then proceed to narrate the annals of Europe in detail, as if nothing important had happened in Asia after that remote epoch and Clio had gone to sleep there for two thousand years. Thus "the world" is regarded as equivalent to "Europe," and the part is unwisely taken for the whole. This curious aberration is due to impudence, indolence, and ignorance, and there is no excuse for it. History is thus misinterpreted and travestied. I wish I could set every historian of this type on

a hill and point out to him what Michael showed to Adam's wondering eyes:—

> "His eye might there command wherever stood
> City of old or modern fame, the seat
> Of mightiest empire, from the destined walls
> Of Cambalu, seat of Cathaian Cham,
> And Samarcand by Oxus, Temir's throne,
> To Paquin, of Sinaean Kings, and thence
> To Agra and Lahore, of Great Mogul,
> Down to the golden Chersonese, or where
> The Persian in Ecbatan sat, or since
> In Ispahan."

(9) Many scholars have cruelly cut up History into "national" fragments and written learned tomes on the history of England, France, Germany, Albania, Armenia, Iraq, etc. They are the brutal butchers of History. Mankind is unfortunately split up into many "nations" at present, but it does not follow that this temporary sectionalism should also invade the domain of History. Kant's great idea of "Universal History" has been forgotten in the last century. Demented Nationalism attempts to desecrate and disintegrate holy History, and to use its mangled and mutilated limbs as decorative embellishments for the bloodstained mansions and monuments of the warring Nations. The nation-states must poison the young citizens' minds with the virulent virus of "patriotism" at a tender age, and History is therefore ruthlessly hacked and hewn into as many pieces as there are "nations" in the world. But what does the scientific historian say? He gnashes his teeth in rage and cries: "You have murdered History; therefore you shall sleep in peace no more. This shall be your doom, that, like the house of Atreus, you shall destroy one another, because you have first destroyed History."

History is really unintelligible, if it is divided into "national" sections to suit the exigencies of political strife at different periods. The mighty movements of the past resemble the great rivers, which flow through several countries and take no account of nationality. The Rhine, the Danube, and the Ganges are thoroughly unpatriotic vagrants. All nations have grown and thriven on fruits, vegetables, cereals, ideas, and institutions that have been imported from other countries. No nation has developed by its own unaided strength. As the Swedish poet Tegner says: "Only barbarism was indigenous in the beginning." A "national" historian cannot explain the origin of the religious, political, and intellectual movements that suddenly appear in the history of his own beloved country. His narrative is always obscure and unsatisfactory; it is also illogical and unscientific. Even Karl Lamprecht, who devoted himself only to German history, admits that " the full historical comprehension of a single change or a single phenomenon, with their historical significance, can only be acquired from the most general principles, that is to say, from the application of the highest universal-historical categories."

Thus Christianity, Chivalry, the Franciscan Order, the Reformation, and the Renaissance were all imported into England. What would England be without these precious gifts of other peoples? But if we read the history of England as it is written, St. Augustine and the friars seem to come from nowhere; the Reformation appears to have no relation to Martin Luther. In fact, politicians like Henry VIII and Elizabeth usurp the place of the prophets, Luther and Calvin, in the reader's imagination! The American historians tell us a great deal about the Pilgrim Fathers, but very little about Calvin, who begat them. Again, Spenser and Milton are inexplicable without a knowledge of the earlier Italian poets, but the latter are not discussed in a " national " historical treatise, because they were not born in England! Similarly, the " national " historian of Japan cannot explain the introduction of Buddhism, Confucianism, Christianity, Democracy, Industrialism, and Socialism into his country. Such an author is like a French geographer, who should observe the Rhône only between Lyons and Marseilles on French territory, and refuse to go and see the majestic Swiss glacier from which it issues as a tiny stream. Such a geographer may be an admirable "nationalist," but he would be a poor scientist. In fact, the device of dividing History into exclusive "national" compartments is utterly absurd, ridiculous, and indefensible. History, which should impress the mind's eye as a vast and stately edifice, adorned with all the gifts and masterpieces of art and science, now strikes our imagination as a disorderly collection of paltry and primitive huts, decorated with the head-hunter's trophies of human skulls and bones. The historians have been compelled to bear the yoke of benighted Patriotism. It is high time that they should boldly declare their independence. They should refuse to march meekly and humbly in the triumphal procession of arrogant Nationalism, as the conquered kings walked behind Julius Cæsar. They must emphatically and unequivocally say: " We are the servants of Humanity and Truth: we cannot dishonour History in order to gratify your vanity and war-lust. We are scientists and moralists, not sycophants and trumpeters."

" National " history also fixes our attention on wars and many minor issues. The master-clue of Universal History is the gradual development of human Civilization; but the patriotic historians, who are the hired thugs of Nationalism, mislead us by attaching undue importance to bloody wars and small movements, *e.g.* the exodus of the Jews from Egypt, the unification of England under Egbert, the wars between Sweden and Denmark, and between Germany and France, the separation of Norway from Sweden and of Portugal from Spain, the local exploits of Bruce and Wallace, etc. All sense of proportion is thus lost, and History is shown to be "red in tooth and claw" with the blood of the slaughtered "patriots" of all nations. The product of such a mentality cannot be true History; it is always a pitiful caricature and a shameful sordid story of mass-murder.

Therefore I warn you, "Beware of the national historians." History is truly like a lustrous diamond with many facets; it loses all value, if it is broken into numerous fragments. The history of the world is marked by fundamental unity: it is not just equal to the sum of the histories of England, France, Japan, and other countries. The topsy-turvy custom of teaching "national" history first and world-history later (or not at all) must be abolished.

If History is studied in a scientific and cosmopolitan spirit, a new era must be employed for reckoning dates and periods of time. There have been several national eras, *e g.* the Hellenic system of the Olympiads, the Roman era which began with the year of the foundation of Rome, the Vikrama era of India, the Jewish era, etc. Several religious eras are used by the different Churches. The Moslem era commemorates Muhammad's flight from Mecca, and the Christian era is associated with the birth of Jesus Christ. But scientific and universal History cannot approve of such eras. We do not believe that the birth of Christ was the most important central event in world-history. We are not Christians or Moslems, and need not pay homage to the Churches in this way. Besides, such eras are extremely inconvenient; we must reckon backward for many centuries of recorded history. This unnatural procedure is most illogical and produces mental confusion. History (as distinguished from Archæology) requires a historical era, which should transport the mind back to the beginning of the historical period of civilization in Egypt and Babylonia. It should roughly measure the length of the historical period. For my present purpose, I may tentatively fix 5000 B.C. as the starting-point of the historical era; but this important question must be settled by a congress of eminent historians. This era should be called the Era of History, and denoted by A.H. (Anno Historiæ).

(4) Some great historians, like Ranke, Droysen, Maurenbrecher, and Freeman, have promulgated the doctrine that "History is past politics." They teach that History should deal only with the evolution of the State, and not with the development of all the factors of Civilization like philosophy, art, literature, science, industry, commerce, etc. Only the record of wars, treaties, constitutions, laws, revolutions, and other political events is thus dignified with the title of "History." All other processes and movements are neglected, as they are regarded as extraneous to "History" proper. Thus J. R. Seeley says: "The historian is a politicist. The political group or organism, the State, is his study. . . . To lecture on Political Science is to lecture on History." This is an unsound and misleading doctrine, as it attaches excessive importance to a single aspect of human activity. The State is important, but it is not all-important. At some crises, the political events are the decisive factors in History and should occupy the centre of the stage. But, at other times, religion, art, literature, science, or economics may be the dominant influence in society, and History must pay homage to it. The noble Art of the Italian Renaissance was historically a more momentous phenomenon than the political intrigues and cabals of the petty Italian despots, who are now forgotten. The sixty-third century A.H. (thirteenth A.D.) in Europe is glorious on account of the Universities and the friars; but who cares for the political annals of that century? The epoch of the T'ang dynasty is remembered in China for its poetry and art, but it was not very eventful in the political sense. Who was more important for history, Jesus Christ or Tiberius? Buddha or Ajatasatru? Darwin or Gladstone? Auguste Comte or Napoleon III? Goethe or the Duke of Weimar? It is clear that the political history of a period does not always represent its most characteristic activity, which may lie in other spheres. The State at such a time may be a dull and barren institution, while the Church, the Academy, or the Chamber of Commerce may be pulsating with new life. The State may then serve only as the husk, covering and guarding the precious grain within. Lowell has warned us: "Man is more than constitutions." History is much more than mere politics. Why should History confine itself to past politics? History is not merely the pastime of politicians. It is the record of *all* that Man has thought and done, dared and suffered, felt and cherished. Man is not only a subject or a voter: he is also a parent,

a bread-winner, an art-lover, and a thinker. The whole of his work must be known and appreciated.

The Cream of History

You should first read several good treatises on World-history in general, and then concentrate especially on the following periods, movements, and personalities:—

(1) Early Egypt, Sculpture and Architecture.
(2) Akhnaton: his Life and Work.
(3) War between Persia and Hellas.
(4) Greek Democracy and Socialism.
(5) Greek Philosophy from Thales to Plotinus.
(6) Greek Art (Sculpture and Architecture).
(7) Homer's "Odyssey."
(8) Greek Tragedy (Æschylus, Sophocles, Euripides).
(9) The Scientists and Scholars of Alexandria in the forty-eighth century A.H. (third century B.C.).
(10) The Hebrew Prophets.
(11) Origin and Growth of the Christian Church: its Martyrs and Apostles.
(12) Zoroaster and the Rise of Zoroastrianism.
(13) Buddha and Buddhism in India. Asoka. Jainism.
(14) Nagarjuna and the Mahayana. Gandhara Sculpture.
(15) Kung-fu-tzu (Confucius), Mencius, and their movement. Lao-tse and Taoism.
(16) Early History of Rome. Democracy and Republicanism.
(17) Class-struggles in Rome.
(18) The Reign of Justinian. Roman Law. Byzantine Art.
(19) The Rise of Monasticism in Egypt. The Orders of St. Basil and St. Benedict.
(20) Spread of Christianity in Europe. Irish Saints and Scholars.
(21) St. Francis and his Order. The Spiritual Friars.
(22) Muhammad and early Islam.
(23) The Islamic Renaissance; Moslem Philosophy and Science (fifty-ninth to sixty-second centuries).
(24) Sufism and its Saints.
(25) The Dervish Orders.
(26) Persian Didactic Poetry.
(27) The T'ang Dynasty in China. Progress of Buddhism Chinese Painting.

(28) The Gupta Empire in India. Indian Literature and Art. The Ramayana.
(29) The Sassanian Period in Persia.
(30) The Renaissance in the Byzantine Empire (fifty-ninth century A.H.) (ninth A.D.). Photius and Arethas.
(31) Early Renaissance in Europe (fifty-second and fifty-third centuries).
(32) The War between the Communes of Lombardy and the Emperor.
(33) The Great Renaissance in Italy and Europe (sixty-fourth, sixty-fifth, and sixty-sixth centuries). The New Schools and Colleges. Democracy at Florence. Italian Painting, Sculpture, and Architecture.
(34) The Vaishnava Saints of N. India. Reformers. Modern Hindu Sects. Tamil Saints.
(35) The Buddhist Religious Leaders of China and Japan; their Sects and Schools. Japanese Sculpture.
(36) The Sung Philosophers in China.
(37) Discovery of the Cape route and of America. Columbus.
(38) The Protestant Reformation. Luther, Calvin, Zwingli, Anabaptists, Puritans, Socinians, Nonconformists in England and America. Gustavus Adolphus. The Dutch War of Independence.
(39) India's Wars of Independence against the Moguls. Mogul and Rajput Painting. Mogul Architecture in N. India. Hindu Architecture in S. India.
(40) Progress of Science since 6400 in Europe and America.
(41) German Music from Bach to Wagner.
(42) Modern English Poetry. French Tragedy and Comedy. German Drama, Lyrics, and Short Stories. Russian Novels and Ballet. French and English Landscape-Painters.
(43) Modern Democracy. English, American, and French Revolutions. European and South American National Movements. Parliaments. Abolition of Slavery.
(44) Socialism in Europe. The Russian Revolution. The Jesuits in Paraguay. The Communist Colonies of N. America.
(45) Modern Philosophy and Religion. Positivism. Spinoza. Spencer. Freethought and Ethical Movements in Europe and America. Theosophy. The Brahmo samaj. Bahaism. Oomoto in Japan.
(46) The Peace Movement. Esperanto. The League of Nations.

These are the really important and instructive periods and movements in history. If you wish to extract the very cream of History for your personal development, you may go further and concentrate only on the following abbreviated list:—

(1) The "Odyssey." Greek Tragedy. Greek Philosophy. Greek Art (Sculpture and Architecture).
(2) Lives of Rama, Krishna, Zoroaster, Confucius, Mencius, Laotse, Mahavira, Buddha, Mani, Muhammad, Yuan-Chwang, Rabia, Nanak, Bodhidharma, Chi-Kai, Luther, Calvin, Fox, Bab, Baha-ullah, Honen, Shinran, Nishiren, Wesley.
(3) History of Early Christianity.
(4) The Order of St. Benedict and its work.
(5) The lives of Petrarch, Erasmus, and the other Scholars of the Renaissance. Vittorino and other Educationists.
(6) Chinese and Italian Painting. Japanese, Gandhara, and Italian Sculpture. Gothic Cathedrals. Islamic Architecture in Spain and India.
(7) German Music.
(8) English Poetry. Shakespeare. French Comedy. German Lyrics. Goethe. Russian Novels. Tolstoi and Dostoievsky.
(9) Modern Democracy.
(10) History of Modern Science and Education.
(11) Modern Socialism and Communism.
(12) Modern Philosophy. Rationalism, Positivism, and Freethought.
(13) Modern Internationalism and the League of Nations.

Some Lessons of History

If you study History in this way, you will learn a few necessary and salutary lessons.

(1) You will become a convinced cosmopolitan, like Goethe, who said: "Above all nations is Humanity." The Unity of Mankind will shine forth like sunshine on your mind, and destroy the malevolent microbes that breed such destructive plagues as Nationalism and Race-pride. Kant taught that World-history should enable us to realize the unity of the human race, and Tennyson expressed the hope that it would find its consummation in "The Parliament of Man, the Federation of the World." History shows you how all nations and races have striven through

sore toil and travail to conquer Nature, eliminate evil, and improve society and the individual, as far as they could. History also proves the interdependence of all races and nations. The Greeks learned much from the Egyptians, and the Romans from the Greeks. The Chinese and the Hindus borrowed from each other. The Moslems were the pupils of Greece and India before they became the teachers of Europe. The modern Europeans owe an enormous debt to Greece, Rome, and Islam. We are indebted to Italy for the Renaissance, to Germany for the Reformation, to France for the Revolution and Positivism, and so on. The races and nations have also thriven through blood-mixture in the past. The Aryans and the aborigines mixed in India, the Etruscans and the Romans in Italy, the Arabs and the Spaniards in Spain, the Celts and the Teutons in England, the Slavs and the Teutons in Prussia, the Europeans and the Americans in Brazil, etc. The historian joyfully cries with Terence: "I am a Man, and nothing that relates to Man is alien to me."

World-history will thus cure you of the intellectual myopia, from which some squinting patriots and "race-philosophers" suffer. They can see only a part of Humanity, but not the whole of it. They love to sing the praises of a small nation, or a group of nations, or a single race. They indulge in exaggeration and sophistry in order to prove that a particular nation has been, is, or will be superior to all the others, or that a nation or a race has contributed much more than the others to the development of Civilization. Some of them would indeed claim a monopoly of culture and achievement for one nation or race! Such grotesque megalomania is a phenomenon of spiritual pathology. The "nation-worshippers" and the "race-maniacs" are the pitiable victims of brain-disease. Thus J. Michelet declared that "logic and history" had proved to him that "his glorious country was henceforth the pilot of the vessel of humanity." He added that he was not influenced by patriotism in reaching this conclusion. A drunken brawler always swears that he is not drunk. F. P. G. Guizot wrote: "To France, therefore, must be ascribed the honour, that her civilization has reproduced more faithfully than any other the general type and fundamental idea of civilization." In 6807, Fichte declared that the progress of culture and science would depend on Germany! H. S. Chamberlain is obsessed with the notion that the "Teutons" are the chosen people. He says: "The inhabitants of northern Europe have become the makers of the world's history. The great Italians of the rinascimento were all born either in the north, saturated with Lombardic, Gothic, and Frankish blood, or in the extreme Germano-Hellenic south. . . . Our whole civilization and culture of to-day is the work of one definite race of men, the Teutonic." Some race-fanatics even assert that Jesus Christ was of Teutonic origin! (But what about Moses and Confucius?) Others laud "the Aryans," and belittle the Semites. They forget that the Semites of Egypt and Mesopotamia were the first pioneers, whose pupils the Aryans became. A Hindu has dedicated his book, entitled "Hindu Superiority," to "India, paradise on earth; thou gavest Civilization and Religion to the world; Eternal, Immortal, Everlasting." Purblind patriotism can find such lyrical utterance! M. N. Dhalla makes this untenable claim: "Zoroastrian Persia enjoyed an importance quite unique in the world's history, from about 1000 B.C. to the seventh century A.D." All such historians are like lovers and lunatics, who are "of imagination all compact": they have learned to love only a part of Humanity very passionately. Let us now learn to love Mankind as comrades.

(2) You will become tolerant and humane in your judgment of the dead. History judges all persons by the standard of their age and environment, and not by our advanced ideals. Thus perhaps you will learn "to speak nothing but good of the dead," who cannot reply to an attack on their honour. You will sympathize with both Calvin and Servetus.

(3) You will become an ardent but discriminating reformer. History will convince you that all elements of permanent value in the old institutions must be preserved, and that every ancient institution is not altogether rotten. It is an amalgam of good and evil. You will discover all the good that should be cherished and preserved in the historic religions and customs. You will not act as a thoughtless root-and-branch iconoclast. At the same time, you will recognize the necessity of reforming and overhauling all institutions at frequent intervals, "lest one good custom should corrupt the world." You will ruthlessly abolish and suppress all institutions that have outlived their usefulness, as the gardener lops off the dead branches from the tree. You will not tolerate the ancient abuses, anomalies, anachronisms, absurdities, and monstrosities that stifle and smother the human spirit in all countries and among all nations. You will understand that the Architect of Progress must demolish some old dilapidated houses before beautiful modern buildings can be erected on the site. Then you will not be afraid to pull down in order to construct anew, while

you keep intact everything that is valuable in the old systems. Whittier says very wisely:

> "I looked · aside the dust-cloud rolled.
> The Waster seemed the Builder too;
> Up springing from the ruined Old
> I saw the New
> 'Twas but the ruin of the bad,
> The wasting of the wrong and ill,
> Whate'er of good the old time had
> Was living still."

(4) You will be convinced of the validity of the following general propositions:

1. Personal despotic rule is a curse. Government by assembly is the only safeguard against misrule (*e.g.* Greece, Rome, India, England, France).

2. Monotheism breeds intolerance (*e.g.* Islam, Christianity).

3. The maximum of personal freedom is the mainspring of progress (*e.g.* Athens, England, India, United States, France, Scandinavia, Switzerland).

4. Organized monastic institutions, based on the rule of celibacy, are harmful (*e.g.* Catholic and Buddhist monasteries).

5. Oligarchies are always very selfish and cruel, and also lead to perpetual internecine strife (*e.g.* the Romans, the feudal Barons, the French bourgeoisie, the Japanese landlords).

6. Self-denial and the simple life are necessary for the success of new movements (*e.g.* Buddha, Jesus, Muhammad, Dayanand, Mazzini, Marx).

7. Martyrdom must sometimes be endured for the sake of Progress (*e.g.* St. Stephen, Etienne Dolet, Vanini, Ferrer, Teg Bahadur, Qurrat-al-Ayn).

8. Economic inequality leads to disorder or stagnation (*e.g.* Peru, Greece, France, Russia).

9. Standing armies are a menace to the freedom of the people (*e.g.* Mogul Empire, Russia, Prussia, Turkey).

10. Polytheism, monotheism, and metaphysics are inimical to Science and Progress (*e.g.* Peru, Mexico, Egypt, Babylonia, Byzantium, India, Islam, medieval Europe).

11. Great art is the product of great social ideals (*e.g.* Periclean art, Gothic cathedrals, Buddhist scupture).

12. The conquest of Nature can be enormously accelerated through the systematic encouragement of scientific research (*e.g.* Europe in the last century).

13. The people can be led to happiness or to disaster by their leaders (*e.g.* Themistocles, Nicias, Alexander, Cromwell, Washington, Napoleon, Chatham, Charles XII, Banda, Caliph Omar, Lenin).

14. Resolute armed minorities can impose new religions, laws, and institutions on the people by force (*e.g.* the Moslems in Persia and Kashmir; the English Protestants; the Bolsheviks; the Fascists; the Incas).

15. Able and energetic men will exploit the people by fraud or force, if they are not trained in high ideals of personal conduct. Every movement tends to produce a gang of charlatans and parasites, however noble its aims may be at the outset (*e.g.* Christian bishops, Trade Union officials, Socialist leaders).

16. Imperialism always involves cruelty and injustice, and leads to the degeneration of both the conquering and the conquered peoples (*e.g.* Assyria, Persia, Rome, Spain).

17. Progress is facilitated by the contact of different cultures (*e.g.* Greek, Indian, and Chinese culture in Central Asia; Greek and Hebrew culture in the Roman Empire; Greek, Roman, and Christian culture in Zoroastrian Persia; Moslem and Indian culture in the Abbaside Empire; European, Hindu, and Islamic culture in India).

18. Political fusion and aggregation are inevitable (*e.g.* abolition of the Heptarchy in England; Union of England and Scotland; the German Empire; the United States of America).

Theories of History

You should reject all theological, metaphysical, and fatalistic theories of History.

(1) In the "philosophy of History," St. Augustine, Orosius, Tabari, Bossuet, Buchez, Ravaisson-Mollien, Keshub Chunder Sen, and others have advanced the theistic theory, which attributes all historical events and movements to the will of "God" and the dispensation of "Providence." Thus Bossuet regards all History as the prelude to the establishment of the Roman Church. He says: "God made use of the Assyrians and Babylonians to chastise His people; of the Persians to restore it; of Alexander and his immediate successors to protect it . . . and of the Romans to maintain its liberty against the Kings of Syria, to avenge its rejection and crucifixion of Christ, and to secure the spread and triumph of the Christian faith." Buchez teaches that God has guided the course of History by four revelations, that had been given to Adam,

Noah, an unnamed prophet, and Christ! Carlyle regards History as "a mighty drama, whose author is God." Keshub Chunder Sen said: "History is a most sublime revelation of God, and is full of religious significance." Matthew Arnold has expressed the same fantastic idea in verse:

> "Before Man parted for this earthly strand,
> While yet upon the verge of heaven he stood,
> God put a heap of letters in his hand,
> And bade him make with them what word he could.
> And Man has turned them many times · made Greece,
> Rome, England, France: Yes, nor in vain essayed
> Way after way, changes that never cease.
> . . . .
> One day, thou say'st, there will at last appear
> The word, the order, which God meant should be."

Thus History is reduced to a display of marionettes, a vast Punch-and-Judy show, in which "God" pulls all the strings!

(2) G. W. F. Hegel, V. Cousin, A. Fouillée, B. Croce, and other thinkers have interpreted History according to their misty and musty metaphysics. Hegel's logical Idealism, as applied to History, "postulates the world-spirit striving for Consciousness, and then freedom, its essential nature." This spirit assumes successive forms, which it successively transcends. These forms are exhibited in the peculiar natural genius of historical peoples In the Persians, the world-spirit attained unlimited immanence of subjectivity; in the Greeks, "individuality conditioned by beauty"; in the Romans, "subjective inwardness." The German spirit is the spirit of the new world; its aim is "the realization of absolute truth, as the unlimited self-determination of Freedom." This immense metaphysical cobweb, spun out of the philosopher's capacious mind, should be swept away by the besom of historical insight and gentle ridicule. V. Cousin divides History into three epochs, corresponding to the three essential elements of thought: the epoch of the supremacy of the Infinite, of the Finite, and of the relation of the Infinite and the Finite! He opines that a fourth epoch is impossible! B. Croce is responsible for such a rigmarole as this: "The spirit itself is history, and, in every one of its moments, the maker of history, and at the same time the result of all foregoing history, so that the spirit carries within itself the whole of its history, which in fact coincides with the spirit itself." Alfred Fouillée explains history by his doctrine of the "Idea-Forces," which are supposed to be the prime movers of social change. He says: "The ideal contains the elements of possibility, which lead to the result

that, when it is present in thought, it finds the means of passing into reality."

Metaphysical conceptions have also been employed by some historians to "explain" many historical phenomena, which are certainly not made more intelligible by this ingenious method. The "spirit" or "genius" of a nation or race has been mentioned as a determining cause without any reference to the economic, geographical, social, and personal factors involved. Such "explanations" are not helpful. They merely mean that a nation or race did something because it could do it, or failed to do something because it could not do it. Thus Grote and Gilbert Murray speak of "the Greek mind," "Hellenism," and "the Hellenic spirit." Paparrigopoulo "explains" all Greek history by "Hellenic character." E. Renan attributes the characteristics of the Arab civilization to "the Semitic spirit." J. Morley declares that the Greeks and the Jews were "devoid of the sovereign faculty of political coherency." Cunningham speaks of "the principles which the Greek and the Phœnician respectively represented." Such superficial interpreters throw no light on historical causation: they only assume the existence of certain metaphysical entities, and fob us off with mere words. Such thinkers live in the Cloud-cuckootown that was celebrated by Aristophanes. Let us come down to solid earth and deal with the scientific theories.

(3) Among the scientific views of History, all the mechanical or fatalistic theories must be rejected, as they ascribe historical phenomena only to the influence of Environment (and exclude or neglect Personality). They may be described as semi-scientific theories, which should be revised and amplified. They are not wrong, but one-sided. If you come across a historian who teaches that Environment is omnipotent, you may regard him as a one-eyed wise man. If he had been blessed with two eyes, he would also have recognized the power of human Personality in History. I teach that History is the product of two forces, Environment and Personality. Personality is the father, and Environment is the mother. Personality is the active spermatozoon: Environment is the passive ovum.

Some scientific thinkers have exaggerated the influence of Environment upon the development of mankind. Bodin discussed the northern, middle, and southern nations and their habitat. Montesquieu tried to explain history principally by the geography and climate of different countries. He repudiated fatalism, but he frequently suggested that all laws and institutions were the products of soil and climate. He expressed the opinion that the people of the tropical regions were inevitably doomed to slavery and misery. He wrote: "Great heat enervates the strength and courage of men. The effeminacy of the people in hot climates has almost always rendered them slaves; the bravery of those in cold climates has enabled them to maintain their liberties. . . . Political servitude depends on the nature of the climate, like that which is civil and domestic. . . . The barrenness of the Attic soil established there a democracy; the fertility of that of Lacedæmonia an aristocratic constitution." J. G. von Herder also attached excessive importance to natural Environment; he described human history as a branch of natural history (*eine reine Naturgeschichte*). He suggested that history only exhibited the operation of the laws of external Nature through human beings. He said: "Climate is a chaos of causes, very dissimilar to each other, and in consequence acting slowly and in various ways, till at length they penetrate to the internal parts and change them by habit, and by the genetic law itself." T. H. Buckle over-estimated the potency of the purely physical factors even in the early stages of human progress, though he recognized the increasing power of Personality in advancing civilization. He wrote: "The various Aspects of Nature have caused corresponding varieties in the popular character. . . . Climate, Food, and Soil have originated the most important consequences in regard to the general organization of Society." H. Taine taught that race and environment were the main factors in History, and said: "History is a mechanical problem. . . . Our preferences are futile; Nature and History have determined things in advance." L. Feuerbach boldly based History on gastronomy and declared: "Man is what he eats." Karl Marx and F. Engels over-emphasized the economic conditions and forces that mould society and its institutions, though they also clearly indicated the limitations of the "economic interpretation" of History. Marx said: "The manner of production, of material life, conditions in general the process of social, political, and spiritual life. . . . The hand-mill gives you society with the feudal lord, the steam-mill, society with the industrial capitalist. . . . The ideal is nothing else than the material world reflected by the human mind and translated into forms of thought." Engels wrote: "In every historical epoch, the prevailing mode of economic production and exchange, and the social organization necessarily following from it, form the basis upon which is built up, and upon which alone can be explained, the political and intellectual history of that epoch." Many socialists and communists have attempted to explain all ideas, movements, and events entirely and exclusively according to the "materialist conception" of History. But they forget that Engels himself rejected this method as unsound, when he wrote: "Marx and I are partly responsible for the fact that the younger men have sometimes laid more stress on the economic fact than was necessary." (We should never forget Marx's inimitable saying: "I am not a Marxist.")

It must be admitted that Environment is a very potent factor in History. It must be so. It would be absurd to suggest that the early civilizations could have developed in the arid deserts of Arabia or the bleak highlands of Tibet. The character and institutions of mountaineers will always distinguish them from the people of the plains; and the seafaring folk must have a peculiar outlook on life on account of their work on the water. Athens, Rhodes, and Sidon could not resemble secluded, land-locked Sparta. The Swiss supplied mercenaries to the European princes, and also preserved their democratic institutions in the Age of Despotism. The rugged children of the Himalayas bear the stamp of the snowy peaks and glaciers on their faces and in their souls. No one expects to find a flourishing civilization in Greenland or Tierra del Fuego. The people of tropical and semi-tropical countries like India, Java, and Brazil must differ in their physique and mentality from the denizens of the high latitudes of England, Germany, and Siberia, as the burning, blazing sun is a fundamental fact that can never be ignored. Tennyson has even ventured to generalize thus:

> "O tell her, Swallow, thou that knowest each,
> That bright and fierce and fickle is the South,
> And dark and true and tender is the North."

This dictum may not be acceptable to all; but it stands to reason that there will always be certain marked differences between North and South, as their climates and foodstuffs cannot be the same. Man cannot defy Nature altogether. In China and France, North and South have really given birth to two different nations. The Roman eagles could not penetrate far into Germany and Great Britain, while they were irresistible in the South. The plastic Arts have found a congenial home in the South, while they have been somewhat of exotics in the North. The North appreciates quantity in food and drink, and produces "gourmands"; the South values quality and breeds refined "gourmets." The North must conquer Nature: the South can enjoy her. The North must witness more bitter and protracted class-conflicts than the South (other things being equal), as those two silent agitators, Hunger and Cold, can assert themselves more powerfully and persistently in Scandinavia than in Sicily or Ceylon. Apart from climate and geographical situation, the economic and political institutions of a people must also partially determine its laws, customs, and ideas. The inhabitants of an agricultural country like Argentina, India, or Southern France must think and act in a different way from the highly industrialized peoples of England, Germany, and Northern France. Even in the same country, particular groups like fishermen and miners have certain peculiar characteristics. Our daily bread not only fills the stomach, but moulds, colours, and controls our minds and hearts and souls in their deepest recesses. The victims of landlordism in Bengal, England, and Germany must be more servile than the free peasants of the Punjab, France, and Sweden. The members of the semi-socialistic Jesuit settlement in Paraguay developed greater social virtues than their compatriots, who were not so fortunate. The citizen of a republic is less snobbish than the subject of a monarch. Demosthenes declared long ago: "The polity of the State educates and trains the people." Herodotus clearly indicated the beneficial effects of Democracy on the Athenian citizen, and wrote: "When the Athenians were governed by tyrants, they were not superior to their neighbours; but when they were free, they excelled all the others. It is seen what an excellent thing equality of rights is, not only in one instance, but in every way." Similarly, the political institutions of England, France, the United States, and Japan must produce different types of character Thus Environment, in all its various forms, affects men's lives at every point from the cradle to the grave. It is as impossible to escape its influence as it would be to get out of one's own skin. With your birth in a particular country at a particular epoch, your horoscope is definitely fixed for a larger or smaller number of the planetary houses; in the case of many persons, it is determined for almost all the houses. Environment is indeed one of the ever-active potters that mould our human clay.

There is another potter too, and that is Personality. The semi-scientific philosophers, who exaggerate the power of Environment, forget that History, like Sparta, is governed by two rulers. Environment and Personality are the two creative and causative forces in History.

The fragile fatalistic theories of the omnipotence of Environment are completely smashed, when they encounter the hard facts of history, like a glass dropped on the ground. The same Environment has produced different types of men, different customs and laws, different religious and philosophical ideas, at different epochs. Similar institutions are found to flourish among nations living in the midst of widely divergent Environments. This undeniable fact proves that Environment cannot be all-powerful. Thus Buckle was led to the demonstrably false opinion that the civilizations of Egypt and India must have been very similar, as he knew that the *milieu* was similar. Montesquieu assigned political despotism to the tropical regions, but we know that free republics existed in India in the forty-sixth century A.H. (fifth century B.C.) and that despotism has wrought havoc in France, England, Germany, and Russia, which are miles away from the tropics. The Arabs lived in a country that is like a furnace, but they conquered the people of colder regions. Renan held the view that the Semites developed a monotheistic instinct as a corollary of their life in the desert; but the desert had been the home of the Arabs for countless generations before Muhammad, and they never thought of Monotheism. Akhnaton, Moses, and Anaxagoras, who are among the earliest monotheists known to history, were not born in the desert. Wordsworth believed that liberty was particularly associated with the mountains and the sea, and Schiller wrote: "Freedom dwells upon the mountains." Montesquieu also associated democracy with mountainous regions. But national or tribal freedom has flourished in ancient and modern Hellas, in Germany and Spain during the Napoleonic era, in Maharashtra, Nepal, and the Panjab in the sixty-eighth and sixty-ninth centuries, in Montenegro and Afghanistan, in modern Italy and Japan, in Switzerland in the sixty-fourth century, in the Congo during the war against the Portuguese, in Michoacan among the Tarascas, in the Atlas range among the Berbers, in Haiti, Holland, Scotland, and Ireland. Civic freedom, based on democracy, has been a less frequent phenomenon: it has been known in imperfect forms at Athens and Florence, in Northern India, and in Holland, England, Scandinavia, France, and other countries. Now it is clear that liberty has not been the exclusive possession of sea and mountain. The mountains of Kashmir, Tibet, and the Caucasus have not bestowed freedom and democracy on the people. Liberty has been established in north and south, east and west, on mountain and plain, on sea-coast and hinterland, under palm and pine, wherever and whenever Personality acted on a certain Environment with success. During the fifty-ninth, sixtieth, and sixty-first centuries A.H., the Moslems of torrid Iraq, sweltering in an enervating climate, were more active in the pursuit of science and philosophy than the Europeans of the bracing North. The indefatigable Italian scholars of the Renaissance, born in warm and sunny Italy, were infinitely more industrious than the learned monks of chilly England and Germany. The Anglo-Saxons in the sixty-first century A.H. were not noted for energy and vigour. Climate need not inevitably and universally produce lethargy or activity among the people; it tends to do so, but this tendency can be counteracted by Personality. As regards the economic factor, it does not reign in solitary grandeur. It *is* only one among many forces, and its effects can be modified and even nullified by Personality. The economic processes and methods of agriculture, domestic industry, and transport did not undergo many fundamental changes from the early period of history down to the end of the sixty-eighth century A.H. (eighteenth century A.D.). They were remarkably uniform over the whole world during those long centuries. The ploughs and the scythes, the horse-carriages and the sailing-vessels, the spinning-wheels and the water-wheels were employed by all civilized nations before the very modern era of steam and electricity. The technique of economic life was altogether stationary and unprogressive; there was not much difference in this respect between the tenth century A.H. and the fifty-fifth century. But we find an immense variety of experiments and achievements in religion, literature, politics, art, and philosophy during those five or six thousand years. The human race has been gladdened or saddened by monarchy, oligarchy, democracy, city-states, nation-states, empires, astrolatry, zoolatry, polytheism, monotheism, atheism, pantheism, tragedy, comedy, epics, lyrics, Greek and Gothic architecture, etc., etc. This wonderful diversity of intellectual, artistic, and political experience stands in sharp contrast to the immobility and uniformity of the "economic basis" of society. Surely all these various phenomena in the kaleidoscope of History could not be produced by a single factor, which changed very little or not at all. A pyramid cannot be reared on a point.

In the domain of Psychology and Ethics, strict "economic determinism" can be shown to be an utterly untenable hypothesis. Hundreds of enthusiastic Russian students worked and suffered with burning zeal for the triumph of Socialism, a movement that was directly antagonistic to their class-interests and incompatible with their bourgeois education. In fact, many leaders of Socialism have come from the upper and middle classes; they have unconsciously refuted the specious pleas of the out-and-out "economic determinists" by their own work and worth. St. Simon, Robert Owen, Louis Blanc, Marx, Bakunin, Kropotkin, Engels, Hyndman, Branting, Jaurès, Matteotti, Ernest Jones, and other self-sacrificing leaders have spent themselves in the service of Socialism, and thus exposed the fallacy that the "materialist conception" of History is universally valid. According to the pedantic pundits of mechanical "Marxism," the Socialist revolution should have broken out in the most advanced capitalist countries; but the explosion actually occurred in Russia, where Capitalism was least developed! K. Kautsky was therefore bewildered and took refuge in dogmatic denial, like the boy who visited the Zoo, saw the giraffe, and exclaimed "There isn't no such animal!" But K. Kautsky's gospel of "Marxism" was only a half-truth, as it exalted mechanical Environment and belittled living Personality. In the sphere of religion, it is true that the Reformation failed in Poland, because there was no commercial and industrial middle-class in that country. Jainism and Puritanism have been accepted chiefly by the urban trading-class. But Calvinism succeeded in Scotland, which also lacked a middle-class; and the merchants of the towns in India have divided their allegiance between Hinduism, Jainism, and Buddhism. The people of Java passed from Hinduism to Islam in the sixty-fifth century, though there was no change in the economic system. The early Christian Church drew its adherents chiefly from the urban traders and the working-class, but the same religious doctrines found ready acceptance at a later period among the farmers, noblemen, and kings of northern Europe. Their conversion to Christianity was not associated with any economic movement. In China and Japan, the introduction of Buddhism was not preceded by any economic revolution. Islam arose among prosperous middle-class people, but the farmers and labourers of Persia and Egypt are to-day the most devout of Moslems. History proves that many religious opinions and movements can make headway without any necessary connection with economic forces or class-interests. Man is a composite creature: he needs not only Money, but also Morality, Mirth, Music, and Mystery. Sometimes he must react to new stimuli according to his class-psychology and his economic situation, as a landowner or merchant or labourer. At other times he must respond and act as Man pure and simple, such as he would be in a classless society. When classes have been abolished, what will become of this dogma of "economic determinism"? Will there be no progress in philosophy, ethics, and art in a classless society? Will the human mind stand still, when no new technical inventions are made? The Mind, and not its product the Machine, is at the helm of History. A working-man now belongs to a class, but Nature created the species Man long before greed created the proletarian class. Class shall disappear one day; but Humanity will abide for ever. When a labourer enjoys a beautiful sunset or a delicious apple, listens to music or kisses his wife, receives a guest at his home or attends the funeral of a friend or relative, reads Poetry or ponders on the problems of life and death, he acts in virtue of his indefeasible humanity, and not in pursuit of his temporary class-interests. When the people bore Cimabue's "Madonna" in procession through the streets of Florence, or shouted that Diana of Ephesus was great, or assembled in their thousands to acclaim Garibaldi and Mollison, or came to blows over *Hernani*, or followed the funeral of Victor Hugo in solemn silence, or celebrated the life and deeds of Rama in annual pageants, or fled from Persia to India in order to keep their ancestral faith, or flocked to Palestine at the call of Zionism, or marched to Jerusalem in response to the appeal of Peter the Hermit, or voted money to build the Parthenon, or stubbornly refused to yield to Xerxes and Mardonius, or starved and shivered in Valley Forge, or fought like heroes at Valmy, Lützen, and Tours, or followed Voltaire's carriage in procession, or celebrated a festival to receive the relic of Buddha, then, at such moments, they were not thinking of Money, but of something else, which is far greater than Money.

The theorists of "economic determinism" mutilate and calumniate human nature, which is a rainbow of many hues; but they see only the yellow tint of gold and nothing else. History, properly and honestly interpreted, provides the cure for such lamentable colour-blindness.

Further, I ask, What or who changes the economic structure? Do new machines invent themselves? Did the hand-mill and the steam-mill, referred to by Marx, make themselves? Do new methods of production and distribution establish themselves? Do new social classes arise mysteriously and mechanically? No, men and women alter the economic structure of society by promoting technical progress, distributing commodities in new ways, and recognizing certain rights of property on the ground of labour, occupation, conquest, acquisition, bequest, etc. All these economic activities are not undertaken and accomplished by implements and instruments, but by living men and women. Thus, in the last resort, "economic determinism" (even if it were true) would depend on the minds and wills of human beings, on Personality. The mechanistic philosophers just stop short of the final question, "Who did it?" If they pushed their enquiries to the logical conclusion, they would discover that "What" always leads to "Who," and every "it" points to a "he" or "she." They forget that a man always lurks behind every machine, as there is a spider somewhere in every web. Even if Machines and Classes determine History, they are created and changed by Personality, which is thus the final arbiter of man's destiny. All economic processes and methods are the products and adjuncts of human Personality, which is the active creative power in History. All the arts and sciences should pay homage to the Mind and Will of Man.

If Environment and economic-political institutions really determined all the ideas and ideals of men, it would be impossible to explain how new ideas could ever arise and how an oppressive régime could ever be overthrown or modified. Environment must produce only such concepts as are compatible with it. Economic-political institutions must mould men in a certain pattern, which is congruous with their purpose. Thus monarchy breeds loyal subjects, and feudalism teaches that a good vassal must follow and serve his lord. But if these external influences were paramount and all-powerful, how could institutions ever be changed? Who could rebel against them? What force would be there to create malcontents and innovators? How could the Roman Empire witness the rise and growth of the Christian idealists, who obstinately refused to worship the Emperor's statue? Whence came their strange idea, which could not be the natural product of that economic-political system? How could the heretics of Provence, Valais, and Bohemia grow within the Catholic Church? How could Capitalism give birth to its opponents, the Socialists? As a matter of fact, the vast majority of people do tend to remain the passive slaves of Environment and economic-political institutions for a long time, as they are lacking in free creative Personality. But a minority always begins to criticize and condemn the old régime: these few rebels finally succeed in establishing new institutions. But whence come their new zeal and insight? It is idle merely to affirm that Thesis must lead to Antithesis. I ask, "Why so?" The Thesis must preserve itself. How can the Thesis itself produce something that negates and destroys it? Clearly there must be some potent hidden force besides the Thesis. That force is human Personality, which can be great and creative only in some souls in each epoch. The Antithesis is not produced only by the Thesis, but by the Thesis and Personality put together. Similarly, Personality unites Thesis and Antithesis into a new Synthesis, which can never be created otherwise. Personality is responsible for the dialectic of History.

I shall illustrate the combined influence of Environment and Personality in the causation of great events. The Persian War and the subsequent events in Greece and Athens necessitated the rebuilding of the temple on the Acropolis, but the genius of Pheidias created the immortal frieze of the Parthenon. There would certainly have been a frieze of some kind if Pheidias had never been born; but it would not have been the unique masterpiece that we owe to the peculiar genius of that artist. The political activity of the Turks, the need of spices for the population of Europe, and the economic interests of a section of the trading class led in the sixty-fifth century A.H. to the genesis of the idea that a new route to India should be discovered. But the adventurous spirit of Columbus, the sagacity of Isabella, and the heroism of the sailors realized the idea. The Puritan movement in England was responsible for the choice of an unsuitable subject for Milton's "Paradise Lost"; but Puritanism did not create the peculiarly constituted brain of the "mighty-mouthed inventor of harmonies." That brain was an adjunct of Personality. Every Puritan of that period did not write a great poem. The French Revolution was the result of certain economic and political conditions, combined with the propaganda of Rousseau, Voltaire, Diderot, and other thinkers. That Revolution gave Napoleon his chance; but can any serious scholar maintain that all the Napoleonic wars would have been fought just the same, if a man of Napoleon's genius and ambition had never existed? That genius and that ambition were as necessary as the general movement of economic and political forces at that time. Capitalism produced the necessary external circumstances for the growth of Socialism, but Capitalism did not go every morning to the British Museum in London for many years, and write "Das Kapital." It was a particular individual, named Karl Marx, who did it. Capitalism did not enable Marx's parents to give birth biologically to that original brain.

The equal importance of Environment and Personality was clearly indicated by Themistocles long ago. Plutarch relates the incident thus: "Once an ordinary citizen of the small city of Seriphos said to Themistocles: 'You owe your glory, not to yourself, but to your great city of Athens.' He replied: 'Very true; I should not have become famous, if I had been born at Seriphos; but you would not have become great and powerful, even if you had been an Athenian.' "

Environment may be compared to the cold candle, and Personality to the match, without which it cannot be lit. Both together produce the light that lightens the world.

(4) Some philosophers have tried to discover a general, necessary, and comprehensive law, which should explain the whole of the past. But alas! History reveals no absolute and universal "law" of social evolution. There is no inevitability in historical phenomena. It is, of course, possible to be wise after the event, and say with Spinoza that whatever happened could not be otherwise! History was not made to order according to any preordained plan.

No single "law" or theory can explain and interpret the vast and complex repertory of human experience that is History. All such sweeping generalizations must be rejected as unsound. Every so-called "law" is applicable only to a small group of phenomena; it does not cover the whole of the past. There are many highways and byways in History, and some of these may be mapped by different thinkers. But History cannot be stretched on the Procrustean bed of a single generalization, however useful it may be. This mental aberration has been due to the fallacious idea that History must ape the exact sciences of Physics and Chemistry. Every ambitious Newton of Sociology has tried to discover an all-embracing "law" of historical development. But History need not be degraded to the level of the "exact" sciences that investigate sound and selenium, and light and lutecium. History is proud of the fact that its phenomena cannot be weighed and measured in grammes and centimetres. She glories in her incompetence for prevision and prediction. She says: "Lo! I do not and cannot deal with nebulæ and solar systems and Milky Ways, that can be gauged and counted so precisely, because I tell of that which counts and gauges them and is far greater than they, even the Mind of Man, that no law can bind."

(*a*) Auguste Comte set out in search of an exact science of Sociology. He formulated the "law of the three stages," which had been stated by Turgot. He affirmed the necessary passage of all human theories through three successive stages: first, the theological or fictitious, which is provisional; secondly, the metaphysical or abstract, which is transitional; and thirdly, the positive or scientific, which alone is definitive. He wrote: '" This law is the most precious intellectual acquisition of the human mind. With its ascertainment, that long search after the laws of the Universe, which began with Thales at the first awakening of Reason, is completed." Unfortunately, Comte himself deprived this "law" of its alleged universality, when he admitted that some tribes might pass directly from fetishism to positivism. He declared that medieval society was "metaphysical and feudal": but surely the prevailing Christian philosophy of the Middle Ages was theological, as "God" was the centre and the circumference of all thought in that benighted epoch. He deduced the corollary that the modern age would be peaceful and industrial. What an ironical comment on the events of 1914-18 A.D., and after! He leaves out of view all Central and Eastern Asia, and does not apply his "law" to those civilizations. He does not mention pantheism, which has deeply influenced India and Persia. How can Protestantism be considered a "metaphysical" phenomenon? It is theological to the marrow. A Catholic may pray to a beatified saint, but a Protestant always cries only to God for succour. Further, how does this "law" enlighten us as to the real cause of historical events and movements? Does it explain why and how theology is supplanted by metaphysics and metaphysics by science? It appears that this "law" is itself a product of metaphysical modes of thought. Comte does not go to the root of the matter.

(*b*) Herbert Spencer also formed the ambitious project of discovering a universal law. He simply borrowed K. E. von Baer's formula of embryonic development, and applied it to all Nature and also to human society. He was guilty of a grave philosophical crime and misdemeanour. The eminent historians C. V. Langlois and C. Seignobos have warned all sociologists against "the temptation of applying biological analogies to the explanation of social evolution, which is not produced by the operation of the same causes as animal evolution." Spencer compared human society to an "organism," a hackneyed and utterly unscientific device, which reduced his philosophy to verbal jugglery. He elaborated this portentous formula: "Evolution is an integration of matter and concomitant dissipation of motion, during which the matter passes from a relatively indefinite incoherent homogeneity to a relatively definite coherent heterogeneity, and during which the retained motion undergoes a parallel transformation." History reveals no such general law. All institutions do not develop from simplicity to complexity and from homogeneity to heterogeneity. This process can be observed in some cases, but the reverse is equally true. *The Family* has not evolved from simplicity to complexity. The unwieldy joint-family of ancient societies has been simplified, until it consists only of the man and his wife and children. The family now does not include uncles, aunts, nephews, nieces, brothers-in-law, and sisters-in-law in the progressive countries of the world. *Language* has not evolved from simplicity to complexity. Primitive languages and the classical languages like Sanskrit, Greek, Latin, and Arabic are very complex in structure, while modern languages like French, English, and Hindi are relatively simple. *Religion* does not illustrate Spencer's so-called "law." Early religion inculcated the worship of a complicated hierarchy of gods and demons, as we may learn from Hesiod's "Theogony," and the Vedas. Religion has been simplified from polytheism to Zoroastrian dualism and Semitic monotheism. Religious ceremonies were also very complex and elaborate in ancient times, like the Vedic sacrifices described in the Brāhmanas, and the ritual of the Mysteries in Greece and Rome. But modern religion prefers simplicity in worship, and the Quakers have discarded even baptism and holy communion. *Government* has sometimes evolved from simplicity to complexity, and at other times in the reverse direction. Thus Athenian democracy, with its councils, assemblies, and juries, was more complex than the bureaucracy of Roman imperialism, which consisted only of officials. Despotism and Bureaucracy are always simpler than Democracy. Modern democratic governments tend to acquire a complex structure again. Thus Spencer's generalization is found to be only partially valid.

(*c*) Some thinkers have attempted to deduce a universal law of growth and decay by comparing society to an individual, and the historical epochs to the different stages in an individual's life. Pascal said: "The whole succession of men through the ages should be considered as one man, ever living and always learning." C. Fourier divided the imaginary period of 80,000 years of history into four parts corresponding to the infancy, youth, manhood, and old age of the individual. St. Simon and Littré thought that Infancy was represented by Egypt, Youth by Greece, Manhood by Rome, and Mature Age by the moderns. A. Toynbee has elaborated the analogy in detail. He says: "The germ of Western society first developed in the body of Greek society, like a child in the womb. The Roman Empire was the period of pregnancy. The 'Dark Age' was the crisis of birth. The Middle Ages were the period of childhood. The fourteenth and fifteenth centuries may stand for puberty, and the centuries since the year 1500 for our prime." I may ask, "And when was the time for teething, measles, and chicken-pox?" J. W. Draper said: "Social advancement is as completely under the control of natural law as bodily growth. The life of an individual is a miniature of the life of a nation."

All such reasoning is vitiated by poetical allegory. Society is not an organism in the biological sense, because it is composed of many self-conscious men and women, with their separate Brains and Wills. Hence Society is rent asunder by conflict and confusion, and it is the height of philosophical ineptitude to compare it to a single individual. Sociology cannot be founded on such quaint similes. One may as well call a fat boy "a football," and then proceed to deduce the laws of his development from the movements of the ball!

(*d*) Some incorrigible optimists have formulated the "law of Progress." The idea of Progress was adumbrated in the works of Æschylus, Euripides, Aristotle, Seneca, Cicero, Pliny the Elder, Tertullian, Brother Gerard, Hugo of St. Victor, Thomas Aquinas, Roger Bacon, Francis Bacon, Réné Descartes, Pascal, and other writers. But it was distinctly and eloquently expounded first by the brilliant European thinkers of the sixty-eighth century A.H. (eighteenth A.D.). Bodin, Chastellax, C. F. Volney, E. W. Leibniz, Mercier, Voltaire, Restif de la Bretonne, and others showed that the European nations had advanced in civilization during many centuries. The doctrine of necessary and perpetual progress is particularly associated with the names of A. R. J. Turgot and N. Caritat de Condorcet. In Turgot's discourse on "The Successive Advances of the Human Mind," the idea of progress was made "the organic principle of history." He wrote: "The succession of Man offers from age to age a spectacle ever varied. Reason, the passions, liberty, incessantly produce new events. . . . The total mass of the human race, by the alternations of calm and agitation, of good and bad conditions, marches always, though slowly, towards still higher perfection. . . . Like the tempest, which has agitated the waves of the sea, the evils inseparable from revolutions disappear, the good remains, and Humanity perfects itself." Condorcet divided the history of Europe into nine periods, which had been marked by continuous progress and must also lead to indefinite progress, complete equality, and human perfection in future. He said: "No bounds have been fixed to the improvement of the human faculties; the perfectibility of man is absolutely indefinite;

the progress of this perfectibility, henceforth above the control of every power that would impede it, has no other limit than the duration of the globe. . . . The course of this progress may doubtless be more or less rapid, but it can never be retrograde." Pierre Leroux also proclaimed the certainty and inevitability of universal progress. St. Simon and A. Bazard traced the curve of progress through organic and critical periods of history. A. Comte accepted "Progress" as the goal of his "Church of Humanity." Cabanis, Madame de Staël, V. Cousin, T. S. Jouffroy, F. R. G. Guizot, J. Michelet, E. Quinet, Pelletan, and others kept alive this doctrine. H. A. Taine, in spite of his fatalism (or because of it), believed in a definitely guaranteed progress. Vacherot and E. Renan also shared this belief. A. Fouillée insisted on man's progress in knowledge, self-determination, and freedom. In England, thinkers like A. Ferguson, J. Priestley, and W. Godwin disseminated the French ideas. Godwin declared: "There is no characteristic of man which seems at present at least so eminently to distinguish him, or to be of so much importance in every branch of moral science, as his perfectibility." Robert Owen and the early Socialists were ardent optimists, and believed in the early advent of a social system which "will ensure the happiness of the human race throughout all future ages." In Germany, J. G. Herder, who believed in continuous development, prophesied that "the flower of humanity, captive still in its germ, will blossom out one day into the true form of man." G. E. Lessing explained history as the drama of a progressive series of religions. Kant looked forward to the establishment of a "universal civil society founded on justice," though there is also a vein of pessimism in his philosophy. J. G. Fichte deduced the law of necessary progress towards Freedom *à priori* without reference to history. Progress is indeed the principle of ethics in his philosophy. He divided history into five epochs; in the last two periods, progress in science and art is due to "conscious and regnant reason." Hegel traced Progress among different nations in the past, but held that this development was now finished! Buckle took the fact of Progress for granted, and only tried to investigate its causes. John Stuart Mill expresses the opinion that the general tendency of history is in the direction of improvement. H. Spencer based his optimism on the theory of Evolution and said: "Evolution can end only in the establishment of the greatest perfection and the most complete happiness. . . . No accidents, no chance, but everywhere order and completeness."

These are the confident radiant optimists. On the contrary

many thinkers have believed in a law of continual deterioration. They are the inconsolable pessimists. Others have discovered alternate cycles of progress and retrogression: they may be called "semi-pessimists." Pessimism and semi-pessimism have also had their champions. The Hindu priests believe that the world began with a golden age, the "Satya-Yuga," and has been deteriorating ever since. It has passed through two other periods, and is now in the fourth and worst epoch, the "Kali-Yuga." Hesiod also speaks of four ages, "the golden, the silver, the heroic, and the iron"; and his tone and mood are pessimistic. Plato postulated alternate cycles of perfection and deterioration, each lasting 36,000 solar years. The Stoics taught that "in fixed periods of time, a burning and destruction of all things takes place, and the world returns again from the beginning into the very same shape as it had before, and that the restoration of them all happens not once, but often, or rather that the same things are restored an infinite number of times." Aristotle described how States passed through tyranny, oligarchy, democracy, and back to tyranny again. Among the Romans, Ovid speaks of the popular belief in four ages of continuous deterioration, and Virgil refers to a Saturnian golden age. N. Machiavelli, following Aristotle and Polybius, accepted the theory of cycles in the development of political constitutions. G. B. Vico believed that each civilization must end in barbarism, and the cycle would begin again. Rousseau taught that civilization had been a failure, for society had been going from bad to worse since the primitive epoch. Voltaire declared that history was "a mass of crimes, follies, and misfortunes," though he was not a pessimist. T. H. Huxley was saddened by the study of history and held that man's ethical progress would depend on resistance to the amoral Cosmic process. He was thus inclined to be pessimistic, and said (as against Spencer): "The theory of Evolution encourages no millenial anticipations." Byron has interpreted the pessimists' verdict on history thus:—

> "There is the moral of all human tales;
> 'Tis but the same rehearsal of the past,
> First Freedom, and then Glory—when that fails,
> Wealth, vice, corruption—barbarism at last."

I am not a pessimist, a semi-pessimist, or an optimist. I do not believe in the law of deterioration or the theory of cycles. At the same time, I cannot accept the pleasant but fatalistic doctrine at mankind has continually advanced in all countries at all ›chs, and must infallibly continue to advarce. There is no inherent universal law of progress, which must operate for our benefit, whatever we may do or be. I hold that History is a medley; it reveals a mixed patchwork of progress and retrogression in different countries at different epochs. During certain periods, some peoples have advanced in some directions, but they have also at the same time retrograded in other important respects. At the end of the epoch, they are both better and worse than their ancestors. I cannot discern all-round, uniform progress in every part of the world during each decade and each century. Couéism is not applicable to History. Humanity has never been in a position to say: "Every day, in every way, I am getting better and better." The march of Humanity has been irregular, disorderly, and haphazard. It has not been in a straight line, or in a circle, or in a spiral, or in any curve of a definite shape. It has been an up-and-down, down-and-up, forward-and-backward, right-to-left, left-to-right lawless and chaotic movement, according as men and women have been virtuous or wicked, active or lethargic, wise or foolish, creative or conservative. I proclaim the power of human Personality. I do not believe in any mysterious invariable law of progress, which is independent of Personality. If Personality is maintained at a certain standard of excellence, society will advance in civilization. If Personality is allowed to sink to a low level, society will decay and stagnate. Civilization may be compared to a garden, and Personality is the gardener. If the gardener is an active, well-trained craftsman, the garden will grow in beauty and splendour; but if the gardener is lazy and ignorant, weeds and thistles will choke out the flowering plants.

A Survey

I shall now briefly discuss the merits and demerits of the civilizations of the past, and indicate the causes of their progress and decline. I shall attempt to sum up the results of this inquiry, which should teach us what traits of Personality are most conducive to Progress.

Egypt and Babylonia rose and flourished, because the economic situation was very favourable to social development. Food was easily obtainable in the fertile countries. The Egyptians early achieved greatness in art (sculpture and architecture) and ethics. But they declined on account of militarism, superstition, and social inequality. The priestly caste at first promoted science, but they degenerated into a parasitic and conservative class, and encouraged degrading zoolatry. The obsession of a future state paralysed energy and activity in this life. There was no democracy and no safeguards against oppression. We read of a few strikes and insurrections, but they were sporadic. Women held a high position in society and enjoyed much freedom. The people had no sense of personal dignity and independence. They therefore acquiesced in social servitude, and did not resist the cruel exploitation to which they were subjected by the kings and the noblemen. Egypt produced several sages and philosophers (Ptah-Hetep, Kaqemna, Herutataf, Tuauf, Ani, Amen-hetep). In Babylonia, similar causes were at work. The Babylonians made contributions to science (astronomy), art (sculpture), and government (Hammurabi's code). They were not victims of fear and worry about the life after death; but they were as pious as the Egyptians in worshipping their gods and goddesses. Despotism and priestcraft arrested the growth of civilization, as in Egypt. We owe the signs of the Zodiac, the division of time into months, hours, and minutes, the epic of Gilgamesh, and the week of seven days, to the Babylonians.

In Assyria, selfish and brutal Imperialism undermined character and led to degeneracy. But the Assyrians established great libraries of Babylonian literature. The Assyrian Empire borrowed the culture of Babylonia and diffused it among the adjacent nations. Greece also came into contact with it. The Empire incidentally served this useful purpose. But unjust war brought its own nemesis.

Egyptian and Babylonian culture was also spread abroad by the Phœnicians, who were great navigators and traders. Their alphabet has been transmitted to us through the Greeks and the Romans.

Ancient Persia developed a noble civilization on the basis of the Zoroastrian religion, which offered a great prophet's life as a model for imitation and a permanent source of inspiration. This was a great advantage, as Personality is the foundation of progress. Zoroastrianism also inculcated a doctrine of religious dualism, but foretold the triumph of Good over Evil in the long run. It taught the importance of purity in thought, word, and deed. It honoured agriculture, and laid stress on physical culture and veracity. But it was an intolerant creed. Its priests invented many superstitious ideas about heaven, hell, resurrection, and judgment, which were borrowed by the Hebrews and thus transmitted to the Christians and the Moslems. Persia has been the source of rank superstition. The ethical standard was high during many centuries, but no democratic institutions were established. Herodotus relates why the Persians preferred despotism to democracy. The magnificent ruins of Persepolis, the life of Mani and his ideas, the elements of Mithraism that were incorporated into Christianity, the names and actions of Cyrus and Naushirwan, the precepts of Zoroaster, the epic of Firdausi, and the moral influence of the Parsis of India are the legacy of Persia for us. Imperialism sapped the moral strength of the upper classes, and superstition and servility held the people in bondage. So the vast country could offer no resistance to the Macedonians and the Arabs. The Persians borrowed the Indian literature of fables and the game of chess, and passed them on to Europe. They have been efficient culture-bearers.

The Hebrews found a wise guide and legislator in Moses; this bond of union was valuable for social unity and moral training. They also secured the ten commandments, and a definite ethical code was thus accepted by the whole nation. They had a spirit of sturdy independence, which was reflected in their laws and their revolts. They cared more for happiness in this life than for felicity after death. They had the honour and glory of being the obstinate martyrs slain by Roman Imperialism. When almost all other peoples in Asia bowed to the Roman yoke, the Hebrews defied the tyrants again and again, and paid the penalty for their love of freedom. They produced the group of eloquent prophets, Isaiah, Amos, and others, whose writings may still be read with profit, though they are couched in theological terms. The ideas of a cosmopolitan society and universal peace were developed by the advanced Hebrew thinkers. The futility of all formal rites and ceremonies was also proclaimed. But the Hebrews are also responsible for intolerant monotheism and its terrible consequences. They learned much from the Persians and the Babylonians, and passed it on to the Christian Church. We owe our Sunday rest, the achievements of Jesus and Paul, and the noble ethics of the Talmud to this people. Their religion teaches them charity and chastity. In spite of dispersion, proscription, isolation, and suffering, the Hebrews are still alive and active. Modern music, science, and socialism owe much to them. To Philosophy, they have contributed the supremely lovable figure of Spinoza. Maimonides, Mendelssohn, Marx, and Einstein are also the gift of this people to the world.

The history of the Hebrews shows that good leaders, a well-defined ethical code, a this-worldly creed, a living historical tradition, and unity of fundamental ideas will enable a people to accomplish great things.

Ancient Mexico was enslaved by cruel superstition, and the

warring tribes there sacrificed their prisoners to the gods. Imperialism on a small scale caused perpetual strife. Material culture was developed to a certain extent, and temples, aqueducts, and causeways were built. Pictorial historical records were kept. The Mexica were easily defeated by Cortez, because Aztec society was much weakened by superstition and political tyranny. The tribe of the Tlaxcalans even aided Cortez! In Peru, the Incas, a highland people, developed the earlier civilization of the Tiahuanoco folk, and established an empire. They worshipped the Sun, and compelled the subject tribes to adopt their cult. They built a great Sun-temple at Cuzco, which forms the foundation of the present Cathedral. Like the Egyptians, they preserved the dead bodies of the rulers as mummies, and attached great importance to the cult of the dead. They lived under a kind of State-socialism, administered by a bureaucracy. All the produce was state-property, and every one was required to do some work. An equal food-supply for the empire was thus secured, and no one suffered from hunger and poverty. But there was excessive State-supervision, and personal freedom was very much restricted. The quarrels and jealousies of the leaders weakened the State, and Pizarro took advantage of this condition of affairs. Superstition and despotism contributed to the downfall of this interesting state.

China developed a stable and progressive civilization that is still living. The Chinese were fortunate in the early stage of development, as several great leaders arose among them. Confucius finally gave them their ethical code. He was not superstitious, and taught only social duty and practical ethics. He insisted on the importance of economic progress and education. He is among the few religious teachers who were also scholars and appreciated learning. He organized a class of well-educated philosophers, who were entrusted with the task of administering the State. This great idea is a precious legacy of Chinese civilization for us. Intellect should be combined with noble character, and both are to be devoted to the service of the State. But Confucius neglected the principle of democratic control: he did not establish democratic institutions. His administrators were thus benevolent despots, and they degenerated on account of the absence of popular government. In China, the democratic spirit is deep-rooted in society, but it has not been embodied in political institutions. Despotism has undone the good wrought by Confucianism. But China was progressive until the end of the Sung Dynasty. Confucius also attached excessive importance to the family; hence public spirit has not developed among the people. The sense of duty to the family is very keen; but the ideals of citizenship have not been highly appreciated. Ancestor-worship has tended to make the nation conservative. China made some bold experiments in feminism in the past. Drama has exercised a permanent influence on the people. Chinese painting is China's supreme gift to the world.

Taoism has spread pernicious mystical ideas in China, but it is more humane and universal in spirit than Confucianism. It has degenerated into charlatanism. Confucianism is eminently sane and sound, but it lacks the spirit of moral enthusiasm and exaltation that makes apostles and saints. It is also not a universal gospel: it is Chinese nationalism organized into a system.

The history of China teaches us that it is very important for society to have a well-organized rationalistic religion, founded by a wise prophet. Personality unites the people and ennobles them by its pervasive influence. The unity and stability of the family are also a safeguard against decay and disorder. Voluntary combination for social purposes is the seed-plot for many virtues. This liberty of association must be preserved as an essential condition of progress. Superstition, derived chiefly from Buddhism and Taoism, has been rife in China, and has contributed to the decline of the old civilization. Lack of contact with other progressive civilizations has also arrested the growth of Chinese culture. Isolation has always hastened decay and produced stagnation. Religious freedom and toleration have been securely established in China, though Buddhism was persecuted in 5426–51, 5560, 5714, and 5845 as an anti-social and foreign creed. An admirable eclectic spirit has prevailed, so that a Chinaman can derive full benefit from Confucianism, Buddhism, and Taoism. Some foreigners, brought up in exclusive sects, say that the religion of China is "Confusionism"! China demonstrates the advantages of spiritual eclecticism.

India developed a progressive civilization on account of the energy and valour of the Hindu people. The Hindus appreciated two qualities in a special degree: bravery and truthfulness. They preserved the biographies of the great men of old in two epic poems, which are the vehicles of moral teaching to this day. They held up Rama to the admiration of the people as the ideal man. He is described as an all-round, well-developed personality, uniting strength and beauty to a keen intellect and noble character. The ancient Hindu ideal was the same as the Hellenic. A high ideal of domestic duty and stability was inculcated. The Hindus also developed the doctrine of religious toleration, and Emperor Asoka enunciated it explicitly in his edicts. Since that date (forty-eighth century A.H.), the Hindus and the Buddhists have not persecuted any one for his doctrines and worship. This tolerant attitude also enabled them to give shelter to the Persians, who fled to India in the fifty-seventh century A.H. Zoroastrianism as a living creed flourishes in India even more than in Persia. The caste system, the long-continued internal peace, the accumulation of wealth, the luxury and corruption of the upper classes and the priests, the despotic state-system, and the absence of a centralized administration contributed to the partial downfall of Hindu polity in the sixty-third century A.H., when the Afghans overran Northern India and established Moslem Kingdoms. Under Moslem rule, various religious reform-movements aimed at the abolition or mitigation of caste and priestcraft. Noble architecture adorned the country. This Afghan-Mogul architecture is one of India's supreme gifts to civilization. The tyranny of the Mogul emperors provoked national resistance to foreign rule, and the Sikh and Mahratta movements re-established national independence over a large part of the country The Sikh movement combined religious and social reform with revolutionary politics, and resembled Puritanism in this respect. In recent times, the impact of British culture on India has produced new movements and thought-currents. India has been the home of mystical and metaphysical pantheism, which is a tolerant but inert and anti-social creed. The indolent "spirituality" induced by this philosophy has been a main cause of India's backwardness in the medieval and modern periods. Priestcraft and despotism have kept the people in bondage during many centuries. Vegetarianism has been prevalent in India among a very large section of the population. It has made the people mild and gentle and compassionate, though it has perhaps not been an unmixed blessing for the urban classes.

The history of Hellas is the most interesting and important in the ancient world. Hellas has given mankind the best epic and dramatic poetry, the best sculpture, and the best philosophy that we possess. It has also produced excellent architecture, lyric poetry, oratory, and history; and it developed the sciences of geometry, medicine, and mechanics. Its philosophy emphasizes the importance of Rationalism, Justice, Liberty, and Science. It also attained to the conception of cosmopolitan citizenship. But the Greeks did not advance beyond the city-state in politics, though they organized some federations at critical periods. Their cities were always fighting among themselves, and the laws of war were cruel and barbarous. Slavery was a recognized institution, and even Plato was once sold as a slave. The problems of the class-struggle between the rich and the poor were clearly understood, and theories of Socialism and Communism were freely discussed. As in China, great importance was attached to music as a subject of education. The evils of Hellenic civilization were slavery, internecine war, unnatural homosexuality, and lack of tender compassion for weakness and suffering. But Greek culture is really the backbone and vertebral column of true Civilization. It has only to be developed and fulfilled with the aid of Buddhism, Christianity, and modern Rationalism in order to serve as the intellectual and moral basis of the Civilization of the future.

The Romans were really a well-organized band of ruthless brigands. Roman "civilization" was only the thin veneer of Hellenic culture on the coarse and repulsive visages of cruel and besotted exploiters and sensualists. But they contributed the fact and the idea of political organization, and also inculcated the necessary subordination of the individual to the interests of the State. The unity of the Roman Empire was the marvellous achievement of the Italian people. The ideal of cosmopolitanism, preached by the Stoics and the Christians, could be realized in practice only within the framework of such an international State as the Empire became in the course of its development. When the Gauls were admitted to the Senate, a new political principle was introduced into the world. Citizenship was held to abolish the barriers of race and nationality. The Romans also welded the eastern Mediterranean peoples into one State, while Christianity rendered them socially homogeneous. Thus was born the Byzantine State, which, though ugly and venomous, yet bore the priceless jewel of Greek literature and philosophy in its head at Constantinople. After the closing of the Athenian schools of philosophy in 5529 A.H. (529 A.D.), Greek culture was kept alive only at the University of Constantinople (and also partially at Edessa by the Nestorians). From Constantinople, Italy received the gift of Greek learning in the sixty-fourth and sixty-fifth centuries A.H., and our modern civilization began. Thus Florence is linked through Constantinople to Rome and Athens. The Latin language boasts of the great work of Lucretius, which is the only poetical masterpiece of Rationalism. The evils of Roman "civilization" were political tyranny, economic exploitation, administrative plunder, coarse and brutal amusements, rampant militarism, and widespread superstition. The overthrow of the Western Empire by the Teutons (who were not " barbarians ") was a blessing and a step in advance.

The Eastern Roman Empire was the careless guardian of Greek culture; but it was also the bulwark of Europe against the Saracens and the Turks during many centuries. If the Asiatic Moslems had captured Constantinople before Europe had produced the commercial middle-class that initiated the Renaissance, the Greek manuscripts would perhaps have been destroyed. Greek learning might have perished altogether, like the Zoroastrian literature of Persia. Byzantium has thus played a very important part in History, and we must be grateful to her. The Byzantine missionaries also converted Russia and the Slavs to Christianity, and these barbarous tribes were brought into line with the other European nations. The Christian Church in Russia taught the people the ordinary virtues of gentleness and charity, and the higher virtues of martyrdom and self-abnegation for the good of Humanity. Christianity paved the way for Herzen, Tolstoi, and the socialist leaders of the Revolution. Thus Red Moscow is connected with imperial Byzantium. The beginnings of art in Italy are also closely associated with Byzantine models (*e.g.* Cimabue's Madonna). It was also Constantinople that supplied the Greek scholars to the Arab court at Baghdad, and Greek books were thus translated into Arabic. Byzantium was the source of the Renaissance in the Islamic countries too: but that Hellenic movement was suppressed by Moslem orthodoxy and did not bear fruit in Islamic society. The evils of Byzantine civilization were despotism, bureaucracy, landlordism, intolerance, excessive addiction to theology, and ignorant monasticism.

The history of Medieval Europe has often been described as the " Dark Age " and " a thousand years without a bath." But great and wonderful achievements stand to the credit of the generations that lived and died between the fall of the Western Empire and the Italian Renaissance. A new type of moral excellence was evolved; it was defective, but so very magnificent in its own way. In 5529 A.H., St. Benedict established his monastery at Monte Casino. Every Benedictine monk set the example of a life devoted to simplicity, manual labour, study, and education. They combined some of the best aspects of Hellenism and Christianity. Christianity in their hands was a progressive movement, when they converted the Northern European nations to the Church. Their asylums and hospitals struck a new note of social compassion in that brutal age. These unselfish philosophers had to adopt the rule of celibacy at that epoch, as birth-control was not known. Monasticism also enabled some poor men and women to escape the curse of common drudgery, and attain to eminence in literature, art, and science. The Church, in the first half of the Middle Ages, was a democratic institution, the organization of the people as opposed to the kings and the feudal barons. A poor peasant's son could be elevated to the Papacy, which held the noblemen in check. At a later period, the Church joined the exploiting classes as their ally. But Canossa was a victory for Democracy, and not for clericalism. Democracy could be organized only in a religious and paternally bureaucratic institution at that time. As lasting visible monuments of that democratic and socially harmonious population, witness the superb Gothic cathedrals, which have not yet been surpassed in sublime beauty and grandeur by any modern buildings. The secret of their charm and power is that they represented the townsmen's ideal of Democracy and Ethics, which was summed up in Faith, Hope, and Love. As soon as a town grew and flourished, it freed itself from feudal tyranny and erected a Cathedral, which was its social club and church and concert-house and picture-gallery and school and college all in one. It is a great mistake to regard these Cathedrals as merely "religious" buildings, like a Methodist chapel. They were social buildings, in which the complete life of the community was centred. They symbolized that social unity, which we alas! lack at the present day. The middle-class of the towns also established the democratic Universities of Paris and Oxford, where the poor scholars studied the ancient Greek treatises in Latin translations of the Arabic versions that were accessible at Cordova. Thus the first partial Renaissance was inaugurated in Europe. Oxford and Paris are connected with Athens through Cordova, Baghdad, Constantinople, and Rome. The democratic and ethical movement initiated by that great pacifist, St. Francis, menaced the parasitic classes for a time, but it was compelled to relinquish its economic programme. In medieval society, money and work were not regarded as sacred objects of devotion. The people enjoyed many holidays, though they possessed fewer commodities.

The evils of medieval civilization were despotism, feudalism, serfdom, war, ignorance of Science, superstition, squalor, pestilence, intolerance, excessive authority, and degenerate monasticism.

Islamic civilization, which began with the Arab conquests in the fifty-seventh century A.H., is based on unity of creed and worship, and is therefore intolerant in religion. It could not assimilate the Hellenic Renaissance that Caliph Al-Mamoon initiated. Orthodoxy triumphed over freethought, and the Islamic nations remained stagnant. A certain democratic spirit has prevailed in society, as in China. But political democracy has not been known until quite recently. Monotheism has also robbed this culture of the arts of sculpture and painting, as Prophet Muhammad was anxious to prevent a relapse into idolatry. The prohibition of wine has made the common people sober and thrifty. If the Moslems cared as much for themselves as they care for the "glory" and "honour" of "God," they could build up a fine civilization, for they have cultivated simplicity, fraternity, and charity. The seclusion of women has contributed to the decline of Islamic society in the past, and a sensual view of Love prevails among large circles. Scientific studies have been discouraged during many centuries, and the arts and crafts have remained stagnant. Bahaism has proved a serious rival to Islam in Persia, where the revolt against Islam has been helped by French literature and philosophy. Turkey has disestablished the old Church and abolished Moslem law, which was really a relic of medievalism. Rationalism is now making rapid progress among the Moslem nations. The evils of Moslem civilization have been superstition, intolerance, despotism, landlordism, bureaucracy, nationalism, and lack of popular education.

Modern civilization began with the great Renaissance in Italy in the sixty-fifth and sixty-sixth centuries A.H. It had its origin in a revival of the study of Hellenic culture, the art, literature, history, and philosophy of Greece. Thus did Hellas take its revenge on the Christian Church, whose leaders had believed that they had killed Hellenism for ever. But Hellas can never die. The people of Florence, and especially the new commercial and financial class, encouraged the study of Greek. Erasmus was the apostle of the new gospel for the nations of Northern Europe. Education was reformed, new schools and colleges were founded, art was revived, literature and science were cultivated, and political questions were discussed in a rational spirit. Since that period, modern civilization has gone from strength to strength. The State has been democratized and secularized in an increasing degree. The Churches have been losing their prestige and popularity. Education has been brought within reach of the people. Sanitation has been improved. Scientific discoveries and inventions have enriched society. Rationalism and rationalistic Ethics are replacing dogma and superstition. The Reformation was a popular movement, as contrasted with the Renaissance, which was confined to the upper and middle classes. The Protestants inherited many superstitions from the old Catholic Church, and they added a few of their own. In some ways they led a retrogressive movement; but, on the whole, the balance of Progress was in favour of Protestantism. It broke the thousand-year-old monopoly of the priests and monks. It abolished organized monkery and ecclesiastical privilege and exploitation. It made men more earnest and honest than they could be under a system of ceremonialism and graft. By multiplying sects, it discredited Christianity altogether. By organizing the middle-class and the common people, it fostered the democratic spirit. The fissiparous tendency of Protestantism led to the triumph of secularism in the constitution and the educational system of the United States,—an event of crucial importance in world-history. Protestantism divides the Christians, and also removes all the defences of Christianity except unintelligent Bibliolatry. Rationalism thus finds its task easier in the long run, though the partial and specious rationality of Protestantism at first hinders the progress of scientific Rationalism. But the Protestant Church did not appreciate Art, or the value of historical tradition and continuity, or the necessity of deeper ethical experience, or the importance of Science. In the hands of Calvin, it championed political democracy, and helped to establish popular government in America. It also insisted on popular literacy (though not on popular education). Calvinism was the least pernicious form of Protestantism, though it produced such monstrous aberrations as witch-burning. The Renaissance had no direct message for the common people at that time, and we find that the Renaissance and the Reformation overlapped at several points. Melanchthon, Erasmus, Dolet, and other eminent leaders took an active part in both movements. The Baptists were the first Christian sect in England to advocate a doctrine of general toleration, and the multiplicity of Protestant sects finally made even Lutheran intolerance impossible and impracticable. When the Reformation had exhausted its force as a progressive movement, the precursors of the French Revolution appeared on the scene. At the same time, Capitalism began to develop. The French Revolution ended the rule of the feudal landlords and the priests, and installed the middle-class in power, with the working-men as humble allies It proclaimed the individual's rights of free speech and free association, and condemned paternalism in the State. It established Deism and Atheism as organized forces in the social system. It laid the foundations of popular education, as Democracy came first, and universal schooling followed in its wake. It encouraged the study of economics and politics, and drew its inspiration from Greece and Rome, not from Palestine. It may be called the political fulfilment of the Renaissance. But it let loose Nationalism on the world. Nationalism has served the useful purpose of breaking the power of the Catholic Church and shielding the nations against imperialistic greed and aggression. But now it has outlived its usefulness. Capitalism also obtained a charter of licence from the French Revolution, which glorified individualism and competition. These two forces, Capitalism and Nationalism, which led the world forward in the last century, have now plunged it into the abyss of war and poverty.

I hold that the Renaissance has been the great watershed of world-history, dividing all civilizations based on superstition from the still incomplete and imperfect modern civilization, which is founded on Rationalism and its ally, Science. Hellenism is the main highway of History: other movements are by-ways and blind alleys. Through English and French teachers, it has spread in a diluted form even to Persia, India, China, and Africa, and shaken the old creeds and ideals in those stagnant and moribund civilizations. Thus the eternal empire of Athens continues to expand. But the Renaissance needs fulfilment. Hellenism must add unto itself some elements, which were indeed implicit in it, but which were made explicit in Christianity and Buddhism. The Renaissance also awaits its ethical and social fulfilment. Hellenism cannot be fulfilled without its new Platos, Aristotles, and Zenos, its new Academies, Lyceums, Stoas, and Gardens, its new visions of the perfect Citizen in the perfect State. The Renaissance is not finished. It has not yet come into its own. It must be fulfilled in the ethical and social spheres, as it has been fruitful in Art, Science, and Literature. Now it demands the new Philosophy, Politics, and Economics of Reason and Freedom. This is the way out of the present *impasse*. Hellenism has undermined the old foundations of Ethics, which were theological or metaphysical, and it is now called upon to build up the new Ethics and the new State on the basis of Rationalism.

The Conclusion

I have shown that History does not record continual uninterrupted progress, but rather uncertain and indeterminate periods of progress and retrogression in all countries. Civilization rises and falls, and falls and rises, like the barometer in the climate of England. What, then, should be your philosophy of History? Well, you should be neither a gloomy pessimist nor an ignorant optimist. You should be a Meliorist. Meliorism should be your creed. Meliorism is the gospel of Progress-plus-Personality.

History reveals two antagonistic Principles in Nature and in Man, and these Principles are in eternal conflict. The principle of Good (or Progress) and the principle of Evil (or Retrogression) are ever at war in the individual and in society. Now, Progress, or the victory of Good, does not depend on the Environment, or on Evolution, or on "God," or on the Life-Force, or on the Absolute World-Spirit, or on economic forces, or on any inherent tendency or law of Nature. All these are not the decisive factors. The triumph of Good depends entirely on the individual, on you and me. The law of Progress is in your mind and heart: seek it not elsewhere. Social progress corresponds directly and proportionately to personal improvement, and vice versa. The individual is the mirror of Society. Humanity is only the individual writ large. History is only your own Brocken-shadow magnified for your vision. Humanity is an abstraction: you and I and other persons are the concrete realities. Thus the individual is the only architect of Progress. You can accelerate or retard the march of the race towards Perfection. You can help to inaugurate glorious eras of rapid progress and development, or dreary epochs of degeneracy and decline. You can strive and struggle for the Good; or you can waste vital energy in frivolity and lethargy, thus abetting Evil in History. You can decide to make the best use of your life in the service of noble ideals and become the ally of Progress; or you can choose to be a slothful and selfish sensualist, and thus act as an accomplice of Evil. You can work with zeal and energy for health, beauty, knowledge, virtue, love, and peace, thus ensuring and achieving Progress; or you can actively or passively increase ill-health, ugliness, ignorance, vice, hatred, and strife, and be responsible for Retrogression in History. You make History every minute and every second of your life. Your daily life *is* History: what else is it? Hence you must choose between Good and Evil, and enlist under the banner of Progress or Retrogression. As you choose, so will History be made. Every moment Progress is anxiously asking you: "Are you working for me or against me?" As your reply is, so will History be made. Wisely has Longfellow warned and advised us:—

"All are architects of Fate,
Working in these walls of Time;

. . . . .

For the structure that we raise,
Time is with materials filled;
Our to-days and yesterdays
Are the blocks with which we build.

Build to-day, then, strong and sure,
With a firm and ample base;
And ascending and secure
Shall to-morrow find its place."

Section III.—PSYCHOLOGY

You should study this important science both from books and in the laboratory. You will learn many valuable lessons.

(1) You will realize that Psychology and Physiology are interdependent. The mind affects the body. As Spenser says: "Of the soul, the body form doth take." But it is equally true that the body moulds and controls the mind. There is no thought or feeling that is not accompanied by corresponding changes in the body and the brain. The old idea of a disembodied "spirit," that can think and feel without a brain and a body, will thus become as unintelligible to you as vision without eyes, mastication without teeth, and digestion without a stomach. There is no Psychology without Physiology, and, I may add, there is no Physiology without Psychology. This latter truth is not sufficiently emphasized by many scientists.

(2) You will come across the controversy between "substantialism" and "actualism." Are the psychic elements, such as percepts, thoughts, feelings, and purposes, to be regarded as the states or modifications of a unitary immaterial Self or Soul, which "possesses" or "experiences" them, or in which they inhere? Or are they the very constituents of the Self, which is only a name for the sum-total of these psychic elements? The actualists deny the existence of a permanent "spiritual" reality or substratum behind or above the psychic states. The early Buddhists also taught this doctrine. You should follow a middle course between these rival schools. It is clear that there is no immaterial entity called the "Soul," which exists apart from the psychic states, like a musician playing on a piano. Such an imaginary metaphysical entity need not be assumed. The theory of "substantialism" explains nothing and creates new difficulties. It cannot be reconciled with the phenomena of dual or multiple personality and loss of memory. But you should not accept the rather comic and paradoxical doctrine that only the psychic states exist as a sequence of psychic events, and that there are thoughts and feelings, but no one who thinks and feels! The mental experiences and phenomena are organized with reference to a Centre, which is Self-consciousness,

the "I" that knows and affirms himself or herself without the aid or sanction of the scientists. The fact of Self-consciousness is a necessary postulate of all knowledge and life. "I think: I feel: I act: I am," thus speaks the Ego, and no further proof is required. The Ego is like light: light reveals all things to our eyes, but it is invisible. What will show us light itself? You may try to prove the existence of your own Ego by arguments; you may refuse to believe in your own being unless the how and the why of it can be demonstrated by reasoning. But then you will act like the honest bureaucrat, who could not admit the fact of the birth of a traveller, as the latter had lost his birth-certificate. He said: "Sir, can you produce a document to prove that you were born? I know as a private individual that you were born at some time; but, as an official, I do not know it." Similarly, you should recognize the existence and activity of the Ego as the basis and centre of Personality, even if the analytic scientists cannot find it in the continuous stream of thoughts and feelings. I prove all things by and through the Ego; but nothing external to me can demonstrate to me that I exist. It is unnecessary to inquire how and by what process Self-Consciousness arises and inheres in the psychic states. It is an ultimate fact, beyond which we cannot penetrate.

(3) You should possess up-to-date knowledge of the facts and theories of psycho-analysis, but don't be morbidly obsessed by it. S. Freud, Alfred Adler, Carl Gustav Jung, and other thinkers are one-sided philosophers, like Marx and Comte. They try to explain the complex and varied phenomena of human nature by a simple theory, which must be ridden to death and then expire in general ridicule. Appreciate the truth in psycho-analysis, but reject its excesses.

(4) Take a proper interest in "psychic" phenomena (also called "spiritualistic"), and read about the recent researches of Charles Richet, H. Price, and others. But maintain the attitude of the Scientist. Don't be prejudiced for or against anybody or anything. It is necessary to observe and accumulate facts, and more facts, and nothing but facts; then Science will attempt to explain and co-ordinate them. To the dogmatic superficial critic, who denies the possibility of telepathy, clairvoyance, levitation, and other such strange phenomena, you should say, in Hamlet's words:

> "There are more things in heaven and earth, Horatio,
> Than are dreamt of in your philosophy."

If these phenomena are genuine, they would not be more wonderful and mysterious than electricity and wireless. You must be open-minded and curious, but beware of credulity and superstition. Science claims this domain too, and trained scientists should explore it. It has nothing to do with religion or metaphysics.

(5) Behaviorism also denies or ignores Personality. It is sound and effective as a method for the scientific study of certain phenomena, but it is not the whole of Psychology. In fact, it is not Psychology at all. It should be described as a branch of veterinary science. A statesman said to his doctor: "Please examine me, but don't ask any questions." The physician replied: "Sire, I am not a veterinary doctor." You should appreciate the services of this school of scientists, but reject their exaggerated claims. They are good so far as they go, but they don't go far enough.

(6) As you are conscious of your Ego, so you should also admit and proclaim that the human Mind possesses creative Power, which helps forward the process of Evolution. It is not merely a passive recipient of impressions and influences, but can originate and create what has never existed before anywhere at any time. It does not simply discover and reveal what has already existed in some form, as Columbus discovered America but did not create it. It actually gives birth to that which was absolutely non-existent before; it does not just re-arrange and re-cast the previously existing elements and experiences and facts of the universe. This great truth must be proclaimed anew in this age, when Science tends to apply physico-chemical and biological concepts to Psychology. But Psychology must be mistress in her own home.

SECTION IV.—ECONOMICS

You should give much time and thought to Economics. It is one of the basic sciences. The task of finding food, clothing, and shelter still takes up the greater part of the energy of Mankind. The production, distribution, and consumption of commodities are worthy of serious study, like the phenomena of external Nature and of Mind. Economics will give you a deep insight into history, politics, and sociology. It will explain the origin of many wars, revolutions, religions, and parties. It will reveal to you, as with a flash of lightning, the motives and methods of contemporary politicians and industrial leaders. It will help you to clear your mind of cant. I was present at a gathering where someone asked "Who really rules England?" Several different answers were given to this question: "The Parliament," "Christianity," "Public Opinion," "The Press," "The Schoolmasters," etc. When my turn came to speak, I said, "Money rules England, and also Europe." The respectable ladies and gentlemen were evidently shocked and disgusted. They were ignorant of Economics. You cannot understand Politics and Sociology without a thorough knowledge of Economics, as you cannot study Physics without Mathematics. If the people had been conversant with Economics, they would have known that the Great War was not fought for liberty, democracy, justice, or peace, but only for Money. Then many would have stayed at home. Now they are buried somewhere in France or Mesopotamia.

The study of Economics will make you think of the function of Wealth in the State. You will consider Production, which depends on Consumption. Many economists do not discuss Consumption adequately, but you should avoid that mistake. Economics is both a descriptive and a normative science. It must ask the question, "What *should* we consume? How much?" Economics must not be divorced from Ethics and Psychology, otherwise it will degenerate into a tangled jungle of figures and curves, in which the mind is lost. Wealth is a means to an end; it is not an end in itself, for the individual or for the State. It is to be used as the instrument of Personality under your control and direction. It must be limited in quantity according to the purpose that it is intended to serve at any particular time. It is not true that the State will promote the greatest efficiency and happiness if it produces as many commodities as it can. There are many things that are far more important than commodities. This truth will save you from the error of the one-sided economist, whose mind is deeply coloured by his subject, as a miner is covered with coal-dust. Study Economics, but condemn the modern cult of "Economism," which teaches that the highest happiness is to be attained by the multiplication of goods and material objects of enjoyment. This may be the gospel of the industrious ant and the busy bee; but it is a false and vicious creed for Humanity. On the contrary, you will realize that too many Things may and do crush and smother human Personality, as a heavy load bends the porter's back. Therefore, master Economics as a science, but beware of "Economism," which is a present peril for mankind, especially in its American version.

When you study the problem of Distribution, you will understand that Civilization is based on injustice and robbery. Your heart will go out in sympathy and compassion to all the millions of the exploited slaves, serfs, and labourers, dead and living, whose pathetic plaint has been thus rendered by Ernest Jones, the great Chartist leader:-

> "The land it is the landlord's,
> The trader's is the sea,
> The ore the usurer's coffer fills—
> But what remains for me?"

Then your blood will boil with indignation at the thought of the injustice and suffering that have been and are still allowed to prevail in society. You will resolve to champion the cause of the poor and the oppressed, and to live and teach the gospel of equality. The study of Economics will convert you to Socialism. You will also express the metaphysical wish that all those oppressed workers may be re-born in the Socialist Commonwealth of the future, and complete their frustrated lives, if possible. Beware of the "classical" and capitalistic economists, who are hired or deluded apologists of Capitalism. There is no such thing as a cold impartial "science" of Economics. No professor can teach Economics, as a scientist teaches Physics and Chemistry. He must directly or indirectly condemn or justify rent, interest, and profit, even if he takes care to be very cautious and neutral. The secret will out. Love and political opinions cannot be concealed. Therefore, if you read the treatises of the capitalistic economists or attend their lectures, remember that they have a conscious or unconscious bias in favour of Capitalism. They may formulate such sophisms as " the iron law of wages," " laissez-faire," " the social function of private capital," etc. Money will always find its slaves and hirelings, whose mind is in their stomach. Above all, give your days and nights to the works of Fourier and Marx, who have analysed capitalist society with the marvellous insight of genius. They are among the founders of socialist Economics. Read the writings of Gray, Bray, Thompson, and Hodgskin; these early English thinkers suggested many ideas to Marx. You will also learn much from Th. Veblen, the solitary original American thinker, almost a voice crying in the wilderness. Revise your Marx frequently, and appreciate the value and significance of true Marxism. If you do not understand Marxism, you cannot march in the vanguard of progressive Humanity.

SECTION V.—PHILOSOPHY

You must devote much time and thought to Philosophy. Don't be afraid of Philosophy; she is not so dreadful as she is said to be. She is simply "Love of Wisdom" in a Greek garb. If you think at all, you are a philosopher. Every man must be either a philosopher or a fool.

Philosophy deals with many questions and problems, some of which are very important, while others are futile and unnecessary. You need not trouble about the latter. Philosophy has got a bad name, because many philosophers have wasted too much energy on unintelligible and insoluble conundrums, which are of no use and interest to the average citizen. The modern thinkers are worse sinners in this respect than the ancient sages. You can dismiss such questions with a knowing smile, as you understand that some of them are only verbal puzzles, while others are meaningless, unprofitable, or even impossible. Such controversies have led to much deplorable misuse of talent in the past.

(1) The pursuit of "the Absolute," "the Unconditioned," "the Eternal," "the Immutable," and "the Everlasting" has been a wild-goose chase, on which many philosophers have started; but, like Milton's fallen angels, they have "found no end, in wandering mazes lost." They may be called the Don Quixotes of Philosophy. The Indian metaphysicians of the Upanishads sought to discover "that which changes not" and to know "that by which everything else is known." Plato and Plotinus also attempted to probe the mysteries of the unseen "spiritual" realm. The German Idealist thinkers like Schlegel, Fichte, and Hegel explained everything about "the Absolute" as readily as if it were their bosom-friend or next-door neighbour. F. H. Bradley, B. Bosanquet, J. M. McTaggart, J. Royce, and others follow the same tradition.

You should clearly understand that Philosophy must be anthropocentric. It is a human achievement, and it shares the limitations of the human mind. As Science teaches us, there is nothing that is independent of Space-time, Causality, and Flux. Man is incapable of conceiving and comprehending "the Absolute"; his brain cannot fly out of his head. Human personality is strictly limited and circumscribed, though there is, of course, no finality in its development. Man understands more of the Universe than the ape, and civilized Man possesses a broader and sounder philosophy than the neolithic barbarians. You see more of the landscape as you ascend to the several balconies of the Kutab tower, and the horizon recedes into the ever-increasing distance. Even so, Man rises in the scale of Being through the æons of Evolution, and his intellect can grasp more and more of Nature and Life as the years roll by. But, at each epoch, his intellectual capacity and his sense-organs can suffice only for a certain imperfect synthesis. He cannot fathom the entire Universe, which may be compared to an infinitely deep ocean, while Philosophy is Man's sounding-line dropped into its eternal waters.

At present, our eyes can see only the colours between the violet and the red, corresponding to a range of "from about 4000 tenth-metres to 7500 tenth-metres"; but it would be foolish to assert that the rays of other wave-lengths will not produce other colour-sensations in the more highly developed eyes of the Man of a million million years hence. We ask in vain this interesting question: "What colour-sensations correspond to the infra-red or the ultra-violet rays?" The scientists inform us that "ultra-violet rays have been found of wave-lengths less than 1000 tenth-metres, while infra-red rays have been found of lengths varying from 7500 tenth-metres up to 600,000 tenth-metres." Other eyes will see other colours: ours alas! cannot. Our ears can now hear only a few notes of the music of this Universe. J. Duncan and S. G. Starling say: "If the frequency rises very much, the note becomes very shrill. At a frequency of 15,000, the note is little more than a hiss, and, at some frequency above this, it ceases to be heard at all. Some people have a higher limit of audibility than others, being able to hear a note of frequency 20,000 or even 25,000. Young people have usually a higher limit of audibility than older people, and many people are unable to hear the squeak of a mouse owing to its high pitch." What ears will hear the notes of frequency 100,000? How will those notes sound? We cannot tell. We are like prisoners allowed to walk about in the courtyard of the gaol. It behoves Man to be modest. How much he may hear and see and understand after millions of billions of years, we do not know and cannot predict; but to-day, his philosophy must correspond to his own diminutive size. Hence you should distrust and reject all philosophers who claim to "explain" the whole Universe and know everything about it. They are only quacks and charlatans masquerading as philosophers. The wise philosopher must learn to say, "I don't know; I can't know," when certain questions are put to him. This frank confession of incurable and unavoidable ignorance is the first step in Wisdom. Gautama Buddha refused to answer ten or fourteen such metaphysical inquiries: he dissuaded his disciples from discussing them. Herbert Spencer divided the Universe into two parts, "the Knowable" and "the Unknowable." I would prefer to employ the terms "Known" and "Unknown," for no one can set any limits to the potentialities of human development in the infinite future. No one can assert that the Universe will remain "Unknowable" for ever. The time must come, when Man will know and understand everything without exception, and acquire Omniscience, to which the Jainas and the Buddhists aspire. In the meantime, let us build up our philosophy of this epoch on the foundations of Science.

Science is the only safe guide for the philosopher. Philosophy has been too often divorced from Science in the past. The philosophers have been mere logicians and visionaries, while the scientists have lacked the universal vision and the moral earnestness that give birth to Philosophy. Only twice or thrice in the fair story of Civilization have Philosophy and Science been united in holy wedlock, as in the schools of Aristotle, Epicurus, Spencer, and Comte. Philosophy without Science is a mirage and an opium-eater's dream; while Science without Philosophy is myopic and mischievous. A scientist, who is not a philosopher, cannot see the wood for the trees; he collects many facts, but cannot interpret and co-ordinate them. Such a half-educated scientist resembles a printer, who may possess all the letters of Shakespeare's plays pell-mell, and be unable to arrange them in the proper order. To-day, the world stands in sore need of philosophers who are also experimenting scientists. Beware of the superficial and shallow thinkers who have not received a thorough training in both the physical and biological sciences. It is not sufficient to be a physicist or a biologist: a philosopher must stand with one foot on each side, like Shakespeare's Colossus. Before you listen to any new philosopher, examine his intellectual credentials carefully. If he is a stranger to experimental Science, you need not pay much attention to his teaching. Such unscientific theorists as a rule despise the slow spade-work of Science. They pretend to have discovered a short cut to Philosophy through "intuition" or logic. They even claim to be superior to the scientists. They profess to examine and scrutinize the assumptions and procedure of Science and to deduce the most general principles from the laws formulated by the different sciences. But both these latter tasks must also be entrusted to the scientists themselves. They cannot be left in the hands of mere bookworms, who have never touched a test-tube or dissected a frog. I cannot accept the division of labour that some scholars have proposed as between the scientists and the philosophers. Philosophy *is* Science: there is no difference between them. Philosophy is the whole, and the sciences are the parts, as the stones make up the Pyramids. The same persons must cultivate both Philosophy and Science, otherwise the wise men will be fools, as they have been in almost all the historic Churches up till now. We want men like Aristotle, Theophrastus, Albertus Magnus, and Herbert Spencer, who can study Nature in detail, and also discern the general plan and outline of the Universe. The unfortunate philosophers who are ignorant of experimental Science mistake their own fancies and whims for true ideas. They evolve their magnificent systems out of their own minds, as the snail builds its portable cottage. They look inward and close their eyes, like the Indian, Christian, and Persian mystics; they do not look outward and learn from Nature. Their method is subjective and introspective, and their "philosophy" consists for the most part of unreal abstractions and unsound generalizations. It is like a dry well or an empty larder. Such pretentious philosophers try to explain anything and everything, because they are not bound by the facts and laws of Nature. Heine has wittily ridiculed such system-builders:

> "He can well put all the fragments together
> Into a system convenient and terse:
> While, with his night-cap and dressing-robe tatters,
> He'll stop up the chink of the wide Universe."

Therefore, you should not trouble about "the Absolute" and "Reality." Science deals only with the conditioned and the relative: it knows nothing of the "Absolute." Dismiss all such systems with the Swedish poet Gustav Fröding's exclamation:—

> "Weary am I of all this schism
> Betwixt the 'above' and 'under.'
> 'Idealism' and 'Realism,'
> They cleave our brains asunder,
> But trash is trash."

(2) You need not also waste much time on "epistemology" (the "theory of knowledge"). It is not possible to explain how man acquires a knowledge of the environment, or to prove that the external world exists. Such proof is not necessary. It is also futile

to inquire if our ideas correspond to "reality." Man must interpret Nature according to his sensations: there is no other Nature for him. What some thinkers call "Appearance" is "Reality" for the rationalists. Our "epistemology" cannot be absolute: it must be anthropocentric. It is also not necessary for you to decide how the mental activity called "judging" is related to the cognitive processes of "perceiving," "conceiving," and "reasoning." All such subtleties of "epistemology" may be left to the academic professional philosophers, who delight in the battles of words and terms. There is no end to such logomachies. Don't try to imitate the wonderful philosopher, who, according to Butler, could

> "distinguish and divide
> A hair 'twixt south and south-west side."

(3) You need not bother about the problem of "judgments," their classification, and the criteria of their "truth" or "error." The hair-splitting logicians have quarrelled over their theories of "obviousness," "pragmatism or utility," "coherence," etc. You will only be disgusted with Philosophy if you take such vain theoretical problems seriously.

(4) Another meaningless controversy has been carried on between the champions of "Determinism" and "Indeterminism or Free-will." Beware of being lured into this labyrinth, from which there is no exit. The Catholic Church has very wisely included this question among the "non-essential" matters, on which the pious reasoners are free to differ among themselves. We rationalists must go further, and ban this dispute as a foolish and futile pastime. The problem, which we are supposed to discuss, has never been stated in intelligible terms. Do the Indeterminists mean that an honest decent citizen can suddenly choose to pick a pocket or assault a woman? They do not. Do the Determinists mean that the human mind is passive and law-bound like a machine or a planet? They do not. In fact, it is impossible to find out what all the noise is about. Hence I believe that the controversy is devoid of serious significance. We must study the facts of Psychology, and avoid such metaphysical wrangling as the medieval Schoolmen loved. This debate has no bearing on Ethics. We are not interested in fixing "responsibility" in order to punish or reward people in this life or the next. That judicial procedure is no part of our philosophy. Then why waste your time on this ancient squabble? Study Psychology, its facts and laws.

(5) Another time-honoured but meaningless controversy concerns

the relation between "Mind" and "Matter." You can follow it down the centuries, but you need not attach any importance to it. The theories of interactionism, parallelism, epiphenomenalism, and emergence are all wrong; there are seventeen of them, according to Dr. C. D. Broad, and they are all wrong and worse than wrong. We owe a debt of gratitude to the pragmatists for insisting on "the otiose, artificial, and gratuitous nature" of this problem, as Professor J. B. Pratt (himself a dualist) puts it. But you should go further than the pragmatists: you should be neither a monist nor a dualist, but simply a scientist. Discard for ever such old metaphysical rags as "Matter" and "Mind." There is no "Matter" and no "Mind": there are only phenomena and their laws. "Matter" and "Mind" are both abstractions. Remember the two old questions and the new answers. "What is Mind?" "Never mind!" "What is Matter?" "It doesn't matter." You cannot study the anatomy of a camel by measuring and examining its shadow; even so, you cannot learn much about the processes of thinking, feeling, and willing by fighting over an imaginary problem, which is really of theological origin. Avoid such medieval spurious "philosophy," which will be of as little benefit to you as it was to Omar Khayyam.

> "Myself when young did eagerly frequent
> Doctor and Saint, and heard great argument
> About it and about: but evermore
> Came out by the same door as in I went."

When a man moves from one house to another, he generally gets rid of a lot of useless lumber; in the same way, Philosophy must now simplify and modernize itself, as it leaves the old tenement haunted by the ghosts of scholasticism and instals itself in its new abode, which is equipped with all scientific appliances and labour-saving devices. It must free itself from the burdensome encumbrances of such unintelligible verbal puzzles as have been mentioned above. It has already been stripped of some of its outlying provinces, like Logic and Psychology, which are now independent branches of knowledge. It should welcome such a deliverance. It must concentrate upon two central themes, which belong to it by right—viz. Science in its general and universal aspects, and Ethics. With these precious gifts in its hands, it can appeal to our interest and sympathy. We must restore Philosophy to the position of pre-eminence and practical importance that it occupied in Greece and Rome. It taught genuine Wisdom and Virtue, not mere metaphysical rodomontade. It embraced Science and

Ethics, as among the Peripatetics, the Stoics, and the Epicureans. It spoke to the common people through those "athletes of Virtue," the Cynics. Modern Philosophy has become lifeless and jejune: there is no warm blood in her shrunken veins and no bright lustre in her wan eyes. She is almost a skeleton compared with her ancient self; the flesh and fat have been eaten up by her rival, Theology. Now Theology has fallen on evil days, and Philosophy can come by her own again. It must teach the modern Rationalists how to live complete and noble lives; it must not content itself with writing obscure treatises about non-existent entities. It must popularize Science and formulate the new Ethics. It must lay the foundations of the World-State that is to come. Such Philosophy should be your love and light and life, as it was for Marcus Aurelius and Lucretius.

In studying Philosophy, you should devote special attention to the works of Aristotle, Epicurus, Spinoza, Locke, Diderot, La Mettrie, d'Holbach, Ludwig Feuerbach, T. Huxley, Auguste Comte, E. Haeckel, Herbert Spencer, Dietzgen, Th. Ribot, Pierre Janet, Emile Durkheim, Lucien Lévy-Bruhl, Wilhelm Ostwald, Ludwig Büchner, Bertrand Russell, John Arthur Thomson, Frederick Soddy, Conway Lloyd Morgan, Julian Huxley, and other exponents of scientific philosophy. You will be inspired and enlightened by their teachings and personalities.

Don't waste your time on the unscientific metaphysicians, ancient and modern. They do not deserve to be named.

SECTION VI.—SOCIOLOGY

SOCIOLOGY is a very important subject of study. It will teach you how social and political institutions have arisen and developed in the past, and how they are influenced by climate, racial characteristics, economic forces, superstitions, and other factors. It will broaden your mind and prepare you for citizenship. You will learn much from it.

(1) You will cease to believe in the theological doctrine that "God" has established and hallowed certain institutions for all time. The habit of regarding an absolute and eternal lawgiver as the originator of all social customs at any particular epoch has led to stagnation in the past. Theology is static in its ideals: "God" has revealed his will once for all for our guidance. The Christians believe that no prophet is needed after Christ's revelation, and the Moslems look upon Muhammad as the last of the prophets. Some Buddhists teach that there can be only one perfect Buddha in a particular world and a particular age, and all should follow his teaching. But Sociology discusses the value and significance of all institutions in a rational spirit, and discounts and discredits such theological claims. Thus you were taught to believe that the Sunday rest was orally prescribed by "God" on Mount Sinai: but the sociologists trace it back to the Babylonians. Sociology has discovered that similar institutions have existed among many different tribes and nations. Herbert Spencer's "Descriptive Sociology" is a mine of information on this subject. Professor Westermarck's researches will astonish and perhaps shock you, when you learn that all sorts of marriage-customs have prevailed and still prevail among mankind, and that divorce is granted for different reasons in different countries. You will be interested in the problems of Feminism, and study the facts that throw light on the position of Women in society at different times. Sociology will cure you of national pride and self-complacency, if you have been intellectually a frog in the well. It will show you that other nations have some customs that are better than yours. It will explain the origin of some queer and curious primitive practices that survive among civilized nations. You will be con-

vinced that all institutions have been built up by men and women, and are relative to a certain stage of development. They must be changed and developed in course of time. Sociology will expose such fallacies as the " divine " right of Kings, the " divine " prohibition of marriage with a cousin, the " divine " approval of monogamy or polygamy, the " divine law " of the subjection of women, etc., etc.

(2) Sociology will make you a wise social and political reformer. You will not believe that any institution is so perfect and beneficent that it should last for ever. You will try to borrow some ideas and customs from foreign countries, or even from the long-forgotten past. You will find that some custom which is considered dangerous and horrible in your country is approved and sanctioned by another people. This knowledge will open your eyes, and lead you to inquire if it is really as dangerous and horrible as it is said to be. Sociology will help the rationalists to establish new common world-customs, which may make a world-society possible. All of us must leave our old national or religious grooves, and throw all the old customs and institutions into the melting-pot. Let Sociology fabricate the new links that will unite us in the new Society of the future. But first you must study this subject without any religious or national prejudices. Then come out with your plans and projects of Reform.

SECTION VII.—LANGUAGES

THE growing infant learns to speak. The proper use of language is among the earliest acquisitions of childhood. You should acquire a good command of your mother-tongue: you should be able to speak and write it as well as your natural ability will allow. The study of language and the practice of composition and elocution are the first steps in mental culture. It is supposed that the primary school equips us with an adequate knowledge of our national language. But how many people in your country can write an essay in correct and idiomatic language? Many farmers and working-men cannot even write a letter without making ludicrous mistakes! So much conversation around us is slovenly and slipshod, because the study of language is neglected. Conversation is a fine art, and speech is its medium. We dislike shabbiness in dress, but we often tolerate clumsiness and awkwardness in the use of our own language. You should be proud of your mother-tongue, the speech of your ancestors and poets and orators. Learn from the example of the French and the Persians. How they love and cherish their lovely languages!

You must naturally begin with your mother-tongue, but you should not stop there. You should try to learn at least one other modern language. Your choice will depend on the nature of your work or business, your aptitude, and your intellectual interests. If you are not very clever, learn an easy foreign language, which is somewhat similar to your own. Thus a Frenchman may learn Italian, a Bengali may take up Hindi, and a German may try to master English. If you have a talent for linguistic studies, you may choose a difficult foreign language. A gifted Englishman may choose Chinese, and a brilliant German may tackle Persian or Arabic. It is necessary to disseminate a knowledge of all living languages in every country as far as possible. There should be many competent scholars of every language in every country. You should not regard language-study only from the professional standpoint. A commercial traveller, a consul, or a clerk in a Travel Bureau may learn several languages in order to earn his bread; but you should first and foremost look upon language-study as a duty undertaken for Self-culture. You develop your Personality by knowing two languages instead of one. If your knowledge of foreign languages also helps you to make money, you gain a double advantage. But improve your mind first.

Many and various are the benefits that you will derive from the study of at least one foreign language. It will sharpen your intellect, as you will discover that different nations do not express the same idea in the same way. It is curious that such a simple question as "How do you do?" is asked in such different ways in English, French, German, and Swedish. You will be astonished to find that the nations of the world do not even count up to a hundred or read the dial of a clock in the same way as you do. Thus your stay-at-home mind is rudely awakened to a sense of world-culture. You become really conscious of the existence of other nations. Your mind is no longer confined in the comfortable prison of your national language and life. A new world of thought, custom, poetry, and history is revealed to you. You cease to be a narrow-minded, half-educated "Nationalist"; you are on your way to becoming a cultured cosmopolitan. I recall two good sayings: "With each newly-learned language one acquires a new soul"; "A man who knows two languages is worth two men." When you have learned a foreign language like French, you look forward to the pleasure of travelling among the people who speak it. At last, you start on your trip, and you are thrilled at finding yourself in a strange land, with French faces, French names, French costumes, French talk, French gestures, French equality, French fluency, French coffee-and-milk, French tips, even French curses and oaths, all around you. You find that the French are not half so bad as the English historians of the sixty-eighth century A.H. and the Napoleonic Wars have made them out to be. You forget all about the blood-stained past, and think of the French as lovable friends and comrades, not as the "national enemies" of the text-books. You begin to feel that the English people should change the names of "Waterloo" Station and "Trafalgar Square," which only serve to keep alive sad memories of strife and conflict. You discover that the citizens of Paris have named some streets after foreign musicians and poets, and you appreciate their broad-based artistic culture. You are pleased (or shocked) that the minds of the French people are not warped by the irrational and puerile colour-prejudice, which the Germans, the English, and the North Americans cherish as a most precious national tradition. You will also wonder how the French can get on without a Prince of Wales, and why their leading newspaper does not publish a detailed description of the dresses worn by women at a "Court." A few months' stay in France will thus work as a cure. It will eliminate some of the virulent toxic matter that has accumulated in your cerebral centres during many years of purely English education and English society. You will develop an Anglo-French psychology, and lose your old English-and-nothing-but-English mentality. You will say to yourself, "Now I am resolved to be more and more of a Man, and less and less of a mere Englishman." In the same way, a Frenchman who learns English and visits England is improved and transformed for the rest of his life. He admires and appreciates English order, English liberty, English kindness, English sincerity, English public spirit, English tenacity, English moral courage, English love of adventure, English heroism, English punctuality, English honesty and integrity, English outdoor sports, English reticence, English humour, English cider, English tea, and English gardens. He forgets what he was taught at school about "perfidious Albion" and "a nation of shopkeepers." He develops a Franco-English psychology; he is cured of the vice of raving hysterical Nationalism. He says to himself: "Now I am resolved to be more and more of a Man, and less and less of a mere Frenchman."

Similarly, if you are English and learn both French and German, your mind is immersed in an English–French–German cleansing bath. You are healed still more of the leprosy of Nationalism. It is a pity that one cannot learn all the living languages of the world, for time and talent are limited; but learn as many as you can. It is great fun being a polyglot. You can then read many books and journals, receive foreign visitors in your home, translate letters and circulars for your favourite social and political movements, act as an interpreter at meetings and conferences, and render such other service as only a clever polyglot can give. I would advise you to master several foreign languages before you are thirty. This accomplishment must be acquired early in life. At a later period, you will not have the time or the aptitude for such study. Lay the foundations well in the years of youth and early manhood, and you will be rewarded a thousandfold in intellectual, moral, and practical benefits that will accrue to you throughout your life.

Esperanto

When you have learned several languages, you realize that it is not possible to know all the languages of the world. You also begin to understand that this diversity of tongues keeps the nations apart and fosters suspicion and distrust. You are disgusted at the Babel of confusion at the international congresses of different movements. Speeches must be translated and interpreted, and the gathering never develops the living spirit of unity and spontaneity. It remains a dead and dull affair, and often ends in disillusionment. Only a mechanical mixture of nationalities takes place, as all the delegates can never speak to one another. A real union of minds and hearts cannot be attained without unity of language. True comradeship cannot grow and flourish in an atmosphere of dumb gestures and smiles. Effective discussion is also out of the question in an assembly when a member cannot speak and appeal directly to all the others. Even the League of Nations lacks real vitality for this reason. The Roman Catholic Church, which is an international organization with its centre at Rome, teaches all its priests the Latin language as their common medium of communication. It could not maintain its unity for a week without Latin. It is strange that many socialists, pacifists, trade-unionists, protestants, theosophists, freethinkers, feminists, and other modern leaders have established so-called international organizations, with "branches" in many countries, but they have not at the same time insisted on the adoption of a common language as the vehicle of their world-wide propaganda. The consequence is that all these movements are not really international; they are composed of loose agglomerations of national sections, which can be rent asunder by the slightest centrifugal force. They cannot unify and organize the human race, even if they preach the ideal of universal unity. They lack the indispensable material instrument of world-wide organization, viz a common language.

Thus you will be led to consider the problem of the auxiliary world-language. It should be chosen and cultivated by all genuine practical cosmopolitans. Some cosmopolitans suggest that a living language should be adopted as the medium of international communication, like Greek in the ancient Mediterranean countries, or French in the world of modern diplomacy. Auguste Comte recommended Italian; others prefer English. English is spoken by many millions in many countries. Some scholars have offered a simplified form of English with phonetic spelling and scientific pronunciation. Spanish has also its advocates, as it is spoken in Central and Southern America. But there are two unanswerable objections to the use of any modern language in the service of cosmopolitanism. First, all living languages are very difficult to learn on account of the irregularity of grammar, spelling, and pronunciation. How many young men and women can speak English, French, or German with real fluency and facility, even after several years' daily drill in the secondary schools? The average boy's mind is lost in the chaotic wilderness of rules and exceptions and counter-exceptions. Secondly, we shall rouse national prejudices and passions by trying to impose one living language on all the proud and sensitive nations of the world. No nation is likely to accept a foreign modern language as the auxiliary tongue. Can you imagine Russia meekly submitting to English linguistic Imperialism, or China introducing Spanish in all her schools and colleges? There is not an iota of practicability in this fantastic fad.

We must, then, invent a new universal language. At present, you are assailed and admonished by the champions of English, Esperanto, Ido, Anglic, Basic, Mondo, and other obscure inventions. You have a wide field of choice. But perhaps you will decide in favour of Esperanto, as it is very easy to learn, and also possesses the momentum of fifty years' propaganda and service. An international auxiliary language must be simple; it must be free from difficulties and complexities of grammar; it must be capable of development and adaptation; and it must be supported by a living movement, in which many enthusiastic men and women participate. This last condition is very important. A scholar may invent a wonderful language, perfect in every part; but it has no future, if he cannot inspire many zealous disciples and colleagues to devote themselves to his propaganda. In history, nothing succeeds like success. Esperanto is not a faultless creation. I doubt if any one could invent a perfect language free from all defects and difficulties. An arm-chair critic can always criticize this or that feature of Esperanto, and even suggest considerable improvements. But such objections are irrelevant. We do not need an absolutely perfect language. We require a sufficiently simple and easy language, which can be mastered by ordinary men and women in their spare time during one or two years. Many scholars can invent a new language: they possess all the necessary grammars and dictionaries. It is easy to give birth to an artificial language, but it is very difficult indeed to make it live even for a few years. Just as many ordinary preachers have started ephemeral religious sects, but only a great prophet, aided by external circumstances, can found a successful Church, even so a universal language requires a great personality and favourable environment for its inception. Zamenhof, the inventor of Esperanto, must have been a remarkable leader, as he secured the co-operation of many intelligent disciples and colleagues. The French and Russian enthusiasts of the eighties of the last century spread the new gospel with all the ardour of true apostles. Esperanto has now definitely succeeded: no one can deny this amazing and encouraging fact. It possesses a considerable literature. Many Chambers of Commerce and evening schools offer instruction in it. Esperanto Lectureships have been established at the Universities of Liverpool, Geneva, and Cracow. It is taught in over a thousand schools in thirty-two countries. Many religious, educational, and professional organizations have adopted it, and the League of Nations Committee has recommended it. Even the world-war did not kill it. Some villages in the south of France have set up sign-posts on the roads in French and Esperanto ("*Halto por autobusoj*"). Esperanto is flying into many homes on the wings of the wireless, and Russia has given it official sanction and patronage. No other proposed language can show such a record of actual achievement. If we are vain or fussy or ultra-patriotic, we shall continue to advertise our brand-new plans or an unsavoury hash of English, and thus divide the true cosmopolitans into hostile camps. But if we are sagacious and sincere, we should accept Esperanto (with all its faults) as a superb historical *fait accompli*, and unite in its defence. Under the sign of the green star (*la verda stelo*), we will conquer!

The Ancient Languages

So much for the living languages. As for the dead classical languages, you may choose one or two of them (preferably only one) for some particular purpose, if you are an exceptionally gifted linguist. If you can easily learn formidable grammatical declensions and conjugations, and are keenly interested in some special subject, then I wish you good luck in your attack on one of these citadels of the ancient giants. You may wish to come into close touch with the inspiring personalities of Plato, Aristotle, or Lucretius. You may choose to dig deep into the mysteries of the Mahāyāna, or live in continual communion with Confucius and Mencius. You may be attracted by the reverberating thunder-peals of the mighty-mouthed Prophet of Arabia and the luminous encyclopædic wisdom of Alfarabi and Ibn-Rashd. If you have such intellectual projects and aspirations, then you may study Greek, Latin, Sanskrit, Chinese, Arabic, or any other classical language. It must be thoroughly mastered in all its details before you can get at the kernel of thought and life hidden away under the rough and tough shell of the grammar and the vocabulary. Some talent and very hard work are required.

If you are an able linguist, but have no special subject of study, you may desire to learn the one classical language that should be most useful and helpful for your personal culture. If this is your quest, you need not hesitate at all, but choose Greek for your life-long devotion. The most valuable ancient poetry, drama, philosophy, rhetoric, biography, and history are enshrined in the subtle and supple tongue of Hellas. One of the other ancient languages may offer some masterpiece that is superior to anything in Greek: but no other ancient literature contains so much of the very best of everything that is needed for culture. Greek is especially valuable for modern Rationalists, as Greek philosophy is largely based on Science and Humanism. The great philosophers of Greece are nearer to us in spirit than the saints and teachers of other countries. They are the immortal precursors of modern Rationalism. Greek should be studied by the leaders of Rationalism in the same way as Hebrew is mastered by the Jewish rabbis, Latin by the Roman Catholic priests, Arabic by the Moslem scholars, and Sanskrit by the Hindu Brahmins. It is the sacred classical language of Rationalism.

I may add the testimony of famous scholars and poets with regard to the supreme and unapproachable excellence of Hellenic literature and philosophy.

Goethe: "The work of the Greek tragic poets is marked by grandeur, excellence, sanity, complete humanity, a high philosophy of life, a lofty way of thinking, a powerful intuition. We find these qualities in their surviving lyric and epic poetry as well as in their drama. . . . Beside the great Attic poets, like Æschylus and Sophocles, I am absolutely nothing."

P. B. Shelley: "Their very language . . . in variety, in simplicity, in flexibility, and in copiousness, excels every other language of the western world."

T. B. Macaulay: "I have gone back to Greek literature with a passion quite astonishing to myself. . . . I felt as if I had never known before what intellectual enjoyment was. Oh that wonderful people!"

Robert Bridges:

"There is now no higher intellect to brighten the world
Than little Hellas own'd; nay scarcely here and there
Liveth a man among us to rival their seers."

("The Testament of Beauty.")

Professor Gilbert Murray: "The Greeks of the fifth century B.C. produced some of the noblest poetry and art, the finest political thinking, the most vital philosophy, known to the world. . . . There is hardly any type of thought or style of writing which cannot be paralleled in ancient Greece. . . . The conception of Freedom and Justice, freedom in body, in speech and in mind, justice between the strong and the weak, the rich and the poor, penetrates the whole of Greek political thought. . . . Greek is a finer language, because it expresses the minds of finer men."

J. A. Froude: "On long voyages, I take Greeks as my best companions. . . . I have a few volumes of pocket classics, which I always take with me in distant expeditions. Greek and Latin literature is wine which does not spoil by time. . . . These finished relics of the old world shine as fixed stars in the intellectual firmament."

Professor R. C. Jebb: "The thoughts of the great Greek thinkers have been bearing fruit in the world ever since they were first uttered. . . . They were the first people who tried to make Reason the guide of their social life. . . . We find writers of all sorts, poets and historians and philosophers, habitually striving to get at the reason of things."

Professor R. Flint: "Greece discovered the universal principles of all high purely human culture, and embodied them in forms of almost perfect beauty, to remain as objects of admiration and models for imitation to educated men of all ages in all lands."

Translators

Apart from your personal enjoyment and culture, you can render a valuable service to progress and civilization by translating some books from ancient or modern foreign languages into your mother-tongue. You should help in building a bridge between the past and the present, or between a foreign nation and your own people. You will thus play a very important part in the history of your country. A good translator is a great benefactor of the human race. At present, the literature, philosophy, and science of each nation can be interpreted to all the others only by means of translations. In the past, talented linguists have thus introduced new religious, political, and scientific movements into their countries. They have enriched and enlightened their people, and enabled them to participate in the progressive movements of the world. As the mariners have transported the spices and silk of the East to the far West, even so industrious translators have enabled the great creative nations to exchange their ideas and ideals, which are far more precious than the cargoes of perishable commodities.

In the course of history, the great translators stand out as international interpreters in each momentous epoch. We owe a heavy debt of gratitude to all of them. Cicero and Lucretius popularized Greek philosophy among the Romans. Jesus Christ spoke Aramaic, but his words have come down to us in Greek. St. Jerome translated the Bible into Latin. The Nestorians translated Greek treatises into Syriac. The Buddhist religion was introduced into China by means of numerous translations from Sanskrit and some Indian dialects into Chinese. Kumārajiva, Yuan-Chwang, and others devoted long years to these fruitful labours. The medieval Renaissance in Islamic countries was based upon Arabic translations from Syriac and Sanskrit, which were made by Hunayn-ibn-Ishaq, Ibn-al-Baluk, Costa ben Luca, and others. The early European Renaissance of the sixty-second and sixty-third centuries A.H. originated in the devotion and zeal of such translators as Dominic Gundisalvus, Gerald of Cremona, Mark of Toledo, Ibn-Dawud, and others. During the sixty-fifth and succeeding centuries, the real Renaissance in Europe was ushered in by the great translators, who learned Greek and then faithfully rendered the Hellenic masterpieces into Latin, Italian, English, and French. Such were Ficino, Amyot, North, Erasmus, and others.

In recent times, the Pali literature of Buddhism, the works of the Chinese philosophers, Persian poetry, the Bahai scriptures, the plays of Ibsen, the writings of Tagore, and other important masterpieces have been rendered accessible to the whole world by the indefatigable European translators.

The translators have always contributed to the efflorescence of culture in new countries, as the bees carry pollen from flower to flower. You should join this noble company of the learned Messengers of Culture.

Section VIII.—COMPARATIVE RELIGION

You are probably born in a family that professes one of the great living religions: Buddhism, Hinduism, Jainism, Positivism, Christianity, Taoism, Judaism, Islam, Zoroastrianism, Confucianism, Shintoism, or Bahaism. When you accept the modern gospel of Rationalism, you should winnow the wheat from the chaff in your ancient creed, and take the wheat with you as your contribution to the Harvest-Festival of the new Fellowship. Don't come empty-handed from your old home.

(1) You should study the great religions carefully and thoroughly: their origin, history, and present position. For social progress, they have been what the mighty rivers are for the material prosperity of the nations. They have supplied the life-giving waters of Ethics, which are, however, very dirty and turgid on account of the large admixture of superstition, as the Hoang-ho is yellow with the mud of a continent. The valuable element in each religion is its Ethics, which is always present in varying amounts, as some pure water can be obtained from even the foulest stream by the process of distillation. Rationalism distils the Ethics out of all the old religions. You should condemn and discard the superstition that is found in all the religions, but you should not throw away the Ethics with the superstition. Comparative religion is a fascinating study: it will introduce you into the presence of noble sages and saints, who will teach you the social virtues of self-denial, temperance, patience, simplicity, and love. Most of them were ignorant of Science, and combined the highest Ethics with gross superstition. Borrow their virtues, and reject their errors, as the Arab eats the dates and throws away the stones. Rub and rinse and wash and cleanse the old religions; but don't rub and wash away the Ethics altogether.

(2) All religions prescribe certain social customs and inculcate some political ideals. They approve of various marriage-laws, and prohibit some kinds of food. They insist on the performance of rites and ceremonies. All these appurtenances of the old religions must be judged on their merits from the standpoint of modern Science and Rationalism. The *ipse dixit* of the ancient prophets

cannot be accepted to-day. We cannot prohibit divorce, or abstain from pork and fish, or sanction polygamy, merely because some venerable holy teachers said something about these matters long ago. Such social institutions must change from age to age. So think for yourself on these questions, and don't follow Jesus, Manu, Zoroaster, Muhammad, or Buddha. They cannot dictate our social laws and customs, though we learn Virtue from them. If a Church approves of Democracy (like Calvinism), you should obey its political precepts. But if it supports despotism or oligarchy, you should reject its teaching in that respect. All religious utterances that militate against democracy, liberty, equality, and fraternity in politics and economics must now be consigned to oblivion. No dead spiritual leaders can now induce us to pay tribute to Cæsar or Caliph.

(3) The rites and ceremonies of all the religions must be spurned and condemned. External and mechanical acts can never purify the soul and develop Personality. As it is difficult to be virtuous, the priests teach the people to be outwardly pious. Such Pharisaic piety is a serious obstacle to moral growth. In many cases, the people believe that they will escape future punishment in hell or secure material prosperity in this world by the performance of certain ceremonies. The priests are usually paid money for this religious mummery and buffoonery: whoever loses, they always win. You should set your face against all such fraud. Teach your neighbours that nothing is gained by circumcision, baptism, pilgrimages, sacraments, "holy communion," fire-altars, sun-worship, sacred threads, bloody sacrifices, candles and incense, circumambulations and prostrations, river-bathing and stone-kissing, relic-worship and the adoration of tombs, teeth, idols, animal-figures and painted pictures. Away with all such imbecilities! Ye Christians, water and wine will not wash away your sins: receive the baptism of Brotherhood, and drink the wine of Wisdom until you are drunk with it. Ye Moslems and Jews, cut off lust and lewdness: don't mutilate the body! Ye Hindus, don't worship the sun, but love Science that explores the sun. Don't wear the sacred thread, but bind your hearts with the silken cord of love. Ye Parsis, don't feed the holy fire: rather keep the flame of fraternity burning in your souls. Ye Buddhists, don't adore Buddha's tooth: listen to the sweet words that come from his lips. Ye Shintoists, your *obarai* will not expiate your sins. Ye Hindus and Moslems, kill not the dumb beasts in honour of Kali or Allah: slay the wolf and the snake within you. Mutter not the ninety-

nine names of "God" or the thousand names of "Vishnu": repeat instead the names of all the saints and scientists that have lived. Don't walk round the temples: rather travel round the world and be wise. Don't fast at certain periods: be very temperate every day and every night. Don't crush your souls with the coarse material symbols that perish. Love the sublime ethical Verities that endure for ever.

(4) The doctrine of "salvation" in a heaven or many heavens, and "damnation" in a hell or several hells, forms an integral part of almost all religions. Such bliss and such misery may be eternal, as in Christianity and Islam, or they may last only for a certain period of time, as in Hinduism and Buddhism. The rewards and punishments of the future life are supposed to incite the average man to the pursuit of virtue or deter him from vice and sin. All such dogmas are generally based on the notion that a certain portion of human Personality, called "the soul," survives death. It may be reunited with the body, or it may subsist by itself. It has been regarded as "material" or purely "spiritual." The central idea is that something of your Personality as a sentient being will exist after death, and you will be capable of enjoying happiness or suffering pain. What a stupendous structure of superstition has been raised among all nations on this unscientific doctrine! Ethics has been defaced and degraded in supporting and buttressing it. Fear and terror have robbed countless men and women of dignity, peace, and true morality. From the ancient Egyptians down to the most recent ranting Revivalist, ignorant Man has mumbled this question in piteous accents: "What will happen to me when I die?" Cunning charlatans and unscrupulous scoundrels have exploited this ignorance throughout the ages. The priests have stolen the money of the people by promising future happiness of some sort to the deluded worshippers. Perhaps they deluded themselves first, but they made profit out of the delusion. The fear of "damnation" has drawn more tears from the eyes of the human race than would fill all the briny oceans. The hope of "salvation" has filled the coffers of the priest-parasites with more gold and silver than the Spaniards extorted from America or Mahmud from India. Ethics has been reduced to sordid commercial arithmetic, as Virtue has been regarded as the daily premium paid for insurance against the risk of "damnation," each Church being the safe and solvent insurance company for its votaries. A Russian impostor actually sold seats in Heaven to the peasants at the price of five and ten roubles! Masses, prayers, and gifts

for the dead are permanent sources of income for the priestly gang in all countries. Such are the evil consequences of this doctrine of "the soul" and its future existence in another world. Judged by its results alone, it should be condemned and combated by every lover of mankind.

Now, you should liberate yourself and others from such superstition by refuting the dogma of Retribution in all its forms. Man is born in order to develop his Personality, not to be punished with pain or rewarded with pleasure for his actions. You should hit the idea of Retribution on the head, and hit it hard, wherever you find it. Development, and not this hedonistic or vindictive Retribution, is the destiny of Personality. The Universe is not in the hands of brutal policemen or greedy hucksters: it is ruled and regulated by Evolution, growing Life, unfolding Actuality. None will be punished or rewarded anywhere in any way after death. Virtue is its own reward here in this life, as you grow by it. Vice is its own punishment here on earth, as it arrests growth. The Universe keeps no register of your deeds: it does not remember your good actions or your sins. It counts each moment as complete in itself, and hurries forward with its task of Growth. Therefore, get rid of the notion of blissful or painful Retribution after death.

(5) Having discarded all superstition, you can derive benefit from the study of Comparative Religion. Ponder well the lives and sayings of the great saints and prophets. They despised money and property. You can do the same. They sacrificed everything for the good of their fellow-men. You can do the same. They cultivated extreme simplicity in food, drink, and dress. You can do the same. They loved and served the poor and the humble. You can do the same. They were free from lust and craving. You can be the same. They were always patient and gentle. You can be the same. They inspired their friends and comrades with zeal for perfection. You can do the same.

You should cull a nosegay of ethical precepts from the different Scriptures. They will refresh your soul with the beauty and perfume of Virtue.

(6) The superstition in the old religions generally consists of Theology in some form or other. Polytheism or monotheism is their creed. The worship of Siva, Vishnu, bodhisattvas, demons, angels, or one "God" constitutes the core of superstition in them. You should free your mind of the last vestiges of such theological belief.

Polytheism still exists in India, China, and other countries; but, on account of the growing intelligence of the people, it is slowly verging towards extinction. It is easy for them to doubt the existence of those numerous gods with four mouths, three eyes, and elephant-heads. Polytheism paints the gods in human colours, and thus renders itself incredible. But "spiritual" monotheism is a more dangerous and insidious enemy, as it makes pretence of subtlety and rationality. It divests "God" of a body, members, senses, passions, wives, and children; and it presents an invisible, intangible, eternal, omnipresent, wise, benevolent, omnipotent Being, who is supposed to create, sustain, and maintain the entire Universe. This doctrine is more plausible than crude polytheism; it is the basis of Jewish, Moslem, and Christian theology and philosophy. Fortunately, most of the Greek, Hindu, and Chinese philosophers were not caught in this snare. Of the four chief streams of religious tradition, only one is polluted with the impurities of this superstition.

You must reject and repudiate this dogma for the following reasons:—

(i) There can be no First Cause or Prime Mover of Nature, as Aristotle and St. Thomas Aquinas assume. St. Thomas Aquinas says: "The first and most evident way (of proving the existence of God) is the argument from Motion. Anything which is moved is moved by some other thing. We must then arrive at some first source of motion, which is moved by nothing else, and such a source all men understand to be God." Aristotle, in his "Metaphysics," wrote: "The primary motion belongs to the changes; . . . but the First Mover imparts motion to that. Of necessity, in this case, must this Immovable First Mover constitute an entity."

This argument is not valid at all. We cannot conceive of a beginning of motion or of the Universe. Motion in Matter is a physical phenomenon, which has also physical causal antecedents. It is impossible to jump out of this physical chain of events into the lap of a "God," who is a Person.

(ii) The Universe has not been created by "God." Some thinkers teach that "God" created the Universe out of nothing. This doctrine can be found in Genesis, the Koran, and al-Ghazzali's works. Other philosophers assume that God did not create out of nothing: thus Leibniz speaks in the "Theodicée" of "fulgurations" of the Deity. These give birth to the monads by a process, which is intermediate between the absolute creation of the theists and the "emanation" of the pantheists.

Plato, Descartes, and Dayanand teach that God created the world out of pre-existing Matter. If "God" created Matter and the

Universe out of nothing, or only re-arranged and vitalized eternally existing Matter, it is, in both cases, impossible to guess what his motive could have been. Activity denotes the desire for some object and the pursuit of some end that is not attained. But God is supposed to be perfect from all eternity: there was nothing that he lacked or needed. Why did he take the trouble of creating anything? If it increased his happiness, then he was not perfect before this creation. Perfection cannot be enhanced. If the existence of the Universe was necessary for his altruistic activity, then also he was not perfect before the creation, as a new element was added to his personality. Thus creation seems to have been an act without any motive; but even a fool does not act without some impelling motive. Either "God" was not perfect before the creation or he could not have created anything. Further, if "God" created the world, who created "God"? Where did "God" come from? Whence is his origin?

(iii) We have no idea of a Perfect Being that is not a man or woman. The ontological argument for the existence of "God" is a mere cobweb of words. St. Anselm, in his "Proslogium," says: "Our belief is this: Thou art a Being than which no greater can be conceived, *quo nihil majus cogitari potest*. . . . But certainly that very man, when hearing the term, understands what he hears. Now certainly that, than which no greater can be conceived, cannot be in the understanding alone, for, if it were only in the understanding, it could then be further conceived to be also in reality, which would be a greater thing. Something, therefore, without doubt exists, than which no greater can be conceived, and it is both in the understanding and in reality." Descartes also borrowed this argument, and wrote: "Existence can no more be separated from the essence of God than the idea of a mountain from that of a valley, or the equality of its three angles to two right angles from the essence of a rectilineal triangle. Necessary existence is contained in the nature or in the concept of God. Hence it may with truth be said that necessary existence is in God, or that God exists. It is certain that I no less find the idea of God in my consciousness, that is, the idea of a being supremely perfect, than that of any figure or number whatever."

This mode of reasoning can also be employed to prove the existence of demons, chimeras, sphinxes, and dragons, for some persons have had or have a clear idea of these beings. If I can imagine something as existing, it does not follow that it actually exists. Man's brain is not a miniature map of the Universe.

(iv) Personal direct intuition is no proof of the existence of "God." Many mystics and philosophers have asserted that the existence of "God" need not be demonstrated by reasoning, as they "perceived" or "felt" or "apprehended" it in their hearts and souls. This doctrine has been held in various forms by the Quakers, the Sufis, and some modern thinkers like A. Eddington and others. Baba Kuhi (cited by R. A. Nicholson) said:

> "Neither soul nor body, accident nor substance,
> Qualities nor causes—only God I saw."

Such theists claim that they directly experience "a spiritual Power, not ourselves, but around and within us." Dr. T. G. Dunning (cited by Joseph McCabe) says: "Here are data which are overwhelming indeed!" Ramakrishna, the Hindu saint, said to Vivekananda: "I see God as I see you or that wall."

This plea really means that the theists run away from the fight. You cannot argue with a man who will not reason. Philosophy is based on discussion and reasoning; it appeals to facts and experiences that all can test and verify. But if some one refers me only to his inner consciousness, I reply that I cannot penetrate into his private harem and zenana of favourite feelings and intuitions. He cannot convert me, as I cannot convince him. He does not want to listen to what I say, and I cannot experience what he has inwardly experienced. So we may both go home. A person's subjective experience cannot prove the existence of "God," who is supposed to be an externally existent Being. Luther not only felt, but saw the Devil, and threw an inkpot at him; but most theists now do not believe in that once-famous personage. The Hindu devotee asserts that he "experiences" his beloved deity, Siva or Vishnu, in the same manner as these intuitionists know their one "God." In this way, every one will be confined in his own little mind, and every opium-eater will enjoy his own pleasant hallucination. We must appeal to our common universal human Reason, which is the final arbiter in Science and Philosophy. An accused criminal may as well say, "I feel I am innocent," and the policeman may retort, "I feel you are guilty." Who will decide, if Reason is not to be the Judge? It is better to declare, like Kapila: "God has not been proved."

(v) Many theists adduce the familiar but fallacious "argument from Design." Udayana, the Hindu philosopher, says: "The world is a product, as it consists of component parts; and so it must have had a maker, an intelligent being possessed of that combination of volition, desire to act, and knowledge of the proper means which sets in motion all other causes." Prophet Muhammad says in the Koran: "Glorify God; he quickeneth the earth after it hath been dead. . . . He hath created you out of dust, and behold, ye are become men. He hath created for you, out of yourselves, wives that ye may cohabit with them." The Talmud of the Jews (cited by Edwin Collins) says: "God has formed a world full of beauty and order; a universe full of exquisitely adjusted laws that work together for good. There is nothing in it useless or evil, or even superfluous." Epictetus declared: "God has made all the things in the Universe and the Universe itself, completely free from hindrance and perfect, and the parts of it for the use of the whole." Cicero expounded the Stoic view of Providence thus: "How bountiful is Nature, that has provided for us such an abundance of various and delicious food! . . . the great utility of rivers, the flux and reflux of the sea, the salt-pits remote from the sea-coasts, the earth replete with salutary medicines. . . . Examine thoroughly into the structure of the body, and the form and perfection of human nature. . . . The teeth are there placed to divide and grind the food. . . . The stomach is wonderfully composed. . . . As in buildings, the architect averts from the eyes and nose of the master those things which must necessarily be offensive, so has Nature removed far from our senses what is of the same kind in the human body. The revolutions of the sun, moon, and all the stars . . . may be considered also as objects designed for the view and contemplation of Man. . . . Of what utility would sheep be, unless for their wool? Why need I mention oxen? We perceive that their backs were not formed for carrying burdens, but their necks were naturally made for the yoke. What is the pig good for, but to eat? As it is proper food for man, Nature has made no animal more fruitful. . . . Everything in this world, that is of use to us, was made designedly for us." Leibniz emphasizes the idea that the Universe forms one system, and says: "There must also be a sufficient reason for contingent truths or truths of fact—that is to say, for the sequence or connexion of the things, which are dispersed throughout the universe of created beings, in which the analysing into particular reasons might go on into endless detail, because of the immense variety of things in Nature and the infinite division of bodies. . . . As this necessary substance is a sufficient reason of all this variety of particulars, which are also connected together throughout, therefore, there is only one God, and this God is sufficient." Paley, Paul Janet, and other thinkers have also advocated this theory of Design or Adaptation, which is based, (1) on the apparent design in biological organisms, (2) on the invariable laws of Nature, and (3) on the operations of animal instinct. The theists assert that Design implies a Designer; laws point to a law-giver; and the bees could not make hives of a perfect geometrical pattern without the help and guidance of "God."

This argument is very weak and unconvincing. Let us ask all the sciences. Each science cries that Nature is not made by a wise and benevolent God. *Geology* teaches us that the earth has been adapted for Life during a certain period of time: during many millions of years it was hot and fluid. Why is there no Life on the Moon or on Mercury? Even on this tiny earth there are vast deserts where not even a rat can live, and Man would wish that the salt ocean were smaller in extent. If the Earth is a home presented to us by "God," the architect cannot be given much credit for wisdom. Even the vilest jerry-builder does not build houses that shake and topple over at intervals, like the ground on which the Japanese and the San Franciscans live. *Seismology* makes the unthinking theist blush with shame (or ought to). Earthquakes are purely "divine" phenomena: no human agency is concerned in the production of these shocks and tremors. How many thousands of men, women, and children have been slain in earthquakes and their attendant disasters! In Japan, 99,331 persons died in 6923, and 576,000 buildings were destroyed. The desert of Gobi was once fertile land, as the ruins and remains of ancient cities show. *Meteorology* also seems to prove that rain and the weather are not controlled by an intelligent and benevolent Being. What is the wisdom of dropping rain into the oceans, from which it came? There is no regularity in rainfall, as there is in the supply of water through man-made irrigation-works. Sometimes the people are ruined by floods and inundations; at other times, drought kills the cattle and destroys the crops. A clergyman prayed for rain. It soon began to rain heavily, and the downpour continued. The country was inundated. Then he said in his prayers: "O Lord! we did pray for rain and thou hast heard us, we know. But *this* is really ridiculous." Lightning strikes innocent men, women, and children, and burns them up. It also reduces many homes to ashes. Hail blasts the gardener's hopes, and hurricanes lay the poor farmer's cottage low. In 6933 A.H., a storm destroyed two million banana trees in Jamaica. What cruel sport! What a pestiferous "breath of God"! The typhoons, simooms, siroccos, dust-storms, and other similar phenomena do not make our short life very pleasant on this earth. Some places like Cherapoonji are too wet: other regions like Arabia are too dry. Extremes of heat and cold plague us: very few countries have the equable and mild climate of Honolulu and Madeira. The climate changes in course of time: what "divine" department is in charge of this business? *Biology* also shows no trace of wisdom or benevolence. In the plant-world, a constant struggle for light and food is going on. Hungry plants, growing in poor soil, become cruel insect-eaters, and kill their victims by artifice. Millions of buds never blossom into flowers: a frost nips them, or a wind makes them homeless, and they die. What a wanton waste! What a floral tragedy! Billions of seeds are produced, and only a few can sprout and grow into trees. Others are lost. Many plants and trees perish in storm and drought. Parasites like the mistletoe and the rafflesia rob other plants, and the murderous embrace of the ivy strangles the oak. The big trees of the forest prevent the small ones from getting their share of sunlight. A tropical jungle is a scene of incessant cut-throat competition among the plants and the animals. Thus does *Botany* deny "God"! *Zoology*, which used to be the stronghold of the teleologists, has now been surrendered to the atheists. The devices of adaptation to environment in animal organisms, the sense-organs, the protective colours, and the defensive habits have been explained by Darwin and other scientists as the products of natural causation. The animals that could not adapt themselves to the environment perished in untold numbers. What a holocaust of sentient beings! What an orgy of slaughter! Vile vivisection is only a pin-prick to it. The environment killed billions and billions: other billions of animals have slain one another. The carnivorous and venomous animals are sorry specimens of "perfect wisdom and love": the dinosaurus and other reptiles, the lions, tigers, wolves, jaguars, giant cobras, hawks, eagles, condors, whales, and sharks. How many lovely antelopes have been devoured in the jungles during millions of years! The honest small fishes earn their living, but all the other fishes live on the small ones. Besides these open bandits and highwaymen of zoology, there are the small sneaking parasites and poisoners, the microbes of disease and suppuration, the pneumococcus, the gonococcus, the Koch bacillus, the actinomyces, the cholera spirillum, the spirochæte pallida, and other creatures, minute in size but mighty for mischief. There is one terribly tragic phenomenon which should shame the theist into sense. In Biology, the lower animals can and do kill the higher. Cholera germs, despicable vermin, poisoned Hegel and turned his mighty brain to dust and ashes. Keats was also the victim of the bacilli. Several thousand persons die of snake-bite each year. Many are mauled by tigers and leopards. Here is neither wisdom nor love, and not even common sense. What is the use of creating a man, if he can be destroyed by the tsetse-fly? I call it a mean, malicious, idiotic procedure altogether. Zoology reveals a world of ruthless egotism, bloodshed, rapine, violence, and slaughter, before which even Jenghiz Khan would stand aghast. By a refinement of despotic cruelty, some animals like leeches must suck the blood of other animals in order to live; they cannot do otherwise. An enormous number of eggs and offspring is produced by every species, so that a few may survive. Some are killed by Nature, and others are destroyed by the competing organisms of the same species or of other species. If the environment were favourable, they would multiply like the rabbits in Australia and the horses in Patagonia. This law of necessary, inevitable, wholesale destruction of Life is fundamental in Zoology. This is the blood-stained road, resounding with the piteous cries of suffering, starving, agonizing creatures, that Life has travelled The Appian Way, lined with the crucified slaves, was an avenue of delight in comparison with Life's upward path.

Thus speaks Zoology, and then comes Man on the scene. He has no reason to thank an imaginary Deity for the pains and pleasures of Life. His life is short and uncertain. Transiency hangs like a pall on human life. As the Chinese poet Li Po says:

> " Life slips away,
> A dream of little joy and mean content "

Po-Chüi laments thus.

> " I cry aloud—
> Alas! how grey and scentless is the bloom
> Of mortal life "

How many babies are still-born or die in infancy! There is not much sense in creating lovely children, if they are to be destroyed in a few days or weeks or years. Disease takes a terrible toll of human life. How many millions have suffered and are suffering to-day from

> " all maladies
> Of ghastly spasm, or racking torture, qualms
> Of heart-sick agony, all feverous kinds,
> Convulsions, epilepsies, fierce catarrhs,
> Intestine stone and ulcer, colic pangs,
> Demoniac frenzy, moping melancholy,
> And moon-struck madness, pining atrophy,
> Marasmus, and wide-wasting pestilence,
> Dropsies and asthmas, and joint-racking rheums? "

The moans and groans of all the sick patients at this moment would, if collected and concentrated at an acoustic focus, swell into a roar of agony more thunderous than that of Niagara. Famine stalks as a spectre across the pages of history: the "Father" does not seem to care for his hungry "children." Above all, vice and anti-social instincts have been implanted deep in man's soul, and we do our best now to eradicate them. If "God" loves Virtue, why has he not made Man wholly virtuous? Why has he burdened us with hatred, envy, gluttony, lust, sloth, pride, anger, avarice, cruelty, and other sins too heavy to be borne? Why has Man to wade his way through blood to social peace? Why must he often eat his bread in tears? Why is history partly a record of folly, slavery, murder, and strife? The author of such a grim tragedy of real life cannot be wise or benevolent. The Zoroastrians and the Manichæans were at least logical, as they attributed Evil to Satan, and only Good to the Divine Being. The Devil is also mentioned in Christian and Islamic scriptures, but his claim to recognition has been neglected. There is no answer that the theist can give to the sagacious schoolboy's question: "Why did God not kill the Devil?" Some thinkers like Plato and J. S. Mill have assumed the existence of a "God" of limited powers. Mill wrote: "This Being, not being omnipotent, may have produced a machinery falling short of his intentions." This idea will soon lead us back to Zoroastrian dualism. It is not necessary to personify the forces and principles of Good and Evil in the universe. We need neither "God" nor "Devil." All the so-called theistic "solutions" of the problem of Evil are unsatisfactory and mischievous. It is asserted that "partial evil is universal good." Our sin and suffering promote a higher end known only to "God." Virtue is impossible without vice, as an object must have a shadow. Pain is a punishment for our past sins and a warning for the future. It is also inflicted to try our patience and piety, and reward us later on, as in the case of Job. Evil brings out some good qualities of character, like courage, fortitude, and sympathy. Dante declared that Hell was created by perfect love! (What do you think of such sadistic love?) Evil is even said to be non-existent and illusory. Robert Bridges says: "Yet to the enamoured soul, Evil is irrelevant." There is no end to such specious sophistry. If "God" could achieve his purposes without all this suffering, and yet prefers these cruel methods, then he is a monster of iniquity. If he cannot devise any other plan, then he is not omnipotent. Why should we have to "explain" or "explain away" Evil? Why is it there at all? Even if it shall be eliminated after a long period, how can the theist justify all the pain and suffering that must be endured in the meantime? Leibniz pays "God" a very poor compliment when he teaches that this world is the best of all possible worlds that "God" could create. Theism does not convince or console at all: it only adds insult to injury. It also delays and hinders the suppression of Evil in the world by trying to paint it as a blessing in disguise. If there is no real Evil, what are we to fight against? If disease is a visitation of Heaven, why should we not let it run its course? If "God" calls the dead babies to himself, why should we try to diminish infant mortality? It would be sheer folly, presumption, and impiety. Thus Theism has paralysed Man's feet and disarmed his hands in his ceaseless struggle against Evil. In the Middle Ages, the saints saw "the finger of God" in every plague that raged, and exhorted men to repentance and prayer; but they did not study hygiene and preventive medicine. Theism refers everything to the "will of God," and thus dissuades men and women from exerting themselves strenuously to stamp out Evil. Only Rationalism can conquer Evil. A deist has said, "If God did not exist, it would be necessary to invent Him." But I believe that, even if "God" exists, it would be best for mankind to deny his existence and ignore him.

(vi) Some thinkers teach that "God" must exist, as Virtue must be certain of the reward of happiness in another life, celestial or terrestrial. Kant and Udayana have expressed this view. Kant says: "The same moral law must lead us to affirm the possibility of the second element of the summum bonum, namely, Happiness, proportioned to that morality, and this on grounds as disinterested as before, and solely from impartial reasons; in other words, it must postulate the existence of God. It is morally necessary to assume the existence of God." Udayana connects Theism with the Indian doctrine of rebirth and retribution. Professor S. Radhakrishnan explains thus: "A non-intelligent cause, like *Adrsta* (the unseen result of the individual's actions) cannot produce its effect without the guidance of an intelligent spirit. God is said to supervise the work of *adrsta*."

A wise rationalist should reject the whole doctrine of rewards and punishments, as I have already shown. So we can take leave of these superficial logicians.

(vii) "God" is supposed to supply a model of moral character for us. Jesus Christ said, "Be ye perfect, even as your Father in heaven is perfect." Even J. S. Mill thought that a "God" of some sort might be regarded as a "morally perfect Being." He wrote: "This idealization of our standard of excellence in a Person is quite possible, even when that Person is conceived as merely imaginary." Now it is not conceivable how "God" can teach us Virtue. He is not exposed to the temptations of gluttony, sloth, theft, adultery, murder, envy, pride, and other deadly sins, as he lives alone and has no physical body or property. He lacks nothing. How can a Person in such utterly non-human circumstances set an example to us? Jesus Christ, Rabia, Buddha, Louise Michel, and other virtuous teachers can inspire us by their example, as they were men and women like ourselves. But a purely "spiritual" Being cannot embody the moral Ideal for us. It is said that God "loves" us, and this "love" should be our principle of action. But "love" implies service, sacrifice, sharing, company, and devotion. If you "love" your neighbour, you are willing to sacrifice something for him, your work or money or time. That is the test of love. But God is infinitely powerful and possesses the Universe. It is no sacrifice for him to give us life or rain or flowers. He practises no self-denial in bestowing these boons upon mankind. How can "God" then show us what human love can and should be? Man can love Man. This is our gospel.

(viii) The metaphysical arguments of some thinkers are more curious than convincing. Berkeley argues that there must be a "God," as all things are only ideas in an eternal Mind. Geulincx and Malebranche think that "God" alone can cause and regulate the interaction of Mind and Matter. Cousin believes in the existence of "God" as the personification of the principle of Beauty, and bases Theism on Æsthetics.

You should dismiss such far-fetched theories with gentle ridicule.

(ix) Theism is not the basis of Ethics, and it has not been universally accepted, as some theists imagine. The Jainas, the Hindus, the Buddhists, and most of the Greek philosophers reject the doctrine of a creator of the universe. The Jainas and the Buddhists have developed a noble system of Ethics without assuming the existence of a creator. The Confucians were at first indifferent to supernaturalism, and later became hostile to it. Aristotle expounds Ethics in his famous treatise without speaking of any divine commands. In fact, Ethics has been founded on Theism only in the Moses–Jesus–Muhammad–Bab line of religious thought. India, China, and Greece have not accepted Theism in any sense whatsoever.

(x) Finally, there cannot be a living Person without a physical body, some sense-organs, and a brain. It is absurd to suppose that any Person can think without a brain and a nervous system. If "God" can plan and think and love, where are his brain and nervous system? We cannot conceive of a living Being who is not similar to ourselves in this respect. The uneducated "anthropomorphic" theists really conceive of "God" as an old majestic sultan, as painted in Michael Angelo's "Creation of Adam." Of course they are wrong, but their belief is more intelligible than this impossible and meaningless doctrine of a thinking Being, who has no brain and no stomach, who does not eat but can cogitate perpetually, a "spiritual" giant-skeleton whose bones are made of vacuum or ether. All the specious arguments of the theists are knocked to pieces against this one undeniable and inescapable fact—that I find it impossible to conceive of a Being, who is spread out sprawling from the farthest nebulæ up to this earth, who hears my conversation without ears, who sees everything without eyes, who works without food and drink, who fabricates things without hands and tools, and thinks and feels without a head and a brain in that head. I cannot conceive of such a living Person, and there is an end of the whole matter for me personally. However much I may try, I cannot visualize him. I cannot help it. I ask: "Where is he?" "How does he work?" "How can he perform some human actions and experience human psychic states without a human body?" I cannot believe what I cannot conceive. It sounds like a fairy-tale, a story of spectres and ghosts and *jinns* and *pretas*. In fact, this old notion of "disembodied spirits," who nevertheless act in every way like us "embodied" people, is simply magnified and universalized by the theists. Their "God" is a ghost, infinitely attenuated and expanded, coterminous with the entire Universe. Children believe in ghosts, and adults with children's mentality believe in "God." "God" is a meaningless and mischievous monosyllable, and nothing more.

All the theoretical arguments for Theism are very bad indeed, but its practical and social consequences are infinitely worse. Superstition is never harmless, and this dogma is a veritable Pandora's box of calamities and sufferings for mankind. Theism hinders Progress and inflicts misery on the world, for the following reasons:—

(1) Theism discourages and thwarts the progress of Science. We believe that Science is the friend and benefactor of Mankind. But the pious theist looks askance at Science. He is not inclined to observe Nature and make experiments. This attitude may seem

to be curious and illogical, as the theists assert that Nature proclaims the glory of "God." But the fact is that the minute and detailed study of natural phenomena always undermines the belief in a Creator and a benevolent Providence. Science emphasizes the idea of impersonal, invariable Law in Nature, while Theism postulates a living Person's Thought and Will behind or above or in Nature. The uninstructed man just looks up at the sky and begins to worship the stars and the sun, or their "Maker," in awe and humility. But the astronomer, who observes the heavenly bodies and their movements day after day and night after night, ceases to regard them as gods or to think of a wonderful Creator. For him, they are only enormous fire-balls. A hasty, superficial glance at Nature may suggest the idea of "God"; but close and continual study leads the mind slowly but inevitably to Rationalism. When Laplace was asked why he had not even mentioned "God" in his treatise on Astronomy, he replied, "I had no need of that hypothesis." The theists honestly believe that faith in "God" is absolutely necessary for social morality and order. They think that an atheist cannot be a virtuous man or woman. Hence they must support Ethics according to their ideas. If Science produces atheists, and Atheism undermines morality, then they conclude that Science is dangerous and undesirable. They naturally prefer Virtue (as they conceive it) without Science to Science without Virtue. This lamentable error resulted in the suppression of scientific studies in medieval Europe and the Islamic countries. It was found that the students who read Aristotle's works generally accepted his teaching that the universe was eternal and uncreated. Aristotle was therefore condemned by both the Catholic Church and the Moslem orthodox theologians, who believed in the dogma of creation by "God" as taught in the Bible and the Koran. Scientific studies also lead to disbelief in the miracles, on which many theistic churches lay much stress. Professor Maurice de Wulf says: "Constantly and bitterly did he (Roger Bacon) reproach his scholastic contemporaries with their negligent attitude towards scientific observation and research. The scholastics held aloof from the progress of the sciences." Dr. T. J. de Boer writes: "Aristotle, with his doctrine of the Eternity of the World, was regarded as dangerous. Moslem theologians of the 9th and 10th centuries wrote therefore against Aristotle. . . . The library of a certain philosopher was burned in Bagdad. The preacher threw into the flames an astronomical work of Ibn-al-Haitham."

It is clear that there is an everlasting and irreconcilable conflict between Science and Theism: they can never be harmonized. The theists will always believe that morality is impossible without belief in "God," and they will neglect and oppose Science as an anti-social force. Hence Science must throw down the gauntlet to Theism and be prepared for a fight to the death. Mankind must choose between Science and its triumphs and gifts on the one hand, and "God" and his imaginary favours and blessings on the other. Science gives us Power, Plenty, and Peace: Theism rejoices in Prayers, Poverty, and Pestilence. Make your choice.

(2) Theism leads to stagnation and decay in society, as it regards the laws and ideals of a certain religious system as divinely ordained for all nations and epochs. Authority in its most pernicious form is thus established as the arbiter of social destiny, and free criticism and discussion are prohibited for ever.

(3) Theism robs mankind of all the advantages and benefits that Science confers upon us. It also blocks the forward-moving traffic on the highway of History. What an immeasurable loss! What a suicidal policy it has been to pray to "God" and despise Science! Mankind has paid dearly for this folly. But worse is behind. Theism not only deprives us of knowledge, sanitation, wealth, and inventions, but also foments strife, hatred, and discord among men. It is a tremendous anti-social force. The theists chant: "God is love." That is their theory. In practice, Theism has led and must lead to bloodshed and cruelty by its own inherent logic.

The theistic churches are very intolerant and fanatical. They teach the doctrine of "exclusive salvation." Their dupes believe that the votaries of all other religions will be "damned." They also approve of two codes of morals: the one to be practised among themselves, the other to be applied in dealings with the "infidels," whom a "believer" may sometimes cheat or murder without incurring guilt. The whole human race is divided into only two classes: the believers and the unbelievers. The former will crowd into paradise after death; the latter will suffer torments in hell. If you are born in such a Church, you should reject and repudiate this anti-social dogma, which breeds hatred and uncharitableness among neighbours and fellow-citizens. Study the biography of Gautama Buddha, and note how he treated the members and leaders of other sects. Read the edicts of Asoka, and imbibe the spirit of religious toleration. The literature and history of Buddhism and Hinduism provide the best antidote to the ingrained and ineradicable intolerance of Islam and Christianity.

Theism has fomented many wars and persecutions. The seamless garment of Humanity has been rent and torn by the different Churches into which superstition has divided mankind. The belief in many gods and goddesses has often made men hard and cruel towards one another. The worshippers of one god or goddess have regarded the devotees of another divinity as rivals and enemies. The tribal gods have served as the battle-flags of the different tribes, *e.g.* Yahweh, Baal, Indra, Thor, etc. But ancient polytheism, exclusive as it was at the outset, did not beget so much discord and persecution as medieval and modern monotheism. Monotheism, like Attila, is a veritable scourge of Man. It is a upas-tree, blighting peace and friendship wherever its baleful shadow is cast. When the old local gods are combined and consolidated into one omnipotent universal Deity, then the exclusiveness, aggressiveness, and intolerance of the old cults are multiplied a thousandfold and a millionfold The *one and only* God of the Jews, the Moslems, and the Christians then emerges from the muddled and bewildered minds of uneducated prophets and theologians. This " God " is a really monstrous creation, a hideous hybrid generated by political despotism and ignorance of Nature. He is the magnified image of the capricious tyrants of Egypt, Assyria, Babylonia, and Persia. This " God " is supposed to be above all law and ethics: he is an arbitrary, ferocious, pitiless, arrogant creator and destroyer. He is the very apotheosis of unbridled personal Power. He is indeed said to be merciful and compassionate: but his mercy and compassion, as exhibited in earthquakes, tempests, and plagues, seem to be much more dreadful than the cruelty of the ravenous beasts of the jungle. This idea of a despotic Monarch in the sky has bred fierce and unrelenting intolerance among the various monotheistic Churches and sects. The earth has been time and again drenched in blood by his deluded worshippers. All " theists " hate and despise the polytheists, who happen to believe in the numerous ancient gods, and not in this new universal " God." The monotheists of Islam have taken pride in butchering and plundering the polytheists and " kafirs " of Persia, India, and China in the name of Allah. The stern monotheists must also smite and slay the pantheists and atheists, who believe in no divinity at all. It is written in the Koran: " O true believers, wage war against such of the infidels as are near you; and let them find severity in you. If there be a thousand of you, they shall overcome two thousand by the permission of God, for God is with those who persevere." The wretched victims of the murderous superstition of monotheism are inflamed with savage hatred against all who do not bow down to their imaginary invisible fetish. But worse is to follow. Having fought the polytheists, the pantheists, and the atheists, the pious monotheists turn against one another in their zeal for the "glory of God." The Moslems think that the Christians do not worship "God" in the right way, and the Christians believe that the "God" of the Moslems is unworthy of adoration. Hence perpetual sanguinary strife between these two Churches. The doctrine of "one God and none other" necessarily breeds intolerance, as there must then be only one book of revelation and one accredited prophet, who lives in constant communication with the unseen "God" If other wise men also claim to be "prophets," they must be sheer impostors, as "God" can send only one "messenger" at a time. As the whole system is based on direct "divine" revelation, and not on human reason and conscience, everyone must accept the exclusive "revelation" as the only authorized teaching, and obey the oracular "prophet" blindly in all matters and on all occasions. Thus at the present time there are several competing prophets offering their rival "revelations": Moses, Jesus, Muhammad, Baha-ullah, Mary Baker Eddy, Joseph Smith, Freytag, and others of less note. Each of these leaders is supposed to be the only genuine "prophet," to whom "God" has directly revealed the entire truth and nothing but the truth. The priests who represent these different churches must make war on one another with the pen and the sword in order to establish the supremacy of their unique, all-devouring divinity and their all-sufficient, infallible "holy book." The blood-stained story of the Crusades, in which even so virtuous a man as Saint Louis appears as a homicidal warrior, is an awful warning to us all, as it demonstrated beyond a peradventure the inevitable consequences of the blood-thirsty creed of monotheism. The philosophers of Athens and India taught different doctrines, but they could work together in peace and friendship for common ends. A Moslem mullah and a Christian evangelist, however, must at least bark at each other, when they cannot bite. The Christian Church must attack the Moslem Church by the fatal necessity of the logic of Theism.

Two rival prophets cannot live together in the world, as two kings cannot reign in a kingdom. But there is a lower deep beneath the lowest deep. The followers of the same prophet begin to quarrel among themselves, as they cannot interpret his "revelation" in the same way. This idea of an absolute "revelation" again leads to war among the different sects of the same Church.

Theism must insist on uniformity, and also try to establish it by force, if necessary, as the laws enacted by a Government are enforced by the police and the army. The annals of Islam and Christianity are partly written with blood spilled in internecine strife. The "orthodox" Catholics persecuted the pagans, the Donatists, the Arians, the Waldenses, the Paulicians, the Cathari, the Fransciscan Spiritual friars, the Hussites, the Lollards, the Beghards, the Petrobrusians, the Henricians, the Arnoldists, the Lutherans, the Calvinists, and other Christian sects. In the sixty-third century A.H., the Catholics massacred all the inhabitants of the town of Béziers, and burned four hundred "heretics" together on one day at Laval. Llorente, the historian of the Inquisition, estimates that more than 363,000 persons were condemned to death or other penalties in Spain from 6478 A.H. to 6808 A.H.

Such were the Catholics! But the Protestants also persecuted the Puritans and the Scottish Covenanters; the Calvinists in their turn tried to suppress the Quakers and the Unitarians as a religious duty. The Greek Orthodox Church harassed and maltreated the Nestorians, the Stundists, the Molakani, the Doukhobors, and the other sects. A Moslem dissenting preacher was half buried alive in the ground and stoned to death only a few years ago in Afghanistan. Lucretius has branded such superstition with infamy for all time:

> "Tantum religio potuit suadere malorum."
> (To so much evil could religion prompt.)

Cruel intolerance is, indeed, the very life-breath of Theism. It steels the hearts of the pious worshippers against friendship and family affection. If a man does not believe in "God," and also in a particular revelation of "God," he is shunned and hated even by his parents and brothers. Philip II of Spain said: "I would send my own son to the stake, if he were a heretic." Matthieu Orry, a Catholic priest, denounced his own nephew, who was burned as a heretic. Many ardent theists have been only too ready to kill the "infidels" and the theists of other sects and Churches. Some Babis murdered in cold blood other Babis, who belonged to a rival group within the same movement! Theism incites to murder, and even glorifies it. This tragedy of the human spirit is a well-attested fact of psychology. Theism teaches men to love "God" so much that they begin to hate, abhor, and outlaw those who honestly and sincerely cannot accept that incredible doctrine. So long as this abominable superstition prevails, the unity of Mankind cannot be realized. Theism is the negation of both Reason and Ethics. Down with this Moloch!

CHAPTER II

PHYSICAL CULTURE

CHAPTER II

PHYSICAL CULTURE

It is one of your first duties to take care of your body. Keep it in good health and develop strength and endurance. Try also to make it as beautiful as you can. Place a small statue of Apollo Belvedere or Venus de Milo in your room for inspiration. Everyone is handicapped by inherited defects and latent tendencies to disease and weakness; but you should do your best. As the poet Kalidasa says, "The body is indeed the principal instrument of Duty." If you are not born with the gift of beauty, you can at least endow your body with the charm and grace that come of sound health and a noble and happy mind. Beauty is not skin-deep; it is deep as the soul.

Life without good health is a sore burden. You need strength and physical stamina for your strenuous work in life. You must feel what the French call "the joy of living" in every nerve and fibre of your being. Then dark thoughts and gloomy forebodings will not assail your mind. Optimism is as natural to a healthy person as breathing and sleeping. Dyspepsia has produced more pessimism than all the arguments of Schopenhauer and Hartmann. Only the sick and the ailing ask the foolish question "Is Life worth living?"

If you do not keep the body in normal health, you will lose time in illness. Time is often money; and Time is Life always and everywhere. Life is very short, even if you live a hundred years. You cannot afford to lose the smallest portion of it in illness. From the social point of view, illness interferes with production and causes enormous loss of wealth in every country. A sick person also puts his relatives and friends to needless trouble. He may even spread disease around him, if he suffers from a contagious or infectious malady. It is really a crime against society to neglect your body and diminish its capacity of resisting the onslaught of chronic disease or acute sickness. How many people unwittingly make a gift of coryza and influenza to their friends! If you fall ill through no fault of your own, you deserve the sympathy of all citizens; but if your misfortune is due to your own carelessness or intemperance, you must face unfriendly criticism. You then wrong yourself and others. All avoidable sickness is a sin.

You need not try to be an athlete or develop abnormally powerful muscles. You can leave that kind of Physical Culture to the professional runners, wrestlers, and boxers. You should aim at attaining average health, strength, efficiency, and longevity. You should have the legitimate ambition of enjoying freedom from disease and living to the age of a hundred years, if not longer. The Psalmist thought that the average length of human life was seventy years; but now we must aim higher. Always think of the famous men who were active and hale and hearty even in old age, *e.g.*, Plato, Buddha, Sophocles, Voltaire, Goethe, Frederic Harrison, Robert Bridges, Annie Besant, Bernard Shaw, Dr. J. Oldfield, John Dewey, and others.

A few men and women in all countries live to be centenarians: why should you not do the same?

You should read a few text-books of Anatomy and Physiology in order to know your own inside. How many people are content to remain completely ignorant of the structure of their own bodies! But if they purchased a motor-car, they would surely try to learn everything about its mechanism! I suppose the reason is that they have paid money for the car, while their body is a free gift from Nature. Lay the foundation of Physical Culture on an adequate knowledge of Anatomy and Physiology.

You should also read a few books written by some experts, but use your common sense in applying their theories to your own life. All specialists tend to become one-sided, and you should test their precepts by your own experience. You may read the various treatises on fasting, vegetarianism, Aird diet, Salisbury diet, milk diet, "Fletcherism," mono-diet, Mazdaznan rules, Kneipp's water-cure, Ebbard's method, Ehret's mucusless diet, Dewey's no-breakfast plan, colon-cleanliness, sun-bathing, pandiculation, unfired food, Lust's Marathon bath, radium-emanation cure, the Schroth cure, etc. But you should think twice and thrice before launching on the interesting experiments recommended by these teachers. Remember that Hygiene is made for man, not man for Hygiene. Health is only a means to a higher end. Do not be obsessed by Hygiene all the time. Don't imitate those well-meaning but intolerable bores who are always talking of calories, vitamins, and toxins. Such a mania for health is also a disease. Give the body its due, but not more.

I shall not trouble you with minute and detailed rules that you may find it impossible to follow in practice. You do not perhaps live in ideal surroundings; you have to practise Physical Culture as your means and opportunities permit. I may direct your attention to a few general principles.

I. Pure Air. Your lungs need pure fresh air. The vitiated air of modern towns is rank poison. Try to live in the country, or in the suburbs of a town, if you can do so. Sleep with the bedroom window open even during the winter. Cold air will not hurt you, if you are warm in bed. Sleep in a porch or a balcony in summer, if you have access to it. Your skin also needs air quite as much as your lungs. You breathe through the skin too. Expose the skin to the air a few minutes daily, and also for a longer time during the summer holidays. Don't wear too much thick clothing, which keeps out the air. Choose porous underwear of meshy cloth.

Learn how to breathe properly. Practise deep breathing for a few minutes daily. Oxygen will keep you young. Professor O'Shea and Dr. Kellogg say: "The actual daily ration of air, that is, the amount of fresh air each person requires, is about forty to fifty thousand cubic feet." Eustace Miles writes: "I must emphasize the importance of practising the deep and full breath at frequent intervals throughout the day. The ordinary breath of the ordinary civilized person is neither deep nor full."

II. Water. "Water is best," said Pindar long ago. It is indeed a great tonic both for the outside and the inside of the body. Wash the entire body daily with cold water, and also take a hot bath once or twice a week. Drink plenty of pure water, preferably warm, in the morning and between meals, but not during meals. If it is impure or too hard, use distilled water. Distilled water is a potent medicine. The time will come when it will be more commonly used than it is at present. Bathe your eyes in cold water occasionally. Clean out the colon with cold or slightly warm water at frequent intervals; this hygienic measure will prolong your life. Colon-flushing must not be neglected.

III. Sunshine. You should be in close touch with Dr. Sun, who cures without a fee. Expose the skin to the rays of the sun regularly for a few minutes in the morning. In the absence of sunshine, use a sun-lamp (carbon or mercury), which should be an article of household furniture in the northern latitudes. Dr. C. H. Tyrrell says: "Sunlight is one of Nature's greatest therapeutic agents and she bestows it ungrudgingly, without money and without price. . . . A valuable lesson on this point may be learned by observing the lower animals, none of which ever neglect an opportunity to bask in the sun. . . . There is a curative power in the chemical rays of the sun. . . . By the sun's healing and rejuvenating rays, a woman will gain colour warranted not to wash off."

The exposure of the body to electric light is also beneficial, especially when you induce perspiration. Such a "sweat-bath" eliminates the toxic matter and promotes better circulation. It has been called "the family doctor." If you cannot buy the electric apparatus, you may sweat in over-heated air, as in a Turkish hammam.

IV. Food. Your health will depend in a very large measure on what you eat and drink. Gastronomic wisdom is eighty per cent. of Hygiene. There are three questions: How to eat and drink? How much? What? How? Slowly and cheerfully. Masticate your food well. The stomach cannot do the work of the teeth. Solid food and even milk must be thoroughly insalivated before they are swallowed. You need not follow Horace Fletcher's example, but chew as much as you can. For this purpose, you must avoid mushy starchy foods that cannot be masticated. Take smaller morsels than most people do at present. Sir Andrew Clark says: "Thirty-two teeth in one mouth, thirty-two bites to every mouthful, and for any tooth that is gone, the number of bites to be proportionately increased" Eat only when you are hungry; don't eat by the clock. Cheerfulness should also be a guest at meals. Herbert Spencer found that a meal could be digested more easily if it was eaten in pleasant company. Dr. W. B. Cannon, speaking of experiments on cats, writes: "The stomach movements are inhibited, whenever the cat shows signs of anxiety, rage, or distress." Dr. L. H. Gulick says: "Worry, hurry, unsettled mind, low spirits, all tend to delay or stop the activities of the alimentary canal." Simplicity in diet is also essential for health. Too much variety upsets the digestion. Don't eat many courses at a meal, and don't cook very rich and complicated dishes. Dr. A. Haig says: "Simple food of not more than two or three kinds at one meal is another secret of health."

How much should you eat? With great moderation. Saadi, the Persian poet, wrote: "Eat not so much that the food comes out of thy mouth again: and eat not so little that the soul comes out of thy body." If we except the very poor class, most people eat and drink too much, especially after the age of thirty. In some countries, a heavy breakfast, a hot lunch, a high tea, and a substantial dinner are consumed during the day. To these repasts, some add eleven o'clock coffee, six o'clock cock-tails, and a late theatre supper. So much food is the shortest cut to an early grave. Remember the true story of Luigi Cornaro of Venice, who regained lost health by a drastic reduction in the quantity of food and drink; he died in 6565 at the age of 104 (or 98, according to some authorities). He wrote: "Finding myself, therefore, in such unhappy circumstances, between my thirty-fifth and fortieth year, I resolved to live sparingly. . . . Galen, who was so great a physician, led such a life and chose it as the best physic. The same did Plato, Cicero, Isocrates, and many other great men of former times; and, in our own days, Pope Paul Farnese led it, and Cardinal Bembo, and it was for that reason they lived so long; likewise our two doges, Lando and Donato. . . . I now find myself sound and hearty at the age of eighty-six. . . . What with bread, meat, the yolk of an egg and soup, I ate as much as weighed in all twelve ounces, neither more nor less; I drank but fourteen ounces of wine. . . . A temperate and regular life, in less than a year, rid me of all those disorders which had taken so deep a root in me."

The safe rule is that one should avoid a feeling of repletion at meals. You should be able to eat half as much again, when you leave off. As L. Cornaro said, "What we leave after making a hearty meal does us more good than what we have eaten." This principle will help you more than the weighing-machines and the tables of proteins and calories.

What should you eat and drink? This is a very important question indeed. Many diseases are caused by the lack of some foodstuffs that are necessary for proper nutrition; others are due to the consumption of unwholesome and injurious food and beverages. We commit sins of omission and commission in diet. Hence misery, suffering, and premature death! Dr. R. C. Macfie says: "Food is the basis of man's body. Every bone, every muscle, is made of food. . . . No question, therefore, can be more important than the question of food."

The various articles of diet may be divided into four classes:

(1) Some things must be regarded as absolutely deleterious and dangerous to the body and the mind, and these must be altogether shunned like poison. In fact, they *are* poisons. You should abstain from them at all times. No civilized country should manufacture them, except perhaps for medical purposes, if necessary. Such destructive concoctions are opium, cocaine, heroin, hashish, and other drugs, distilled liquors (brandy, whisky, rum), absinthe, etc. All persons, who are the victims of such drugs, lose physical strength and mental vigour, and wreck their lives on the hidden

rock of drug-addiction. Let us all shout with a mighty voice of compassion and indignation: "Down with all drugs!"

(2) There are some injurious things that should not be consumed by the wise and the temperate. It is best to abstain from them. They are unwholesome and pernicious, and also cost money. But they are not so dangerous as the drugs mentioned above. If you have contracted the habit of using them daily, you should try to free yourself from this slavery. Then you may enjoy them in extreme moderation on special occasions like a free agent, if you so desire. You must not remain a slave of such seductive enemy-friends of mankind. Only the free man, who can do without them in the daily régime, can really enjoy them at proper intervals. Such pleasure is not strictly hygienic; but, after all, it is not your highest duty to become a hygienic robot. If you wish to partake of such unwholesome but allowable things, you must do so in perfect freedom, and not as a slave of habit. Test and prove your freedom by abstaining from them altogether for short periods. Such bitter-sweet foods and drinks are the following: (i) Mild fermented alcoholic beverages, like light wines, cider, beer, and mead. (ii) Tea and maté. (iii) Coffee. (iv) Cocoa. (v) Betel-leaf. (vi) Tobacco. (vii) Meat and fish. (viii) Spices and condiments. (ix) Pastry and sweets.

It has been established beyond a shadow of doubt that alcohol, theine, tannin, caffeine, theobromine, nicotine, and purin are harmful even in small quantities. Cigarette-smoke contains nicotine, pyridine, picoline, collidine, acrolein, furfurol, etc. Tobacco-smoking is also an anti-social habit. It poisons the air in the homes and restaurants. It has the Marxian quality of dividing the world into two hostile classes, especially in travel, viz. the smokers and the non-smokers. Bernarr Macfadden says: "Tobacco, and more especially cigarettes, are a source of protoplasmic poison, actually causing degenerative disorders of the brain, heart, blood vessels, and kidneys. Smoking lessens mental activity, especially in students. It is a pernicious, life-shortening vice, contributing nothing but degeneration to the human race." T. A. Edison, the famous inventor, wrote: "Unlike most narcotics, this degeneration is permanent and uncontrollable. I employ no person who smokes cigarettes." Dr. T. B. Scott speaks of the "tiredness, the feebleness, and the absence of initiative that we see so often in the man saturated with tobacco," and adds: "Moderation in smoking is very rare, and difficult to maintain." Dr. J. H. Kellogg is of opinion that "nicotine is known to be one of the worst heart poisons." Tobacco also causes degeneration of the sex-glands, and women inflict irreparable injury on the race by poisoning themselves with nicotine. Dr. Lichty says: "Nicotine-saturated and poisoned tissue cannot beget a standard healthy progeny."

Alcohol is also a stimulant and should be avoided. Sir Lauder Brunton says: "All the alcohols tend to dilate the vessels, to lessen blood pressure, and ultimately to diminish activity of the nervous tissues, although at first they may seem to have a stimulant action." The daily habit of drinking wine or beer must weaken the body, even if we do not accept Upton Sinclair's dictum: "Alcohol is, I think, the greatest trap that Nature ever set for the feet of the human race." Light wine may be permitted for social cheer on festive occasions in Europe, but it is never indispensable. Tea and coffee affect the brain and nerve-centres, and also impair digestion. If you take them occasionally, they should be very weak. China tea is the least harmful, and a slice of lemon is always useful. Strong tea and coffee are to-day slowly undermining the health of millions of men and women of all classes. Some persons are abject slaves of the morning or afternoon tea and coffee: they cannot live and work without them. Such a vicious habit must be broken at once. Under no circumstances must the weak tea or coffee be taken more than once a day. Above all, you should always protest by example and precept against the use of strong tea and coffee, which are really responsible for so much illness and suffering around us. Strong tea and coffee, which are now drunk several times daily, are insidious enemies that are sapping the vitality of the human race. Too much coffee killed Schiller at the early age of forty-five. S. Kneipp says: "Coffee produces violent disturbances of the organism. The whole nervous system can be shattered. It causes melancholy, weakness, worry, etc. When women drink it, it may rightly be called a slayer-of-men. The same is nearly true of tea and chocolate."

Meat and fish also belong to the category of unwholesome foods, which must be taken in small quantities, if you do not abstain from them altogether. They produce acidosis and toxæmia, and overtax the stomach and the kidneys. Dr. R. L. Graham says: "Only those engaged in vigorous manual labour can with safety eat much meat. Others should, as a rule, eat very little of it, and should also touch beans and nuts very lightly." Pastry and sweets are delicious but dangerous. Spices and other condiments should be used very sparingly, if at all. Dr. L. H. Gulick says: "To put reliance upon a drug or a stimulant is evidently to put reliance upon a treacherous ally. A stimulant is very much like a whip. What it really does is to increase a man's energy-spending power. A drug does not create the energy in the man, any more than a whip creates the energy in a horse."

(3) Some articles of food are wholesome and necessary, but they should be consumed in very moderate quantities. Such are eggs (especially the yolk), wholemeal bread, maize, millet, natural rice, boiled wheat, oatmeal porridge, nuts of all kinds, cheese, butter, cream, peanut-oil, soya beans, olive oil, yeast, agar-agar, chestnut flour, peas, beans, pulses, honey, brown unrefined sugar, and maple sugar.

Two white things are really cheap calamities sold over the counter and must always be avoided—viz. white bread and white sugar. These devitalized false foods cause constipation, malnutrition, decay of teeth, kidney trouble, and premature senility. Analyses by W. O. Atwater show that wholemeal contains twice as much mineral matter as white flour. It has been proved by Broadbent and others that this mineral matter is exceedingly valuable both as a nutrient and on account of its neutralizing effect upon proteid wastes.

(4) Some things are so wholesome that they may be taken in large quantities, so long as you are not guilty of undue excess. Such beneficial foodstuffs are milk, buttermilk, yoghourt, kefir, whey, soured milk, all fruits (especially grapes, raisins, figs, prunes, and oranges), all green vegetables and root-vegetables (raw, baked, and steamed), alfalfa, and malt.

Fruits are Nature's own ready-made delicacies, prepared in the kitchen of the City of the Sun. They should be tree-ripened as far as possible. Dried sweet fruits need not be stewed: they should only be soaked in water. The fig was the favourite fruit of the Greek philosophers at Athens. Some raw leafy green salad must be eaten daily, *e.g.* lettuce, watercress, cabbage, endive, etc. This very important rule is observed in feeding the pigs on the farm, but it is often neglected in the home in rearing the children. For a plentiful supply of the alkaline salts, use vegetable soups and juices, alfalfa, and grape-juice.

A wag has hit upon a few good slogans: "Eat lots of greens and keep in your teens." (Here are indeed both rhyme and reason!) "Boiled vegetables are spoiled vegetables." "Eat 14-carrot soup and be worth your weight in gold." "More than one picture of beauty is done in vegetable oil."

Milk should be a staple food, though some experts condemn it. It is indeed indispensable, if you do not eat meat. Drink plenty of pure milk and fortify your system against disease. Dr. W. L. Mackenzie, M.A., M.D., says: "Whatever happens to meat, milk will maintain its place, for the children must be fed. For adults, too, it is practically as indispensable, and, as time proceeds, will become increasingly a necessity. In every country in the world, milk has risen in dietetic importance." Goat's milk agrees better than cow's milk with some people. If your stomach cannot tolerate fresh milk, try good dried milk. Yoghourt is particularly useful for preventing intestinal putrefaction. Professor E. Metchnikoff says: "Lactic acid lessens intestinal putrefaction. . . . Favourable results follow the use of lactic acid in many intestinal diseases."

A proper dietary should therefore include a little of each of the Sections Nos. 1—4, and a large quantity of Nos. 5—8.

(1) Nuts. Legumes. Cheese. Eggs. (Meat and Fish, if desired occasionally.)
(2) Cereals, both baked and boiled.
(3) Butter. Nut-butters. Oils.
(4) Brown sugar. Honey. Maple sugar. Treacle. Malt.
(5) Fresh and dried fruits.
(6) Green leafy vegetables (raw).
(7) Root-vegetables (carrots, turnips, beetroot, potato, etc.), both raw and baked (or steamed); also soups.
(8) Milk and Yoghourt.

Persons who are troubled with constipation may add a little yeast and agar-agar.

It is not advisable to eat too much proteid food from Section (1). Excess of proteid food overburdens the system and causes gout, rheumatism, and other diseases. Professor R. H. Chittenden conducted his famous experiment on thirteen men during six months, and wrote: "The experiment-results presented afford very convincing proof that, so far as body-weight and nitrogen equilibrium are concerned, the needs of the body are fully met by a consumption of proteid food far below the fixed dietary standards, and still further below the amounts called for by the recorded habits of mankind."

Be careful also to eat only moderate quantities of starchy cereals, fats, and sugar (Sections 2, 3, and 4 above). Too much starch and sugar produce flatulence and several chronic diseases. As Upton Sinclair says: "Excess of starch, so my experience has convinced me, is the deadliest of all dietetic errors. It is also the commonest of errors, the cause, not merely of the common throat and nose infections, but of constipation, and likewise of diarrhœa and anæmia."

It is a good plan to eat only fresh fruits and no other food one day in the week. The body thus gets a much-needed rest, and elimination is facilitated. The stomach must also have its Sabbath. Some Churches prescribe daily fasts during several weeks at a certain period of the year; but a fruit-fast once a week is more beneficial. If you suffer from some chronic disease like rheumatism, you may cure yourself by fasting for many days under medical supervision. But if you eat and drink moderately every day, and also observe a fruit-fast once a week, you will not accumulate toxins, and need not resort to long fasts at all. Remember also that a feast (if indulged in) must be followed by a fast in order to restore the balance. Dr. J. Oldfield says: "To abstain from food for a short time is never injurious, and is nearly always beneficial. A short fast is eliminative and curative, and restful to every cell in the body. A short fast may be undertaken at any age and by every one."

Above all, whatever you eat and drink, always consume a very moderate quantity and masticate thoroughly. Moderation and Mastication are the two universal and invariable rules of diet. Remember Milton's wise precept:—

> "If thou well observe
> The rule of 'Not too much,' by temperance taught,
> In what thou eat'st and drink'st, seeking from thence
> Due nourishment, not gluttonous delight,
> Till many years over thy head return·
> So may'st thou live, till, like ripe fruit, thou drop
> Into thy Mother's lap, or be with ease
> Gather'd, not harshly plucked, for death mature"

V. GYMNASTICS. Indoor gymnastics, with or without apparatus, is a daily duty. A few minutes suffice for the different movements that must be practised. Sanford Bennett of San Francisco has demonstrated that regular muscular exercise can help wonderfully in restoring health and prolonging life. At the age of 72, he was described in his doctor's clinical report as "having the appearance of an unusually well-preserved man of middle-age; his movements evidence an elastic body, and the entire muscular structure is remarkably well developed."

Always sit in an erect posture and walk with an erect carriage. Muller's system and wrestling may be tried with advantage. Stretching without straining is very useful; a "pandiculator" may be employed.

Dr. D. A. Sargent says: "Exercise is the chief agent in the renovation and repair of the tissues. Through its influence on respiration and circulation, new material or liquid food is hurried forward in the blood, and the waste substance resulting from the oxidation is borne away more rapidly by the same agency. Thus it may be easily shown that judicious exercise not only improves the condition of all muscles brought into action, but, through its stimulating effects upon the vital organs, the health and tone of every other part of the system are improved. . . . The best means of furnishing these necessary exercises are the ordinary calisthenics, free movements, and light gymnastics with dumb-bells, wands, and Indian Clubs." So you must exercise the muscles daily, otherwise you will deteriorate both in body and mind. Professor G. Stanley Hall has wisely said that "the flabby muscle is the chasm between willing and doing." Friction and massage are also very useful. Friction of the skin with a rough towel or gloves should follow the morning bath. The scalp should be massaged with the fingers and a brush for healthy hair-growth. The gums should be rubbed vigorously in order to prevent pyorrhoea. Massage of the stomach and intestines promotes digestion and peristalsis. It is perhaps a useful practice to rub oil into the skin, as the Greeks and the Romans did.

VI. Sport. Outdoor sport is both a pleasure and a duty. According to Dr. T. B. Scott, "walking at a moderate pace" is the best exercise for most people. It costs nothing but shoe-leather. You should be regular in your daily walk, like the great philosopher Kant. Learn also to walk in the town as much as you can; don't be a slave of tramcars and omnibuses for short distances, if you are not pressed for time. Other excellent sports are tennis, badminton, football, cricket, hockey, golf, riding, swimming, rowing, running, basket-ball, cycling, pole-vaulting, baseball, lacrosse, skating, skiing, gardening, open-air dancing, etc.

VII. Conservation of Energy. In Hygiene, as in Physics, one may speak of the conservation of energy. Continence or extreme moderation in the sexual life will conserve vitality and energy far better than many tonics and nostrums. The vital fluid is your very life-blood in a different form. If you waste it heedlessly and needlessly, you diminish your power of resisting disease, and your life will be short and inefficient. It behoves every thoughtful person to reduce sexual activity to the absolute minimum that Hygiene and Love require. Any excess above that minimum will be paid for in Nature's currency of sighs and tears. Don't sleep on your back, as involuntary emissions are more likely to trouble you in that posture. Conserve your energy more carefully than you keep your money. Don't squander it. This is one of the great secrets of health and longevity.

VIII. Optimism and Altruism. The mind makes or mars the body, as the body affects the mind. Optimism and kindliness should be cultivated as essential elements of Physical Culture, even apart from their ethical significance. Too much anxiety, worry, and mental gloom impair the digestion and ruin the nervous system. Shakespeare clearly indicated the interdependence of mind and body :

> "A merry heart goes all the day,
> Your sad tires in a mile-a."

A happy mind makes a healthy body. Love and gentleness are also powerful therapeutic agents. Kind words and deeds not only help others, but also keep your own body fit and strong. This physiological aspect of altruism has been elucidated by modern scientists. Professor Elmer Gates says: " My experiments show that irascible, malevolent, and depressing emotions generate in the system injurious compounds, some of which are extremely poisonous; also that agreeable, happy emotions generate chemical compounds of nutritious value, which stimulate the cells to manufacture energy."

Therefore, always smile and be kind. That habit will also bring you good health as a blessing that is well deserved.

CHAPTER III

ÆSTHETIC CULTURE

SECTION I. THEORY AND FUNCTION OF ART.
II. ARCHITECTURE.
III. SCULPTURE.
IV. PAINTING.
V. MUSIC.
VI. DANCING AND ORATORY.
VII. POETRY.

CHAPTER III

ÆSTHETIC CULTURE

Section I.—THEORY AND FUNCTION OF ART

Æsthetic culture should be commenced early and directed according to sound principles. It is like an immense ladder stretching from the zenith to the nadir: you can climb or you can descend. Its aim is the appreciation and enjoyment of the best Art. Art stirs our emotions. Emotion is its domain. The Intellect has nothing, or very little, to do with it. Science is related to the Intellect, while Art appeals to the Emotions. Some cold, over-intellectual people hold that æsthetic appreciation is an intellectual and rational judgment. This is a fallacy. Beauty does not pass through the gate of the Intellect: it has its own short cut to the soul. Art and Science are independent, but they are interdependent.

The noblest Art is a source of unalloyed happiness and perennial inspiration. As Richard Wagner says: "Art is pleasure in itself, in existence, in community." It rouses deep feeling and gives zest to life. In this way, it furthers the process of Evolution.

You need not trouble much about the theories of Beauty and Art, though you should study them. In Art, practice precedes theory. The artist creates by spontaneous inspiration, and the theorists then analyse his masterpieces. "Homer" did not compose his hexameters after learning the rules of prosody in a Greek grammar. But you should reject all theological and metaphysical theories of Beauty. I warn you against the metaphysical definitions of Beauty that are found in the writings of Plato, Plotinus, Hegel, Cousin, Bradley, and other philosophers. Plato, in the "Symposium," speaks of "beauty absolute, separate, simple, and everlasting, which, without diminution and without increase, is imparted to the ever-growing and perishing beauties of all other things." In the "Phaedrus," Plato defines Beauty as a supersensible essence, which is realized in the state of ecstasy. Plotinus says: "The soul, being what it is, and belonging to the world of true reality, when it sees what is akin to it, or a trace of kinship, acknowledges it with transport, and is reminded of itself and its own things. . . . Bodies become beautiful by sharing in the rationality that comes from the Divine." Hegel writes thus obscurely: "The beauty of Art is a beauty that has not only been born of the mind or spirit, but born again of it. . . . Art has the function of revealing truth in the form of sensuous artistic shapes and of presenting to us the reconciliation of the contradiction between sense and reason." Cousin obtrudes his theology on Art, and says: "As we have found God to be the principle of all things, He must be the principle of perfect Beauty. He is the principle of the Beautiful, both as Author of the physical, and as Father of the intellectual and moral worlds. . . . It is in God that the Beautiful and the Sublime combine." C. E. M. Joad says: "The artist is created by the Life-Force." According to F. H. Bradley, Beauty is "an image of infinity." G. Gentile defines Art as "the soul of thought." Ruskin declares that Beauty is "the expression of the creating spirit of the Universe." All such theological and metaphysical theories misrepresent the origin and function of Art. There is no such thing as absolute Beauty in a transcendental realm. Art has nothing to do with "the Infinite," "the Absolute," etc. It is also not connected in any way with such an imaginary being as "God." You should take a common-sense empirical view of Art. Art is a human achievement for this life.

Many attempts have been made to define and describe Beauty in terms of something else. Thus fitness, suitability, and utility were regarded as the elements of Beauty by Socrates and Berkeley. Harmony, proportion, order, and symmetry have been emphasized by Aristotle and Kant. Congruence of parts and unity have been indicated by Schiller, Hume, S. Alexander, and Langfeld: unity of form and unity of content. Pleasure has been considered the essential feature of Art by Lotze and Ruskin, and also by Santayana, who says that Art is "pleasure objectified" and is perhaps remotely connected with sexual stimulation. All such doctrines are irrelevant and superfluous, as they attempt to represent Beauty as dependent on something that is not Beauty. Others have even equated Art with science (like H. Taine), or with history (like the "verists"), or with mathematics (like the Herbartian formalists). But Beauty is *sui generis*; it is an ultimate category. Art is for Beauty, and for nothing else. An object may be useful, symmetrical, unified, and pleasure-giving, and yet lack Beauty. Genius invents the technique of Art, which may vary in different epochs and countries. But the technique is not the essence of Beauty, which may be created through disproportion as well as proportion, through variety as well as unity. Pleasure is not the greatest gift of Art, which can and should also awaken the emotions of awe, wonder, and mystery. Pleasure is, indeed, only a by-product of Art. There is profound truth in Coleridge's remark: " The Apollo Belvedere is not beautiful because it pleases, but it pleases us because it is beautiful."

I believe that the only adequate and universal criterion of Beauty is its power of producing self-oblivion in the percipient. Art makes you forget yourself. It is the antithesis of self-consciousness. This essential function of Beauty was indicated in the well-known remark of Dio Chrysostom about Pheidias's statue of Zeus at Olympia: " Any man, who is heavy-laden in soul, who has suffered many misfortunes and sorrows in his life, and who has no comfort of sweet sleep, even such a one, I think, if he stood opposite this statue, would forget all the dangers and hardships of this mortal life." This unique power of taking you out of yourself, out of your petty personal self, is the peculiar quality of Art. This is its essence, and not utility, pleasure, proportion, and other external and variable attributes. If a work of Art so affects you that you are " lost " in the contemplation of its beauty and are not fully conscious of your own existence, then it is a genuine masterpiece indeed, whatever its form and technique may be. If it leaves you cold, self-conscious, and critical, then it is not good Art, even if it possesses usefulness and proportion, and also gives pleasure. Great Art proclaims itself by the effect that it produces on the soul: that is the only valid test. As a joke is not a good joke if it must be explained to make the company laugh, even so that Art is not living and immortal which fails to lift your soul instantaneously and irresistibly out of the region of self-consciousness. With a work of true art, you can live as with a friend, as Winckelmann wished to do. By this touchstone you can judge them all, from the Palæolithic art of the Dordogne to the latest salon: ancient, medieval, and modern art, Impressionism, Post-impressionism, Vorticism, Numeralism, Orphism, Integralism, Pointillism, Divisionism, Surrealism, Neo-impressionism, Cubism, Dadaism, Futurism, Rodinism, abstract art, Oriental and African art, imitative and idealizing art, and all possible and impossible varieties of new Art. You can apply this rule to all the major and minor arts: architecture, painting, sculpture, music, drama, dancing, acting, oratory, poetry, etc. If new artists proclaim new ideals and adopt new methods, you should not condemn them, but wait and see if they can create genuine Art. Art cannot stand still, or only repeat the past. New developments are to be encouraged and welcomed.

Let the artist employ any material that he chooses, work with any tools that he likes, use any lines, colours, tones, forms, curves, patterns, and designs that he prefers; but if he creates a masterpiece that moves, thrills, enchants, and captivates us to the extent of complete self-oblivion, then he is a great artist, whatever the old men and the newspaper critics may say. His inspiration is communicated to us, and we are also transported to another psychological plane with him. Such art is truly immortal, as Théophile Gautier sings: "All things pass. Great Art alone cannot perish. The city dies, but the Statue remains."

Why does Art produce self-oblivion? Because it takes us out of our small individual selves, and facilitates communion and communication with the Social Self, which is common to all men, women, and children. As each home has its water-cistern and its tap, but the municipal reservoir is one, even so the Social Self is unitary and universal for all mankind, while the individual self is limited and personal. Art enables us to develop and realize the unity of these two Selves, which are fundamentally identical. Some thinkers have gone down into the cellar and basement of the sub-conscious and the unconscious in search of the psychic unity of Humanity. But it is not necessary or desirable to be atavistic in this way. The Superconscious is the highest and topmost terrace, to which we all may ascend, when we leave the workaday rooms of our individual selves. That Superconscious is open to the sky and sun, and is a tonic for Personality. Art takes us up there quickly and safely, like a lift in a vast mansion. This is the creed of Social Pan-psychism, and the artist is its priest and prophet. The smaller artists, who have more talent than genius, are the humble priests; the great artists, who possess or are possessed by genius, are the seers and prophets.

Great Art has therefore a profound and permanent social significance. It is a social product, like Ethics, though its vehicle may be an individual. Isn't it a remarkable fact that social appreciation is of the very essence of all Art? If a picture or a statue is admired only by the artist himself, but not by a single visitor to the gallery; if a poem pleases only the poet who has written it, and no other person at all; if a building is considered beautiful only by the architect, and by no other citizen; if a sonata thrills only the composer, and no other listener; then we conclude that such a work of Art is inferior, spurious, and transient. It is like a child who is liked only by its parents, but not by the friends, relatives, and neighbours. Our conception of Art includes the social appeal.

Hence all artists anxiously ask if their work is appreciated by the community or at least by a small group; the greatest of them even aspire to immortality and posthumous fame. Tolstoi was wise in laying stress on the social origin and import of Art. Art which is not social is only a personal pastime or hobby.

Hence it follows that great Art has its roots in universal Humanity, and not in personal or national idiosyncrasies, or in the passing catchwords and shibboleths of parties and Churches. The best Art is that which is praised and cherished by the greatest number of men and women over the longest period of time. Such Art has also the best chance of survival, as more people will take pains to preserve it. Inferior Art belongs to a certain class or coterie or Church; it is restricted and temporary in its social basis. When that class or Church disappears, its Art perishes with it. Such are the sculpture of the Assyrian military class, the Corinthian column of the putrid Roman aristocracy, the hell-pictures of Orcagna, the royal portraits of Van Dyck, the condottieri statues of Donatello and Verocchio, the Old Testament scenes of Ghiberti, Signorelli's "Judgment of the Damned," Velasquez's "Surrender of Breda" ("Las Lanzas"), Watteau's fashionable picnics and balls, Millais's "Yeoman of the Guard," Burne-Jones's "Wheel of Fortune," Greuze's "Morning Prayer," Chardin's "Grace before Meat," Cézanne's "Card-Players," Renoir's "Opera-Box," Bourdelle's "Leda," de Segonzac's "Drinkers," Manet's "Bar of the Folies Bergères," and the nudes (or more correctly "nakeds") of Manet, Degas, Rouault, Corinth, and Epstein. Such Art is local, short-lived, and evanescent. So is also propagandist Art, which has been described by C. E. M. Joad as a means "to bring new ideas into the world." He says: "Beauty, in fact, is for me nothing more than a contrivance of the Life-Force for securing that its ideas shall win acceptance. It is the sugar on the pill." But new ideas have their origin in the Intellect, which plays a very subordinate rôle (if any at all) in Art. As A. E. Housman has remarked: "The intellect is not the fount of poetry." Novelties are necessary and useful, but there are also the approved and acceptable verities, which have already been recognized as permanent principles of Life. Art cannot deal only with social Dynamics; it must also celebrate and idealize social Statics. Propaganda is one duty and one pleasure; but surely it does not exhaust the whole of Art. What propaganda value has a glorious sunset, or the Matterhorn, or a lovely child's face, or Claude Lorraine's superb Landscape, or Paul Potter's Bull, or even the Taj Mahal? Art must rouse deep Emotion; its direct aim is not intellectual persuasion or propagandist preaching. Even when Art makes the grand mistake of teaching Ethics by exhortation, like Pope and Tupper, it trespasses into a stranger's field. Art is not for the sake of Morality as such; it is for the sake of Beauty. Both Beauty and Morality are equal and independent constituents and factors of Personality. Art is not like a beautifully dressed country vicar, who pelts you with didactic texts every time you meet him in the street; it may be compared to a noble and tactful friend, whose very presence improves and ennobles you without a word. Art does not preach: it inspires. Oscar Wilde defended the independence of Art, when he said: "No artist has ethical sympathies. No artist desires to prove anything. All Art is quite useless." Art is indeed "useless" for the purpose of direct propaganda, homilies, argumentative appeals to the intellect and the conscience, and inartistic ethical or political advertisements masquerading as Art. But, in a deeper sense, Art and Ethics are one. Art releases and liberates you from your individual self, and merges you in the Social Self. This psychic experience or upheaval is the essential condition of moral growth. The highest Art and the highest Ethics are thus identical.

On account of the social origin and function of Art, its greatest achievements are possible only in such communities and periods as are noted for social idealism. If many citizens of a State are pondering on great problems and working for great ends, that State will bequeath a priceless legacy of noble Art to Humanity. When the people strive for personal improvement, earnestly seek better ways of life, and zealously reform their political and economic institutions, then great Art is sure to be born among them. Art is the offspring of an upward-climbing community, not of one that is standing still or sliding down. The Art of a conservative or hedonistic community only imitates Nature, but progressive Art idealizes Nature without wandering away too far from it, certainly never farther than Michael Angelo in the figures that decorate the Medici tombs. The sculpture of Gandhara and Japan and the masterpieces of Chinese painting were the artistic symbols of a community that was deeply influenced by the social idealism taught by Gautama Buddha. Of such Art has Victor Hugo said:

> "True Art can free from slavery,
> And give true greatness to the free."

The active progressive Athens of the forty-sixth century A.H.

produced Æschylus and Pheidias, creators of the most sublime Art that the world has ever known. But the pleasure-loving, easy-going Athenians of the forty-eighth century A.H. could boast of nothing better than Menander and Philemon. The democratic Italian Communes, full of eager, forward-looking, noble citizens, have given us Giotto, Michael Angelo, Fra Angelico, and Raphael: but stationary, self-complacent Venice can offer only the inferior art of Titian, Veronese, and Tintoretto. As the Italian people lost their social idealism, the dwarfish epigoni, like Moroni, Dosso Dossi, Ammanati, and Gian Bologna appeared. Modern works of art (with a few exceptions) are second-rate and soulless, simply because there is very little social idealism in this age. Men and women try frantically to become richer, but not better and nobler. They hanker for Pleasure, not Progress. The incubus of a corrupt and sensual capitalist class, which pays most of the artists, is crushing out all seriousness and sublimity from Art. Even if a prophet-artist is born among us, he is soon reduced to the position of a humble vassal and lackey of this Capitalism in order to earn his bread, like the Greek philosophers in ancient Rome. Oligarchy, plutocracy, and tyranny are fatal to great Art, as social idealism cannot flourish in that asphyxiating atmosphere. It is idle to blame our artists for their mediocrity, banality, artificiality, egotism, sensationalism, and sensualism, when we maintain the political and economic institutions that foster those vices of a decadent Art. Compare the medieval cathedrals with our restaurants, railway stations, and skyscrapers! Sir Michael Sadler notes the rise of a new spirit of freedom and earnestness in modern art, and says: "Much of modern art, having been conceived in revolution, seems prophetic of revolutions still to come. But we, who live in a revolutionary age, know how quickly we get acclimatized to change. . . . Thus modernism seeps into general taste."

May the prophecy come true! You are thus personally responsible for Art, and not the artist only. If you are virtuous and earnest, your epoch will produce great Art. If you are mean and vulgar, Art will also be mean and vulgar. Art is your own social image. There are four varieties and types of Art, that correspond to four different social and ethical atmospheres or environments. These are: (1) Sublime Art. (2) Sympathetic Art. (3) Sensational Art. (4) Sensual Art.

SUBLIME ART is the best of all. Sublimity, solemnity, and grandeur awaken the feelings of awe, wonder, and earnest aspiration. The more you assimilate and enjoy sublime Art, the better and wiser and happier you will be. Devote your days and nights to Pheidias in sculpture, Michael Angelo and Giotto in painting, Bach and Beethoven in music, and the Gothic cathedrals, the Parthenon, and the Indian buildings of the Afghan period in architecture. Sublime Art is created, when a great genius is also a great man.

SYMPATHETIC ART is charming and graceful; it aims at pleasure and refinement, and not at elevation and edification. Such Art is delightful and useful, as the valley is green and lovely, while the sublime mountain-tops are lonely in majestic grandeur. Such agreeable Art is seen in the works of Praxiteles in sculpture; of Raphael, Luini, Rossetti, and others in painting; in the Taj Mahal, the Alhambra, the Temple of Nike at Athens in architecture; and in Mozart, Puccini, Verdi, and Rossini in music.

SENSATIONAL ART is violent and passionate. It loves movement and unrest, and disturbs and agitates the soul. It is liked by those shallow people who want " thrills " and excitement. It is harmful. Such mediocre and paltry Art is represented by Scopas and his contemporaries in sculpture; Wagner, Stravinsky, and the jazz-masters in music; Chirico's dream-horror pictures and all war-pictures (like Meissonier's " Friedland "), Kandinsky's violently coloured pictures, Paul Nash's war-drawings and El Greco's works in painting; and the modern American architects in architecture.

SENSUAL ART is the worst of all. It is a sink of vice and iniquity. It degrades and brutalizes the soul. It is always the product of a corrupt and decadent civilization, *e.g.* the Greek Venus Callipygus, the " Leda " (wrongly attributed to Michael Angelo), the libertinage of Boucher and Fragonard, the vulgarities of Goya, Rubens, and van Ostade, the brutalities of Jordaens, the sensuality of Manet (in " Olympia "), Degas, Louis Corinth, and other artists. Such debasing Art should be shunned and condemned.

Section II.—ARCHITECTURE

Architecture is the most social and magnificent of the Arts. It combines utility with beauty, and promotes social communion and unity. Unity of design, harmonious proportions, and imaginative idealism are the marks of great Architecture. Noble buildings are often adorned with statues and pictures: thus the three plastic Arts can unite in the service of Beauty.

You should study the history of Architecture and its technical problems. Buy photographs or small models of the great buildings that you should contemplate frequently, *e.g.* the Parthenon and the Temple of Nike, the Paestum Temple, the Cathedrals of Lincoln, Lichfield, Amiens, Chartres, Cologne, and Strassburg, the tomb of Altamsh, the Mosque and the Kutab Tower at Delhi, the Taj Mahal and the Buland Darwaza, Brunelleschi's Dome of the Cathedral at Florence, St. Peter's Church at Rome, St. Sophia at Constantinople, the Alhambra at Granada, St. Mark's Church at Venice, the Mosque at Ispahan, the Forth Bridge, the Panthéon and the Sacré Cœur Church at Paris, the Capitol at Washington, the Houses of Parliament at London, the Woolworth Building at New York, the Stadshuset and Konserthuset at Stockholm, etc.

As a citizen of the Municipality, you should demand beautiful buildings for all local purposes. The Town Hall, the Post Office, the Police Station, the School, and all other public edifices should be made as beautiful as possible. Beauty is not a question of size and splendour, but chiefly of design and spirit. Everything in our environment should be beautiful—our houses, our shops, our monuments, our lamps, our pots and pans.

Section III.—SCULPTURE

Beautiful Sculpture is a source of the purest joy and inspiration. It has rendered a great service to Humanity by preserving the portraits of the Greek philosophers, poets, orators, and statesmen. We do not know what Buddha and Christ looked like, but we are familiar with the serene faces of Socrates, Plato, and Marcus Aurelius. Sculpture has also given us idealized types of physical beauty and strength, and also of intellectual and ethical beauty. The contemplation of these busts and statues inspires us to persist in regular Physical Culture, and instils the balm of repose, calm, serenity, and peace into our souls. Sculpture deals chiefly with living forms and figures, and it combines imitation and idealization in about equal proportions. Its material has been marble, stone, alabaster, terra-cotta, wax, wood, ivory, metals, and even gems. It can incarnate an ideal in an immortal chiselled visage or body, though it is more dependent on its material than the other arts. It can express living character and thought in dead stone and wood. It is less successful with motion or historic groups and scenes, which are better handled in painting. The Laocoön and the Niobe group are not very impressive. Simplicity of form, expression, and attitude are the characteristics of this art.

Modern Sculpture has also preserved for us the portraits of eminent persons. Such are Rude's "Jeanne d'Arc," Boehm's "Bunyan," Bega's "Schiller," Barba's "Cervantes," Canova's "Washington," Houdon's "Voltaire" and "Washington," Barrias's "Victor Hugo," Bartholome's "Rousseau," and others. You should study the history of Sculpture, and purchase photographs or replicas of the famous statues. Look at them from time to time; place some of them in your room. Pay special attention to the following works:

(1) Greek Sculpture. Greece and Japan share the honours of supreme excellence in Sculpture. They complete and complement each other. Japan supplies what is lacking in Greek Sculpture. To Greece, we owe the statues of athletes and sporting-women (Diana), which should now adorn all gymnasia. The type of Athena is a unique contribution to sublime Art. The faces on the coins of Sicily should be made familiar to your mind. Study

Venus de Milo, Venus de Medici, Apollo Belvedere, and the Hermes of Praxiteles, which is the only attested original work of Praxiteles. Zeus of Otricoli and the Elgin marbles should be contemplated frequently. Travel to Greece and see the Parthenon and the "Hermes" before you die. Professor H. N. Fowler says: "The sculptures of the Parthenon, even in their fragmentary condition, are among the greatest monuments of human genius." Buy photographs of the statues of Sophocles, Demosthenes, and others. A replica of the fine statuette of Socrates is available in the market.

Remember Professor Percy Gardner's words: "All ages must owe a debt to Greece for the simple beauty, the sanity, the healthfulness of the ideal element, which she introduced into Art, making it, for the first time in history, a true exponent of the human spirit."

(2) Japanese Sculpture. Japanese Sculpture owes its inspiration to Buddhism, and represents ideal types of saints and sages. It has produced statues and statuettes of Buddha in metal and wood. The colossal bronze statue in the temple at Nara dates from the fifty-eighth century A.H (eighth A.D.). It is one of the wonders of the world, not because of its size, but because of its artistic merit. The impression produced by the Buddha statue at Kamakura has been thus described by C. F. Holland:

"It tells of passion long subdued,
Of wisdom's calm repose,
Of patience born of pain and strife,
And strength to him who knows
It tells an all-embracing love,
Of joys that never cease,
And how from sorrow, grief, and fear
Emerged eternal peace."

The Bodhisattvas are also represented, such as Ashikou (faith), Ho-sho (perfection of conduct), and others. The statues of Kwannon, the Goddess of Mercy, and the Dhyani-Buddhas are masterpieces of idealization. J. F. Blacker says of the Dhyani-Buddhas: "Whether we regard the hold it had over millions of people, or merely look upon it as a matter of philosophic study, we cannot help being impressed with the beauty and dignity of the magnificent Buddhas of contemplation, the Dhyani-Buddhas."

(3) Gandhara Sculpture. This Art was born of the union of Buddhist ideals with Hellenic technique in Central Asia and North-western India. It combines physical and ethical beauty, like Japanese sculpture. V. A. Smith says: "Many of the good Gandhara sculptures may be fairly held to express with admirable

feeling and sincerity the ideal of a saintly Indian man. . . . The best works of the Gandhara school are intrinsically beautiful and skilfully executed. . . . The Gandhara school achieved a grand success by becoming the parent of the Buddhist art of Eastern or Chinese Turkestan, Mongolia, China, Korea, and Japan." Thus was Hellas wedded to Buddhism. The sculptured biography of Buddha at Bara-Budur in Java is worthy of study.

(4) MODERN SCULPTURE. It is a sad truth that most Christian sculptors have not succeeded in producing a satisfactory statue of Jesus Christ. The best figure is the "Christ" on the western façade of the cathedral of Amiens, called "the beautiful God of Amiens." You should secure a photograph of this statue. Thorwaldsen's "Christ" has also some merit. Michael Angelo's "Moses" and "David" may be recommended as types of wisdom and manly beauty respectively. The four recumbent figures on the tombs of the Medici at Florence represent sublime tragedy in Sculpture, and may be contemplated as such.

In the modern epoch, the Sculpture of Labour and Socialism should be appreciated, *e.g.* the works of de Groot and Cathier at Brussels, and, above all, the masterpieces of Constantin Meunier, "the Sower," "the Smith," "the Stevedore," and his reliefs representing labourers in various industries.

Section IV.—PAINTING

Painting is distinguished by the vastness of its scope and range It deals with both Nature and Man. It can tell a story, depict a historical scene, or embody the aspirations of a whole nation or class. The religious pictures of the Middle Ages were called " the Bible of the people," who were illiterate. History and Biography should be illustrated by the painters, who can enable us to visualize the past. Painting can thus be a most active and useful ally of Ethics.

It is a pity that all the Greek paintings have perished, except the few that survive on terra-cotta vases.

Study the history of Painting, and pay special attention to the following works:

(1) Chinese Painting. In Painting, several nations have made masterly contributions. Chinese Painting derives its inspiration from Buddhism and from Nature. The Chinese painters depict landscape, flowers, birds, plants, and insects, and use silk or paper. Buddhism fostered a spirit of charity for all living beings, which is reflected in Chinese Art. The disciples of Buddha, called Lohans, are the subjects of many paintings. The great artist Wu Tao-tzu created the Chinese type of Kwanyin, the goddess of Mercy and Charity, during the period of the T'ang dynasty. Li Lung Mien painted Buddhist pictures and also landscapes. R. Petrucci says: " He challenges comparison with a facile genius like Raphael." Mi Fei is also a great landscape-painter. The period of the Sung dynasty saw the efflorescence of landscape-painting in China, which evolved a new conception of Nature. In the sixty-fifth century A.H., Lu Fu headed the famous group of painters of the plum tree. Simplicity and freedom from non-essentials are the *characteristics* of Chinese Painting. *Chinese Painting is comparable* to Italian Painting in its depth, its variety, its beauty of form, and its national and universal appeal. I may mention Li Lung Mien's " Arhat with Lion," Wu Tao-tzu's " Kwanyin " and " Sakyamuni," Ma Yuan's " Pines and Rocky Peaks," Sheng Mou's " Sage in the Forest," etc.

Some Japanese colour-prints are also masterpieces, *e.g.* Hiroshige, Hokusai, and others. Get a few.

(2) Italian Painting. The Italian Renaissance gave many masterpieces of Painting to the world.

For Christianity, study only Fra Angelico's paintings, Leonardo da Vinci's "Last Supper," and Luini's fresco at Milan. Most Italian paintings of Christian subjects are insincere and false. Fra Angelico was a saintly monk, and therefore succeeded in painting truly, though his techique is not perfect. Sodoma's pictures of "Life of St. Benedict" at Monte Oliveto are important. Giotto's frescoes of the "Life of St. Francis," his figures of the Virtues and Vices, and his Allegories are noble, both in theme and form. He is a pre-eminently ethical painter.

Some remarkable masterpieces, which should be purchased in coloured reproductions, are Guido Reni's "Aurora," Palma Vecchio's "Sta. Barbara," Dolci's "St. Cecilia," Botticelli's "Birth of Venus" and "Primavera" (which was suggested by Lucretius), Sodoma's "St. Sebastian," Raphael's "Madonna of San Sisto," Michael Angelo's "Isaiah," Ambrogio Lorenzetti's frescoes on the Commune at Siena, Leonardo da Vinci's "Mona Lisa," and a few others.

There is one picture that should be in every Rationalist's house, Raphael's "School of Athens." It glorifies Greek philosophy and represents the spirit of the Renaissance. Poetry is celebrated in Raphael's "Parnassus." Perugino's figures of the heroes and philosophers of Greece and Rome at Perugia (Sala del Cambio), and Luca della Robbia's bas-reliefs of Plato, Aristotle, and the sciences are valuable contributions to the art of Humanism as distinguished from Christian art, which has many undesirable themes.

(3) Among modern paintings, I would recommend David's "Death of Socrates," Hofmann's "The Rich Young Man and Christ," Anderson's "The Woman taken in Adultery," Millais's "Christ in the Carpenter's Shop," Madox Ford Brown's "Work" and "Christ Washing the Feet of the Disciples," Biedermann's Buddha pictures, Feuerbach's "Plato's Symposium," Romney's "Lady Hamilton," Pryse's "Towards the Dawn," Fausto Zonaro's "New Turkey," Jacob Maris's grand Landscapes, Brangwyn's Labour pictures, Van Gogh's "The Reaper," Balla's "Centrifugal Force," Carrière's "Maternity," Ginner's "The Great Loom," Picasso's "Mother and Babe," etc.

Section V.—MUSIC

Music is a wonderful art indeed. It lifts us out of the individual self into the Social Self without any effort on our part. It is a bond of social unity. Molière even expected it would unite the whole human race in love and peace. He said: "If all men learn Music, would it not be a means of agreeing together in concord and establishing universal peace in the world?" All men love Music. Even some animals respond to it. It is Nature's direct wireless message. From the blackbird to Beethoven, all musicians are harbingers of joy and life. They confer upon us a kind of happiness that can be attained by no other means. Music lightens labour and promotes harmony and concord among men. It solaces us in adversity and inspires us in prosperity. It enlivens our leisure moments, and adds a touch of refinement to all our pleasures. It rescues us from coarseness and vulgarity, and lifts us to a higher mental and ethical plane. It awakens in us that inner rhythm which adds to the zest of life and increases our energy and vitality. It weans us from the trivial material pleasures that are so treacherous and deceptive. It accustoms us to keen and deep emotional pleasures that never pall or satiate. Who ever got tired of good Music, even after the millionth repetition? Music expresses for us what speech cannot convey, even in the mouth of Demosthenes, Shakespeare, and Victor Hugo. As speech is superior to gesture, so does music transcend speech. Music appeals directly to the fundamental human nature in us; it does not depend on words and thought-processes. It can rouse or benumb us, calm or perturb us, make us laugh or weep, rejoice or mourn, according to the technique employed by the genius of the Master. The Hungarian Government had to prohibit the Racoczy March in 6848. Such power is in Music! In the opinion of Plato and Confucius, music even makes or mars character, and instils virtue or vice in all the institutions of society. Music accompanies all social events; there is Music for marriages, for funerals, for religious worship, for dancing, for war, for peace, for life, and for death. Isn't it marvellous that rhythm can have such power of expression and interpretation? Music covers the whole gamut of human feelings and emotions, aspirations and ideals.

In modern Music there is much "musical journalism," which is intended for the vulgar people of all classes, rich and poor. These undeveloped persons regard Music as an amusement or a distraction, and not as a fine Art. They want a thrilling and interesting kind of noise. As an occasional diversion, it is allowable; but, as the daily food of the soul, it is poisonous. For the greatest message of Music, you should always go back as often as possible to Bach and Beethoven. Purchase a good gramophone and many records, if you can afford it. Take every opportunity of hearing noble Music on the wireless or at concerts. Don't grudge the expense. Learn to play on some instrument, if possible. The mandoline is said to be the easiest to learn. If you play for your own pleasure at home, you will appreciate the experts better. Music was an essential part of Greek education. Every child should be taught to play on some instrument as well as he or she can. Let our homes and halls be full of good Music: then our hearts will also be full of sweetness.

In choosing your Music, you should prefer the sublime music of Bach, Beethoven, and Brahms, the exquisite and delightful music of Verdi and Mozart, or some passages of Wagner, but keep sensational music only for very occasional use. We get enough excitement from the hurried and flustered life around us: this generation needs sublime Music as a tonic and a sedative. Remember the three B's of sublime Music. We need copious daily potions of Beethoven's Sonatas, Symphonies, and the "Mass in D," and Bach's "48 Preludes and Fugues." In addition to these, accept the Trauersmusik (Siegfried's Death March) from Wagner; the "1812 Overture" from Tchaikowsky; "Scheherazade" from Rimsky-Korsakov; "The Damnation of Faust" from Berlioz; the "Sonata in A" from César Franck; the orchestral prelude to "L'après-midi d'un faune" and the prelude for pianoforte entitled "La Cathédrale Engloutie" from Debussy; the "Death and Transfiguration" from Strauss; "The Dream of Gerontius" and the "Second Symphony" from Elgar; "Finlandia" from Sibelius; the "Overture to William Tell" from Rossini, the first Peer Gynt suite from Grieg; the "Unfinished Symphony" from Schubert; the "Concerto for Piano and Orchestra" from Schumann; "The Messiah" and the melody known as "Largo in G" from Händel; the "Fifth Symphony" from Dvorak; the "Prelude in C Sharp minor" from Rachmaninov; the "Pavane pour une enfant defunte" from Ravel; the "Fire Bird" from Stravinsky; and other masterpieces of sublime or sympathetic Music. But beware of the sensational and sensual Music, which is popular in certain circles to-day.

Section VI.—DANCING AND ORATORY

Dancing is often regarded as a "minor Art": but I include it among the major Arts. It combines music with rhythmical movement. It is one of our most ancient and universal arts. It is easily accessible to all. It enhances the delights of social life. But group-dancing is preferable to couple-dancing. In group-dancing, the artistic enjoyment is the principal attraction. In couple-dancing, the erotic element predominates. Our popular Dancing-Halls are only purveyors of sexual stimulation and excitement. If young persons wish to spend some time together, it is much better to take a walk in the country than to whirl round and round in the impure air of the public Dancing-Halls. The Saturday habit of dancing is an obstacle to personal improvement among the young people of all classes. Sex-sublimation should be taught and encouraged, not artificial and premature sex-stimulation. Occasional dancing at private gatherings is an unobjectionable social pastime. But the public Dancing-Halls undermine moral stamina by selling the weekly dose of degeneracy. Don't dance too often and too much. It is an insidious habit. Group-dancing as an art should be encouraged, especially in the open air. An intelligent working-man said to me, "Alcohol and dancing keep the working-class in slavery."

Oratory is a great art. It can affect the mind and the soul like poetry and music. It is the message of Personality. In a democratic State, the popular orator attains the position of a political leader. Hence it is very important to train the orators in Philosophy and Ethics, so that they may not use the wonderful gift of eloquence for selfish ends. If Oratory is not guided by Ethics, then it is indeed a curse for the State. You should hear some great speakers and preachers. Try to develop your talent for public speaking, if you have any. Join a debating society. Learn great speeches by heart, and declaim them. Read Demosthenes's "On the Crown," Quintilian's "Institutes of Oratory," the speeches of the orators of the French Revolution, Wendell Phillips's speeches against slavery, Burke's speeches against Warren Hastings, and the discourses of Jaurès, Ingersoll, Keir Hardie, Bradlaugh, and other enlightened orators.

SECTION VII.—POETRY

POETRY is an essential element of a liberal education. You need not trouble about the many definitions of poetry; it is more important to read and love poetry than to define it. You do not define a flower or a sunset; you enjoy it. Several thinkers and poets have tried their hand at this game. Thus Ebenezer Elliot described poetry as "impassioned truth," while John Stuart Mill approved of the definition of poetry as "man's thoughts tinged by his feelings." Coleridge wrote: "A poem is a species of composition opposed to science as having intellectual pleasure for its object or end, and as attaining its end by the use of language natural to us in a state of excitement." Matthew Arnold regarded poetry as "criticism of life, mainly on the side of morality." William Hazlitt said: "Poetry is the language of the imagination and the passions." According to Shelley, "poetry expresses those arrangements of language, and especially metrical language, which are created by that imperial faculty whose throne is curtained within the invisible nature of man."

Apart from such formal definitions, a great deal of exaggerated praise has been lavished on poetry. You should beware of being swept away by the torrent of theological, metaphysical, and sentimental phrases in which some writers have extolled poetry to the skies. I cannot agree with Novalis, who declares that "Poetry is absolute Reality," or with Schiller, who says: "The poet is the only real man and the best philosopher is but a caricature by the side of him." Philip Sidney speaks of a poet's "force of divine breath" and regards poetry as infinitely superior to philosophy or history. Aristotle also preferred poetry to history, "as poetry speaks more of universals, but history of particulars." Shelley talks sheer metaphysical nonsense, when he says: "A poet participates in the eternal, the infinite, and the one: as far as relates to his conceptions, time and place and number are not. Poetry is at once the centre and circumference of Knowledge." In Plato's dialogue, "Ion," Socrates is represented as teaching that the poets were divinely inspired and possessed by the Muse, and did not compose by art, but through a divine power. Milton was also a theologian, and taught that good poetry required "prayer to the Eternal

Spirit" who "sends His seraphim with the hallowed fire of His altar, to touch and purify the lips of whom He pleases." Carlyle, mixing up theology and metaphysics, glorifies the poet as one "who has penetrated into the Divine mystery, the Divine Idea of the World, which lies at the bottom of Appearance." V. Cousin also takes a metaphysical view, as he says: "Poetry is the first of the Arts because it best represents the infinite." Emerson tries to foist his crude metaphysics on the art of poetry: "Poetry is the perpetual endeavour to express the spirit of the thing, to pass the brute body and search the life and reason which cause it to exist. . . . Poetry was all written before time was." G. Santayana is of opinion that "religion and poetry are identical in essence, and differ merely in the way in which they are attached to practical affairs." But I think that poetry has no such necessary relation to theism of any variety, and Santayana's piety-in-poetry is mere superstitious irrelevance.

While the theologians, metaphysicians, self-complacent poets, and over-enthusiastic critics have hysterically hailed poetry as something "divine," "transcendental," "spiritual," and "supreme," some philosophers have gone to the other extreme and condemned poetry as a debased form of imitation or mere mendacity. Plato dragged the poets down from their ancient lofty pedestal, when he wrote in the "Republic": "All poets, beginning from Homer, are imitators of the images of virtue, and of other things about which they compose, but yet do not attain to the real truth. . . . Imitation is a sort of amusement and no serious business. . . . Imitation, being depraved in itself, and joining with that which is depraved, generates depraved things." Nietzsche also castigated the poets in these scathing words: "Poets tell too many lies. They know too little and are bad learners. They make their water muddy that it may seem deep. A poet is a sea of vanity." Prophet Muhammad said in the Koran: "It is the poets whom the erring people follow. Dost thou not see that they rove distraught through every valley, and say that which they do not?" The exegete Al-Beidawi adds the caustic comment: "Their compositions are as wild as the actions of a distracted man, for most of the ancient poetry was full of vain imaginations."

Thus poetry has been blindly and unduly eulogized, and also unjustly decried and belittled. You should steer a middle course between these two extremes. Know that poetry is not derived from any "God" or Goddess. It has also nothing to do with the "Absolute," the "Infinite," and the "Eternal" of metaphysics.

It is just one of many human achievements; it appertains to Man on earth. It has its use and abuse, its advantages and its limitations. This is the common-sense view of poetry according to the philosophy of Rationalism.

Poetry is essentially rhythmical speech that gives delight through rhythm, harmony, and melody. Poets have made use of alliteration (as in Anglo-Saxon), or metre with rhymed or unrhymed verse (as in Sanskrit, Greek, and English), or *vers libre*, whose rhythms are based on cadence. Great poets may invent other beautiful forms of rhythmical speech in future. Rhythm is the starting-point, but poetry must illumine, interpret, and irradiate Nature and Humanity with the light of Imagination. Rhythm is the body of poetry, but Imagination is its soul. Shakespeare has described it thus.

> " As imagination bodies forth
> The forms of things unknown, the poet's pen
> Turns them to shapes, and gives to airy nothing
> A local habitation and a name "

Imagination is the power of penetrating into Nature and interpreting it. It is intermediate between intellect and emotion; it combines and harmonizes what may seem to be discordant and contradictory. It perceives subtle aspects of truth, and discovers hidden relations and far-reaching analogies. It enables the poet to clothe intellectual conceptions in appropriate forms. But Imagination must be orderly and synthetic; it must be under the control of the poet's creative genius. It must not degenerate into mere wild fancy and chaotic sensation and impulse.

Besides Rhythm and powerful Imagination, poetry is based on intense Emotion. It is the language of passion, feeling, sentiment, pathos, enthusiasm, rapture, ecstasy, inspiration. Prose is sufficient for the humdrum needs of the intellect, but poetry is indispensable for the expression of deep and spontaneous feeling. Whenever and wherever men and women have been touched, moved, and thrilled in their innermost souls, to the very core of their being, then and there they have always burst into song. Poetry is the cry of the human heart. Whatever affects Mankind very deeply will create noble poetry as soon as the genius is born among them. Prose is like the daily work-clothes of human speech; poetry is its festive garb donned for solemn feasts and festivals. All vital interests and basic institutions that are supremely important for the happiness of the race are cherished with a deep and abiding love: they evoke profound emotions that safeguard them at all times. Thus love, liberty, virtue, justice, the charm of Nature, mercy, self-sacrifice, and other fundamental ideas and ideals have inspired the poets of all epochs and countries.

Rhythm, Imagination, Emotion: these three enter into the texture of poetry, but Beauty is its very breath of life. Good poetry is suffused with Beauty, as the tropical landscape is bathed in sunshine. Without the power of creating genuine Beauty, a versifier may become what Hotspur called a "metre-balladmonger," but he cannot be a poet. A poet is first and foremost an artist; he fascinates us by the witchery of words.

Now you may ask, "What is the use of Poetry?"

1. Poetry gives deep delight and perennial pleasure on account of its rhythm. Rhythm is one of the mysteries of Nature. We breathe and our hearts beat according to what Herbert Spencer has even named "the law of rhythm." Poetry, music, and dancing all depend on rhythm, and these arts are closely related. In inanimate Nature, too, wave-motion is a kind of rhythm that pervades the entire Universe. It seems that rhythm affords us such exquisite and ineffable delight because it is a life-increasing and race-preserving force. Even the new-born babe feels the soothing effects of the lullaby. Thus poetry finds its ally in biology. Some modern critics have expressed the opinion that the charm of poetry depends on the frequency of the sounds "j" and "sh," which induce a copious flow of saliva in the mouth! However that may be, joy is something that is worth having for its own sake. Poetry adds to the joy of life. It pleases and gladdens us through the ear. The pleasures of poetry never cloy or satiate: we always ask for more of them. Goethe says truly:

> "And who the voice of poesy disdains
> Is a barbarian, be he who he may."

2. Poetry stimulates your imagination and widens your spiritual horizon. You willingly follow the sweet poet in his world of images, dreams, and visions, as the children of Hamelin followed the Pied Piper. Your daily life is dull, narrow, and commonplace; the poet lifts you with him on the wings of his Imagination and reveals to you Nature and Humanity in all their glory. To Peter Bell, a primrose was a yellow primrose and nothing more; but we know what daffodils could be to Wordsworth, and through him to us too. Great poets have given us new eyes to see the wanderings of Odysseus, Rama, and Buddha, the training of Jesus, the fall and redemption of Faust, the heroism of Tell, Sertorius, and

Horatius, the public spirit of Brutus, and the deeds of Zoroaster. We can derive moral benefit from the storied past of the race only with the help of the poets, whose Imagination can breathe life into the dead bones of the old chronicles and annals. Of course, Imagination may be abused, as when Dante employed it to visualize non-existent regions of the Universe, or when Tasso rescued from oblivion the blood-stained figures of uncouth barbarians. Misguided Milton also created his stupendous Satan and presented him to us, a grievous gift, altogether profitless and unacceptable. But through the wise poet's Imagination you can survey the immensities of Nature, or move among the noble scenes and characters of history, or penetrate into the glories of the future of mankind. As the telescope aids the physical eye, so Poetry is a tonic for "the eye of the mind."

3. Poetry intensifies your emotions, and thus gives you a fuller and deeper life all round. Emotion is the central dynamo of human Personality: it gives zest to life and drives you to action and adventure. Without strong emotions your life would be an arid waste, in which only the thorns and thistles of impotent intellectualism or swinish sensuality could grow and thrive. The great poets are inexhaustible wells of deep feeling. They were extremely sensitive men and women who loved or hated, suffered or enjoyed, greatly and whole-heartedly. As the thirsty soil of India needs bountiful showers of rain, so do our shrivelled souls, parched with dull and carking cares, require the quickening and fertilizing influence of the mighty hearts of the poets. If you have no dominant feelings and passions, you cannot be said to live: you simply vegetate. Your vitality is low and should be replenished. Go and revivify your Personality by letting a little of the true poet's powerful electric current pass through your being. Then you will be rejuvenated in every pore.

4. Poetry makes philosophy and ethics interesting and effective. It portrays or creates noble characters for our inspiration, and directs our sympathies and antipathies into the proper channels. The great nations of antiquity honoured their poets as wise teachers. Aristophanes, in the "Frogs," puts these words into the mouth of Æschylus:

> "See there, what a blessing illustrious poets
> Conferred on mankind in the centuries past!
>
> . . . . .
>
> Orpheus instructed mankind in religion,
> Next came old Hesiod, teaching us husbandry,
> Homely morality, labour, and thrift."

The Persians of to-day regard their great poets as inspired prophets and can recite beautiful verses as readily as a Christian priest can quote texts from the Bible. The best poets describe past events and delineate character, and thus improve and elevate us by acting on our feelings. They teach us without directly preaching to us or at us. But even the inferior variety of "philosophical" and "didactic" poetry is very helpful in the pursuit of Truth and the cultivation of Virtue. Verse serves to imprint indelibly on our minds the ideas and ideals that we love. Rhyme and rhythm make it easier to memorize the noble precepts and instructive aphorisms that shed light on our path in life. As the prosaic poet Alexander Pope says: "Truth shines the brighter, clad in verse." Memory has some subtle affinity with rhythm. It is no difficult task to learn and remember a few hundred lines of philosophical and didactic poetry, while it would be impossible to retain and repeat the same quantity of bare prose. The Chinese primer called the "Three Character Classic," which is written in rhyme, has been learned by heart during six hundred years by almost all literate persons in China. Such memorized verses are of immense service in every civilized person's life: they are for the average citizen what pemmican is for the Arctic explorers. They are the concentrated essence of wisdom in a portable shape. When we repeat them in solitude or in conversation more than a thousand times each year, we fortify our Personality against the insidious attacks of error and sin. Lucretius cast the halo of poetry about the dry-as-dust dogmas of Epicurus, and Caedmon told the story of Christ in verse to the rugged Northumbrians. You will find that Horace, Bhartrihari, Saadi, La Fontaine, Hsieh Chin, and Ssu-Kungtu, who have provided us with wise saws and maxims, are really better known than greater poets who have only told a story with perfect art. Even Shakespeare's sententious "quotations" are at least as popular as his immortal characters. A didactic poet mints the raw ore of Ethics into current gold coin for the people by casting it into the mould of rhythm and attaching the superscription of his name to it. He is not a creative poet; but he helps to conserve and disseminate the truth and virtue that have already been created by the prophets and the philosophers. Thus he renders inestimable service to society.

Such is Poetry and such are its advantages. You should begin by cultivating a liberal and catholic taste in poetry. Do not degenerate into a narrow-minded partisan of a coterie. Do not shut your eyes to the beauty of new forms of poetry, which the daring innovators may invent in your lifetime. All great poetry is a boon and a blessing, whatever form it may assume. You should love blank verse and rhymed verse, and even modern "free verse" and "cubist poems," epics and lyrics, ballads and odes, tragedies and comedies, pastorals and elegies, and all other genres of poetry. Enjoy both the "Classical" and the "Romantic" poetry of France, as the soul of man has affinities with both Racine and Victor Hugo. Attune your ear to "the surge and thunder" of the "Odyssey," but at the same time find pleasure in simple songs and even in the Sunday hymns of the rationalists. Let your soul be responsive to all the tones and under-tones of good Poetry.

I say "Good Poetry." And thereby hangs a tale. There is good poetry and bad poetry, as there is good wine and bad wine. What makes poetry good or bad? Well, every poem has its Theme and its Form. The Theme is the subject-matter; the Form is the style. A poem can be bad if its Theme is bad, or if its Form is bad, or if both are bad. A poem may have an excellent Theme and an inferior Form; it is like Socrates, a virtuous man with an ugly face. Another poem may have an admirable Form and an objectionable Theme; it is like Alcibiades, a vicious man with a handsome countenance. A really great poem must have both a noble Theme and perfect Form; it is like Milton, endowed with both virtue and beauty.

Now you should not care much for the poems that have a bad Theme, even if the style is excellent. In fact, a bad Theme and a beautiful style form a very destructive combination. Such attractive and debasing poetry is like the dynamite of art placed under the noble ideals and institutions of society.

What Themes are bad and harmful? It is sad to reflect that many poets have abused their genius by singing of ignoble themes in noble verse. Such poets must be shunned, as they are more dangerous to mankind than plain prose-writers. They are like venomous cobras clad in a skin of glittering colours. The bad Themes are Pessimism, Superstition, Cruelty, Hedonism, and Servility. Alas! Much poetry is so fetid and putrescent that it cannot be read without infecting the soul with loathsome maladies. More's the pity!

1. *Pessimism* is a thoroughly bad Theme. Life is already full of trouble and tribulation; we do not need poetry to fill us with gloom and sadness. The pessimistic poets are good men gone astray. Leopardi, whom Alfred de Musset called "dark lover of Death," was tormented by chronic ill-health, and his verse reflects his incurable melancholy. Lenau and other hooting night-owls

simply depress and disturb us; their poetry has no message for us. James Thomson's dirges in "The City of Dreadful Night," Pushkin's and Shelley's occasional outbursts, and Wang Tsan's laments are also the Dead Sea fruit of petulant and inconsistent Pessimism.

2. *Superstition* has often found an ally in poetical genius. It has then derived immense power and potency from rhythm and imagery, like an ogress draped in beautiful raiment. Homer gave a new lease of life to Zeus, Hera, and the other Hellenic divinities. Milton wrote a magnificent epic in order "to justify the ways of God to man," a pitifully superstitious and ill-fated enterprise. Dante helped to bolster up the cosmogony of Catholicism through his allegorical poem; the intangible ethics of the allegory was submerged in the palpable superstition of the story. Tennyson enshrined many superstitious ideas about "God" and Death in his masterpiece "In Memoriam"; they will, unfortunately, be transmitted to posterity in his sweet music like flies in amber. Umar Ibn Al-farid of Cairo wasted his genius on mysticism. Many Nature-poets are grievous sinners in this respect. Victor Hugo compared Nature to a musical instrument and the poet to the player. He wrote: "O holy poets! Art is the sublime sound, which Nature, the immense piano, emits under your powerful fingers." But if the poet is a theist, a pantheist, or a polytheist, his music is sure to be as fatal as the strains of the sirens that lured the sailors to their doom. You must always ask, "How does this poet interpret Nature?" "Is he a safe and sane guide?" Wordsworth's pantheism expresses itself in metaphysical drivel, as in the famous "Lines written above Tintern Abbey." Walter Scott would have us believe that Nature mourns a poet's death and "celebrates his obsequies"—a fantastic and puerile notion altogether. Victor Hugo begins to shriek of "Infinity" and "Eternity" on seeing the mountains: nothing less will satisfy this voluble metaphysician. Jelaluddin Rumi also suffers from the illusions and delusions of pantheism. Goethe regards Nature as "the living garment of the Deity": his Spinozism makes him a false and misleading interpreter of Nature. Robert Browning is incapable of reading Nature aright on account of his incurable monotheism: he sees "God" everywhere and is therefore blind to Nature. I warn you against all such superstitious high-priests of Nature. Read simple and straightforward descriptive Nature-poetry, such as is found in the works of Kalidasa, Shakespeare, Crabbe, and the Chinese and Japanese poets, who combine Art with common sense and rationalism. Beware of the theists, the metaphysicians, and the irrational mystics in poetry.

3. *Cruelty and Hatred* disfigure a great deal of fine poetry. Great poets have employed their genius for the glorification of war among different nations and Churches, with all its inevitable horror and bloodshed. They have also sung songs of hate. All such poetry must now be relegated to eternal oblivion, as you support the League of Nations and work for perpetual peace on earth. The old ideal of belligerent patriotism and race-pride produced such hideous masterpieces as Homer's "Iliad," Virgil's "Æneid," Camões's "Os Lusiadas," and Firdausi's "Shahnamah." The sanguinary conflicts of warriors, factions, and Churches are the themes of the "Mahabharata," Tasso's "Gerusalemme Liberata," "Nibelungenlied" and "Chanson de Roland." All this poetry of war and conquest should be buried "deeper than ever plummet sounded," as Prospero got rid of his books. You should not take delight in reading how Diomede struck Phegeus in the breast with his javelin, or how Arjuna slew his enemy with his arrow. Homer's "Iliad" must make men cruel and callous indeed, when they read of such exploits as the following: "First Agamemnon, king of men, hurled from his chariot huge Hodius, chief of the Halizonians, who turned in flight, and Agamemnon fixed the spear between his shoulders and drove it through his breast; and falling, he made a crash. . . . Next Idomeneus killed Phaestus; as he was mounting his chariot, the spear-famed Idomeneus wounded him with his long lance in the right shoulder; he fell from his chariot and hateful darkness seized him. . . . Menelaus, son of Atreus, slew with his sharp spear Scamandrius; . . . Menelaus wounded him, flying before him, with a spear in the back, between the shoulders, and drove the spear through his breast. Prone he fell, and his arms resounded upon him. . . . Meriones slew Phereclus, whom he struck in the right hip, but the point went right through beneath the bone, near the bladder, and on his knees he fell lamenting, and death overshadowed him," etc., etc.

The poetry that reeks of the shambles and revels in ghastly images of slaughter and bloodshed is not true Art, but a morbid and miasmic exhalation from the worst and lowest elements of human nature. In fact, such a terrible holocaust as occurs in the closing scene of Shakespeare's "Hamlet" must also have a brutalizing effect on the spectators. I wonder if the ancient Hindus were not well advised in prohibiting the representation of death on the stage. They also demanded that all plays must end happily. They thus ruled out tragedy as a legitimate form of literature, but perhaps they won in gentleness and refinement what they lost in Art.

Cruelty and Art do not mix well together. I must therefore also warn you against Dante's "Inferno," where the highest Art is employed to describe imaginary scenes of devilish torture and punishment. Such a nightmare will not move sinners to repentance: it will only turn them into brutes.

The poetry of hatred and scorn should also be discarded for ever. "Patriotic" poems are generally full of vanity, falsehood, and blood-curdling threats against other nations. The different "national anthems" are a nuisance in this age. The old themes of "England," "France," "Deutschland," etc., should now be deposited in a literary museum of antiquated poetical specimens. Do not keep alive such poems as "Rule, Britannia," "Deutschland über alles," Kipling's "Recessional," Lowell's "Ode for the Fourth of July 1876," Victor Hugo's "Waterloo," Leopardi's "All' Italia," Henley's "England," etc. Such singers have really sown dragon's teeth broadcast on the earth. Away with such marauding and murderous verse! The "patriotic" poets have a dreadful responsibility for the wars that rage among the nations, as they corrupt the minds of the young. A savage song can kill more than a million bullets, and the pen can pierce farther than a bayonet. You must set your face resolutely and implacably against nationalistic poetry of all sorts. Let us now sing of Humanity and the Unity of Mankind.

Even in the poetical literature of the movements for the emancipation of oppressed nations and classes, the ominous note of hatred should not be heard. If some small souls must hate in order to be able to strive for justice, let them hate in prose. Poetry is the sacred vehicle of the highest and noblest human impulses. It cannot be dragged in the mire of temporary enmities and animosities. Georg Herwegh, in his fury and despair, cried out: "Love cannot free us. Arise, O Hate, and break our fetters." Even if such an invocation be considered necessary, it must not be made in poetry: it jars on the ear and on the soul. Poetry must not be desecrated by the bitter anathemas of hatred and cruelty among nations, classes, or individuals. On the portal of the white-flagged temple of Poetry, it is written: "Abandon all hate, ye who enter here."

4. *Hedonism and Sensuality* are also unworthy themes for a true poet, who should always shout "Excelsior!" as you climb upward. He should teach you the beauty of self-control and temperance; he should inspire you to sacrifice and service. If a singer portrays vice in pleasant colours, excites the imagination with prurient and seductive images, and adds fuel to the flame of your lusts, then he

is a pander and not a poet. Poetry is the handmaid of purity and activity; it should not be prostituted to the service of suicidal vice and brutish sense-bound lethargy. I must warn you against such enervating verse as Omar Khayyam's "Rubaiyat," Byron's "Don Juan," Bhartrihari's "Çṛngāra-cataka," Martial's many obscene epigrams, the poems of Ibn-al-Habbariyya and Anacreon, Muslim ibn el-Walid's wine-songs, Li Tai Po's demoralizing lyrics, the comic drama of the Renaissance in France and Italy, and of the Restoration in England. Omar Khayyam's refined and indolent hedonism must weaken the moral fibre of impressionable youth, and so lead slowly but surely to spiritual atrophy. Bread, wine, a sweetheart, and self-centred repose cannot long satisfy an earnest and aspiring soul. Khayyam should be honoured as a mathematician, not as a poet. Men and women are only too prone to slip and slide down the inclined plane of hedonism, on which they all stand at the moment of birth. They need good poetry to encourage and sustain them in their upward ascent, as the earthward pull of their animal ancestry is continually powerful and persistent. Woe to the base poet, who pushes them down instead of pulling them up! Such malodorous and malarial poetry need not be preserved. The leaders of the Church at Constantinople destroyed Sappho's sensuous and passionate lyrics. Have we lost much thereby?

5. *Servility*. Some poets have sold their genius for a salary or a gift. Despotism, landlordism, and capitalism have afflicted many countries at different periods in the world's history. Some poets have practised the debased and debasing trade of singing the praises of the despots, landlords, and capitalists. Such fulsome flattery earned some crumbs and bones for these gifted curs. Thus the Muse was bound in golden chains and bartered for tainted money. The slobbering panegyrics composed by sycophants like Al-Ghazzi, Mutanabbi, Anwari, Minuchihri, Hilali, and Khakani are steeped in nauseating venal servility. Hilali thus addressed the Vizier of the Sultan: "The majesty of thy countenance has stricken me to the earth; I shall never rise again till the last judgment." Minuchihri at least was conscious of his own degradation, for he wrote: "My critic says, 'Why dost thou pay thy court to the King?' I answer, 'Should not the foxes pay court to the lion?'" Feizi fooled Emperor Akbar to the top of his bent, and wrote: "Although Kings are the shadow of God on earth, Akbar is the emanation of God's light. How, then, can we call him a shadow? See Akbar and you see God." To such depths of infamy can genius descend, when it is enslaved by Mammon! In Rome, too, Martial earned

the wages of obsequious adulation. He declared that he would rather dine with Domitian than with Jupiter, and that there never was so much freedom under any other Emperor. Li Tai Po, the Chinese poet, was also a spoiled court-favourite. All such mercenary poets betrayed their trust, and their insincere effusions must be left to perish.

Such are the soul-destroying Themes that are found in the poetry of all nations. But there are many good and noble Themes too, and they are the subject-matter of the finest poetry.

As regards the best methods of reading and enjoying poetry, with full spiritual benefit, you should make a practice of reading at least a few lines every day, preferably as part of your morning Meditation. This will be your daily stimulant. You should also set apart a little time each week for reading longer poems. Poetry must be read aloud; it must not be read in dumb silence like prose. It is meant for the ear as well as the eye and the mind. Learn many verses by heart, and cite them as often as you can. A man, who cannot quote at least a few verses, is like a destitute traveller with no cash in his pocket. It is advisable to keep a notebook for poetical extracts that interest you. Thus your home will be a hive filled with the honey of the Muses, that you have gathered from many flowers. You will soon discover your favourite poems and your best-loved poets. Go back to them often, and thoroughly master and assimilate them. Poetry demands that you must diligently chew the cud. Frequent repetition will make your soul vibrate in harmony with the poet's lyre. Do not waste your time on second-rate poetasters. In poetry, only the best is good enough for you. Inferior verse is a torture to the ear and a weariness to the spirit. Join a Poetry Society or Literary Association, and keep in touch with the latest developments in poetry. Attend many meetings at which good poems are recited by well-trained elocutionists: this is one of the greatest pleasures that you can have. Try to arrange such meetings, if none are held in your town. The revival of poetical recitation is one of the crying needs of this prosaic age. Let the people hear the best poetry, and it will bring joy, calm, love, and hope into their dull or distracted lives. A University professor confessed to me that he had not read a line of poetry for ten years! I said, "I don't understand how you can live like that." Another friend said to me, "I read so much about politics that I can't find time for poetry." I replied, "Then your politics can't be worth much." Be not like unto such one-sided men.

You will, of course, begin with the poetry in your own language.

Poetry is a peculiarly indigenous product, and it is fully appreciated only in the mother-tongue. Like fruit, it has the best flavour when it has grown and ripened in the homeland. Read as much good poetry as you can find in your own literature. That is your first duty. It is foolish and absurd to compel English boys and girls to swallow Greek and Latin hexameters before they are thoroughly familiar with English poetry. The love of poetry must grow and take root in the tongue that you speak at home. Then, if you have learned a foreign language, ancient or modern, you may taste of its poetry. Finally, you may wander further afield and salute the great foreign poets whose masterpieces are available to you only in translation. First read an accurate translation in prose, so that you may know exactly what the poet actually wrote. Later, you can read the best verse translation that has been made. A prose rendering will give you all the ideas, stories, images, and similes of the original. It lacks only the rhythm and the sound-effects; but you can never get these in any translation, unless the translator is also a great poet. This is very seldom the case. Most translators are only clever and learned versifiers. Some "translations" of foreign poems bear as little resemblance to the original as the head of Bottom the weaver before and after he had been "translated." You may read a translation in verse, but remember that it is always like a convex or concave mirror, and must distort the original out of shape.

In choosing your poetry for study, examine the Theme first. Reject all poems with an objectionable Theme. If the Theme appeals to you, you should consider the style. Most famous poems are written in a good style. Slovenly or inartistic verse never becomes popular. Further, enquire if the poet was a sincere and earnest man, whose deeds were to some extent in harmony with his poems. If the author is known to have lived as he sang, the value and power of the poem are enhanced a thousandfold. We read "The Isles of Greece" as a religious hymn, for we know that Byron died at Missolonghi. Victor Hugo's "Châtiments" stands as a literary monument of Democracy, because it was composed in exile. Tulsidass's poetry rings true as the message of a pious saint. Ssu-Kung-tu's verses move us, as we learn that he actually became a hermit. Poetry is most powerful when it is the true voice of a living soul. You should always study the biography of the poet whose works you read. If you find that his life did not belie his poetry, you will derive additional pleasure and profit from his inspired words. As a general rule, if both the theme and the style are noble, the poem is a masterpiece. If the poet himself is also noble, it is a priceless possession for Humanity.

I may suggest a few great poems that should be read. Pindar, the greatest lyric poet of Hellas, devoted his genius to the glorification of beauty, strength, and athletics. He is unique in this respect. His contribution to poetry is as great as that of Myron and Polyclitus to sculpture. It is our good fortune that he should have chosen the theme of Physical Culture. Virgil's "Georgics," which treats of the joys of country life, is perhaps the only famous masterpiece on this important theme. His "Æneid" is not valuable, as it has only fine Form, while the themes are quite undesirable: war, patriotism, and passion.

Among philosophical poems, Lucretius's "De Rerum Natura" holds the first place for Rationalists. He expounds the Epicurean philosophy, which is based on Science. This poem must be read and re-read. Mr. M. S. Dimsdale says: "Such is the intrinsic importance of the topics treated, such the writer's adequacy to deal with them, such his enthusiasm, his imaginative power, in a word his genius, that he has left in the 'De Rerum Natura' the most impressive poem in the Latin language." Swinburne, Shelley, and Sully Prudhomme are also great poets of philosophic Rationalism. As all the works of Shelley should be read, I need not especially mention "Queen Mab" here. "Prabodhacandrodaya" (in Sanskrit) is also a philosophical drama of considerable merit.

Goethe's "Faust" (Parts I and II) must be studied carefully. It is a philosophical drama of vast scope and profound significance. It will teach you the importance of the all-round development of human Personality through philosophy, emotion, passion, art, science, and altruistic activity. As Professor G. Robertson says: "To know 'Faust' is one of the most elementary and obvious duties of modern culture."

Ssu-Kung-tu's short philosophical poem on Taoism may be read with interest.

Dante's "Divina Commedia" is a philosophical poem set in a framework of superstition. There is much wisdom to be gleaned from "Inferno," if you can forget the horrible images. But the most instructive part is "Purgatorio," which is a beautiful ethical poem in itself.

Milton's "Paradise Lost" is valuable only in parts.

The plays of Æschylus and Sophocles are to be read as philosophical poems. They deal with the problems of Evil and Necessity or Fate, and their conquest by Man. Milton recommends them as "teachers of moral prudence, high actions and high passions best describing."

Among the singers of freedom, equality, and justice, I may direct your attention to Æschylus's "Persæ," Euripides's plays, and the works of Langland, Victor Hugo, Shelley, Byron, Burns, Crabbe, Goldsmith, Swinburne, Whittier, Lowell, William Morris, Galsworthy, Alfieri, Freiligrath, Herwegh, Schiller, Nekrassov, Walt Whitman, and others.

For biographical and semi-biographical poems and plays, you should read Acvaghosa's "Buddha-carita," Milton's "Paradise Regained," Edwin Arnold's "Light of Asia" and "Light of the World," Valmiki's "Ramayana," Al-Busiri's "Qasidat Al-Burda," Corneille's plays, Shakespeare's "Julius Cæsar" (for Brutus, not for Cæsar), John Drinkwater's "Abraham Lincoln" and "Cromwell," Gunn's "Spinoza," Laurence Housman's "Death of Socrates," Voltaire's "Brutus," Schiller's "Wilhelm Tell," Kleist's "Die Hermannschlacht," etc.

For didactic verse, you may read Hesiod's "Works and Days," Horace's "Odes," Bhartrihari's "Niti-Cataka," Saadi's "Gulistan" and "Bustan," Jami's "Beharistan," Jelaluddin Rumi's "Mesnevi" (in parts). "Panca-tantra" and La Fontaine's "Fables" are also didactic in aim and spirit. Molière's plays are witty sermons against avarice, hypocrisy, snobbery, and other vices; he improves your character while you laugh. For the proper use of leisure, study and ponder Milton's "L'Allegro" and "Il Penseroso" again and again. For women and their problems, read Molière and Racine, Ibsen's works, especially "Doll's House" and "Rosmersholm," Bernard Shaw's "Man and Superman," Tennyson's "The Princess," Brieux's plays, etc.

For the thorny question of love, with its various aspects of freedom, jealousy, sacrifice, and bliss, you should read Kalidasa's "Sakuntala" and "Kumarasambhava," Shakespeare's "Romeo and Juliet" and "Othello," Nizami's "Laila and Majnun," Jami's "Yusuf and Zuleikha," Catullus, etc. But you need not read much on this subject. I especially recommend Kalidasa's "Kumarasambhava" for ideal love.

For heroic character, read Homer's "Odyssey," Corneille's plays, Milton's "Samson Agonistes," Bhavabhuti's "Mahavira-caritam," Ibsen's "Peer Gynt," etc.

Let good Poetry be your constant companion in life. Like your wife, she will help, cheer, guide, and inspire you at all times. She is always sweet and sincere, gentle and debonair. She bears the gifts of all the great singers in her hands and offers them to you. She is perennially fresh and bright.

> "Age cannot wither her, nor custom stale
> Her infinite variety."

Time writes no wrinkles on her beauteous brow. She sings eternally, and she sings for you and me and all of us. Listen to her strains, and be happy and wise.

> "Poetry's realm is e'er the realm of Truth
> Ope wide the sacred doors. Let there be light"
>
> (A v. Chamisso.)

CHAPTER IV

ETHICAL CULTURE

CHAPTER IV

ETHICAL CULTURE

ETHICAL Culture includes and embraces all the other branches of Self-Culture. Ethics teaches the whole duty of Man. It is the sole mistress of Life. All your thoughts and actions belong first and foremost to the domain of Ethics. Your thoughts may be ethical or un-ethical: so Ethics penetrates into the deepest recesses of your Personality. Your actions may be good or bad, and all of them are moulded and judged by Ethics. You do right or you do wrong every moment. As you stand, sit, talk, work, or even dream, you are serving Ethics or defying it. Nothing in your life can escape Ethics, which is omnipresent and omnipotent.

Ethics may be divided into two sections: (1) Personal Ethics, which deals with the individual and the Family; (2) State-Ethics, which treats of the State and its institutions. State-Ethics may be further sub-divided into Politics and Economics.

These two sections of Ethics are inseparable and interdependent, like a pair of scissors. Personal Ethics rises and falls with State-Ethics, and State-Ethics also varies with Personal Ethics. Virtuous individuals create and maintain good political and economic institutions; and good institutions produce virtuous citizens. Personal Ethics cannot flourish under evil institutions; and noble institutions cannot exist among a corrupt and degraded people. There is perpetual action and reaction between the individual and the State. The needs and activities of the individual and the World-State are essentially the same, as the atom seems to be the solar system in miniature. Perfection of personal character is possible only in the perfect State, as sound health can be maintained only in a salubrious climate. Some teachers have preached Personal Ethics, but they have not realized the importance of State-Ethics; they seem to believe that Character can be developed under all institutions alike. They insist only on personal virtue of a certain type, and do not discuss political and economic problems. The Christian, Bahai, and Buddhist Churches adopt this method. A Bahai preacher said to me, "We live peacefully under all governments." I replied: "We try to reform all governments." Experience shows that the average man and woman cannot be truthful, honest, and unselfish under a tyrannical government or a capitalist régime. Even the noblest saints and sages must commit some sins, if they live in a society based on autocracy, injustice, and inequality. No one can entirely escape the influence of the political and economic environment. The Greek and Chinese philosophers recognized the fundamental relation between Personal Ethics and State-Ethics. They attempted to discover and elucidate the Ideal both for the Individual and the State. In modern times, some thinkers have fallen into the opposite error of devoting exclusive attention to political and economic institutions and neglecting the development of Personal Ethics. They believe that good institutions automatically generate Personal Ethics, which is regarded as a by-product of State-Ethics, and not its equal and interdependent ally. They are always altering and rearranging the political garments worn by the citizen, but they do not teach hygiene for the proper care of the Man himself. They forget the great truth that Personal Ethics and State-Ethics rise and fall together. You should devote yourself to personal development and the reform of political and economic institutions at the same time, as a physician prescribes medicine for the sick man, but also orders that the room should be well heated and ventilated. Improve your Personality and the social Environment together: even a high-priced new motor-car cannot be driven well on bad, neglected, muddy roads. Politics and Economics are thus integral parts of Ethics and cannot be separated from it.

Section I.—PERSONAL ETHICS

Personal Ethics has three mansions: (1) Discipline; (2) Development; (3) Dedication. Discipline is negative, and it aims at the control of the passions, impulses, and appetites, as a gardener prunes the plants. Development is Growth, unfoldment of Body, Mind, and Soul, expansion and enrichment of Personality to the utmost extent. It is positive, as the gardener gives the plant manure, sunshine, and air. Dedication consists in the consecration of the disciplined and developed Personality to the service of Humanity and the World-State, as the tree brings forth luscious fruit in abundance. Such is the threefold task of Ethics.

Theories of Ethics

You need not trouble much about the various theories of Ethics that have been propounded by arm-chair philosophers in their barren books and tedious tomes. In Ethics, theory comes after practice, not before it. Virtue is first born spontaneously of Life in its fullness, and then the thinkers and theorists begin to enquire into the why and how and wherefore of Virtue; but they do not and cannot create it. Goethe has hinted at the futility of such post-factum speculation:

> "All theory, dear friend, is grey,
> And green, alone, life's golden tree"

In the history of the race, practice preceded theory, as men and women began to practise Virtue long before Plato, Aristotle, and Kapila commenced to reason about its origin and nature. In the individual's life, too, morality is taught in childhood and depends on good habits, which are formed long before the mature intellect can enjoy the luxury of philosophical inquiry For the progress of Ethics and the discovery of new ethical concepts, we owe very little to the purely academic thinkers. Such vital creative activity has been the miracle-sign shown only by the great prophets and sages, who have founded new Churches, Orders, and Fellowships. Thus ethical theory is only an unimportant and ancillary subject of study.

You should study the different ethical theories: the natural intuitionism of the Stoics; the theological intuitionism of the Christians; the humanistic intuitionism of Kant; the metaphysical intuitionism of Plato, Plotinus, and Cudworth; the personal hedonism of Aristippus and Max Stirner; the social hedonism of Epicurus, Helvetius, Bentham, and Mill; the altruistic energism of Aristotle and Comte; the egoistic energism of Nietzsche; the ascetic theory of Schopenhauer, the Cynics, and the Buddhists; the evolutionary doctrines of Spencer, Huxley, Bergson; the conscience theory of Butler; the moral-sense theory of Hutcheson; the politicism of Thrasymachus and Hobbes; the altruistic intuitionism of Sidgwick and Rashdall, etc., etc. But all such theories are mere speculative pastimes, as they attempt to explain why we should do what we already know to be right. No theory has created or developed Ethics. Ethics is indebted to Practice and Personality for its origin, growth, and vitality.

You will find that general and comprehensive ethical formulæ are also not very helpful. You should, of course, know of Kant's famous rule of universal ethics and Bertrand Russell's new precept: "Act so as to produce harmonious rather than discordant desires."

Epictetus devised the test of self-sufficiency: "What kind of thing do you imagine the Good to be? That which flows easily, that which is happy, that which is not impeded. . . . The wise man attempts to avoid everything that is independent of his will. . . . He who desires or covets the things which are not in his power can be neither faithful nor free." The Stoics appealed often to Nature, and Diogenes Laertius says: "Zeno said that the chief Good was confessedly to live according to Nature, which is to live according to Virtue, for Nature leads us to this point." Aristotle taught that "Virtue is a mean state between two vices, one in excess, the other in defect." The "Golden Rules," positive and negative, of Christianity, Confucianism, Hinduism, and the Mahayana are also such portable pellets of ethical theory. But you cannot learn much about practical morality from such slogans: "Do unto others what you wish that others should do unto you"; "Don't do unto others what you don't wish that others should do unto you"; "Do unto others what you would wish to do unto yourself," etc. Bentham and the Utilitarians invented the formula: "The greatest happiness of the greatest number." Herbert Spencer wrote: "Ethics has for its subject-matter the most highly-evolved conduct as displayed by the most highly-evolved being, Man." Comte said: "Live for others; live openly." All such succinct generalizations are interesting as intellectual pastimes, but they cannot guide you in your daily life. You need Nature's food and drink to live, not such concentrated pills and potions prepared in the laboratories of philosophy.

The Summum Bonum

What is the highest Good, the Summum Bonum? You should reject all theological and metaphysical doctrines of the Summum Bonum. The end of man's life is not "to do the will of God," or to "imitate God," or to "seek union with God," or "to enjoy God," as the theologians tell us with dogmatic assurance. It is as impossible for a man to imitate "God" as it is for him to imitate a comet or a crocodile. Man cannot also obey "God," as the commands of "God" are not known and cannot be known. Dante wrote: "In His will is our peace." John Gerson, the medieval philosopher, said: "God does not require actions because they are good; but they are good because he requires them, just as others are evil because he forbids them." This is pure theology in its absolute form. This slavish ideal is unworthy of free men and women. "Islam" means "submission" to the will of God. But why should Man submit to another being? And how can the will of God be ascertained? The Persian and other mystics teach that union with God is the highest goal. Nasafi says: "O Dervish! dost thou think that thy existence is independent of God? This is a great error." "Love of God" is regarded as the best means of achieving this much-coveted union. Jelaluddin Rumi sings sweetly, but alas! falsely thus:

> "O thou pleasant madness, Love!
> Thou Physician of all our ills!
> Thou healer of Pride,
> Thou Plato and Galen of our souls"

Remember that all theories of the Summum Bonum, that are derived from the conception of "God," are like the quicksands on the seashore in which the unwary wayfarers sink and perish. They consist of mere words, words, words, all empty and glittering like so many soap-bubbles that delight little children. Whenever you hear that meaningless term "God" mentioned in any discourse on Ethics, you may be certain that the speaker will treat you to a lot of nonsense and balderdash.

The metaphysical doctrine of the Summum Bonum has been developed chiefly by the Hindus, the Christian mystics, and the Platonists, who postulate a fundamental Dualism in human personality. The body and the mind are regarded as perishable, while the "Spirit" is supposed to be immutable and immortal. We are taught to suppress the body and the mind, and to develop and unfold the "Spirit." The body is reviled and condemned as the "prison-house of the soul." The ideal is supposed to be the final liberation of Spirit from Matter, which causes evil and suffering. Plato says in the "Phaedo": "Surely the soul then reasons best, when none of these things disturb it, neither hearing, nor sight, nor pain, nor pleasure of any kind, but it retires as much as possible within itself, taking leave of the body, and, as far as it can, not communicating with or being in contact with it, it aims at the discovery of that which is." This "spiritual" ideal mangles and mutilates human personality in a horrible manner, as the unfortunate criminals were formerly hanged, drawn, and quartered. The Body, which is the basis of Personality, is despised; the Mind, which is the light of Personality, is ignored, Society, which is the cradle of Personality, is neglected; while the imaginary "Spirit" is considered to be the real essence of Man. The highest duty, therefore, consists in abnormal asceticism, quietism, meditation, and isolation from society. The Buddhists too, while denying the reality of "the soul," aim at the same goal, as they long for "nirvana," which may be attained through monastic celibacy and meditation without physical or intellectual development. The perfect man should eat and drink very little, and must fast often; he must not marry and beget children; he must not devote himself to science, education, or art; he need not render social service or engage in political activities. Such mischievous teachers really destroy all the elements of human Personality, like the fool who should chew the shell without the nutritious nut-kernel in it. As a consequence, ignorant and sickly "saints" have been adored as "perfect men," if only they could become sufficiently lean and haggard through malnutrition and maintain physical chastity throughout life! Such are the Indian Yogis, the Sufi dervishes, the Christian mystics, and all who believe in fundamental opposition between "soul" and "body." This metaphysical Summum Bonum also produces those lunatics of Religion, the self-torturing fakirs and monks, who macerate and torment the body for the good of the soul, sometimes even mutilating it like Origen and the Russian fanatics. True Social-Ethics is sacrificed to a morbid orgy of celibacy and underfeeding. Tragi-comic caricatures of Personality are admired as "holy men." Such "holiness" is really hollowness and nothing more. Stunted, stupid, selfish, sterile simulacra of Humanity stalk up and down the world as revered "spiritual" leaders. They know nothing; they do nothing; they undermine their own health; they are as ignorant of economics and politics as an illiterate farm-labourer; they are not interested in science and art; they strive to attain the absolute zero of Life, where cold and death reign. The folly and futility of this disastrous doctrine are exhibited in the pathetic tragedy of the wasted lives of such ascetics as Simeon Stylites, the raving maniacs of the Thebaïd, the immured Buddhist monks of Tibet who never leave their dark caves and cells, the Hindu fakirs who make long pilgrimages by measuring their length along the ground, the Trappists who never speak, the nuns who never go out of their convents, etc. These are the earnest men and women condemned to slow suicide by "spiritual" Metaphysics.

The Summum Bonum has also been described as "salvation in heaven after Death," "eternal bliss in Paradise," "rebirth in Amitabha's realm of Sukhavati," etc. This mirage of "Paradise" in the Sahara of theology has led many a pious caravan of truth-seekers to death and disaster. Christianity, Islam, and some Buddhist sects specialize in such tempting offers and promises. Virtuous conduct is regarded as the price paid in advance for the pleasures, blessings, and felicities of "Paradise," "Valhalla," "Elysium," "svarga," "jannat," as you book a seat at the theatre. This essentially vulgar and hedonistic doctrine teaches ordinary men and women to expect material rewards for Virtue, and thus makes them even more selfish and sensual than before. It puts a premium on calculating egotism and mercenary morality of the lowest type. It also hinders and hampers social progress by shifting the centre of gravity of Ethics from "Here" to "Hereafter." This life and this world are endured and belittled as a "vale of tears," "a sojourn in exile," "a passing pilgrimage," while "Heaven" is spoken of as the true "home" and "refuge." W. Wilberforce, the pious Christian philanthropist, wrote to his sister: "One should endeavour to . . . establish a practical feeling of the vanity and transitoriness of all human things, and of this life being but a passage, and our home that rest that remaineth for the people of God." He also wrote in a letter to Hannah More: "To my poor wife, death would be a translation from a world of sin and sorrow to a region of perfect holiness and never-ending happiness." This pathetic delusion has been thus versified by Bowring:—

> "There is a land where everlasting suns
> Shed everlasting brightness. . . .
> Oh! how blest
> To look from this dark prison to that shrine,
> To inhale one breath of Paradise divine."

Such "other-worldliness" induces the people and their leaders to neglect sanitation, economics, education, and democratic government, while they try to secure their "salvation" in the mythical abode promised for all time. The hungry poor are thus invited to the Barmecidal banquet of theology, and they make no determined efforts to improve their condition here on earth. The Philippine Islands were under the complete control of the Franciscan friars during several centuries, but they paid no attention to hygiene and public instruction, as these things were not "necessary for salvation." St. Francis taught his friars that they should not learn to read and write, as knowledge would be of no use in Heaven. Brother Lucido, one of his disciples, is described in the Franciscan chronicles as "unwilling to stay in one place for a month"; "when it pleased him to stay in any place, he would straightway withdraw from it and would say, 'Here we have no place of dwelling, but in heaven.'" This universal hallucination of "Heaven" has made true morality and continual progress quite impossible. Science must teach these deluded ignoramuses that the biggest telescope has not discovered "Paradise" anywhere in the universe; and they would not like the idea of living in the hot stars and nebulæ after death, even if they believe in survival. Astronomy must slowly undermine the current conception of "Heaven," and thus usher in the first beginnings of Ethics. While this superstition clouds the mind, Virtue cannot be truly appreciated, as the electric lamps in the street cannot be seen in a thick fog. Modern man must cease to dream of this "Heaven."

Ponder the Japanese poet Omi Okura's wise precept:

> "The ways of shining Heaven are far;
> Turn thee! ah! turn to things yet near;
> Turn to thy earthly home, O friend!
> And try to do thy duty here"

Scientific Ethics is entirely different from theological and metaphysical Ethics in its scope and purpose. It does not define the Summum Bonum in terms of "God," "Spirit," "salvation," "nirvana," or "mukti." It is related to this life on this earth as lived by Mankind in the environment produced by Nature. Its ideal is *the complete and harmonious development of human Personality in all its four aspects—physical, intellectual, æsthetic, and ethical.* "The Perfect Man in the Perfect State": "Full Growth, free Activity, and Happiness"; "Truth, Goodness, Beauty, and Health": such are its precious formulæ.

Methods of Ethical Culture

You will discover that several methods of moral training are practised by the earnest people around you.

Some practical teachers will advise you to hang on to a fixed doctrine and a certain unique Personality for your guidance, if you wish to cultivate Virtue. Thus most Christians believe that monotheism and the "imitation of Christ" are necessary and sufficient for the highest moral life. The Moslems likewise insist on theism, but follow Muhammad as the great exemplar. The Buddhists have also fallen into this groove: they may couple their theory of "anatta" and "karma" with the acceptance of Gautama Buddha's conduct as the very "mirror of perfection." In ancient Greece and Rome, Diogenes and Socrates were held up to the admiration of all aspirants. In the same way, other sects and communities have based practical Ethics on some theoretical doctrine and the life-story of some one Prophet or Philosopher of the past. This popular method is very deceptive, though it is good as far as it goes. It has yielded some satisfactory results, but it should not be adopted in future. It is a wrong assumption that practical Ethics depends on one dogma or doctrine, without which it cannot flourish at all. Many pious Christians, Moslems, and Bahais believe that Virtue is impossible without belief in "God." Bossuet wrote: "A man who does not love God cannot love his neighbour." A young friend said to me: "I don't trust people who do not believe in God." Kant declared that theism was a postulate of practical morality. Voltaire also thought that a servant who did not believe in God would cut his master's throat. The Hindus and the Buddhists do not attach much importance to theism, but may perhaps link Ethics indissolubly to the theory of rebirth and "karma." Montalembert claims that the self-sacrifice of St. Benedict and his disciples demonstrates the truth of the dogmas of Catholicism, which gave birth to their virtues. Now it is a dangerous fallacy to suppose that Virtue is the humble handmaiden of any speculative theory about the origin of the universe and the future life. Virtue is thus painted as an old cripple supported by the crutches of Theology, Metaphysics, or Science. But this view is entirely and utterly absurd. Great men and women have been polytheists, monotheists, pantheists, and atheists; they have held conflicting opinions about man's destiny after death. Noble character was the only thing they had in common, as different flowers of many hues have sweet perfume as their common gift. No Church or sect has a monopoly of Virtue. I was much amused, when my landlady in Boston said to me one day: "Judging by your ways and habits, I thought you were a Christian; but you say you are not." Poor soul, she had been brought up to believe that a "heathen" could never be a "kind and quiet gentleman," as she described me. History shows that supreme Virtue has often ennobled and sanctified the hearts of many saints, whose minds were darkened with the densest mists of superstition on account of their ignorance of Natural Science. The head and the heart do not always seem to stand on the same plane of development. Socrates believed in sacrificing a cock to Æsculapius; St. Paul condemned polytheism and swore by one "God"; Buddha did not deny the existence of many gods; St. Francis accepted the doctrine of transubstantiation, while Calvin vehemently denounced it; Robert Owen, Comte, and Herbert Spencer were not theists at all. But all these leaders were among the élite of Ethics. If you live for a year among a heterogeneous population like that of Bombay, Constantinople, or London, you learn soon enough that honest folk and dishonest scoundrels are to be found in all the churches, congregations, and communities, which differ so widely among themselves in point of dogma and doctrine Experience proves that Virtue does not depend on any particular religious or philosophical doctrine for its vitality and vigour. It is as foolish to regard Virtue as the slave or progeny of Doctrine as it would be to suppose that the beneficent water of the Ganges is produced by the stony Himalayan rocks from which it issues and whose sediment sullies its purity. Ethics has gained nothing and lost much by this *mésalliance* with Doctrine, which has been forced upon it by the purblind priests and philosophers Virtue has its source in Society and is fed by the Emotions and the Will; Doctrine of all varieties originates in the Intellect and attempts to interpret the Universe. Right Doctrine is precious, but practical Ethics is not derived from it by any process of reasoning. They may be compared to the two legs of a biped: both belong to the same body and share in its life, but one leg is not produced by the other and does not branch off from it. Virtue is independent of both Theism and Atheism. It is its own -ism. Ethics is not a planet shining by the reflected light of Doctrine; it is like the sun, self-luminous and world-illuminating.

The second precept of the ordinary moralists is also unsatisfactory. They advise us to imitate one great person in every particular, Jesus Christ or Muhammad or Gautama Buddha or Confucius. Ignatius Loyola follows the career of Jesus step by step and inch by inch in his "Spiritual Exercises," as a faithful dog follows its master. This method is also adopted in the "Retreats" of the Christian sects. The Moslems have collected Muhammad's reputed sayings as "Hadis," which is accepted as authoritative. Such loyal concentration on one example of Virtue certainly helps the neophyte in his moral evolution. The mind and the soul can easily reproduce the ideal pattern inwardly in thoughts and feelings, and externally in deeds, if the attention is firmly fixed on one sole object of devotion, as the painter paints and the sculptor chisels from one woman-model. The doctrines of Incarnation, of Prophethood, and of perfect Buddhahood also tend to the exaltation of the Founder of the Church as a unique and faultless Personality, who attained the highest possible Perfection, the very stratosphere of ethical upward ascent. The Jainas even believe that their prophet Mahavira was omniscient! Thomas à Kempis says: "Let our chief task be to meditate on the life of our Saviour Jesus Christ." Dr. Mgr. Albert Farges writes: "What more glorious calling for man is there than to imitate God? . . . We have before us the example of a man mortal like ourselves and yet God; the example is God made man, a model of absolute perfection."

This practice of imitating one Teacher and no other may be described as "henolatry" (the worship of One). It simplifies and facilitates the arduous task of self-improvement; but alas! it also leads men astray. No man or woman has lived a complete and perfect life, which should be copied in all its details. To err is human. No Teacher has been flawless and sinless. Jesus Christ was somewhat vain, irritable, inconsistent, and irresolute: he whipped the money-changers out of the Temple, but he could not whip avarice out of their souls. Both Christ and Buddha preached as single celibates; but celibacy is a mark of imperfection, for such unburdened guides cannot set an example for normal married persons to follow. Celibacy also shows that Personality has not been developed fully and harmoniously, for a celibate prophet is not born a eunuch. Christ, Buddha, Mahavira, and Socrates did not cultivate Science and attached no importance to Nature-study. Christ and Buddha lacked the political wisdom of Confucius and Aristotle, and their precepts are intended only for the personal life. They did not understand that Virtue could not thrive under political tyranny. Thus it can be demonstrated that no one Teacher has done all that a perfect man should do. All prophets have made mistakes, committed sins, neglected important duties, and thus failed to attain Perfection. Their lives have been only parts of the great whole, which is the Ideal. Learn from each Teacher, but don't be enslaved by any. As Corneille said: "O Moses, be silent! And thou Truth, eternal and immutable Truth, speak to me." You may also appeal from the partial lives of the great men to the Ideal, in which alone Perfection is found.

This henolatry is a great curse. It often bars the way to further progress. The devout Christian not only tries to do what Jesus did, but also thinks that it is unnecessary and even impious to attempt other things that the Master omitted to do. This negative imitation is fatal to the evolution of Ethics. Teetotallers and vegetarians are often confronted with the argument that Jesus Christ drank wine and ate meat, as if Christ had exhausted all the possibilities and potentialities of Ethics for all time to come. The Christian monks did not study Science, because Christ never learned mathematics like Plato or dissected animals like Aristotle. The pious Moslem does not purchase a picture or a statue, because Prophet Muhammad proscribed Art thirteen hundred years ago. The Buddhist continues to worship the old gods, because Buddha declared that they existed. Divorce Reform is opposed, because Christ uttered some words long ago. Polygamy is regarded as lawful, because Muhammad sanctioned it; it is not a sin to marry four wives, but it is wicked and immoral to marry five! And so on. The doctrine of the infallibility of some one Teacher of the past has led to the lop-sided development of many earnest souls, as they could never dream of looking over the walls of the traditional enclosure, within which they were penned. It is considered blasphemous to suggest that all the Prophets were only wise men, with some human weaknesses and defects. Their wisdom was lofty and sublime, but it was also limited and circumscribed by their environment, as an Alpine lake must reflect both the high heavens and the mountains that surround it. No Teacher has taught the absolute and immutable Wisdom that would last for ever: there is no such Wisdom. The Wisdom of to-day will be the folly of to-morrow. Both Virtue and Wisdom are without end or limit in time. There is a bottom to the Pacific Ocean and there may even be Einsteinian finitude in space: but the Ideal of Personality partakes of mathematical Infinity, which can be approached in an increasing degree, but can *never* be reached. Such is its very nature and essence.. An Ideal that can be realized is a contradiction in terms. When it is attained, it is the Ideal no more. It has then been converted into the Actual, and the Ideal is still far away, beckoning us on and on and on. It is blasphemy against the Holy Spirit of Humanity to assert that any man or woman has attained the Ideal. Don't thus reduce the Ideal to a cold corpse, wrapped and embalmed in the shroud of biography and actuality. The Ideal must not be thus turned into the Egyptian mummy of Ethics. The excesses and exaggerations of "henolatry" must be condemned and discarded, otherwise Ethics will be always looking behind at the beacons and lighthouses of the past, and wreck its bark on the rocks and reefs that lie ahead of us.

It is also clear that even the best and wisest Teacher can never set an example of all the virtues, as he cannot get the opportunity to exhibit all of them in his short life. Jesus, Socrates, Mani, and the Bab teach us the courage that can face martyrdom, but how could Buddha possibly give us such a lesson? He preached among a tolerant people and was not arrested and prosecuted. He was also never in a position to display the dignity and fortitude of Jesus Christ during the trial before Pilate. Christ could not prove that his love for mankind was stronger than his affection for wife and child, as he never had a family; but Buddha could pass that severe test. From Buddha you can learn how to leave your wife, but Socrates teaches you how to live with her. Socrates could practise the civic virtues in the republic of Athens; but Christ and the Bab had no such rights of citizenship. St Francis had to recognize the authority of a murderous and predatory Church. Thus even if a Teacher possesses the latent capacity for many different virtues, he can never practise and develop all of them, as all the circumstances are often beyond his control. Hence it is absurd to ascribe absolute Perfection to any man or woman, dead or living. Even the sun has his spots.

I must reject the traditional method of moral culture, which consists in administering to you a daily dose of a mixture of one dogma and one biography. I admit that Biography is indispensable for ethical training, but I regard all dogma, theological or rationalist, as irrelevant in this connexion. I propose the following course of preparation.

(1) Character is developed in a social *milieu*. You must be in living contact with other men and women if you wish to learn Virtue. You must belong to a society or sect that aims at the realisation of your Ideal. That society will be your "Church." As an isolated individual struggling by yourself, you cannot make much progress. Join a group or band, as the Arabs travel in caravans in the desert. In modern times, Auguste Comte, F. Adler, and K.

Marx have attempted to establish such societies of like-minded earnest men and women.

(2) Character is influenced by the example of a living teacher even more than by the historical record of a dead prophet. Life begets life, in the moral as well as in the biological realm. Virtue can be passed from man to man. Moral growth is a process of suggestion and adaptation, and not of ratiocination. If you can find a good guide, you are fortunate, as Plato and Antisthenes found Socrates and Pierre Laffitte found Auguste Comte. The Persian mystics follow a teacher ("pir"), and the Hindus are taught to obey a "guru" (instructor). The Catholics exact the vow of absolute obedience from all novices and monks. You should make the acquaintance of the different religious leaders, who preach and work in your town. Attach yourself to the one who is most virtuous in his daily life. He should be noted for simplicity, gentleness, temperance, patience, and active benevolence. A simple test will also suffice. Observe if there is one among them who does not belittle or slander the other rival teachers. If you find such a humble and generous soul, keep in close touch with him, and you will soon grow in all the virtues. Your attitude towards the self-selected teacher should be one of mingled deference and independence. Before beginning to exercise your judgment, you should for some time follow and obey your teacher in all matters, as an aeroplane runs along the ground for a short distance before rising into the air. This brief phase of unquestioning obedience must be passed through, as it responds to certain needs of the human soul. But don't be permanently slavish and uncritical, as the disciples are taught to be in certain sects. The Persian poet Hafiz inculcated such servility, when he wrote: "Stain thou even thy prayer-carpet with wine if the old man commands thee." Be you willing to learn, but not to obey. Aristotle was Plato's reverent pupil, but not his unthinking gramophone. Such should be the relation between you and your elderly guide, who can enlighten and inspire you in the early stages of ethical self-culture, as the parent-birds feed their young. Temporary discipleship is the prelude to high moral achievement. There are few wholly self-made "autodidacts" in the ethical world. But beware of excessive deference, which may end in spiritual harakiri for the honour of the poor teacher. Remember Aristotle's great saying: "Plato and Truth are both dear to us; but it is a sacred duty to prefer Truth."

(3) The living guide is only the last link in the chain of the virtuous men and women who connect you with the great prophets

of the past. He learned Virtue from his teacher, who surely sat at the feet of his Mentor, and so on through the generations. You will thus be introduced to the great men and women, whose names shine even like Sirius and Canopus in the dark firmament of History. The best way to absorb and assimilate their Virtue is to read of their lives and deeds in connection with the social and political Movements that they really represented. This is the genuine ethical doctrine of transubstantiation: let us eat and drink of the immortal personalities of all the ethical heroes and heroines of the world. The method of interpreting their actions and words as those of isolated holy individuals is unsound and misleading. Ethics must be studied historically and socially, as its significance is essentially social and historical. You aim at creating for your own soul a permanent pure atmosphere of Virtue, rich in the ozone of earnestness and aspiration. You should not try merely to imitate this or that action of some prophet or philosopher: that would be a quack's remedy for moral weakness. Endeavour to create an ethical inner environment for yourself, in which you will gain and maintain moral health and vigour as surely as the sturdy hill-folk thrive in the bracing air of Zermatt and Ladakh. The examples of the dead sages are to be used for the development of your free Personality, not for the mechanical reproduction of certain actions done in the dead and distant past. "Assimilation, and not Imitation": this should be your guiding principle.

No one Movement in history can give you all that you need. As your body is fed and clothed with foodstuffs and cloth bought from different countries, so your soul must draw its sustenance and cover its nakedness with material gathered from various sources. You should make a special study of the following eight Movements:

Confucianism, from Confucius to Chu-hsi. (Sixty-second century A.H.; also called Chu-Fu-Tzu.) In this movement you will learn from Confucius, Mencius (forty-seventh and forty-eighth centuries A.H.), Han Wên-Kung (fifty-eighth century A.H.), Fu I, Chen Tzu-ang, and other great thinkers, who were practically rationalists in belief and sages in conduct. Professor H. A. Giles says of Chu-Fu-Tzu: "Under the hand of Chu-Fu-Tzu, the idea of a personal God, the supreme ruler of the Universe, disappeared for ever." From the Chinese philosophers, you will learn that man is good by nature, that virtue is social in its scope and aim, that economic and political reform is essential for moral progress, and that education and music are indispensable for the higher life.

Buddhism, from Buddha to Asoka (forty-eighth century A.H.).

The early Buddhist and Jaina movements will teach you the necessity of combating priestcraft and sacerdotalism, the futility of prayer and worship addressed to one or many deities, the importance of conquering hatred, sensuality, and ignorance, and cultivating charity, universal compassion, sweet speech, religious toleration, social equality, and abstinence from intoxicating beverages and flesh diet. Meditation will also reveal its marvels and mysteries to you. You will feel the ethical influence of such mighty personalities as Gautama Buddha, Mahavira, and Asoka. A European friend said to me after reading the "Gospel of Buddha": "I give more in charity now than I used to do."

Greek Philosophy, from Thales to Plotinus.

This movement is in some respects the most glorious and fruitful in the history of Ethics. You will learn the value and necessity of rational thought and discussion, all-round personal development, civic freedom, sound ethical theory, economic reform, physical and æsthetic culture, scientific research, temperance, self-control, and optimism. Greek Philosophy presents a vast and fascinating gallery of different representatives of pre-eminent Virtue and Wisdom. Diogenes Laertius has written short biographical sketches of about eighty leaders belonging to more than ten schools of thought. This movement has also bequeathed to us such classical treatises as Aristotle's "Nicomachean Ethics," Plato's "Republic," Marcus Aurelius's "Thoughts," Lucretius's poem, Cicero's "de Officiis," and Boethius's "Consolation of Philosophy." No other movement has produced so many wonderful men and masterpieces. Greek Philosophy is the real precursor of modern Rationalism. Give your days and nights to it, until you are thoroughly familiar with it. You may devote special attention to the Peripatetic and Stoic schools, as they are more important than the others. Aristotelianism may be said to be the "Old Testament" of the gospel of modern Rationalism.

Early Christianity (until 5325 A.H.).

Early Christianity was partly a progressive movement, based on the ideals of cosmopolitanism, compassion, purity, simplicity, anti-militarism, and anti-imperialism. The political aims of the Church are clearly adumbrated in the Book of Revelation, which contains violent propaganda against the intolerable Roman tyranny of that epoch. These three centuries will introduce you to such great personalities as Jesus, St. Paul, St. James, St. John, Polycarp, Ignatius, Irenæus, Justin, Montanus, Marcion, Origen, Clement, and others. They will also suggest to you many fruitful ideas that may be applied in your work at present.

The Order of St. Benedict.

The only other instructive and progressive epoch in the history of Christianity is the early medieval period, during which the Benedictines converted the Teutonic nations to Christianity. In this way, these peoples were first initiated into Hellenic and Roman culture. The heroic figures of St. Benedict, Augustine, Boniface, Anskar, and others stand out clear and bright against the background of violence and ignorance.

After the sixty-third century A.H. (thirteenth A.D.), the Church began to be a reactionary force.

The Arab Philosophers and the Sufi Saints.

The union of Islam and Hellenic philosophy gave birth to the great Renaissance movement in Islam, which began with Al-Kindi. The philosophers, Al-Farabi, Ibn-Sina, Ibn-Tufail, Ibn-Rashd, and the saints like Rabia and Shams-i-Tabriz were partly Moslems and partly Hellenists. This tradition is still living in Islamic countries, and it has produced many noble and beautiful characters.

The Sikh Movement in India (sixty-sixth to sixty-ninth century).

This religious movement aimed at a complete social and political reorganization of society after the overthrow of the Mogul tyranny. It produced leaders who were distinguished both in ethics and politics. It is also aglow with the passion for sacrifice and martyrdom. You will learn from Nanak, Arjuna, Teg Bahadur, Govind Singh, Banda, and others.

Modern Democracy, Socialism, and Rationalism.

You should study the lives and achievements of the pioneers of the Italian Renaissance, Petrarch, Guarino, Vittorino, Niccoli, Aurispa, Filelfo, and Ficino, and also Erasmus, More, and other northern scholars. The deeds of the martyrs Vanini, Etienne Dolet, and Giordano Bruno should be reverently pondered. The Protestant Anabaptists and the voluntary communists of America will interest and inspire you. Modern Philosophy and Science have given us such true sages as Spinoza, Spencer, Comte, Cavendish, and others. Modern civilization has not yet produced any great synthetic ethical systems for our guidance, like the Hellenic Schools of Philosophy. Comte is the only modern philosopher who has attempted the difficult task. Other thinkers have only written books; they have not established new fellowships for the practical philosophy of Rationalism. The different elements of modern Ethics are thus found in various unrelated and unco-ordinated movements; you must get them all where they are to be found. The pioneers of the French Revolution, and of Democracy and Socialism, have written a new epic, which you should often read and enjoy with keen wonder and admiration. Such characters as Marat, Buonarroti, Mazzini, Fourier, Owen, Jones, Considerant, Blanqui, Louise Michel, Karl Marx, Bakunin, Kropotkin, and others will cure you of your cowardice, selfishness, and worldliness. I may especially recommend the biographies of Karl Marx, Peter Kropotkin, and Louise Michel, who combined personal greatness with political wisdom in an unusual degree.

If you assimilate the spirit and temper of the leaders of these eight Movements, you will be able to create the right ethical atmosphere for your own growth and happiness. It is a good plan to buy portraits of the great men and women, and hang them on the walls of your room, with short maxims from their writings. Thus you will ever live in the delicious aroma of the highest Ethics.

(4) *Friendship.* Virtue is a social product. You should join a society or fellowship of like-minded persons. But, within that society, you should have your little group of friends; and within that group, you should have your two or three dearest and closest friends. Friendship is useful for ordinary purposes like social intercourse, conversation, mutual aid in trouble, walks, dinners, etc. But the highest use of Friendship lies in mutual encouragement and inspiration for the development of Personality. A true friend advises and helps you to make the best of your life. He knows your merits and your weaknesses, your talent and your capacity, your habits and your opportunities. He rejoices in your success, and tells you to achieve more. He warns you lovingly of your besetting sins (we all have them). The old custom of priestly confession should be replaced by a system of voluntarily accepted Censorship, exercised by one's best friends. You should ask two friends, a man and a woman, to act as your Mentors and Monitors during a certain period. They must then discharge the duty of criticizing you privately on a certain day of the month for your conduct; and they must also report to you what they have heard

from others. At present, there is no safe method of complaining to a person of his or her anti-social actions and words. Everyone blames him or her, and mean censorious gossip flourishes. But no one is any the better for it. If you announce that you have appointed such-and-such persons as your Monitors for the year, and that all complaints against you should be addressed to them, then the polite people, who would never dream of talking to you of your faults, would gladly convey their criticism to you indirectly through your two Monitors. Their names need not always be disclosed to you. Just criticism will help you, and unjust slander will be silenced, for you will always be informed of what other persons are saying about you. You can privately explain or defend your conduct or apologize for it, as the case may be. At present, every one of us does something wrong or improper, but no one rebukes or warns us. There is a conspiracy of politeness to conceal your defects from you: but everyone speaks of them in your absence! Through the institution of social Monitors, who are chosen by each individual, social criticism can be directed into the proper channel for the purpose of personal improvement. You cannot see many of your own faults, as a person cannot see a wart on his forehead except in a mirror. The friendly Monitors are to serve as your ethical mirrors. The man will notice some shortcomings and the woman will observe others. Men will complain about you to the male Monitor and the women to the female Monitor: but this need not be a fixed rule. Thus you will be able to see yourself as others see you. This method will nip your faults in the bud, remove misunderstandings, prevent the spread of slander and calumny, and maintain social harmony almost automatically. The systems of public confession and criticism, which have been adopted by the Oneida Perfectionists, the Buchmanites, and the Buddhists are crude and theatrical devices; this Monitor system will work smoothly, silently, naturally, and effectively. Thus can Friendship be the handmaid of Ethics.

(5) *Meditation.* Daily Meditation is as essential for moral health as the daily cold wash is for physical efficiency. The Monotheists resort to "prayers," those "litanies of flattery and fear, ascending day by day like wasted smoke," as Edwin Arnold has fitly described them. We do not pray: we meditate. Meditation should be practised every morning and evening (at bedtime). More time should be devoted to it in the morning than in the evening. In the morning, you should begin it on an empty stomach before breakfast. Attend to your soul before your stomach. The mind is more receptive of noble ideas and suggestions when there is no food in

the stomach. After a meal, the energy of the body is taken up with the process of digestion. A full stomach makes an empty head.

Meditate on the following themes:

(*a*) The Fourfold Ideal of Self-Culture: physical, intellectual, æsthetic, and ethical. Think how you can realize it more and more.

(*b*) The Four Principles of political and economic organization: Democracy, Liberty, Equality, and Fraternity. Think how you can work for their triumph more and more.

(*c*) The eight great movements mentioned above, and the virtues of the great men and women associated with them.

(*d*) All who are afflicted with poverty, sickness, bereavement, unemployment, imprisonment, exile, and oppression at this moment. Send them your thoughts of love and sympathy, and wish earnestly for their relief and release from suffering.

(*e*) All who are rejoicing at this moment:—the wives who have become mothers, the betrothed, the wedded couples, the youths starting on a career, the farmers reaping the harvest, the friends gathered at a feast. Send them your thoughts of love, and rejoice in their happiness.

(*f*) The Unity of Mankind. You should have a globe in your room, and also portraits of your friends belonging to different races and nations. The daily contemplation of the globe will help you to cultivate the cosmopolitan ideal.

(*g*) Some great precepts and maxims culled from the scriptures of all religions and the poets of all countries. Such precepts may be printed or written in large type on a card and repeated slowly. You can make your own selection. Some noble ideas are embodied in the following sayings:

Socrates: "An unexamined life is not worth living."

Aristotle: "Not merely to live, but to live well."

Buddha: "Hatred ceases by Love."

Christ: "By this shall men know that ye are my disciples, that ye love one another."

St. Paul: "Love never faileth."

Goethe:

> "Sich vom halben zu entwöhnen
> Und im ganzen, guten, schönen, resolut zu leben."

(Give up the habit of living a half-life: live a complete, virtuous, and beautiful life.)

Goethe: "Nun der verdient sich Freiheit, wie das Leben, der täglich sie erobern muss." (Only he deserves Freedom and Life, who must conquer them every day.)

Shakespeare : "To thine own self be true."

Rousseau : "Man is born free and is everywhere in chains."

Marx : "Workingmen of the World, Unite."

"The knell of capitalist property sounds. The expropriators are expropriated."

Mazzini : "Sacrifice is never fruitless."

Muhammad : "Be thou patient with becoming patience."

Confucius : "At fifteen years of age, my mind was bent on learning; at thirty, I stood firm; at forty, I had no doubts."

The Virtues and Vices

The two chief Virtues are Earnestness and Unselfishness (or Sociability). All the other virtues are comprised in these two, as all the spokes are in the two wheels of a bicycle.

I. *Earnestness.*

Earnestness consists in choosing Development instead of Pleasure as the principal aim of Life. These are the two lights that beckon to all young men and women, leading their footsteps in different directions. Pleasure allures them with a fair but false light that casts a glamour over all things; but at the end of that path are Ennui, Disease, Ignorance, Frivolity, and stunted Personality.

They who choose Pleasure spend too much time and energy on gossip, indoor games, whist, bridge, novel-reading, inferior cinemas and tobacco, flirtations and sex-stimulation, eating and drinking, indolence and irregular habits, dandyism and debauchery. They are disinclined to exert themselves strenuously in any way except for the necessary task of earning their livelihood. They hate serious exertion and application, physical or mental. They try to live for the moment, catching the froth and foam on the surface of Life, because they are too lazy and indifferent to dive deep in search of the pearls and hidden treasure. They wish also to experience as many pleasant sensations and "thrills" as they can manage to get. They make everything easy and smooth for themselves; "taking trouble" and "working hard" are frightful bugbears for them. They wish to be either tickled and titillated in the senses and nerves all the time, or they prefer to do nothing. The latter class (according to the Ceylonese proverb) would rather sit than stand, rather stand than walk, and rather walk than run. A young man used to say during a walk: "Let us have only *soft* conversation." He meant that he preferred light gossip and chatter to useful conversation on science, politics, or religion. Another friend looked at my bookshelves and said, "You haven't got many novels." I replied, "No, but there are other books." He liked only novels, as he sought Pleasure and disliked mental exertion. Effort, assiduity, concentration—all these are anathema to the man or woman who is wedded to Pleasure. Effort darkens the sky for them and robs life of all joy and zest. Time is for them something to be "killed" as painlessly as possible. They believe they "enjoy themselves" immensely, while they are only making fools of themselves. They may be compared to the children, who play with pretty toys and coloured pebbles; but an adult with an infantile mind is a pitiable spectacle indeed. If you choose Pleasure, you may have much fun and frolic, but you will remain a dwarf in mind and soul. And whose lot is sadder than a dwarf's?

The Development of Personality is the aim of the earnest men and women, not mere momentary Pleasure. Growth is the universal law of Nature. The acorn fulfils its destiny in the oak; the tiny egg finds its unfoldment in the beautiful bird of paradise or the majestic eagle; and the new-born babe grows up to be a complete Man or Woman. As Aristotle has taught us, each living being must be measured by the highest possible development of that type and species. That is why we pity the dwarf, though his food and clothes cost him less than if his body were fully developed. But he is not a complete Man. Development gives us deep joy and fills our hearts with pride, as we watch the process in the lives of our children. But we forget that we must not stop growing when we attain the age of puberty. Growth must be continued throughout life, as we breathe and eat. Arrested development is the penalty of all those who do not cultivate Earnestness. They do not enjoy all the flashing facets of Life: they are content with only a few of them. They do not know what they miss, as a man born blind cannot measure his loss. If they neglect the development of the Body, they lose all the joys of sound health, good digestion, outdoor sport, and dreamless sleep. They cannot greet each new morning with a boisterous and hilarious "Welcome!" If they are remiss in mental and æsthetic culture, they deprive themselves of science, literature, and art. They cannot travel far from the zoological origin and starting-point of the race, as high mental and æsthetic culture is the special privilege of Man as distinguished from the animals. Man may be a biped, but he is to be defined as a living being endowed with well-developed Reason and Emotion. Science and Art in all their forms and ramifications elevate *Homo sapiens* above the anthropoid ape. If you are lacking in Earnestness, you are more of an ape than a Man. If you sacrifice moral development for transient Pleasure, you will never feel the happiness and exaltation that are the gifts of love, altruism, self-discipline, and aspiration. Thus deficient Development is its own grievous punishment, as a dwarf or deaf person must suffer from the lack of the complete equipment of human Personality. Growth,—unceasing and uninterrupted Growth,—all-round harmonious Growth,—lifelong, perpetual Growth,—Growth that ends only with death (and perhaps not even then?),—such steady natural normal Growth is the duty and destiny of every child that is born.

Development has its roots in Earnestness, but its sweet fruit is Happiness. Pleasure may be mistaken for Happiness, as the poisonous toadstools are sometimes eaten instead of the nutritious and delicious mushrooms. Pleasure, which depends on the senses and the nervous system, is suicidal and self-stultifying: it cloys and ends in bored satiety. It only deadens or over-stimulates the nerves and the senses, and finally leads to lethargy or fatigue. It cannot satisfy you by simple repetition, as a stronger "thrill" is needed every time to produce the same pleasurable sensation as before. Thus Pleasure is like the usurer, who demands compound interest and enslaves the unwary debtor. If you pursue Pleasure in the hope of being happy, you really pour water into a sieve, and try to charge an earth-connected body with electricity. You will never have done with it. You may as well drink salt sea-water to quench your thirst. Pleasure follows the Law of Diminishing Returns that is known in Economics. More and more of it is required as time passes, and at last even the maximum stimulus fails to produce the minimum of nervous and sensuous response. Pleasure ends in disillusionment and cynicism. Solomon, who enjoyed regal luxury and is said to have possessed seven hundred wives, cried at last: "Vanity of vanities! All is vanity." The victims of Pleasure find no peace and repose, but are constantly driven hither and thither by the chance gusts of passion and impulse, like the unfortunate spectres mentioned by Dante:

> "As in large troops
> And multitudinous, when winter reigns,
> The starlings on their wings are borne abroad;
> So bears the tyrannous gust those evil souls.
> On this side and on that, above, below,
> It drives them, hope of rest to solace them
> Is none."

Pleasure deadens the finer instincts and sensibilities, and converts its votaries into selfish sensualists. They lose all faith in human nature, all enthusiasm for noble ideals, all capacity for sacrifice, social service, and heroic action. They boast of their indifference to all progressive movements, while they wallow in the mire of self-indulgence. They ask the old question of the Lotus-eaters: "What pleasure can we have to war with evil?" Such was the pleasure-loving Rinaldo, whom Ubaldo thus rebuked in the burning words put into his mouth by Tasso:

> "What sleep, what lethargy, what base delights
> Have melted down thy manhood, quenched thy zeal?
> Up! Up!"

So transitory and treacherous is Pleasure, which appeals to the senses and the nerves. But Happiness, which depends on Reason and Emotion, is a permanent possession that makes Life a priceless blessing. In fact, Happiness is Life and Life is Happiness. It grows and expands slowly and steadily, enveloping and suffusing your Personality with that ineffable bliss which is its own *raison d'être*. For its sake, all other things are sought: there is nothing beyond it or above it. It resembles a tree that strikes its roots deeper and deeper into the soil, while it also grows higher and higher like a tall palm, crowned with the sweetest date-clusters, that announce the oasis of peace and rest to the weary wayfarer in the Arabian desert. Deep-rooted it is in the mind and heart, which provide the rich and fertile soil for its hourly and yearly downward push and upward ascent. Happiness never cloys or palls: it never loses its charm and power. Its edge is never dulled, nor is its brightness ever dimmed. Even the stars of minus-magnitude will lose their light and lustre some day, but Eudaimonia, holy Happiness, will always keep its youth and loveliness and splendour, whatever Time may creep or fly. It is this imperishable wealth of Personality that you should acquire and amass day by day. Everything that you do should add to your treasury of true Happiness, as the touch of Midas turned all objects into gold. For this supreme Eudaimonia, which enriches Personality, you should be as ambitious and avaricious as an American millionaire is for his bank-account and investments. Try to be the Croesus and Kuvera of Eudaimonia, a multi-multi-millionaire of the inexhaustible and undiminishable riches of Personality. This wealth cannot be stolen by thieves or confiscated by the communists; it is safe in the midst of all possible crises and catastrophes, wars and revolutions, inflations and devaluations. It is in you and within you, as it is a part of your Self, your very Ego. For this simple reason, it cannot be taken away from you, as no one can ever rob you of yourself. It is always carried on your person, like the beauty of the belle, the knowledge of the scientist, the voice of the singer, the learning of the scholar, the virtue of the saint, the wisdom of the sage. It is not like the external impedimenta that have to be transported on a journey, and not even like the clothes that you wear. It is just You, your body and mind and soul, your genuine Personality, as completely stripped of all adventitious and accidental adjuncts as Odysseus was when he stood before Nausicaa, or St. Francis in the presence of Bishop Guido of Assisi. That is your real wealth, your own property which remains when all your money and possessions and garments are lost. This wealth is in your brain, not in your bank; it is in your heart, not in your hoard. It is the reward of Earnestness and Development. Strive for it with all your might.

Constant unremitting Endeavour is the price paid for this Bliss. Think of the "Socratic vigour" in Ethics. Recall the figure of Socrates climbing the steep hill of Virtue in the painting in the cathedral of Siena. Listen to Schiller's trumpet-call:

> "Restless, onwards must thou strive,
> Never halt nor languor know"

Earnestness is Man's first ethical attribute. It is exhibited in two chief virtues: Simplicity and Conscientiousness.

(1) *Simplicity.* Simplicity is the source of all true greatness. You may have heard and read much about some famous leader, but when you meet him, you say at once: "What a simple man he is!" He is found to be a greater lover of simplicity than many less-known people. Simplicity is for the soul what athletics are for the body. It exhibits itself in many ways. The earnest man is simple in his food and drink. He dislikes expensive and stimulating dishes: he hates complicated concoctions that take a long time to cook and prepare. He spends very little time on eating and drinking; he has more important things to do. He does not eat many times a day, and he does not partake of many courses at a meal. He prefers sun-cooked food to the best masterpieces of the culinary art. He eats what is grown in the country where he lives, if it is cheap. He eats to live; he does not live to eat. Among sauces, he is fondest of "Hunger," the sauce that is given gratis by Nature. He avoids all narcotics and stimulants as far as possible, or uses them with extreme moderation. He learns temperance

from the examples of Socrates, Xenocrates, Zeno, Spinoza, and other saints and sages. Never can the slave of food and drink attain Virtue and Wisdom. His soul is in his palate and his stomach; his will is weak and his brain is always clouded. He becomes a mere physiological machine, insensible to great thoughts and noble feelings.

The earnest man is simple in dress. He spends very little on dress. His clothes are inexpensive, and they are not superfluous in quantity. But they are not dirty or shabby. He does not own half-a-dozen suits and a dozen pairs of boots, as if he were a merchant. He does not take delight in wearing a new costume every day of the week. I knew a gentleman who said proudly: "I have eight suits, and I never use the same suit twice in a week." I replied: "Why don't you have three hundred and sixty-five, one for each day of the year, and three hundred and sixty-six in a leap year?" Cultivate a simple taste in dress: don't be like the vain fops and dandies, who adorn themselves with costly raiment, and wish to display their wealth or borrow a little false beauty by such tricks. True Beauty needs no clothes to set it off. It is only the ugly men and women, who believe that fine clothes make them look less ugly. King Cophetua's beggar-maid was clad in rags, but she was "as beautiful as day." If you are rich and waste what you call *your* money on dress, you strut about with the symbols and emblems of your criminality upon your person: your silk and satin gowns are a convict's garb. Even if you are poor, you may dislike simplicity: poverty does not always teach simple ways and habits. You may in that case buy cheap artificial pearls, gaudy beads, garishly coloured garments, rouge, powder, and lipstick, and thus sin against the rule of simplicity. Remember that the draper and the tailor cannot add a single micron to the stature of your Personality. What you are counts for more than what you wear. As for beauty, sound health and good character are better cosmetics than all the powders and creams sold in Paris. Carrots will give you a fairer complexion than all the quacks of the beauty-parlours. A gentle disposition will make you as handsome as the best-groomed and best-perfumed beaux and belles that ever rode in Rotten Row. Therefore, love simplicity in dress. Eschew extravagance, artificiality, and over-elaboration, which soon excite disgust and derision, as A. v. Platen has truly said:

> "The brightly arrayed, it is true, can enchant, yet it wearies us,
> The simple gives ever refreshment to eyes of the soul."

The earnest man is simple in his Lodging. He likes simple and sufficient accommodation, which shelters him against the cold and the rain, and gives him the necessary comfort for his work. He does not wish to possess a vast mansion with many rooms, which he cannot use for his personal needs. He would not care to walk about from one vacant but well-furnished room to another, like a disconsolate ghost. He knows that he has no right to waste money on superfluous accommodation in hunting for social prestige and position. A normal man or woman should live in a small room or house that is proportionate to human Personality: only an enormous giant should inhabit an enormous apartment, villa, or palace. The palaces of the kings, bishops, noblemen, and millionaires are really magnificent prisons for Personality: but the inmates hug their chains and rejoice in their incarceration. The earnest man's house, however, corresponds to his own needs, as the snail's tent fits its body. He does not encumber his abode with too much furniture; he prefers simple and cheap furniture. He dislikes expensive carpets, chairs, and tables: he does not spend much on them. I once visited a lady whose drawing-room was so full of chairs, vases, and tables that it was difficult to find my way to the sofa on which she sat. I said to myself: "Is this a room in a house, or a furniture-dealer's shop?" Don't make the mistake of buying too much furniture and paying too much for it. Cost and quantity do not make a well-furnished room. Simplicity and artistic arrangement must decorate a lodging in accordance with the demands of your own Personality.

The earnest man is simple in his manners. He does not give himself airs, nor does he delight in formalities and precedents. He is not proud in his bearing, and he meets all with a simple and friendly greeting. He hates pompous titles and honorific phrases in conversation and correspondence. He bows down to none, and he expects none to kowtow to him. He is easily accessible to all his friends and acquaintances, with or without previous appointment. Simplicity bars both servility and haughtiness. It marks the natural mode of social intercourse, which is at present poisoned with artificial conventions, elaborate regulations, and affected manners. Earnest people cut through this barbed-wire fence with the aid of common sense and character.

The earnest man is simple in his speech and style. He speaks and writes directly and simply. He dislikes excessive ornament and circumlocution. Homer, Demosthenes, and Voltaire rank high in literary history: but their style is very simple indeed. If you have something to say, simplicity will give it force and life. Lack of simplicity is the mark of an inferior intellect and a pettifogging, self-conscious soul. Remember Buffon's wise saying: "The style is of the very man."

The earnest man or woman curbs and controls the sex-impulse. He or she is its proud master, not its helpless slave. Like fire, the sexual appetite can consume your Personality and reduce it to dust and ashes, if it gets out of hand. In adolescence, complete continence develops the mind and the body. It enables you to taste the sweet joys of true love at the proper time. Premature sexuality, which is stimulated by the cinemas, the novels, the theatres, and the dancing-halls, corrupts the conscience and enfeebles the body. Defer marriage and sexual experience as long as possible; such self-control will do no harm. On the contrary, it will ensure longevity and good health. It will also develop your Personality by giving you a real zest for art, science, philosophy, and politics. Excessive sexuality in youth is the mark of a weak character and a vacant mind. If you cultivate habits of regular study, social service, outdoor sport, and temperance in diet, you will always be able to tame the dragon of Sex. Above all, don't eat too much of the stimulating foods like meat, fish, and eggs; and don't drink alcoholic beverages daily. Sex thrives on food and drink: it derives its strength from an overfull stomach and over-stimulated nerves. Even when you decide to marry, you should be the master of Sex, not its victim, whether you are a man or a woman. Pitiable indeed is he or she who cannot restrain and regulate Sex according to the dictates of Conscience. Such a sex-ridden, sex-driven person is like a motorist, whose car is running downhill with a defective brake that does not work. He or she will never know peace or happiness. Uncontrolled Sex is like a violent fever, which keeps the sufferer tossing in bed from one side to another. Say to yourself, "I shall enjoy Sex when I will, not when I must." Inordinate self-indulgence is the cause of chronic and acute disease and premature death, as it saps the vitality of the system. I know a young man who survived a severe attack of bronchitis, and the physician said, "Any other young man would have died. I think he is very continent and his blood is not alcoholized." The wise physician guessed right in this case. Sex must be deliberately regulated not only as regards frequency, but also as regards Direction. Roving fancy must not be allowed to run away with your heart and head. Sex is a gypsy vagabond and vagrant, if it is not trained to settle in a fixed abode and follow the routine of a civilized society. Sex must be caged and confined, otherwise it will wander hither and thither like a lion that has escaped from the menagerie. You must aim at its sublimation and its reduction in quantity, and also give it steadiness of Direction. Unsteadiness leads to divorces and secret intrigues, which poison and embitter social life.

Sex can be sublimated and steadied by the sweet emotion of Love. Love is something quite different from the violent Passion that agitates the minds and hearts of the men and women who "fall in love." Beware of "falling in love." Always step into true love. Never "fall" into the abyss of Passion. Passion is a disease: it paralyses Reason and Conscience, and sometimes drives the infatuated, maddened men and women to commit dreadful crimes. Such "lovers" suffer from morbid over-excitement, and should be sent to a hospital. They may neglect their social duties, desert their families, squander their money, kill their rivals or sweethearts, or commit suicide. So dolorous is the complete diapason of the drama of Passion, which rebels against Conscience and cares for nothing but itself. From the love-lorn Antony and Romeo down to last week's adulterer, or murderer, or suicide, or other anti-social agent of what the French call "passionate crime," you can trace a long line of the poor victims of this mental disease. Of such destructive Passion has Shakespeare said:

> "Love is a devil. There is no evil angel but love."

Take heed, therefore, that you are not bitten and smitten with such Passion, which is the hydrophobia produced by that mad dog Cupid. If you see some symptoms of it in your mind, hasten to cure yourself before it is too late. Go away from the place; avoid the dangerous person, in whom Eros is incarnated for you. Open your heart to a good friend, who can help you with his or her advice and company. Don't consume your own smoke: that will make matters worse. Unburden your mind to a wise and sympathetic Mentor. Then flee. The Catholic moralists teach that it is better to beat a retreat before the onslaught of Passion than to stay and combat it on the spot. In such cases, discretion is the better part of valour. Passion is a most potent and persistent microbe: even as a dried-up spore, it is to be dreaded, as it can easily come to life again. Therefore, flee so far that you feel yourself safe. In the new healthy atmosphere, you will soon recover normal Personality.

Flee Passion, but welcome true Love with joy and zest. Passion is chiefly physical and sexual in its origin and content; it often ends in disgust and indifference. But Love is a psychological experience:

it arises in the soul at first, and is then expressed in the body. Love is a gentle emotion, which is always under the control of Reason and Conscience. It enriches, beautifies, and develops Life. Love knows where it is going and what it is doing; it is not blind and deaf like Passion. You should be able to say, "I love because I will, not because I must." Love is a relation between two Personalities of opposite sex; it is Friendship sweetened with sex. Friendship between a man and a woman must precede true Love. You must know and esteem the other person before you can "step into love" for him or her. You must have the same ideas and ideals, the same interests and pursuits. You must not hold very divergent views in religion and politics. You must respect and appreciate him or her as a friend before true Love can arise and grow. Such Love is never sudden. You may see all the beauty of a face in a single glance or a minute's stare, but you cannot know a person's mind and heart and soul so quickly. Hence Passion, which is inflamed by a fair complexion or lovely eyes or a shapely nose or red hair, is often like a fire of straw; it is soon kindled, but it is also soon over. True Love rather resembles hard anthracite, which takes fire very slowly, but lasts a long time, when it has begun to burn. At a certain point in the friendly intercourse of a man and a woman, a deeper personal interest manifests itself, and the nerves also feel the thrill of the sex-impulse. Then both ask, as Shelley asked:

> "Nothing in the world is single,
> All things by a law divine
> In one another's being mingle—
> Why not I with thine?"

Thus is true Love born, and a couple is formed. To such happy and virtuous lovers, one may say, with Freiligrath:

> "O love as long as you can,
> O love as long as you may"

Such love grows deeper, finer, fairer, richer, with the lapse of time. It does not change or vanish like the shallow love that Alfred de Musset mourned, when he cried: "In this place, one day, I loved and was loved." True love is rooted chiefly in the mind and the heart, and not in sex. Sex is indissolubly linked with it in youth, but it is not so after middle age, when it rather resembles the gold that Pheidias put on the statue of Athena Parthenos: it could be taken away without injuring the statue. Such Love is compatible with the highest Ethics: nay, it is an essential part of it. All other so-called "love" is false and fickle, futile and frivolous. Passion and Lust often borrow the name of "Love," but you can easily detect the imposture. True love lasts through life. As Madame de Sévigné said: "The heart never gets wrinkles." Such Love, as defined and delineated by the wise sages, is a priceless blessing. Search for it; find it; keep it, and cling to it all your life.

(2) The earnest man is simple and temperate: he is also conscientious. He has a keen sense of duty. He regards all his actions as so many bricks contributed to the temple of Humanity. All the bricks must be good and sound. He regards his trade or profession as his sphere of Social Service, and not merely as a source of income. He lives in order to work honestly: he does not work only to live. Work is the means and channel of self-expression and altruistic activity; that is its first and foremost function in your personal life. It enables you to earn money for the purchase of the necessaries and comforts of life; that is its second and subsidiary function. What T. Veblen calls "the instinct of workmanship" is deep-rooted in human Personality: we all wish to do something thoroughly and admirably. The creative impulse is only another aspect of Duty, which is accepted, recognized, and fulfilled by the earnest man and woman with joy and pride. Wordsworth spoke of *Duty* as "Stern Daughter of the Voice of God": but you should look upon it as the "Sweet Daughter of the Voice of Self." There is nothing stern about it, and "God" has nothing to do with it. Let Duty be your guide and lodestar. It is the quintessence of Ethics, the very pith and marrow of Virtue, the unified and harmonized Momentum of Personality in Action. As all colours merge in white, so do all feelings, intuitions, emotions, ideas, desires, and aspirations fuse and coalesce in the single and simple concept of Duty. As when a projectile is thrown, it is pushed downward and pulled upward and sideways at the same time, but out of all these warring invisible forces there issues the accurate parabola that must be described, even so, out of the conflict and contact of the manifold instincts, impulses, complexes, motives, and inhibitions of human Personality, there results a single definite, irresistible urge that is called "Duty." This "Duty" is only another name for Conscience. Conscience is the earnest man's safe hurricane-lantern in this jungle of Life: it can never be extinguished by any wind, and it always shows the path that must be taken. Conscience is relative and mutable for Society, but it is unique and absolute for every individual. Conscience merely translates into the imperative mood the experiences and customs of a community at a particular epoch; it is not a creative and independent power or entity. It changes and varies

from age to age and from place to place. It turns the virtue of to-day into the vice of to-morrow. According to the time and the locality, it commands or forbids murder, theft, falsehood, violence, polygamy, and prostitution. Social Conscience is a chameleon. Each community makes its own Conscience, as each country mints its coinage; but, for the individual born on a particular day in a particular place, Conscience is absolute and morally coercive. He can no more trifle with the dictates of Conscience than he can tamper with the currency of the realm. If he did, he would be branded both by the law and in his own mind as a forger and counterfeiter. Conscience may not be fully enlightened at any particular time and place; but, such as it is, it is and ought to be the supreme guide of conduct. There is nothing else to follow. A motorist drives at night by the light of his lamps, however feeble and defective they may be: he would be in total darkness without them. He who acts as Conscience bids him has done his Duty: no man can do more. This is the great law of the Supremacy of Conscience, which is the pivot of practical Ethics. Conscience may lead you astray from the absolutely and theoretically right path, but you must obey it. Like Luther at the Diet of Worms, you cannot "act otherwise." You can know no other Right and Wrong except what your Conscience reveals to you, as you cannot behold any other objects except those whose image falls on the retina of your eyes. What you see is your world, even if others see it otherwise. What your Conscience tells you to do, that is your Duty, and no other. Universalizing the German poet Peter Hebel's sentiment, one may say:

> "Thy life's path to the cross-roads leads
> What way to take? Canst not decide!
> Just ask thy Conscience, he's at hand,
> Knows every tongue. Make him thy guide"

Rückert has well interpreted the message of Conscience in this verse:—

> "Six words there are that plead with me each day,
> I ought, I must, I can, I will, I dare, I may."

Lean not on other people's Consciences, as you do not eat with their teeth or hear with their ears. Even if the saints and sages, priests and politicians, parents and relatives, friends and comrades condemn what your Conscience accepts, you must be true to your Conscience, and not to their Consciences. Those other Consciences are not in your Personality: they are external and foreign to you. But your own Mentor is within you, and it will always be with you, like the heart that beats in your bosom. Therefore, if the priests and politicians, the parents and relatives, ask you to be false to your Self in order to please and obey them, you should always reply: "I am not you, and you are not me. My Conscience is inalienably and unconditionally mine, as your Conscience is yours. I cannot follow your Conscience, of which I know nothing at all, as I cannot wear your clothes or feel your headache. Why should I mangle and mutilate a part of my Personality at your behest? If I smother my Conscience now, it will not let me sleep in peace. Will all your Consciences put together save me then? No; they will not be there at all, as they belong to you and not to me. I shall thus be left in the lurch, exposed to the pain and shame that my Conscience, outraged and disobeyed, is sure to inflict upon me. There is nothing that makes a man so unhappy as a Conscience that is slighted; toothache is nothing to it. An uneasy Conscience is a very cruel and vindictive worm in a man's entrails: its gnawing, clawing, dull pain is more unendurable than the torments and tortures inflicted with all the instruments that are exhibited in the 'Folterkammer' of Nuremberg. If I slay Conscience, it will surely slay me, though itself dying, as Hamlet killed the villain his uncle. Why should I become a helpless victim of my Conscience in order to please you for a moment? No, it is my interest as it is my will to have Conscience for my friend, and not for a lifelong enemy, whose revenge never sleeps." Therefore, it behoves everyone, you and me and all of us, to obey his or her Conscience above all the emperors and prelates of the world, and to respond to that Conscience even more quickly and faithfully than to the loving call of a sweetheart or the solemn advice of parents and friends. What dearer friend will you find than Conscience? What sweeter sweetheart will you caress than Conscience? Conscience is your father and mother, wife and child, friend and neighbour; it is your Self, your Ego, your All-in-all. It holds the talisman of perpetual Happiness in its hands. It is invincible, and conquers pain, grief, suffering, and even Death. All creatures flee Death: but Conscience transcends Biology and works the miracle of Martyrdom. Who and what can resist it, when even Death is defeated by it? Hail to thee, mighty and mysterious Conscience, Sovereign Lord of Life and Death! Thee I obey, whatever befall. With thee, I cannot but be happy, whatever I may do or suffer. Herald and harbinger of pure and perfect Happiness and the highest supreme Good art Thou!

"Lead, kindly Light, amid the encircling gloom!
Lead thou me on!"

The agitation for the abolition of Conscience may be described as an interesting episode in the history of modern thought. Some thinkers have tried to discover a short cut to Virtue. They have therefore pleaded for the abolition of Conscience and Duty. Some of them have even tried to discover four or five substitutes for Duty—a sorry motley group of mutually contradictory impulses. Charles Fourier sets Man's "natural" appetites and emotions on the pedestal, which Ethics must guard and reserve exclusively for Conscience. Fourier conceived the original idea of attaining the goal of moral perfection by the free play and harmonious interaction of our "natural" desires and passions. He believed that gluttony, envy, avarice, pride, lust, and other "vices" need not be curbed and combated, but only directed and impelled in a new direction. Under this system, moral growth is always associated with pleasure. The path of least resistance is followed. The pressure on the Will is reduced to a minimum. Spontaneity makes Virtue as easy and entertaining as a game of cards or a summer picnic.

I admit that Fourier's revolt against the time-honoured methods of suppression and exhortation was a step in advance. Rationalism must declare that Virtue is not morose and ugly, but fair and radiant like the full moon. We must work with Nature and not against her. In moral education, we must link the new precept to the old habit. We must make moral progress easy for the child and the adult of average sensibility and will-power. Let us try to convert all the appetites and passions into the allies of Virtue. It is absurd to declare war on human nature in order to secure the triumph of morality. Such morality would be a poor caricature of the full-blooded, exuberant Virtue, which is the ideal of Rationalism. We should act on the principle that regulation and expression are more fruitful than suppression and prohibition. Fourier has found a clue, which should be followed up.

Now that I have done full justice to the merits of Fourier's system, I must point out its limitations. Ethics may linger and loiter in dalliance with passion, appetite, pleasure, and self-regarding feelings in order to lead the individual up to the craggy summits of Duty and Conscience. But we cannot reach the final goal in such pleasant company. We cannot also trust them as safe allies. We may give the child milk before meat; but Virtue cannot be practised without the exertion of Will-power and the training of Conscience. The early stages of moral growth may be traversed without undue strain on the Will, but each step above a certain altitude requires stronger ethical muscles and lungs in proportion to the heights already attained. The earnest man must not lull himself to sleep in the illusion that self-discipline and self-denial are only philosophical synonyms for instinctive pleasure and emotional gratification. On the contrary, Reason and Conscience must always hold guard over our "natural" inclinations and tendencies. Human nature is not homogeneous. Conscience is not the by-product of the unrestrained operation of our pleasure-giving appetites, passions, and emotions. These forces may be compared to the engines of a steamship, but Reason and Conscience must be the pilots. The Will must be kept awake and alert all the time. Duty may be pleasant, or it may not. There is no device, which can secure the constant concomitance of Virtue and agreeable feeling. These two circles of Life intersect, but they are not always coincident in such imperfectly developed individuals as we all are. In the Perfect Man, citizen of the Perfect State, they will be exactly coincident.

All ethical theories which attempt to lighten the burden of the Will by pushing hedonism to its extreme conclusions are dangerous. Virtue must be wooed and won; she is often coy and difficult of approach.

Much confusion would be avoided if we realize that Reason and Conscience are also "natural" elements of human personality, quite as "natural" as the appetites and emotions. They are feeble and half-grown at the present stage of Evolution, because they have appeared very late on the scene. Nutrition and procreation have played an important rôle in the history of Life for an immeasurably longer time than reflection and social sympathy. The stomach and the generative organs had been functioning furiously for myriads of years before the Brain entered on its snail-march of growth. It is absurd to contend that Egotism, which seeks pleasure and attaches itself to the appetites and self-regarding feelings, is more "natural" than Altruism, which exalts Duty and turns for guidance to Reason and Conscience. Nature has given birth to both forces. The only difference is that Egotism has ruled in the past, while Altruism is just emerging. Egotism must wane, while Altruism shall wax in might with each step forward in the course of Evolution. Max Stirner and Nietzsche have also demanded the abolition of Conscience. Stirner opines that the idea of Duty negates individual liberty. He argues that Ethics enslaves human personality. Nietzsche abolishes Conscience by a different argument. He insists that the conception of Duty lands us in a noumenal world of absolute values. He compares the moralist to the theologian and the metaphysician. He reads the secret of Evolution and finds that Nature aims at the growth and expansion of Life in all its forms, but does not bind herself by any laws of Virtue. But Nietzsche forgets that Nature includes human nature, and human nature finds its fulfilment in Virtue and Wisdom. We regard Socrates, Buddha, Rousseau, and Marx as representatives of Nature, and not the lions and whales and eagles. Let us examine the apex of Evolution. These fantastic theories do not and cannot persuade us to disbelieve our own psychology. We *know* that the idea of Duty is a fact—a fact as self-evident and universal as sunrise and sunset. At each moment of our lives we reflect and judge. We approve and disapprove of our own actions. This curious phenomenon of self-judgment shows that Conscience is no chimera, but a very palpable *fact* of life. Why do these " brilliant " thinkers wage war against *facts*? It is the worst species of suicidal folly. Deep within ourselves, safely ensconced in the innermost recesses of our labyrinthine human nature, secure against the destructive sallies of passion and the mocking jeers of unenlightened intellect, sits the supreme arbiter of Life, the Ego of the Universe, the mighty and irrepressible Power that says " Yea " and " Nay " to the pleadings and promptings of appetite and feeling. Stirner and Nietzsche and other peddlers of puny conceits and ephemeral paradoxes can never impose their crudities and inanities on the human race, which lives and loves and aspires and achieves, while these petulant and self-centred Troglodytes growl amorphous nonsense from their cavernous darkness. Their own " laws " shall judge them. The " fittest " ideas will survive. Life and Time will decide. And what does Life say? Life says " Get ye behind me, ye Perverters and Morphia-mongers. Ye weaken Me. Ye clog and cramp Me. Ye deface My beauty and impair My strength. I grow and expand and wear ever-new forms of surpassing beauty, and Conscience has been my guide in this upward journey. I toddled and stumbled blindly in infancy without this Conscience, knowing not what I did. But as I unfolded myself in the body and mind of Man and Woman, I have waxed strong in every limb and sinew only under the stern régime of Conscience. Conscience has been my Guide in the painful and perilous ascent from the Tasmanian to the Teuton. If Conscience desert me, I perish. Beauty, wit, knowledge, and love avail not to sustain me, if Conscience fall asleep or swoon. Behold! I do not hide my secret from anyone: ye can all read it at a glance. Ye have heard of Socrates: his words and deeds have gone to the ends of the earth But how many have heard of Aristippus and Thrasymachus? Ye have heard of Buddha. His benign features have been carved and chiselled by a thousand million fingers. The parchment which preserves his word is embellished with rubies and emeralds by the wild mountaineers of Tibet. But very few have heard of Brihaspati and Jabali. And why so? Because Socrates and Buddha were real forces of Nature, great Life-builders and Life-evolvers; they proclaimed the sovereignty of Conscience. But those others, Jabali, Aristippus, Thrasymachus, uttered blasphemy against Conscience. Their names are therefore forgotten at my behest. And these hedonistic philosophers of to-day, these hawkers of raw theories and vain syllogisms, they too are creatures of the passing moment, the moths and beetles of my eternal Eden. To-morrow will know them not."

II. Sociability

Sociability expresses itself in several virtues.

(1) *Helpfulness*

The social bond makes you responsible for all, as all are responsible for you. Try to help all whom you know. It has been said, "Love one another," but the precept is better in its concrete form: "Help one another." Grudge not your money or your time when others need it. Lend your money, your umbrella, your books, your bicycle, your motor-car, and your other possessions, to your friends and comrades without a moment's hesitation. Rejoice in all opportunities for such service. If you know that someone is in need, go and offer help before he asks for it.

Start with Personal Service; this duty will be discussed in the next section. But if you are an educated person, perhaps holding a University degree, you should share your knowledge with those who are ignorant. You have received your education at the expense of the People who pay for the colleges that you have attended. It is your duty to diffuse and disseminate the knowledge of Science, History, Literature, Economics, Politics, and other subjects among the farmers and working-men, whose labour has conferred all that learning upon you. Knowledge has this peculiar quality, that it is not decreased when it is given to others. It also remains fresh and bright in your mind, if you teach others. Ignorance is the curse of mankind to-day. No progressive movements can arise or flourish among ignorant people, as no higher animals are found in the dark depths of the ocean. Superstition and priestcraft can thrive only in an atmosphere of Ignorance, as disease-germs multiply in underground cellars where sunlight does not penetrate. Demagogy and tyranny can succeed only among citizens who know nothing of economics, politics, and history. Democracy without education is the rule of knaves over fools. Defective education is one cause of destructive wars. Frivolity in social life and debasing amusements can be counteracted only by better education, which alone can teach the people how to spend their leisure like cultured citizens. Thus the future of Religion, Politics, Art, and Ethics depends entirely on the instruction of the rural and urban workingmen. If you have acquired some knowledge, hasten to pass it on to the ignorant fellow-citizens. You may work as a tutor in the socialist schools and classes, or write short articles, pamphlets, and tracts, or deliver public lectures, or organize study-circles. A University alumnus or high-school graduate who neglects this urgent duty of teaching the common people is only a selfish parasite, unworthy of his academic degree. He or she should at once join a movement for popular education, and serve it in some way or other.

(2) *Patience*

Be patient with all, as a mother is patient with the little baby. Let not the folly, stupidity, ignorance, vanity, and selfishness of ordinary men and women irritate you. Always be sweet and calm. You yourself have some faults, and others have to be patient with you. You know that people cannot help being what they are: they are the victims of Heredity and Education. Their personal responsibility for their mistakes and misdeeds is infinitesimal indeed. If you start to be angry with some one, you should logically go on and vent your wrath upon his father, mother, teachers, grandparents, uncles, neighbours, and many others, who have made him what he is. Anger thus leads you into a pathless jungle. It also hurts yourself; it weakens your body and disturbs your mind. So why be doubly foolish, and offend yourself and another? Anger is also utterly fruitless: it cannot mend a broken mirror or gather up spilt milk in the pail again. It only adds bitterness and resentment to the evil that has already been done, thus changing it from bad to worse and from worse to worst. It is like a rod that stirs your whole Personality and brings up all the mud and slime from the bottom, where it lay buried out of sight. The angry man thinks that he is rebuking and threatening another, but he is really losing Virtue and thus sinning against himself. Like an intoxicated man, he sometimes utters words of which he repents after a short time; but a harsh word, like an arrow discharged from the bow, can never be taken back, even if he should offer a million apologies for it. It is an Act and a Fact that cannot be altogether undone, an anti-social inhuman Act and an eternal, irrevocable, persistent Fact that must engender another similar Fact, and so on for ever. Like undying ether-waves, like the ever-living amœba, every Act and Fact must propagate itself in the Universe: it can never end in itself. Therefore, don't emit angry words and expletives, which escape from you and can never be overtaken, even if you run after them like Nurmi. Think of Cleanthes, the Stoic sage, of whom Diogenes Laertius writes: "He had industry, but no natural aptitude for physics, and he was extraordinarily slow. . . . He used to put up with gibes from his fellow-pupils and did not mind being called the ass, telling them that he alone was strong enough to carry the load of their teacher Zeno. . . . He was present in the theatre when the poet Sositheus uttered the verse: 'Driven by Cleanthes' folly like dumb herds,' but he remained unmoved in the same attitude. The audience were so astonished that they applauded him and drove Sositheus off the stage. When the poet afterwards apologized for the insult, he accepted the apology." It is also related of Aristotle that "on hearing that someone abused him in his absence, he rejoined: 'He may even scourge me, so it be in my absence.'" The German poet Zedlitz has recounted this Moslem story. Emir Hassan, uncle of Prophet Muhammad, sat for dinner. The slave who carried the dishes dropped them on the floor, which was covered with costly carpets. The slave bowed low and said at once: "Our Prophet has taught that he who masters his anger is a wise man." The Emir replied, "I am not angry: go away." The slave continued: "Our Prophet has taught that he who forgives the offender is still wiser." The Emir said, "I forgive thee: go away." The slave then added: "Our Prophet has also taught that he who returns good for evil is the wisest of all." The Emir smiled and said: "I give thee thy freedom and also this sum of money with it. Now go away and be happy."

Anger disrupts and embitters ordinary social life, but it also works havoc in progressive movements. It has ruined many committees and sub-committees. Every association or party consists of all sorts of men and women, and the elected officers are expected to work smoothly and harmoniously. But impatience and anger must always make co-operation impossible. On all committees there are some fools, some dullards, some chatterboxes, some autocrats, and some otherwise-faulty persons. Such teams can succeed only when the members have been trained to cultivate patience as a cardinal virtue. In some committees, angry thoughts have led to angry words, and these latter have been the prelude to angry blows! Patience is indeed the ally of Progress. Without Patience, a committee would degenerate into a friendly club for perpetual wrangling and mutual recrimination. Dante has pictured irascible, ill-tempered persons as naked people standing in a bog:

> " Intent I stood
> To gaze, and in the marish sunk descried
> A miry tribe, all naked, and with looks
> Betokening rage They with their hands alone
> Struck not, but with the head, the breast, the feet,
> Cutting each other piecemeal with their fangs "

(3) *Appreciativeness*

The medieval moralists have warned us against Envy as one of the seven deadly sins; but they have given no name to the virtue that is the opposite of Envy. They only teach us to eschew envy; but I say, " It is not enough to avoid envy; you must learn to appreciate other people's achievements and rejoice in their success and good fortune " Envy is indeed the bane of social life. Molière has even made this mournful prophecy:

> " Envious people will die; but Envy will never die "

Let us hope that Molière will prove a false prophet. Envy has its root in abnormal egotism Try to crush and suppress it by all means in your power. If you see someone who is more beautiful than you are, begin to enjoy that beauty and feast your eyes upon it, instead of thinking of your own inferiority. Just say to yourself, " That is also my own beauty; only it is on another face. Now I can enjoy it more easily than if I possessed it myself, for a beautiful person can behold his or her own beauty only in a mirror." If you do not admire, but are smitten with envy, you are as foolish as the man who was given a delicious apple and a knife; he did not peel and eat the fruit, but cut his own throat with the knife. Similarly, if you meet someone who is more intelligent or erudite than you are, you should say: " That is my own intelligence; only it is in another person's head." You should appreciate that intelligence as a socially beneficent force. Don't be sad and downcast because it is not yours personally. It is yours through the fundamental unity of Humanity. Nature does not concentrate all gifts in one individual: but she bestows a few of them on each, and thus all of them on all together. You cannot be handsome *and* clever *and* famous *and* everything else. Cease to think too much of "I" and "Me," and learn to feel like "We" and "Us." Then Envy will disappear, and sympathetic Appreciativeness will grow and develop. If someone is famous and you are not, just say to yourself: "That is also my fame; only it goes with his name." Whatever Good any brother-man possesses, that is already yours too by the law of human solidarity. You may also reflect that every man is superior to others in some respects and also inferior to them in other ways. Thus everyone is compensated. Envy, which is born of Egotism and Inequality, is an entirely negative and unprofitable feeling, for you cannot acquire beauty, intelligence, or fame by simply envying others. You are like the dog barking at an elephant or a motor-car. As Balzac puts it: "Envy is a vice that yields no return." You gain nothing from envy, and you lose peace of mind and happiness by your own meanness and selfishness. Envy is its own scourge. You may try to decry and belittle others, or point out their shortcomings, or take delight in slander and scandal. Envy engenders such baseness and uncharitableness. But the envious man is like the fool who should look up and spit at the moon; it is his own face that is soiled. He does not understand that he cannot injure another eminent person by malicious calumny or unjust criticism. He is despised by those to whom he speaks. In fact, he produces a reaction of sympathy in favour of the person whom he maligns. When he throws mud at others, it is deflected and falls on himself; but he does not see it, as it falls on his back. Envy turns even great men into pygmies. Diogenes the Cynic was really moved by envy when he pretended to show moral indignation against Plato, as the historian relates: "On one occasion, Plato had invited some friends to a banquet, and Diogenes trampled on his carpets, and said: 'Thus I trample on the pride of Plato.' Plato said: 'Yes, Diogenes, with pride of another sort.'" Saint Kabir has truly said: "It is easy to sacrifice money and even the love of woman: but it is very difficult to abandon envy and jealousy." This difficult feat was actually performed by Goethe and Schiller, whose friendship was not marred by envy, though they were poets.

Envy destroys and disorganizes progressive movements. The second-rate speakers and writers envy the fame of the successful leaders, and try to filch their good name from them. They foment discontent and disputes, and sometimes even break up the organization for their selfish ends. They tell everybody of the real or imaginary faults of their superior comrades, and thus spread demoralization among the members. Envy can kill all parties, churches, and states, as it breeds strife and discord among able colleagues. Spenser has pictured Envy as riding a "ravenous wolf" and chewing a venomous toad:

> "For Death it was when any good he saw;
> And wept, that cause of weeping none he had.
> And when he heard of harme, he waxed wondrous glad."

(4) *Right Speech*

The sociable man avoids all the sins of speech He trains and controls his tongue. He remembers the poet's warning:

> "Boys flying kites haul in their white-winged birds;
> You can't do that way when you're flying words.
> 'Careful with fire' is good advice we know,
> 'Careful with words' is ten times doubly so."

The tongue can be like a scissor-blade for cutting the sweet knot of social intercourse that links you to others. Peace and concord are the gifts of a disciplined tongue. *Falsehood* is a sin that makes social life impossible. Veracity in speech is the essential condition of co-operation and mutual trust. Falsehood is a symptom of moral disease rather than a disease by itself. Men tell lies with some motive and for some purpose; they lie for the sake of money, love, fame, honour, and other baubles. If you combat greed, vanity, and other deadly sins, you will never be tempted to lie. You need not trouble about the casuistry of permissible falsehood (*e.g.* in illness and revolutionary activity, or for altruistic purposes). It is not probable that you will be confronted with such a problem in your life. But remember that it is better to be frank and true than polite and false. Excessive courtesy, that results in insincere talk and downright falsehood, is a social evil; it is more prevalent in Asia than in Europe and America. It is kinder to hurt a person's feelings for a moment than to deceive and mislead him for a long time. Be polite within the limits of veracity.

Slander is a bitter poison exuded by some malevolent tongues. Even if a person has done something wrong, you should not speak evil of him, unless it is absolutely necessary as a social duty. Mere gossip about other people's faults and peccadillos is a most reprehensible anti-social habit. When you hear such slander, true or false, begin to talk of that absent person's virtues as a counterblast to the calumny. If the slander is false, it is a despicable and dangerous device of envy and jealousy. It must be crushed, and the malefactor must be exposed and warned. Such slanderers have been compared to venomous vipers in society. In social conversation, let us try to praise others as much as possible. The good rule is this: if your neighbour has a fault, tell him about it directly or indirectly; if he has a virtue, tell others about it.

Rudeness is a vice for which there is no valid excuse. Do not speak to your superiors in age or ability in a tone of easy familiarity. Cultivate due reverence in speech. Some vain persons claim equality with older or abler or more famous men by speaking of them or to them in a hail-fellow-well-met style. I know a young student who spoke to me of his professor as "Arthur"; this rudeness was due to his vanity. Another young man has the habit of addressing older and abler persons without the customary title of "Mr.," as if he were an equal and intimate friend. He should wait until the others discontinue the formal style of speech in talking to him. Such one-sided, premature informality is really rudeness in a thin disguise. Give everyone his or her due in speech, and be rather modest than presumptuous. No person will ever be offended by proper respect and deference on your part, while curt and rude speech will repel many kind and well-disposed friends. Never be rude in speaking to the poor and to those who are inferior to you in any respect. Be punctiliously polite in conversation with such persons. Rudeness on your part will be regarded as a reminder of their inferiority, and they will resent it as long as they live. Your superiors may forgive your rudeness in speech, but your inferiors will neither forget nor forgive. Harsh speech is always a gratuitous insult to others. You can always say exactly the same thing with sweet and gentle words, which will as a rule be more effective. St. Stephen perhaps marred his great sermon by the harsh peroration, which breathed a spirit of anger and contempt. If you wish to tell a hawker not to call again, you can do so harshly or politely. The words will be different, but the message will be identical. You can always spread love, and not hate, in society. Remember the law of the "Propagation of Speech" in Ethics. If you speak harshly to someone, especially to an inferior who cannot answer back, then he will inevitably speak harshly to someone else, and this latter person will speak harshly to another, and so on. On the contrary, if you speak sweetly and lovingly to another person, he will do the same in dealing with another, and so on. Thus vibrations of love or hate are set up and continually propagated around us. These vibrations are like the waves of the wireless. If your soul were a properly attuned radio set, you could certainly hear how your harsh or sweet words are being repeated and reiterated over and over again in the world. Therefore, avoid rude and harsh speech at all times.

In conversation, always try to talk of serious and important matters. Avoid frivolous tittle-tattle and time-killing, brainless chatter. In social life, some people enjoy foolish or smutty stories, pointless jokes, and unprofitable talk about pots and pans, cricket and football, trade and business. Thus precious time is wasted, and no one is improved or benefited. Always try to turn the conversation into useful channels. The standard of social conversation is a good criterion of the culture of a group. Talk about politics, economics, art, literature, religion, philosophy, history, sociology, poetry, and other interesting topics. Never try to monopolize the conversation, as some brilliant talkers do. Give every one a chance of saying something. Talking too much at social gatherings is one of the worst signs of a selfish temperament On the other hand, don't sit silent all the time: you are not a dummy at the feast. Contribute your fair share of conversation to the party. If you see that some irrepressible person is talking too much, you should particularly ask some other guest to express his opinion; in this indirect way, you can save the company from the tyranny of voluble vanity.

(5) *Modesty*

The medieval moralists condemn Pride, but they have forgotten to include Vanity in the list of the seven sins. As our rationalistic Ethics must be chiefly positive and not merely negative, you should learn to cultivate the virtue of Modesty, which is indispensable for personal happiness and an efficient social life. Don't over-estimate yourself in any way: don't think that you are more beautiful, intelligent, learned, or sagacious than you really are. See your own Personality just with your two eyes, and not through a magnifying field-glass. Vanity is the shadow of a small soul. If you "know yourself" well, you will never expose yourself to ridicule by puerile vanity. Why should you try to acquire greater credit or prestige or fame than you deserve? Vanity is deep-rooted in selfishness and insincerity. Claim what is your due, but not more. Learn also to despise the opinion of unenlightened fools. A vain man or woman is the slave of others; and this slavery is entirely voluntary on his or her part. Most vain people are stupid and shallow. As Sophocles says: "If any man thinks that he alone is wise,—that in speech or in mind he hath no peer,—such a soul, when laid open, is ever found empty." Pride is closely related to vanity, though these two vices are displayed in different ways. Pride has its origin in a false estimate of one's own Personality. It is born of egotism and ignorance. How useful it would be, if you could visit a scientific assayer of Personality at regular intervals, and obtain an exact description and evaluation of your physical, intellectual, æsthetic, and ethical attributes and attainments. Then you can know how-much-carat gold you really are; but a proud man believes that he is 24-carat gold indeed! Pride is psychological cecity of a certain type. It breeds rudeness and coldness in manners and curtness and lack of courtesy in speech; it is a most anti-social force indeed. It produces a ridiculous superiority complex, which is not justified by the facts. Even if you are superior to others in some respect, you should ever be on your guard against the sin of pride, which subtly insinuates itself into the soul, and you don't know it! That is the most dangerous aspect of Pride: it is often unconscious of itself. A proud man as a rule thinks that he is free from Pride, as a lunatic can never understand that he is mad. He is placed in a very difficult situation He believes he is quite normal, while others can plainly discern his weakness and dislike him for it. An Indian poet says with great insight. "An avaricious man sees only money; a lover sees only the sweetheart; a vindictive person sees only his enemy; but a proud man sees nothing." Both vanity and pride often express themselves in self-praise and boastfulness, which render social life disagreeable and unattractive for all. People may like to praise you, but they never wish to hear you praising yourself. Even if you praise yourself with justice and truth, they are offended and begin to think of your faults. When you blow your own trumpet, the listeners withdraw in spirit to a safe distance, where its music cannot be heard.

Modesty is the antidote to vanity and pride. Don't think too highly of yourself. Learn modesty by comparing your achievements with those of the great men and women of history. The tall camel was both vain and proud until he saw a mountain. Try to mix with eminent persons who are superior to you: such friendships will teach you modesty most effectively. Remember that you lose much through Pride: most people do not esteem, help, praise, or love a proud man. Pride also prevents you from developing your Personality: you will *not* strive *to* rise higher, if you fancy that you have already scaled Everest. If you have done something that deserves recognition and publicity, don't begin to talk about it yourself. You will find that others know about it somehow. Thus you lose nothing through Modesty. Your merit will not long remain hidden; you need not proclaim it with your own tongue.

Vanity and Pride also hinder the growth of all progressive movements. Self-advertising lovers of notoriety infest all parties and societies. They spin fine intrigues to be elected to office, and fish for invitations to preside at meetings and deliver addresses. There are often ten candidates for a vacant seat on the Executive Committee. Over-weening pride turns the active members into arrogant autocrats in the committees; and such autocrats ruin and disorganize a movement as surely as a blind conductor would wreck a train. Two autocrats cannot work on the same committee, as two lions cannot live in the same den. Each one always wishes to have his own way, as he thinks he is a Solon and Solomon combined in one. He is not disposed to compromise at all. But compromise is the first principle of co-operation. If there were only one person living on the earth, or only one member on a committee, compromise would not be necessary. But many persons cannot live or work together without the habit of mutual regard and accommodation. Pride renders many able and earnest men utterly unfit for team-work in any movement. Their talent and energy cannot be fully utilized for social progress on account of this one defect of character. Therefore, be modest, tactful, and sociable, so that you may co-operate with your comrades in all forward movements.

(6) *Love of Justice*

Human society is only a herd of beasts, if it is not founded on Justice. In the jungle, the strong prey upon the weak, and the panther devours the antelope. But Justice is the glory of Man and his civilization. Justice gives every one his due She is the parent of peace and harmony. She weans mankind from strife and rapine. She spurs all to work and worth, as she promises the proper reward to all. She is the guardian of organized society, its surest defence and rampart against disorder and violence. Love of Justice is a cardinal virtue that you must cultivate to the highest possible degree. You should try to give everyone what is due to him or her, and you should help others to get what is due to them. Alas! Injustice is so rampant around us that all lovers of Justice have to fight an uphill fight every day. Our civilization is based on injustice. Our institutions are reared on the unsafe and slippery foundations of injustice. We are like the sailors who landed and cooked their food on what they supposed was *terra firma*: but they were really on the back of a whale, which soon began to move and swim. All our States and Churches are vast edifices built up on injustice; they are cemented with injustice; they are painted and decorated with injustice; they are lighted and heated with injustice; they are wired and ventilated with injustice; they are massive memorials and monuments of that inherited unashamed unchallenged universal injustice which rules and reigns over the whole earth to-day. Hence love of Justice will make you a stranger and an alien in this rotten society; but you must not be afraid of that.

Avarice

Love of Justice will root out avarice from your soul. Avarice pervades this society as water saturates the stalactites and stalagmites in limestone caves. The acquisitive instinct, which is praiseworthy within its proper limits, has been allowed to attain disproportionate dimensions. Material things, otherwise called "wealth," tend to crush and strangle human Personality, as the octopus destroys its victim. The devils of Possessions have come to possess our souls: and no religion seems to have the power of driving them out of us. In different countries, the people pretend to worship Christ or Buddha or Siva or Allah; but in all lands they worship gold, like Chaucer's physician-pilgrim of long ago, who "lovede gold in special" Avarice leads them to burden themselves with many external objects, which are unnecessary for Personality or even detrimental to it. They suffer from what John Dewey has called "externalism." They do not try to grow in Virtue and Wisdom like true men and women, but rather take pride in the virtues of well-caparisoned donkeys carrying heavy loads of furniture and clothes and cash and bank-notes. Avarice is to be shunned and condemned, as it undermines both the fundamental virtues: Earnestness and Sociability. It destroys simplicity and seriousness of character, as the money-hunter is always full of plots and plans for increasing his hoard. He thinks and dreams of money, as a lover thinks and dreams of his sweetheart. Avarice is also destructive of Sociability. No honest man can ever become rich. No one can acquire enormous wealth by his own unaided efforts, even if he should work in the most fertile field on the earth, or in a gold mine, or in a bed of pearl-oysters. Large amounts of money are not made: they are taken. All excessive wealth has its origin in the exploitation and oppression of the working-people by armed scoundrels.

There are three classes in society: (1) The justly-remunerated persons, who neither exploit nor are exploited, and who receive about the same amount of commodities and services as they would get in the Co-operative Commonwealth. This is the fortunate lower middle-class, urban and rural, which neither commits nor suffers injustice. (2) The second class consists of the wealthy landlords, capitalists, bishops, officials, professional men, cinema stars, boxers, and others who receive more than their just share of wealth; they are the avaricious exploiters. (3) The third class is composed of the poor underfed working-men, farm-labourers, clerks, and others who are given less than their due reward out of the wealth produced by the community. These are the exploited majority.

Now if a person who belongs to the first (lower middle) class wishes to amass money and join the exploiting class, he is guilty of avarice. The second class is already steeped in greed: it is conceived and engendered in greed, nurtured in greed, spurred to activity by greed, and driven to death by greed. It sees, hears, smells, tastes, and touches Money everywhere. Money is the air it breathes; Money is its food and drink. It works for Money; it cheats for Money; it robs for Money; it lies for Money; it kills for Money. The third class of the exploited poor is not to be blamed for greed, if they claim what is their due. They should strive to increase their wages up to the standard of the properly remunerated middle-class; at present, they are the victims of injustice. But if a working-man dreams of becoming a millionaire, or buys lottery tickets, or gambles, or tries to "rise" into the capitalist class, then he is as avaricious as any exploiter. Avarice can corrode the souls of both rich and poor; it is a heinous sin in either case. Love of justice will teach the lower middle-class to be content with their economic position. It will lead a few members—very few indeed—of the exploiting class to disgorge their ill-gotten gains and employ their wealth for charity and in the service of Socialism. The exploited class, actuated by the love of justice, will organize itself in order to augment its earnings; but it will repudiate and condemn such avaricious individuals as exhibit the capitalistic trait of inordinate acquisitiveness. Avarice will impel such working-men to gamble, or to become accomplices of Capitalism, or to exploit Labour organizations, or to practise theft, housebreaking, forgery, bag-snatching, kidnapping, and other easy devices for getting a lot of money. If they cannot realize their ambition of owning much property, they will be miserable and unhappy every day and every night.

Progressive Movements

Avarice works havoc with all progressive movements. Freedom from this vice is the essential condition for the birth and development of new movements, as rain is indispensable for the crops. A pioneer in religion or politics must say, like the apostle: "Silver and gold have I none." He cannot earn much money in any country, as he must devote much time to free propaganda and also suffer ostracism and unpopularity. If all the ardent well-educated young men and women are avaricious, who will initiate progressive movements? If they all grasp at gold, who will serve Truth and Justice? At present, many able persons prostitute their talents in the service of Capitalism, which alone can give them big salaries and the much-coveted luxuries. They sell their brains for Rolls-Royce cars and costly cigars and wines. Avarice robs the world of many potential prophets, reformers, and revolutionists. There is enormous infant mortality among the young enthusiasts of each generation. Their souls are born into the realm of Virtue and Freedom, when their bodies attain the age of twenty; but, during the next ten years, most of these souls are strangled and slain by Avarice. The well-fed bodies continue to live, stinking cadavers infested with the loathsome worms of Capitalism. Such dead souls are as numerous as the hired intelligent servants of Capitalism, who were born poor and died rich. Therefore, if new movements are to arise, some gifted youths must conquer Avarice and prefer the simple life. If Petrarch, Luther, Rousseau, Blanqui, and Marx had loved Money, the modern world would not have emerged from the slough of medievalism. Avarice hinders the birth of great movements; it also hampers their development. The pioneers and apostles of religious and political movements must live in poverty, as there is no organization that can pay them well for their self-imposed services. They cannot acquire wealth, as they refuse to serve the powers that be. Their supporters are few, and the movements are always in financial difficulties. Only noble men and women, who are free from avarice, can nurse new ideas and ideals into maturity.

Avarice is thus the enemy of all new movements, without which human society would stagnate. It can also ruin and disintegrate such movements after they have grown in strength and won millions of adherents. Like the germs of tuberculosis and influenza, Avarice is in the air all the time, ready to pounce upon the soul that has been enfeebled by selfishness and self-indulgence. Great movements are led by very energetic and intelligent men and women, who are known as "leaders." Such "leaders" are archbishops, bishops, priests, socialist Members of Parliament, trade union officials, Labour party officials, socialist editors, authors, and orators, and other chiefs of the organized political, economic, and religious movements of the People.

If these leaders yield to Avarice, the movements are lost for ever. They then cease to be teachers, and become traitors. They begin to extort money from the poor members of their organizations in return for their "services." Thus many bishops and priests live in comfort and luxury on the money contributed by the working-men in the form of taxes, tithes, freewill offerings, etc. They tell lies and devise subtle schemes for plundering the people: they say prayers for the dead, or pardon sins, or invoke some god, or perform ceremonies for your health and success, or give you charms and amulets, or bless your fields and motor-cars, or pray for rain and victory, or play some other mumbo-jumbo tricks in order to batten on the labour of the poor. Such are, and such have always been, the priests of all religions. They prosper on fraud and superstition; they are hypocritical and sanctimonious thieves, who bless your soul while they pick your pocket. Dante cursed this class in his wrath, when he cried: "Ye have made for yourself a god of gold and silver." They rob the ignorant people: but they do worse. They also help the propertied classes to rob the poor. They teach the people that the predatory kings, landlords, and capitalists have been appointed "stewards" and "leaders" by "God"; that humility and submission are great virtues; that the poor will be rewarded in heaven and should not attack the rich here on earth. With such smooth and honeyed words do the priests of all Churches bewitch the minds of the working-class! They have always been the allies and accomplices of every exploiting class in every country. They have hastened to share the loot with the plunderers, instead of counselling and organizing resistance to injustice and oppression. Greedy, lazy, cowardly, vain, gluttonous, and hypocritical manikins are they, these Reverends, Holinesses, Graces, Ulemas, curés, mevlevis, imams, mahants, marabouts, and lamas, slimy reptiles of the same species, differing only in colour and habitat. Avarice is their bond of union; avarice has turned the shepherds' dogs into wolves. In the Labour movement, too, the same sinister figure of the canting parasite has appeared. The trade union officials are supposed to defend the interests of the poor working-men; but they themselves receive enormous salaries and thus raise themselves and their children into the capitalist class. They acquire the capitalist's psychology with the capitalist's income, and become the champions of "moderation," "class co-operation," and "industrial peace." Their only care is to keep their jobs, and they despise the simple folk whose money they pocket. They are miserable exploiters of Labour, and yet pretend to be the representatives of Labour! As well may the butchers come forward as the representatives of the lambs! A trade union official even embezzled about £10,000! The stupid working-men are thus doubly robbed; they pay these sleek, smart, well-fed, well-dressed rogues, and they also lose money on account of the "moderate" policy of inactivity and compromise that these "leaders" impose on the movement. Avarice thus corrupts the most energetic and intelligent trade-unionists, who are appointed to guide and serve the Labour movement. The socialist politicians have also succumbed to greed. Many socialist leaders were born poor and died rich. They have sold their books to the members of the party, or extorted huge fees for their lectures, or demanded big salaries for their services as editors and authors, or amassed wealth in other ways. No wonder they lose their zeal for the speedy triumph of Socialism! They are really capitalists, as they belong to the exploiting class. It is the size of a person's income that generally determines his politics. A socialist "leader," who was born in a proletarian family and left £15,000 at his death, must be branded as a renegade and a traitor. Where did he get all that money from? How did he differ from a capitalist with the same amount of property? What right had he to condemn the other exploiters, when he was appropriating so much "surplus-value" himself? Avarice also impels the socialists to hunt for lucrative positions and appointments in connection with municipal councils and Government departments. And how their mouths water at the very thought of "office" in Government! How they rush to accept a capitalist portfolio (with a salary), like John Burns and Millerand! How they long to sell themselves body and soul to the capitalist class as puppet Ministers in a "minority Government," which must depend for its existence on the votes of the capitalist parties and can never inaugurate a socialist policy! How they intrigue to form "national" coalitions with the capitalist politicians in order to remain in office as long as they possibly can! Such ruin and devastation can Avarice bring about in a progressive movement! Therefore, if you wish to reform religion and politics, first free your soul from Avarice. Wash it entirely clean from greed, so that it is pure and spotless.

Theft

Love of justice will prevent you from stealing what belongs to others. Theft is a sin that makes social life impossible. An honest working-man must not rob his poor comrades of their money, their clothes, their cigarettes, or anything that is theirs. Even in a socialist community, theft will be regarded as a serious offence. Anyone who takes anything from the public stores in contravention of the accepted rules will be "a thief." Avarice will have to be conquered even in such a society. In Cabet's Icarian community, it was found that some members took various articles from the workshops and magazines in order to give them to their children. Others concealed bottles of wine in their rooms. So difficult it is to root out Avarice from the soul of Man!

Gambling

Love of Justice will teach you that gambling is an anti-social practice. It has its origin in avarice and love of excitement. Under the present system, it is the only chance that many poor people have to acquire a large amount of money. The odds may be one to a million, but still there is that chance of one in a million. As a poor girl said: "It's worth the half-crown," when she bought a ticket in a lottery. Gambling cannot be entirely eradicated in a capitalist society. But you can personally decide to abstain from gambling. Discourage all games played for money, lotteries, betting, raffles, "draws," sweepstakes, etc. In England and China, gambling has become a serious menace Prof. H. A. Giles writes: "Gambling is indeed a very marked feature of Chinese life. A child buying a cake will often go double or quits with the stall-keeper to see if he is to have two cakes or nothing, the question being settled by a throw of dice in a bowl. . . . More homes are broken up and more misery caused by this truly national vice than can be attributed to any other cause" Gambling must create a mental atmosphere of mingled avarice and frustration. A gambler is always dreaming of the great fortune that never comes. The working-men are led away from the right line of action for the abolition of poverty and inequality, and they are tormented by rosy visions of sudden prosperity. If they attain to a position of leadership in the Labour Movement, they will exhibit the avarice that gambling has evoked and intensified in their hearts. An unsuccessful gambler will at last exploit the Movement in order to satisfy the craving for money that has increased year by year. Gambling is a socially insanitary custom, and it should be abandoned by all earnest persons, even if they are poor. Don't run after the end of the rainbow in this foolish manner: we shall all be rich together, when Socialism triumphs.

Your Daily Work

If you are not in the grip of Avarice, you will choose a trade or profession that appeals to you as the means of self-expression and social service, even if you cannot earn much money by it. Your daily duty is not merely money-making drudgery; it is your contribution to social progress and the path of personal development. How sad must be the lot of the man or woman who must do uncongenial work simply for the sake of more money! I know a young professor, who loved literature passionately and taught it admirably; but his salary was small, and he became a lawyer in order to secure a larger income. I tell you that man was guilty of a crime, and he will not be happy as a lawyer, though he may be a little more comfortable, a little better fed and dressed and lodged. A musician who is *born* a violinist can never be personally happy or socially useful as a prosperous merchant or stockbroker, as he will miss the violin all the time. Avarice puts round men in square jobs and square men in round jobs. At present many persons in all classes, rich and poor, are unhappy and restless because their daily work is not interesting. It does not provide an outlet for the creative impulse and the insistent urge of Personality. Therefore, don't ask in youth, "How can I earn the biggest salary?" Ask rather: "How can I be truly happy and do most good to society?" Then you may have less money, but you will have more of Life and Joy.

The Apostle's Call

If you have completely conquered Avarice and Hedonism, you may think of devoting your time and energy entirely to some progressive Movement, and accepting only food, clothing, and shelter as your remuneration. You will not get wages or a salary, and you will have to live a very simple life of active service. You may work as a speaker, writer, and organizer. You will not think of earning money or enjoying the so-called comforts and luxuries that other men and women love so much. You will aim only at Self-Culture and Social Service. If you feel such a call within you, you should defer love and marriage as long as possible. You may wisely choose celibacy, like Spinoza, Mazzini, Louise Michel, and Spencer; or you may marry late, like George Fox and Elsa Brandström. You would prefer a childless marriage, or a family of only one child, so that you may be free from mental distraction, and the Movement may not have to spend too much on your personal maintenance. If you marry, choose a like-minded apostle of Rationalism, not a commonplace avaricious man or woman. Thus you can continue and carry on the tradition of the great philosophers and saints of all the ancient Orders and Churches in modern Rationalism, which fulfils them all.

Murder

Love of justice will lead you to recognize every person's right to life. This is, indeed, the first and most fundamental right of every man, woman, and child. The precept, "Thou shalt not kill" is common to all religions and ethical systems. But it is sad to reflect that Murder still counts its victims by hundreds, if not thousands, each year. In war, the number may rise to millions. Duels are still fought in some countries. Infanticide is openly or secretly practised by a few communities. Rivalry and jealousy in love incite to murder, especially in countries where alcoholic beverages are commonly used and the imagination is over-sexualized by art and literature. Avarice arms the hand of the poor or greedy murderer, who is himself the victim of Capitalism. Striking working-men and unarmed agitators are sometimes murdered by the police and the militia. Prisoners who attempt to escape are shot down under certain circumstances. Among very backward tribes, murder for *cannibalism* or *ritual* still prevails. Many Governments also murder the criminal who has killed a brother-man: this legalized murder is called "justice" and "punishment." But some humane nations have abolished this barbarous custom. Some motorists are guilty of the murder of pedestrians through culpable carelessness. Some working-men are murdered in factory accidents which are caused by the avarice of the capitalists. Racial or "religious" riots result in many murders in several countries. Fascism murders some of its political opponents secretly or openly. Imperialism provokes murder and then retaliates by murder. Capitalism murders millions by slow starvation and premature death.

Thus are men, women, and children killed to-day in peace and war. But do ye vow to have no part or lot in murder of any kind. All can take life, but no one can restore it.

(7) *The Animals*

Sociability should also be exhibited in our dealings with animals. They too are sentient beings, and some of them are capable of attachment and devotion to human beings and to one another. Man killed many animals in the early period of civilization in order to clear the jungle, and the same cruel but unavoidable process can be witnessed in new colonies. There are also noxious, venomous, and ferocious animals like tigers, jaguars, wolves, sharks, snakes, and others, which kill us, and we must kill them. We are not responsible for their appearance on earth, and they cannot be tamed and used. There was only one wolf of Gubbio, and even he did not exist. Rats, flies, wasps, locusts, white ants, and other animals destroy our property or spread disease; they must be destroyed. We cannot afford to feed all these hungry hordes. Zoroaster enjoined upon all his disciples the duty of exterminating such pests, and you should follow his teaching. But all animals which are employed in the service of Man should be treated with the greatest kindness and sympathy. They are your colleagues and comrades. They have also done their part in building up the fabric of Civilization. Feed them well; lay not too heavy burdens on them; give them medicine and a holiday when they are sick; allow them a day of rest now and then; give them a warm blanket in cold weather; speak affectionately to them at times. They can feel the words of love, though they do not understand them. The cow, the ass, the shepherd's dog, the horse, the camel, the bullock, the elephant, the milkman's dog, the pony, the yak, and other domesticated animals are humble and helpless members of the fellowship of Labour. They must not be robbed of their rights, especially as they cannot strike back, or agitate for the redress of their grievances. But do not make useless "pets" of dogs, cats, parrots, and other animals. Don't waste precious human affection and care on such idle parasites. There are many lovely children whom you can pet and fondle. The enormous army of "pet" dogs of all varieties is only a ridiculous appendage to feminine frivolity in capitalist society. What useful purpose do they serve? Their biscuits, kennels, and hospitals represent so much sheer waste of money and time. A prince has even built a palace for his dogs! This foolish cynophilism must cease. No animals should be kept as "pets": children should be our "pets." The animals are to be welcomed only as fellow-workers.

Avoid and eschew unnecessary cruelty to animals in all its various forms. Don't take part in blood-sports like stag-hunting and fox-hunting, or in horse-races, greyhound-races, bull-fights, cock-fights, and bulbul-fights. Such diversions are tainted with both cruelty and frivolity. Don't cut off a steak from a living cow or ox, as some Abyssinians do. Don't buy furs that have been obtained by cruel and atrocious methods. Don't cook shell-fish or any other animals alive. Don't eat them raw and alive. Disapprove of the circus-performances of some animals (like cats), which cannot be trained without cruel tortures. Don't kill birds or worms just for "fun": there is no fun in being cruel. Don't whip any working animal (horse, donkey, or another) at any time; a whip is always the badge of inhumanity. Don't starve them in old age; feed them well or kill them painlessly. In the hot weather, stop frequently at the water-troughs by the road-side. On festival days, give them also a feast of carrots, apples, and other dainties, as you enjoy your Christmas or Dewali dinner. Always be kind, considerate and humane.

As regards the vexed and vexing question of vegetarianism, you should not run to extremes. Vegetarianism or lacto-vegetarianism is a laudable practice, if you can maintain your health and strength without eating fish, fowl, or flesh. But it is doubtful if millions of people in all countries can be cheaply and properly nourished without a supply of fish. Even the Burmese Buddhists generally eat fish, but not fowl and meat. Fish has, indeed, been called a water-vegetable. If you consume milk and cheese, you must answer the difficult question, "What shall we do with the old cows and the young calves?" Animal proteid of some sort (from milk or meat) is perhaps more favourable to growth and mental activity than the purely vegetable proteids of nuts, beans, peas, lentils, and cereals. Thousands of lacto-vegetarians thrive on eggs and milk, but they could not work hard or keep good health as strict vegetarians. It is a wise practice to abstain from all food of animal origin for a short period at intervals, as the Greek Catholic Church prescribes for Lent. Fish and fowl are less harmful than meat from the hygienic standpoint. Our moral sensibilities are also less shocked and wounded in killing them than in slaughtering the mammals like oxen and sheep. The nearer an animal is to

Man in the scale of Evolution, the more keenly we can feel for it. This is a natural law of human psychology. Further, the use of the mammals for food necessitates the erection of slaughter-houses and abattoirs. A slaughter-house in a town is a very barbarous and demoralizing institution. It is altogether undesirable that the children should see the caged animals being taken to the slaughter-house. The employees of an abattoir also become brutal and lose their finer human instincts, as G. Lansbury relates in his Autobiography: "(In Australia), I was then lucky enough to discover a job at a slaughter-house, where I worked driving a van carrying the carcasses of animals from the slaughter-house to town. . . . The men employed were really brutalized by their work. I think they would have been ready to cut each other's throats as easily as they cut up the carcasses of sheep and bullocks. In fact, there seemed no feeling in them." For our own sake, if not also for the sake of the animals, slaughter-houses must be abolished for ever. Several devices for "humane slaughter" have been proposed; but the institution itself is fundamentally wrong and objectionable. The trade of a butcher is not a very noble calling, and his shop is much less attractive than a fruit-shop. It is also asserted that vegetarian food is cheaper than flesh diet; but the prices of cheese, eggs, nuts, and meat may vary in different countries The vegetarians must rely chiefly on the arguments from Hygiene and Ethics, which are indeed very strong and convincing, but not absolutely or universally valid.

You can be a strict vegetarian, or a lacto-vegetarian; you can eat only fish and fowl, or you can be an omnivorous flesh-eater. Of these four food-habits, the last-named may be regarded as the worst. The second and the third are easy and practicable for most people.

Here I must add a word of warning. Temperance and simplicity in diet are the great virtues, not mere vegetarianism as such. Don't over-exaggerate the ethical significance of vegetarianism, which is indeed infinitesimal. A flesh-eater, who is simple and moderate in diet, is a better man than a gluttonous vegetarian, who eats too much or spends too much on food and drink. The vegetarianism of wealthy aristocrats, who live in palatial hotels, has no ethical value whatsoever. Their selfish parasitism is such a terrible sin that the small merit of their vegetarianism is completely lost. They try to be just and compassionate to the animals, but are unjust and cruel to men and women. They may practise vegetarianism for the sake of better health, but they cannot pride themselves on their higher Ethics. Speaking arithmetically, 98 per cent. of Ethics is concerned with our relations to other men and women, and only 2 per cent. may be allotted to man's dealings with the animals. These figures are like the marks for different subjects in an examination. If you get full marks in the Animal Section of Ethics (two only), but do not secure the minimum in the Human Section, you will fail in the examination. Some vegetarians in India are heartless usurers and bloodsuckers. But if you first cultivate the social virtues of justice and fraternity, then your vegetarianism and your kindness to animals have some ethical value as ornaments of Personality. The avaricious, vindictive, wealthy, irascible, or haughty vegetarians and animal-lovers are only like sounding brass and tinkling cymbals. They are the modern Pharisees who boast much of a very minor virtue, while they lack the chief social virtues that are the mainstay of Humanity.

Whatever food-régime you may choose, do not attach too much importance to this question. Cultivate the higher Ethics first, and then you may also perfect yourself in this lower branch in course of time.

SECTION II.—PERSONAL SERVICE

ALL men and women should devote part of their time and energy to Personal Service. This is a debt that each one of us owes to those unfortunate sisters and brethren who have been deprived by Nature or by society of the advantages and privileges that we enjoy. It is not enough to give money: you must give yourself, your time and work. Personal Service is the first step in moral progress, as it teaches you to be unselfish; and unselfishness is the root of all Virtue.

Wherever you may live, you will find these pitiable creatures within easy reach of you. Alas! They are to be found everywhere. No one can have any excuse for shirking Personal Service; there are many opportunities for all, which create duties for all. Bad laws and institutions need not stand between those who love and those who suffer. Direct individual Service oversteps all the artificial barriers of classes, states, nations, and churches. It finds its way as from man to brother-man, from woman to sister-woman. It can work wonders in a Monarchy and in a Republic, under Feudalism and under Capitalism, in Soviet Russia and in plutocratic America. It can heal and bless among the Moslems and the Christians, the Buddhists and the Hindus, the Fetishists and the Freethinkers. Wherever there is suffering, there is the call for Service. Such Service is twice blessed: it blesses him that gives and him that receives it. It does not wait for laws and organizations, institutions and constitutions: it is free, direct, and immediate, flying straight on the wings of Mercy, not crawling and creeping in the crooked labyrinths of politics and legislation. It comes fresh and bright from the hearts of noble men and women; it does not emerge stale and mildewed after a slow and uncertain passage through prating parliaments and blighting bureaucracies. It knows not abstractions and collectivities: it succours and consoles men, women, and children as fellow-sufferers, not as compatriots or co-religionists or fellow-conspirators. It recognizes only one bond, Humanity; it honours only one motive, Love; it hears only one voice, that of human suffering.

Personal Service will always be partial and localized in its effects, as there is a great deal of suffering that can be mitigated or abolished only after the establishment of better economic and political institutions. Far be it from me to suggest that Personal Service can cure all ills or even assuage all sorrow around us. It has its own limited sphere; and Economics and Politics have their mightier orbits. It feels and works for to-day, even for this hour and *this minute*: while Economics and Politics *think* and build for to-morrow, even for the next year, the next century, the next millennium. But Personal Service is quick and practicable, here and now, for every one of us; while Economics and Politics tarry long, and make the heart sick with waiting, waiting, waiting—how long? Oh, how long? When you pass a poor cripple at the street-corner, you help him to get his bread for the day by giving him a small coin; but many years will elapse, and this cripple will not be there, when your progressive political party will establish vast hospitals and asylums for the relief of all such sufferers. There is a time-lag in politics, which can and should be counteracted to a certain extent by immediate personal aid. Science and Politics will one day banish blindness and deafness from the earth: but, in the meantime, you must help the blind and the deaf of your time to live and work as best they can You and I and the blind and the deaf of our time will all be dead and gone when, at long last, the perfect world, entirely free from the blemishes of blindness and deafness, will emerge from the slow-distilling, slow-filtering laboratories of Science. True love works and serves for this miserable To-day and also for the distant golden To-morrow of our dreams.

The triumphs of Economics and Politics are often temporary and precarious, while Personal Service wins what it wills every time. Many admirable institutions and constitutions have been utterly destroyed by brute force in the past. A civilized State may enact varied and complicated laws for the alleviation of suffering, but there comes suddenly the earthquake of a Hun raid, a Teutonic tumult, or a Mongol locust-flight, and where are then all the wise laws of Rome and Baghdad? They are gone, all gone, like a whiff of smoke in the desert air. And what then? For several centuries political wisdom will be dormant and inert; force and fraud will rule the State. Who will then come to the rescue of all the weak and helpless sufferers? Certainly not Law and Politics. In those dark days, only Love, as expressed in Personal Service, can save society from perishing altogether in the slough of pessimism and egotism. When the State could no longer establish hospitals, St. Basil and his disciples created them by the magic of Personal Service. When the "Government" knew only war, wine, and women, St. Benedict and his followers established schools and almshouses for the people all over Europe. All this has happened, and may happen again. The civilized State will remain a feeble and ephemeral institution for a long time to come. Democracy will win and lose, and win again, in the long-drawn-out struggle between the Classes and the Masses, and between Barbarism and Civilization. When Force blots out good laws and institutions, then good men and women must take up the burden of helping all who suffer. Law and Politics will yet rise and fall many a time in the chequered story of our race. Love and Service stand and abide for ever.

No life is complete without Personal Service. If you are a scholar, your learning does not exempt you from this duty. If you are an artist, your genius does not absolve you from this sacred obligation. If you are a politician, your political plots and plans do not release you from this moral conscription. If you are a poet, an orator, or a journalist, your work for different "Causes" and "Movements" is no substitute for this self-imposed *corvée*. I talk to you of living, bleeding, hopeless, helpless men, women, and children, not of abstract "Causes" and "Movements." If you are rich, you cannot run away from your hungry or sick neighbour, and say "Oh, I am giving money to many hospitals and charity societies." On such "patrons" and "philanthropists" falls the curse of Simon: "Thy money perish with thee." If you devote yourself to literature, you cannot leave the blind in their darkness and the deaf in their isolation, and say: "Oh, I am writing a wonderful book on the progress of civilization, or preparing an eloquent speech on the Social Insurance Bill, or composing a beautiful poem on the blessings of Mercy. That is my contribution of Service." No, it is not a contribution at all: it is an evasion. If you are an eminent scientist, you cannot neglect the cripples of your borough and say: "I am carrying on valuable research in physiology, astronomy, and botany, and serve mankind in this way. I shall soon discover a new bacillus or a new star." No, even if you discover a thousand new nebulæ, your life is incomplete and unblessed, if you refuse to give a little time to the Personal Service of those who suffer. You may gaze at stars through your telescope and entrap bacilli with your microscope: but you need no telescopes and microscopes to see these misery-maddened creatures round you, in your own town, in your own street. Your first small duty is to them, not to the stars and the bacilli. Pay your mite of Service to your unfortunate neighbours, and then begin your great and fruitful work in science, politics, and literature. Thus, and thus only, can you prove that your human feelings are not atrophied. Then you will serve mankind as fully-developed men and women, and not merely as soulless machines for the manufacture of pictures, poems, inventions, theorems, speeches, books, laws, or constitutions. Keats has wisely taught us that moral progress depends on deep-felt sympathy and love:

> " None can usurp this height. . .
> But those to whom the miseries of the world
> Are misery, and will not let them rest."

Personal Service must be rendered to the defectives, the sick, and the poor.

1. THE DEFECTIVES. Each one of us must render Personal Service to the blind, the deaf, the deaf-mutes, the cripples, and others who are handicapped in life on account of physical disability and infirmities. They are truly the victims of Fate. You, who are blessed with all the normal organs and limbs, cannot imagine what a sad and drab life the defectives are condemned to live. Think first of the blind. I rejoice to see the glory of sunrise and sunset, the beauty of the starlit sky and the flower-decked meadow, the splendour of painting, sculpture, and architecture, the sweetness of children and maidens that fill me with wonder and delight. I am thrilled at the sight of the snow-clad, sun-lit peaks of the Alps, and treasure the Sistine Madonna and the Taj Mahal in the innermost shrine of my soul as a joy for ever. I am happy to feast my eyes on the love-transfigured faces of my friends and their little children. I have enjoyed the loveliness of the almond-blossoms, the bluebells, the lotus-flowers, and the mimosa-clusters. I can still visualize the silver-sheen of the waterfalls at Lauterbrunnen and the ethereal beauty of the fairyland of Gornergrat. I can recall or behold the sublime grace of Venus de Milo and Zeus Otricoli, when I will. My memory can still revel in the play of lightning in a tropical sky, or that halo round the moon, or that earth-spanning ribbon of the double rainbow, or the artistry of the duck's raiment, or the spacious flower-covered walls of the Riviera, or the rhododendron-dell in the Kew Gardens, or the poppy-fields near Delphi, or the flashing fairy-lights in the white winter of the North. I live over again that moment of rapture, when I caught the first glimpse of the rings of Saturn, or saw the phloem and xylem hidden away in the plants of

the garden. I have seen and enjoyed much that is beautiful and fascinating in Nature and in Humanity. I hope to see and enjoy more of it, because I am not smitten with blindness. But all this world of beauty simply does not exist for the blind: in this respect they share the awful fate of the termites. Let Milton interpret their loss for us. He utters his pathetic plaint thus:

> "Thus with the year
> Seasons return, but not to me returns
> Day, or the sweet approach of ev'n or morn,
> Or sight of vernal bloom, or summer's rose,
> Or flocks, or herds, or human face divine,
> But cloud instead, and ever-during dark
> Surrounds me, from the cheerful ways of men
> Cut off; and, for the book of knowledge fair,
> Presented with a universal blank
> Of Nature's works, to me expunged and rased,
> And Wisdom at one entrance quite shut out."

Henry Fawcett never saw the face of his wife and his daughter. You, who have a family, know what he missed. Well may Schiller put this heart-rending cry into Arnold von Melchthal's mouth: "To die is nothing; but to live, and not to see, that is a calamity."

Now you, who have eyes, owe a duty to the blind. Lend them your eyes for a little time once a day, or once a week, or even once a month. Read to them, or take them out for a walk, or sing and play music for them, or write letters for them, or teach them how to work, read, and write, or cook for them, or make a good cup of tea for them. Do not use your eyes only for yourself: share them with the blind. Be not content only with subscribing money to the fund for the blind: start with that, but do not stop there. Make friends with at least one blind person, and try to serve, help, cheer, and encourage that one friend. Don't worry about statistics and institutions: do your duty to that single, suffering man or woman. You will thus complete and enrich two lives, your own and another's. Remember the Buddhist poet Shantideva's noble wish: "May I be a lamp to the blind!" I once asked a group of blind working-men what I could do for them. I was surprised at their reply: "Please read interesting books to us in our workshop."

The blind must lead a difficult and mutilated life, but the deaf are in some respects even more unfortunate. They are cut off from conversation and social life, and are often shut up in the prisons of their own minds. They are sometimes even shunned by others, as it is troublesome to enter into communication with them. Harriet Martineau's trumpet must have scared away many a friend. Deaf men and women must suffer silent torture at social gatherings.

They see that the people round them speak and laugh, but they have no part or lot in all that talk and mirth. As for music, it does not exist for the deaf. Who or what can compensate them for this terrible loss? You think and say that life without music would be barren boredom, a dull dreary round of drudgery that could not be endured. Even the gypsies, who have no culture, have music and love it. But the deaf can never enjoy music. Not for them the sublime symphonies of Beethoven, or Schubert's lilting Lieder, or Wagner's varied trumpet-tones, or the lyrical strains of Mozart. You have heard much noble music, and can hear it again in your soul whenever you wish to recall it. You hope to listen to more music of the highest order, because you are not deaf. But there is no such hope for the deaf. They are for ever cut off from this perennial source of joy and inspiration. Theirs is a sad and dull life.

You, who can hear, owe a duty to the deaf. You cannot bestow on them the gifts of hearing and of music, but you can serve them in many ways. You can visit them and treat them to interesting conversation by writing or through the medium of a sign-language. You can teach them lip-reading, which will rescue them from their spiritual solitude. You can advise them about possible remedies for their infirmity. You can show them beautiful pictures as a compensation for their misfortune. You can lighten their heavy burden in other ways, and will always find them appreciative.

The deaf-mutes are still more unfortunate than the deaf. Find out how you can serve them, and do something for them.

The cripples are much to be pitied. They cannot walk or work much. They are only half alive and depend on the help of others for many necessary movements and actions. When you walk about in strength and freedom, remember the poor cripples. When you use your hands and limbs for writing, eating, or working, remember the poor cripples. Find out how you can serve them. Perhaps they need your aid for getting up, or sitting down, or going downstairs, or crossing the road, or putting on their clothes, or cooking their food. Try to help as much as you can.

2. The Sick. Most of us are not defectives, but all of us have been ill more than once. We know from experience that the sick need help and comfort. When a person is bed-ridden with fever or pain, he is sometimes unable even to telephone to the doctor or go to his house. Someone—relative, friend, or nurse—must offer his or her services. Then there is the medicine to be bought and given at prescribed intervals, the special food and drink to be prepared,

the temperature to be taken, the bath, etc., etc. Often someone must spend the night in the sick-room, and sacrifice his or her sleep in this ministry of love. Besides the physical care of the sick, the loving friends or relatives must also speak sweet words of sympathy and encouragement, and show the patient that he or she is loved. To know and feel that you are loved—what a difference it makes in the weary hours of sickness! Love is more than half the cure: the medical treatment is less than half. The will to recover is awakened and strengthened in the patient, if the air of the room is vibrant with the unseen thought-waves of love and affection. Much to be pitied is the lonely creature who has no one to tend him or her in the moment of such affliction! For this reason, I must utter my most vehement protest against the cruel modern custom of leaving the sick entirely in the hands of hired nurses and mercenaries, for whom the patient is a mere number in a ward, and not a father, mother, brother, sister, son, daughter, uncle, aunt, cousin, friend, or comrade. It may be necessary to transport the sick to a hospital and employ trained nurses for the technical services that are required. But some relative or friend should also be constantly in attendance, as would be the case if the patient were treated at home. The scientific efficiency of the hospital must be combined with the loving-kindness of the home. I remember that a friend was allowed to spend the night with a class-comrade, who lay ill in a public hospital for several weeks. We took turns at this service. Our mere presence was at least as important as the doctor's prescription and the nurse's visits. The humanitarian feeling of the religiously trained nurses is also no substitute for home-love. You cannot be solaced by a white-robed Sister of Mercy; she may be an angel, but she is not your mother, wife, or sister. She cannot feel keen personal affection for you. You are only an object for her universal benevolence and charity, and her cold compassion cannot surround you with the atmosphere of love. In sickness, deep personal love must be given in full measure by all who are near and dear to the sufferer.

If sickness afflicts your home or your circle of friends, home-treatment should be tried as far as possible. Then you, who are well, should forget your own comfort and repose in the service of the sick relative. You may have to get up in the middle of the night, or go without sleep, or sacrifice your amusements and appointments, or even miss your regular meals. But if you love, you will not find the burden too hard to bear. If you are only a friend and do not serve in the sick-room, don't forget to call and enquire how the patient is getting on and if there is anything you can do. Don't forget to send some flowers, with a kind message of sympathy and goodwill. Don't forget to telephone frequently, if you are unable to call. But you should never be so " busy " that you can't visit a sick friend. Love and Duty find time for everything. During convalescence, you should offer your time for company and conversation. After complete recovery, you may give good advice to the friend or relative. You may remind him or her that prevention is better than cure. You may suggest that illness is usually the penalty for the violation of some laws of Hygiene. Most people in good health resent such homilies from others, but serious illness makes them amenable to friendly advice. They may then be willing to change their habits and take up regular Physical Culture. Through your tactful guidance, an attack of sickness may thus turn out to be a blessing in disguise for your friend. If you give love and service during illness, and wise counsel after it, you have done your duty in full measure.

You may ask, " What should be done if our relatives and friends are in the grip of some contagious or infectious disease, like influenza, tuberculosis, cholera, or the plague? What about an epidemic that may be raging in our town or our country? " Well, your duty is the same as in the case of common ailments, except that you should take proper precautions. That's all. It makes no difference whether your loved ones have to face an ordinary fever or the " million-murdering " cholera. You cannot run away from your family, your friends, or your fellow-citizens, if they are grappling with the pestilence that leaps from man to man. Take all necessary precautions, but stand firm at your post, like a sentinel on duty. Don't be a coward: more people are slain by fear than by the germs. A friend of mine tended many plague-stricken relatives and friends, and nothing happened to him. Think of the Franciscan friars, who lived and served in the filthy medieval towns. Remember John Howard, who visited the death-dealing prison-dens of Europe in the sixty-eighth century A.H. (eighteenth A.D.). Father Damien gave his life for the lepers who were not his kinsmen or friends; and others carry on the noble tradition to this day. Once or twice in life, you may have to face Death in fulfilment of love or duty, and you must not run away. The behaviour of an individual or a people during an epidemic is a searching test of moral calibre. And if you too are struck down, what then? When others are dying around you, you need not be afraid to die. We must all die some day: no one will live for ever. It is in our power to die nobly, like saints and sages, and not like despicable cowards and fugitives. And where will you hide yourself from Death? Where can you flee from him?

You must train yourself to look Death in the face bravely and resolutely, when love and duty may bid you take the risk. If you survive, you live with honour: if you die, you die with honour. It is best so.

3. THE POOR. Under the existing social system, there are many men, women, and children who lack even the necessaries of life. They are found in all countries. They suffer from hunger and cold. They are clad in rags and cast-off garments; they lodge in squalid hovels and dark cellars. They must live on a small pittance, which does not suffice for the barest physical needs. They are always underfed, and their dwellings are dismal and dirty. In cold countries, they cannot buy enough fuel or warm clothing to be comfortable during the winter: they die off like flies through malnutrition and exposure to the inclement weather. In hot climates, their lot is somewhat better, as they can enjoy the sunshine and bathe in the streams. But poverty is a terrible calamity everywhere. Theognis cried: "The worst of miseries, worse than old age or wearisome disease, is Poverty." Such destitution robs life of all joy and zest, and condemns its victims to a very low level of vitality and activity. Such poor people cannot be said to live: they merely breathe and moan. Life without food, shelter, and clothing is only a long-drawn-out agony. Many animals, wild and domesticated, are much better off than this miserable class of human beings. Such poor woe-begone creatures shock and shame us at the street-corners in every country. A starving wretch, clad in rags, who begs money or food, is a very saddening sight that haunts the mind for days.

There are many causes and circumstances that explain the presence of this class in our midst. Some are born in penury and are given only scanty wages throughout their lives. They belong to the ranks of unskilled labour. Others are blind, deaf, or crippled defectives, who have not been trained to work. Others are degenerate drunkards and incorrigible idlers, who have not been properly controlled and directed. Others have been unlucky gamblers who have lost their all. Others are widows and orphans, for whom no one cares. Others are perhaps exiles and refugees, who suffer for some great Idea. Others are the victims of some natural calamity like an earthquake or an inundation. All these form the submerged crowd of poor unskilled labourers, beggars, tramps, vagabonds, street-painters, organ-grinders, match-sellers, and other indigent step-children of the State.

Whatever the cause of their destitution, they are here and now with us. The complete abolition of poverty cannot be brought about by direct Personal Service; new economic and political institutions must be established in order to attain that ideal. The poor will not always be with us; time will blot out Jesus Christ's hasty utterance. But, in the meantime, you, who enjoy the necessaries and comforts of life, and perhaps even some luxuries, owe a duty to your destitute fellow-men and fellow-citizens. You may be a skilled artisan, a factory-worker, a professional man, a merchant, or a capitalist. You feel for the very poor; your heart melts with pity for their sad lot. You cannot bear to think of men, women, and children suffering the pangs of hunger or shivering in the bleak winter, when there is plenty of food and fuel in the world. You are moved to tears, whenever you see the victims of such poverty or hear about their privations and hardships. You would not like to see yourself and your family in such misery. You are a social being, and deep compassion is aroused in your heart at the thought of all those struggling fellow-creatures. This emotion seeks to express itself in deeds of charity. You give a little money, food, drink, or clothes to the poor persons whom you know or happen to meet.

Thus Mercy prompts you to succour the destitute; but Justice also teaches you to give as much as you can. The unequal distribution of wealth in society is unjust and unnatural. Everyone should have an equal share in all the products of social labour. Everything belongs to all. The sum-total of wealth should be distributed in the spirit of love and social service, as the income of a family is spent among its members at present. The father of a family does not starve some of his children, while others are pampered. The wealth of the whole world is the heritage of all who live on the earth. The very poor, who lack even the necessaries of life, are therefore unjustly deprived of their share. They are robbed of what is their due. Some rich people are grabbing too much, and these patient outcasts are given too little. Therefore, if you belong to the upper middle class or to the wealthier group of capitalists and landlords, you are called upon in the name of Justice to make due restitution to those whom you have defrauded and swindled. You possess more than enough: you command the necessaries, comforts, and luxuries of civilized life, while others cannot obtain even the necessaries. A part of what you call your money really belongs to them: you have stolen it from them by force or fraud. It is therefore your duty to restore that money to its rightful owners by giving alms, gifts, and presents to the poor people in your neighbourhood. The spontaneous feeling of pity moves you to give something: then increase your gift by a very substantial amount, when you understand that Justice demands the immediate reimbursement of other people's money. Make haste to give away your superfluous wealth; or live in shame and sin as thieves and robbers. Make your choice. Remember Spenser's wise precept: "Good is no Good but if it be spent."

Thus Mercy persuades you and Justice exhorts you to give much in charity to the poor. Charity is the very first step in moral development, the Alpha of the alphabet of Ethics. If someone were to ask me what he or she should do for moral improvement, I would say: "Set apart a fixed portion of your income (wages, salary, profits, or dividends) for the use of the poor." You will then be on the lowest rung of the spiritual ladder. Do not leave your charity to chance impulse. Do not give what is left after all other possible expenses have been met. Make charity a first charge on your family budget. Place the money in a separate fund, and never use it for yourself under any circumstances whatsoever. You have given it to the poor: do not take it back. One per cent. or more of your income should be ear-marked for this permanent Poor Fund, but never less than 1 per cent. Make up your mind to regard only 99 per cent. of your earnings as your real income: surely this is not a difficult feat of psychology. In this way, you will always have money to help the poor. You will not be tempted to neglect their claims. You will not be obliged to reckon and calculate on every occasion. You have decided once for all to offer that irreducible 1 per cent. to the poor. So you will be ready and willing to act, whenever Mercy and Justice call.

Having established this Poor Fund, you should find out some of the destitute poor in your neighbourhood. Charity should begin in your street, your village, or your borough. Help first the poor people whom you know and meet in your daily life. Your first duty is to them. Do not subscribe liberally to Charity Organization Societies and Mansion House Funds before you have relieved the needy in your little corner of the world. Many philanthropists give very liberally to public charitable institutions, but they often forget the Lazarus at their gate. The best charity is personal, direct, and local; the second best is impersonal, remote, and mechanical. You should go to that poor blind widow round the corner or that old invalid in the almshouse, and offer your gift of money, food, or clothing with love and respect. True charity gives both money and love. Love can never be given through paid secretaries and hired agents of public institutions. You must not mechanize charity. Establish friendly personal relations with the poor neighbours whom you help. Give your gift as a friend to a friend, and not as a soulless company distributing dividends to unseen shareholders. It is the personal touch that counts. Give something of yourself, besides your money. Thus your gift will be twice blessed. Karl Marx gave money to the poor children who lived in the same street, but he also loved them, and they loved him and called him "Daddy Marx."

It is often better not to give money, but food, clothes, fuel, and other necessaries. Love is expressed more naturally by gifts of such things than through the medium of money. After all, the poor recipient of your charity will buy these things with the money. So you save him trouble by purchasing them for him. Besides, you know that your money is not wasted on drink or gambling. Both sentiment and prudence should lead you to prefer gifts in nature to money-presents. But there is no hard-and-fast rule about it. Try to vary the relative proportion of the two kinds of gifts according to the circumstances of the case.

You should also show personal kindness to the poor. They lack not only food and clothing, but often also self-respect, courage, manhood. They are as a rule despised by their prosperous neighbours. They are spoken of as "the scum of society," "the dregs of the population," the "riff-raff," the "ragamuffins," etc. Such abusive epithets exhibit the contempt with which the destitute poor are treated in our capitalistic society. They are made to feel that their poverty is a disgrace and a crime, of which they should be ashamed. You should invite such social pariahs to tea or dinner at your house or at a tea-shop. You should always shake hands with them, and not merely acknowledge their salutation from a distance. You should eat with them, drink with them, play with them, walk with them, and treat them as equals and friends. Scorn no brother-man: never reject and insult the poor and the humble. Say rather with Masefield: "Mine be the dirt and the dross, the dust, the scum of the earth." What is the use of giving money to the poor, if you do not first recognize their common humanity? Buddha and Ananda mixed freely and fraternally with the outcasts, and do you think you are greater than Buddha and Ananda? St. Francis ate and drank with the poor lepers of Assisi. I remember the astonishment of the proprietor and the waitresses of a tea-shop, when I took a London street-painter with me into the shop and ordered tea for two. He himself was agreeably surprised, when we once drank tea together at the corner on the pavement, which was his business office. A millionaire may haughtily throw a gold sovereign into a beggar's cap, as one may cast a bone at a dog. A good-hearted working-man gives more in charity, if he invites a poor widow to a simple supper at his own fireside, as Sir Launfal broke bread with the beggar and learned the great truth that "the gift without the giver is bare." The poor need both material aid and moral help. They are hungry for bread, but they are perhaps even more hungry for love, sympathy, equality, and brotherhood. You must give them both.

As regards the destitute poor, who do not live in your neighbourhood, you owe a duty to them too; but you should be on your guard against professional beggars and impostors. It is difficult to know if a casual beggar or a wandering tramp is deserving of relief and assistance. Many so-called poor men, who stand at street-corners and near the churches, should be sent to labour-colonies or reformatories for their own good. They sometimes earn more than the honest working-man who toils eight or ten hours in a factory. It has been proved that some of these charlatans have substantial bank-accounts in New York. Quintin Hogg personally investigated the cases of a hundred street-beggars. Edward Gilliat thus describes the result of the enquiry: "He found that about fifty gave him wrong addresses; most of the remainder were undeserving; only two were cases of genuine need." It is your duty to discourage such vicious mendicancy. Refuse to give your penny or sixpence to these idle poor. Steel your heart against their appeals. Indiscriminate almsgiving is not true charity: it is a foolish habit. A civilized State should not allow any citizen to beg in public; the deserving poor should be helped by their neighbours, the parish, the municipality, and the State. Beggars and cripples in the streets are the wounds and sores of the body politic; they are symptoms of social disease and disorder. The time must come when public mendicancy, direct and indirect, will be abolished in all countries.

At the same time, it must be admitted that some street-beggars deserve your alms, as they are really destitute through no fault of their own Some of them find it very hard to earn a few pence daily and pay for their night-lodging and their very simple food. They are always under-nourished and scantily clad. You may help a few of them, if you first take the trouble of finding out where they live and what they do. Talk to them and make friends with them. You can thus make sure that your alms are not wasted on scoundrels. In such cases, that general rule also holds good: charity must be based on personal knowledge and interest. It must not be blind and mechanical.

4. Institutions. Some extensive institutions for the relief of the poor and the sick have been established in all countries. You should help them with money, voluntary service, and friendly advice. Subscribe out of your Poor Fund to some hospitals, "settlements," and orphanages. Beware of mercenary institutions, in which more money is spent on the salaries of "secretaries," managers, and staff than on the poor and the sick. Always read the Annual Reports. Give aid and support to such deserving ventures as Dr. Albert Schweitzer's hospital in Africa, the Educational Settlement at Sheffield, Miss Muriel Lester's Settlement in East London, the Cecil Houses for Women, Lady Margaret Hospital, Dr. Barnardo's Homes, the Widows' Home of Poona, the Ramakrishna Mission, the Friends of Armenia Orphanages in Syria, and other properly conducted admirable institutions of the same type, in which the managers are themselves self-sacrificing idealists and not mere hired officials. Do not encourage such institutions as combine reactionary religious or political propaganda with relief-work. Many "Settlements" are not so harmless as they look. They are designed, or at least expected, to hinder the spread of Socialism among the poor or to bolster up some decadent Church.

In your work for such Institutions, you are not in direct personal touch with those who suffer. You should therefore distribute your money among the institutions of several countries. Such impersonal charity should be dispensed impartially to the poor and the sick of all nations. Thus your love will encircle the whole earth. As the seismograph records the slightest tremor of the earth's surface at a great distance, so let your soul respond instantaneously to the cry of suffering all over the wide world.

You should study the lives and appreciate the achievements of the great heroes and heroines of Personal Service in order to keep your own soul-flame always burning brightly. Read some short books about St. Basil, St. Benedict, St. Vincent de Paul, Albert Schweitzer, Bodelschwingh, John Howard, Jane Addams, William Booth, Dr. Barnardo, Dr. Wilfred Grenfell, Elizabeth Fry, J. F. Oberlin, Ramakrishna, J. H. Wichern, E. Schrenk, and others who have served suffering humanity.

Thus you will at all times be ready and willing to do your bit of Personal Service.

> " In silence, . .
> Steals on soft-handed Charity,
> Tempering her gifts, that seem so free,
> By time and place,
> Till not a woe the bleak world see,
> But finds her grace "
>
> (Keble)

SECTION III.—THE FIVE CONCENTRIC CIRCLES

YOU find yourself surrounded by millions of human beings on the earth. There are about 2000 million men, women, and children on this planet. To all human beings, beginning with your parents and your wife and children, and ending with the remotest pygmy in the African forests and the wildest Veddah in the jungles of Ceylon, you owe a duty that is absolute, undeniable, imperative. Humanity is one and indivisible. The Unity of Mankind should be one of the most sacred principles of your creed. If there are men and women on other planets circling round our Sun or other Suns, you are linked to them too; but our ignorance on this point cancels our duties.

The Unity of Mankind.

I say that Humanity is one. There is poetical truth in the old legend of our common descent from Adam and Eve. We need not discuss whether men and women first arose and evolved in one region of the earth or at different localities. That is an archæological technicality. We derive our great principle of the unity of Humanity from present-day facts and experiences. All men have the Earth for their heritage and dwelling-place, this beautiful and bountiful Earth, which is our cradle and our grave. What greater Fatherland could you wish to love? Of what other spacious "Patrie" would you like to be a citizen? This Earth, she is the Mother and Mother-country that we adore. She has given birth to us; she feeds and sustains us; she will take us back into her bosom when we die. Hail, Alma Mater Gea! Thee we salute with reverence and gratitude. Through thee and before thee, all thy children, white and brown and black and yellow, feel their eternal kinship.

Mankind is one. All men and women belong to the species *Homo sapiens*. They can all breed successfully with one another; and blood can be transferred from a white man into a black or yellow man. The slave-owners of the United States attempted to prove that the negroes really formed another species altogether and could be regarded as sub-human creatures. But that argument, born of greed, was doomed to speedy oblivion. All men and women in the five continents have the anatomy and physiology of the same species. No one can doubt or deny the biological unity of the human race as a species, *Homo sapiens*.

All men, even the lowest Bushmen and Papuans, can speak. Speech is the common hall-mark of our race, as *Homo sapiens* has attained the requisite degree of cerebral development. All men and women use tools of some kind and can light a fire. All men and women live in families, and even in tribal society of some type. Rousseau's lonely savage, who "did not know even his own children," is a figment of the untutored imagination. All men and women can count, reflect, draw inferences and conclusions, and adapt means to ends. All men and women have family affection and cherish the relationships of father, mother, brother, sister, wife, and child. All men and women possess some theory of the Universe, its origin and government, its purpose and meaning; they live not at random, but according to rules and laws, customs and ceremonies. All men and women cultivate social memory, look back to the past, and cherish some traditions. All men and women look forward to the future, and provide for their posterity. All men and women feel that they will not perish utterly, but will survive in some way, either personally as self-conscious souls, or impersonally in their descendants. The species *Homo sapiens* may be said to exhibit its fundamental unity through the higher development of two outstanding qualities: Intelligence and Sociability. When a certain stage of Intelligence and Sociability is reached in the course of evolution, Humanity appears on the scene. The Stoics based the unity of mankind on the participation of all in Reason, as Marcus Aurelius says: "If our intellectual part is common, the Reason also, in respect of which we are rational beings, is common." The Christians taught the Fatherhood of God, as "God made of one blood all nations of men." They made Love the bond of unity. Let us now accept both these profound ideas, and recognize that developing Reason (Brain-power) and deepening Sympathy are the two characteristics that distinguish our human race from all sub-human species. You should say with pride: "I am a member of Humanity, a citizen of the Earth."

The Two Barriers.

The unity of Mankind is a fact, but unfortunately it is not clearly recognized and appreciated, as there is no uniformity among Mankind. Unity-plus-variety, but not uniformity: this seems to be the rule of life for us. Some of us would have preferred complete uniformity in all details to this variety-in-unity; others detest absolute uniformity and find that variety-in-unity is interesting. Well, we must face the unpleasant truth that certain differentiating traits among mankind have obscured the fundamental unity of the race and even led to hatred and war. You should be on your guard against these superficial differences, and never allow them to weaken your sense of duty towards all men, women, and children of all continents and countries on the earth. I shall discuss briefly the two chief factors of variety that tend to confuse and obscure our view of human unity. These two factors are Race (with Colour) and Language (with Nationality).

(1) *Race and Colour.*—The anthropologists divide mankind into several "races" according to their complexion, stature, cephalic index, character of face, shape of the nose, texture of the hair, etc. Men are white, brown, yellow, black, and even copper-coloured; they are dolichocephalic, mesaticephalic, or brachycephalic; they are broad-faced or long-faced, prognathous or orthognathous; they are leptorrhine, mesorrhine, platyrrhine, or hyper-platyrrhine, etc., etc. These physical differences have been and are very potent for mischief, as they make men and women look so unlike one another. We are apt to forget our basic unity at the sight of such strange faces and bodies. The tall white Caucasian with the aquiline nose and golden hair looks very different from the short, flat-faced, yellowish Japanese or the thick-lipped, woolly-haired, ebony-hued Negro. Nature has played us a sorry trick here. Although most people know that both the Teutonic blonde and the black beauty of Bechuanaland have the same kind of brain and blood, yet—yet the eye receives such a vivid impression of contrast and diversity that the thinking mind and the loving heart are for the moment defeated and paralysed for all practical purposes. We are compelled by our perfidious eyes to dwell upon the external differences of physiognomy and forget the inner unity. Such visual sensations must be counteracted by Intelligence and Sociability, and you must attain to a keener realization of the fraternal relationship. Remember the well-demonstrated fact that small white children in America are not repelled by the dark complexion of their negro playmates: thus children teach us wisdom. You also know that love between man and woman leaps over all barriers of race. In fact, couples belonging to different races often love each other more passionately than lovers of the same race. Love unites us all in sweet hymeneal bonds. The

Negroes, the Chinese, the Caucasians, and the Americans of Brazil bear witness to the unity of Love. In vain shall the purblind legislators of North America and South Africa say to Love, "Thus far and no further." In vain shall they try to keep Love within the bounds of their wretched laws and ordinances. In vain shall they attempt to imprison the bird of Love in their separate white-coloured and black-coloured cages. Eros will burst the bars and fly as he listeth. Even white and black have been merged into brown Creole beauty in Central America, and Love has affirmed what pride and prejudice would fain deny. Further, you should train yourself to reflect on the many elements of culture that all the races possess in common. Thus you will escape the physiognomic perils that the ethnologists have described in detail. Your eyes will pierce the outer veil of pigment, and the Röntgen rays of love will enable them to see straight into the mind and heart of a brother-man. For now there are no Aryans and Semites, Mongols and Negroes, but only Men and Women; and Mankind is all-in-all.

Of all these external differences, the colour of the skin is often the most terrible obstacle to harmony and concord All honour to the civilized peoples that are free from colour-prejudice: such are the nations of the Mediterranean region and South America. But most people in England, Germany, and North America are lamentably barbarous in this respect. Among them, colour-prejudice in all its folly and fatuity works havoc like a pestilence that nothing can tame. Their belief in their much-prayed-to "God" and their much-trumpeted faith in their "redeemer" Jesus Christ have not availed to cure them of this dreadful disease of chronic *chromophobia* ("fear of colour"). A negro may be a highly educated man, a member of the same Christian sect and a citizen of the same State; but many white Americans, who are fellow-Methodists and fellow-citizens, regard him as "untouchable." The whites of North America insist on excluding the blacks from their schools, churches, and clubs, and even from their cemeteries! The white working-men of South Africa boycott and persecute their black fellow-labourers. Of no worth are such a religion and such citizenship, naked shams and impostures are they, harbingers of doom and dissolution, for they lack the power to save erring men and women from wicked ways and horrible crimes. Between 6889 and 6930 A.H., 3724 persons were lynched in the United States. All colour-maniacs are spiritually sick: they run amok, and wound and kill in savage racial riots and lynching murders. What do the bragging, self-complacent patriots and pious, prayerful Christians say to this?

This mental aberration can be cured by chemical or moral remedies. Some scientists should invent a paint, which should be accepted as the standard authorized colour of the skin for all men and women on the earth. The exact shade does not matter; the chief need is uniformity of hue. Let an international congress choose white or black, whitish-black or blackish-white, yellowish-brown or brownish-yellow, reddish-yellow or yellowish-red, and let us paint all new-born infants the right colour. There should be continual re-paintings throughout life. Let there be absolute uniformity in this respect; all variety is banned. Then the colour problem would be solved for ever. This is the chemical remedy.

If you reject this solution, you will have to resort to drastic measures of moral hygiene and educational reform. You will have to exorcize this destructive demon of *chromophobia* by the magic of sound education, humanitarian ethics, international laws, and fraternal social intercourse.

(2) *Language and Nationality.*

Caliban said to Prospero·

> " You taught me language, and my profit on't
> Is I know how to curse "

It is indeed sad to reflect that the unity of mankind has been marred and mangled by the diversity of languages, which has engendered hatred, suspicion, and bloodshed. It is natural that men should be unwilling and unable to fraternize with strangers who cannot hold converse with them. Mutual intelligibility is a necessary condition of co-operation. Language has erected an almost insurmountable Chinese Wall of separation between one people and another. Here too Nature has been most unkind to us. In the primitive stage, as in Africa to-day, a bewildering multiplicity of dialects prevails, and the sense of social affinity is thus confined to a very limited region. One of the dialects sometimes develops into a national language, and the Nation-State is established as the political organ of each language-group. At present, we are passing through this stage. The thousands of early dialects have been consolidated into about fifty, or fewer, literary languages. The next step in advance will be taken when only one language is employed as the medium of communication throughout the world.

As the unification of language proceeds, strife and hatred are diminished, as the political State is generally founded on the basis of a common language. When many dialects are spoken, many small States are organized, and many small wars are waged. The big Nation-States are rendered possible by the growth of widely diffused national languages, and then fewer wars are fought on a vastly larger scale. It is a historical law that States must fight among themselves. The State has been, is, and will always be a pugnacious beast. So long as there are many States, there will be war among them. The sense of human unity is almost obliterated by the closer and narrower bond of particular citizenship. Men and women cannot be citizens of different States and also live in peace and amity. Peace demands one World-State, which will be reared on the foundation of one world-language.

In the meantime, we should foster and strengthen the sentiment of human fraternity by all means in our power, in spite of the tremendous barriers of the national languages.

Shakespeare has put the complete plea for human unity into Shylock's mouth. The usurer was despised and hated as a Jew on account of his race and creed, and he exclaims: "I am a Jew. Hath not a Jew eyes? Hath not a Jew hands, organs, dimensions, senses, affections, passions? Fed with the same food, hurt with the same weapons, subject to the same disease, healed by the same means, warmed and cooled by the same winter and summer, as a Christian is? If you prick us, do we not bleed? If you tickle us, do we not laugh? If you poison us, do we not die?"

So, if you are ever tempted to scorn or wrong a brother-man of another race and creed, remember the pathetic plaint of Shylock the Jew.

As an air-pilot rises far above the ground and sees the whole landscape at a glance, even so you should rise in spirit above the barriers of race, colour, language, and nationality, and embrace *all* men, women, and children in your love. Let no one be shut out from your loving heart. As the Earth nourishes all and the Sun shines on all, so let your fraternal sympathy extend to all men and women, excluding none. The ancient epic, "Mahabharata," teaches this ideal in Sanskrit verse.

> "Small souls inquire, 'Belongs this man
> To our own race or sect or clan?'
> But larger-hearted men embrace
> As brothers all the human race"

The fundamental rule of social duty is this: Let all your thoughts and actions promote the development and happiness of all mankind, irrespective of race and nationality. Look upon yourself as a very tiny part of the larger whole that is Humanity. At present, for instance, you represent about $\frac{1}{1,000,000,000}$ th of Humanity. Never lose sight of the great Society, with reference to which all your ideas and deeds must be measured and judged. As a criterion of social duty, there is no smaller unit than Mankind in its entirety. For Mankind, we are born, live, think, and work; and for Mankind, we die.

The Five Circles.

Within the great Circle of Humanity, Nature has drawn four other concentric Circles for you. Each Circle lies wholly within the next larger one, and all lie within the biggest outermost Circle. You are the Centre of all the Circles. The Circle of Humanity includes all the others. This geometrical figure is a symbol of the five Social Institutions to which you belong as a human being, viz. (1) the Family, (2) the Relatives, (3) the Municipality, (4) the Nation, (5) the World-State.

The Family.—The family is your smallest sphere of activity in the service of Humanity. It is composed of yourself, your wife, and children. This group is a natural biological unit. Man and woman are attracted to each other by sex-passion and personal love, and the pledge of their love is the offspring.

I need not discuss the alternative groupings that have been proposed from time to time. Plato taught that the personal ties of husband and wife, and of parent and child, made men and women forget their duties to society and the State. He proposed the abolition of the family for the guardian class, as it fostered selfishness and anti-social habits. He wrote: "The fathers and the daughters and the other relations . . . are not to be known at all. . . . This is the community of women and children among the guardians of the State." John Humphrey Noyes, the founder of the Oneida Perfectionist Community in the United States, actually persuaded men and women to give up the practice of living as loving couples. They mated according to a peculiar scheme, and the children were brought up in a common nursery. C. Nordhoff says of these Christian Communists: "Complex marriage means, in their practice, that within the limits of the community membership, any man and woman may and do freely cohabit, having first gained each other's consent, not by private conversation or courtship, but through the intervention of some third person or persons. They strongly discourage what they call exclusive and idolatrous attachment of two persons for each other." There was thus no "family" as an organized institution between the individual and the community.

The monastic orders of the Christian and Buddhist Churches abolish the family by living as childless celibates; they jump over this step of the ladder by means of unnatural self-restraint.

Now I admit that the family must be condemned as a degrading and pernicious institution if it is regarded as an end in itself, and not as a means of rendering service to Humanity. Like all good things, it may be used wisely, or it may be abused. At present, alas! men and women are guilty of wicked, shameless, and criminal abuse of this natural and necessary institution. They suffer from the psychological malady that Gaetano Mosca has called "familyism." Their gaze is so concentrated on their small family that they entirely lose sight of the universal Society, as a penny placed before the eye blots out the sun from the view. The family is very close to us physically and biologically, while Humanity is rather distant, abstract, and intangible. Most men and women love the family too much; and, as a consequence, they love Mankind too little. Excessive devotion to the family breeds selfishness, avarice, meanness, and uncharitableness. Energetic industrialists amass millions by ruthless exploitation of the labourers, to whom they refuse a living wage, while their frivolous wives and children squander all their money in riotous luxury. Wealthy men and women leave almost all their possessions by will to their sons, daughters, nephews, and nieces. On an average, in England, only 1 per cent. of their property is bequeathed to public institutions. What a pitiful story of family-egotism is revealed by these statistics! Most women are tempted to injure other women's children in order to secure some advantages for their own; the name of "step-mother" is a by-word for cruelty. The mothers of the rival candidates in a Beauty Exhibition have sometimes fought with fists and torn each other's hair! Dr. Thomas of Belfast has protested against Baby Shows in these words: "They're the very devil. Every mother thinks her baby is the best in the show. I have seen one mother black another mother's eye at one of these competitions."

Family-egotism prompts many people to rob their neighbours and ruin the State. It makes honest public life impossible, as every politician tries to benefit his family at the expense of the State. This moral failing accounts for the very slow growth of public spirit in such countries as China, Persia, and India. Robert Owen, the socialist leader, was so struck with the havoc wrought in society by this deep-rooted family-egotism, that he stigmatized our "homes" as "dens of hypocrisy and selfishness." The evil effects of familyism brought about a crisis in the English Salvation Army. On a wider stage, the great Marcus Aurelius allowed his worthless son Commodus to succeed him as Emperor. Oliver Cromwell ruined the cause of Republicanism in England by his attempt to establish a dynasty. In contemporary society, marriage and domestic life have robbed many progressive movements of some of their most zealous propagandists. Before marriage, many men and women work for different causes and ideals with exemplary enthusiasm; but they are apt to neglect this higher duty when they have a family to love and care for. Marriage has ruined many a noble character! P.-J. Proudhon found such delight in the company of his three daughters that he seldom attended public meetings after his marriage. I know an able graduate who lost his wife, and then resolved to lead a simple life and devote himself entirely to public movements. But unfortunately he was induced to remarry, and he is now a commonplace successful lawyer with a substantial bank-account John Stuart Mill left England in order to live at Avignon, where his wife died, and he built a house near the cemetery; here was surely an excess of tender sentiment. Herbert Spencer actually declared that he could not have written his treatises on the Synthetic Philosophy if he had married. His celibacy made him a philosopher, as it gave him courage and leisure. I was acquainted with an American physician who went out to Asia as a medical missionary, but he joined himself in wedlock to a lady who also intended to serve in the same Mission. When she fell ill in the tropical climate, he considered it his duty to abandon his life-work and return to America with her. In this case, the family-tie ruined the healthy idealist with the sick one, as the rope sometimes drags down the other Alpine climbers after one of them has slipped. Many brave men are afraid of imprisonment and loss of money, simply because they are blesed with a wife and children. Marriage makes cowards of them all. Surely there is some truth in Bacon's shrewd remark: "He that hath wife and children hath given hostages to fortune: for they are impediments to great enterprises, either of virtue or mischief." Or shall we say with the cynic: "A young man married is a man that's marred."

It is thus clear that familyism is a terrible evil that makes a harmonious social life almost impossible. Shall we then cry, "Down with the family"? Shall we follow the Chinese philosopher, Mo Ti, who taught that one should love all men equally and have no special affection for parents and kinsmen? Before we take up this extreme attitude, we must consider two points: (1) The relation of lovers (as a loving couple) is natural and beneficial. (2) The relation of parent and child is also natural and beneficial. It may be bio-psychological, or purely psychological.

I believe that men and women have a natural tendency to form couples according to the law of affinity (irrespective of the duration of a particular couple-relation, which may be stable or otherwise). They "fall in love" after the age of puberty; and love is a kind of excess, directed towards one object at a time, as Aristotle pointed out long ago. It is desirable that most couple-relations should be permanent and lasting; but that consideration is irrelevant to the argument at this point. It is sufficient to recognize the biological and psychological phenomenon exhibited in the formation of loving-couples, temporary or permanent. The experience of the Oneida community demonstrated the existence of this powerful attraction between men and women. C. Nordhoff says: "The Oneida Perfectionists find in practice a strong tendency toward what they call 'selfish love,' that is to say, the attachment of two persons to each other and their desire to be true to each other. . . . There has been suffering among their young people on this account. They rebuke this propensity, however, as selfish and sinful, and break it down rigorously." J. H. Noyes issued many stringent rules and regulations in order to prevent the growth of personal affection, which would have divided the community into many "*couples*" and their "*homes*." Every man was forbidden to meet a woman alone, and walks were also to be taken in groups. The natural couple-building propensity of men and women was thus kept in check by absurd and artificial restrictions. Such constraint always implies that foolish law-givers are doing violence to Nature and defying her. Human personality is not developed in these tortuous ways: it is only disfigured and distorted. Love is selective and exclusive, and it craves not only sexual intimacy, but also deep personal affection. It is not possible for a man and a woman to fall in love and mate, and then to feel no more interest in each other than in any other ordinary friends and comrades. But this unnatural indifference was exactly what Noyes tried to inculcate in his community, as he wished to abolish "couples" and "homes." He was in such a hurry to climb the spiritual ladder that he took away one of its natural rungs. But men may fall into the yawning abyss beneath, if the ascent is made unnecessarily difficult. I believe that the Perfectionists were most efficient workers; but they could not have been really happy men and women. They lived under an unnatural régime of repression and suppression.

We must accept Nature's law of couple-building, as we accept sex and love. Two lovers must have a certain special relation to each other, which is expressed in complete confidence, deep joy in each other's company, and mutual service. Love is a specialized form of friendship between a man and a woman, whom it unites as a couple. Elizabeth Barrett Browning has well indicated this particular personal aspect of love:—

> "For none can express thee, though all should approve thee,
> I love thee so, dear, that I only can love thee"

Just as we do not demand the annihilation of the individual as a safeguard against personal egotism, even so it is not necessary to abolish the couple-relation in order to counteract the disastrous effects of familyism. We teach each individual to serve the great human Society; and we should teach each couple to do the same. No natural group should be whittled away or condemned: it should *only be subordinated to the highest universal social group*, which is Humanity. Thus all the partial groups (Family, Municipality, Nation) should be harmonized with the complete Society, which must be divided into these component parts in obedience to the inviolable decree of Nature. These parts are futile, meaningless, ineffective, and discordant without the central Whole, which alone can endow them with vitality and permanence. But "Humanity" would also be a lifeless abstraction, devoid of all content and moral appeal, if these various parts were suppressed. In the absence of these intermediate localized institutions, universal benevolence would only end in universal egotism. He who claims to love all can really love none. His social feeling will evaporate and disappear in the vast and vacant void of abstract "Humanity." If all couples learn to hallow their personal relationship by dedicating themselves to the service of Humanity, then the family will be a precious link in the golden chain of Love that should bind together all souls on earth. Beware of the vice of couple-egotism: do not shut yourselves up in your own little world of two. Do not make plans only for your own success and happiness. Do not begin to worry too much about money. Do not neglect old friends, who were dear to you before love shone on your path. Do not retire from social life, because you now wish to spend so much time in each other's company. Do not diminish your contribution of work and money to progressive movements. Do not make too much fuss about each other. Remember that *he* is after all not the most important man that lives, and that *she* is not the most wonderful woman in the world. Do not idolize and idealize each other too much. Do not be jealous and narrow-minded. Do not lose the sense of proportion: give yourselves as a couple what is your due, but nothing more. If your love makes you more selfish and avaricious than before, then it is a curse, and not a blessing. True love should always develop human Personality, and never dwarf it. This is its proper function. It should inspire both man and woman to make the best use of their bodies and minds, and to consecrate them to the progress of Society. Love makes your ascent to the Ideal easier, if you remain its master; but it can also hurl you quickly to perdition, if you become its slave. Higher than love, beyond mere personal joy, sits Conscience enthroned in eternal majesty. Conscience is the Guide, and Love must follow it. Apply this test to every couple's life: Has love improved them physically and morally? Or has it made them worse than before? Remember that each of you is not the other's exclusive property. Each of you belongs to Society first, and to the other afterwards. Love is not an end in itself: it is a means to a social end. Perfect harmony in conjugal life should be aimed at, or as much harmony as can be attained But it is not worth while to form a couple, if you cannot establish permanent harmony. I do not accept a brilliant lady's dictum: "It is better to be unhappily married than not to be married at all." If incompatibility of temperament or of ideas makes harmony impossible, then it is better to separate and revert to single blessedness. But harmony must be striven for: it will not come by itself. Respect each other's individuality: do not try to impose your will on your partner. Never forget Lessing's precept: "Equality is always the strongest tie of love." Be ready to accept each other's plans and suggestions, unless you discern some grave danger in them. Yield to each other in everyday matters: most couples quarrel over trivial affairs. Disarm petulance with a sweet smile, and answer small complaints with friendly silence. Do not attempt always to have the last word. Divine unspoken wishes with the wisdom of true love, and fulfil them as the opportunity presents itself. Reduce personal friction to a minimum. Love starts the married life, but unselfishness sustains and prolongs it. The happiness of a couple depends on character, not on violent emotion and passion. Character keeps love alive: love would otherwise wilt and wither. What Goethe says of Freedom and Life is also true of Love: you must win it anew every day. And how is it won every day? By unselfishness in thought, word, and deed. Work together for noble aims. Read together; attend meetings and conferences together; serve the poor and the sick together; study Nature together; do creative artistic work together; discuss new ideas together; accept or reject them together; travel together; enjoy music together; all that you find good to do, do it together; thus grow old together until your pilgrimage ends.

You should think and speak often of the notable couples who have helped each other in the pursuit of noble aims and ideals. Crates and Hipparchia were philosopher-comrades in an age when most women received no higher education. Diogenes Laertius says of her: "She fell in love with the discourses and the life of Crates, and would not pay attention to any of her suitors, their wealth, their high birth, or their beauty. But to her Crates was everything. She used even to threaten her parents that she would kill herself, unless she were given in marriage to him. Crates, therefore, was implored by her parents to dissuade the girl, and did all he could. At last, failing to persuade her, he got up, took off his clothes before her face, and said. 'This is the bridegroom; here is his property; make your choice accordingly, for you will be no helpmate of mine unless you share my pursuits.' The girl chose; and, adopting the same dress, went about with her husband, and lived with him in public. Menander alludes to him in the following lines:

> 'Wearing a cloak, you'll go about with me,
> As once with Cynic Crates went his wife.'"

St. Lucchesio and his wife Bona Donna were disciples of St. Francis. They served the poor together, and they also died together. P. Sabatier says: "Bona Donna, his wife, became his best co-labourer; and when in 1260 he saw her gradually fading away, his grief was too deep to be endured. . . . When he saw that her soul was gone, he made over her the sign of the cross, stretched himself beside her, and fell asleep for eternity."

In modern times, many couples have grown together in service and achievement: such have been Armand and Claire Bazard, Karl and Jenny Marx, Lenin and Krupskaya, Henry and Millicent Fawcett, Thomas and Caroline Rhys Davids, Bruce and Katherine Glasier, Paul and Laura Lafargue, Sidney and Beatrice Webb, George and Margaret Fox, William and Catherine Booth, John and Lucy Barbara Hammond, Fremont and Cora Older, Bertrand and

Dora Russell, Robert and Elizabeth Browning, Dr. and Mrs. Stanton Coit, Eden and Cedar Paul, and others.

It is a good idea to celebrate your marriage-day each year with your friends, when you can truly and joyously repeat the lines from Spenser's "Epithalamion":

> "Make feast therefore now all this livelong day,
> This day for ever to me holy is"

Love makes couples, and couples beget children. Longfellow has said that children are "living poems"; and so indeed they are. Children are our pledge of immortality; through them and in them we conquer Death. If you have no children of your own, you should adopt at least one child in order to have your share in the future of the race. A couple who have not begotten or adopted any children are like a blind alley in a town, which leads nowhere. They may also be compared to a small stagnant pool on the banks of the free-flowing Stream of Life, which will go on for ever; but alas! they are cut off from it in sterile isolation. Parenthood has a psychological as well as a physiological basis. Life without children or foster-children is bare and bleak indeed. Even an eminent scientist and philosopher like Bertrand Russell has declared: "For my own part, speaking personally, I have found the happiness of parenthood greater than any other that I have experienced." I knew a merchant, who married at the age of forty-five and had two children. He spoke of his past life, and said, "When I was a bachelor, I thought I was quite happy with my club and my dogs and my love-affairs; but I had no children and I did not know what I missed." If ever you have to choose between a baby and a motor-car in the first year of your married life, choose a baby: you will be much happier.

Æschylus teaches us that our children make us immortal:

> "For children save the dead man's name from darkness,
> Like corks that lead along the fishing-net,
> Else in the deep the flaxen lines were lost."

Victor Hugo, the modern poet of Infancy, sings:

> "If I were a King, mine empire, O child,
> I would give, and my sceptre, and them that bow down
> As my chariot rolls by, and my golden crown,
> And my sea-cars wherewith the vast sea waxeth wild,
> For one only smile of thee, child!"

Parenthood opens for us a new world of deep emotions and creative impulses. It is the crowning glory of the long travail of

Evolution. The higher species like the mammals know much more of the joy and responsibility of parenthood than the fishes and the reptiles. In Man and Woman, the feeling of paternal and maternal love has acquired such power and intensity that it can easily become a devastating anti-social force. Parents rear their child with infinite care and self-sacrifice, because they love him or her so tenderly and passionately, with all their heart and mind and soul. But this deep, unfathomable, unquenchable love may and does induce them to neglect or injure the best interests of Humanity in order to secure certain advantages for that one child. They are likely to forget that there are millions of other children, who must all be treated equally and impartially by the State. Now there are three ways of dealing with this powerful elemental force of parental love:

(1) Men and women may be given other persons' children to rear and love, and not their own.

In this case, the biological urge would be eliminated, and only the psychological need would be satisfied. All men and women must do something for some children in order to be happy. If they are given other citizens' children to take care of, they will certainly love and cherish them, as these will be the only children living with them. It is a libel on human nature to assert (as some cynics do) that the average citizen will be cruel or indifferent to another person's children. Every man or woman is so constituted that he or she must seek to establish personal relations of tender affection with at least one child. It is Nature's mysterious and marvellous device for the welfare of the species. Parental love, which is based only on physiology, may become a blind, raging, tearing passion. If it is related directly to the purely psychological need, it will probably be exhibited as a sweet and gentle emotion, which will produce no anti-social effects at all. It would be interesting to enquire in what respects a man's or woman's love for an adopted child differs from the average father's or mother's affection for their own child. There must be a fundamental difference between the two emotions. If a married couple were asked to bring up an adopted child, they would probably experience all the joys and discharge all the duties of parental love without the danger of being overwhelmed and enslaved by that sordid familyism which is the bane of society at present. They will love the child, but they will not try to injure other children or circumvent the laws of the State simply in order to promote the interests of that one child. They will do their best for him or her in perfect harmony with the social principles that have been accepted for the universal Society. Their parental love will thus be "socialized," and the Part (Family) will subserve the purposes of the Whole (*i.e.* Humanity). At present, the Part is regarded as much greater than the Whole by most people.

(2) Some sociologists have proposed the entire suppression of the personal parental relation. They would rear all children in common nurseries under the supervision of trained officials, who would take care of them impersonally and impartially, like the employees in a zoological garden. No adult would be allowed to establish a personal relation of love and affection with any child, and no child would love and revere any particular person as "father" or "mother." This plan has the merit of simplicity, like a logical proposition or a mathematical formula. But it overlooks the great truth that human life is much more complex than logic or mathematics. We must ask two fundamental questions: (*a*) Is it, or is it not, necessary for the happiness and development of adults that they should *personally* love and rear at least one child, if not more? (*b*) Is it, or is it not, necessary for the happiness and development of a child that he or she should be *personally* loved by a couple of adults, and should respond to the stimulus of their affection? My answer to both questions is in the affirmative. If men, women, and children were to live according to the impersonal, mechanical system, they might perhaps turn out to be free from family-egotism, but they would be sorry specimens of humanity. They would bear the ugly scars of moral mutilation and amputation all their lives. It may be easy to avoid certain evils and vices by refusing to grow up to our full stature as human beings, as the monks and nuns try to do. But we aim at perfect, positive, and active virtue in fully developed men and women; we do not admire imperfect, negative, and passive virtue in half-developed caricatures of men and women. The adults who are not allowed to call a child their own will be sad, self-centred, listless creatures. The child who is not fed and fondled by a couple devoted particularly to him or her will fail to develop into a strong, healthy, and normal adult. Human life needs personal emotion as the plants seek sunshine. A child will not thrive in the most scientific nursery, if he or she is robbed of love. In fact, the unfortunate orphans brought up in public institutions do not seem to demonstrate the merits claimed for the impersonal system. That wise and witty teacher, Bernard Shaw, says: "Children in institutions, who receive only what ignorant people call necessary attention, mostly die, whilst home-children, who are played with and petted and coddled and tossed and sung

to, survive with a dirty rag or two for clothing, and a thatched cabin with one room and a clay floor for habitation." We may therefore conclude that the personal relation of parent and child is indispensable for the proper growth of all children and the happiness of the adults. The impersonal plan must be rejected as unscientific and disastrous.

(3) Men and women should nurse and rear their own children, as they do at present; but they should learn to curb family-egotism.

Parents naturally love their children: our task is to teach them not to love too much. You must cut down blind Nature's excess. You should think of all the great men and women who were blessed with a family, but who did not sacrifice the best interests of Society on the altar of familyism. Gautama Buddha left his family in order to enter on his spiritual quest, and he later persuaded his wife and son to accept poverty and dedicate themselves to the service of Humanity. In this case, the Family was subordinated to Society in the true social spirit. Socrates had a famous wife and less famous children; but he never sought wealth for their sake. He lived and died a poor man, true to his call. The annals of Rome shine with the deeds of men and women who subordinated the Family to the larger Society, which in this case was only the Nation, and not the universal human Society of our ideal. But the principle is the same: family-egotism, born of biological affinity, was suppressed in the interests of a larger political group. You should imbibe the Roman spirit of social duty, but reject the national egotism of the Romans, and replace it by loyalty to the World-State. In fact, the triumph of nation-egotism over family-egotism among the Romans, the English, the French, the Germans, the Italians, and other well-organized, warlike nations proves conclusively that it is possible to harness family-love to the service of a higher social group. Now enlarge this higher group until it embraces the entire human race, and the moral ideal will be realized. The awe-inspiring story of Titus Manlius is thus related by Livy:

"The Consuls issued orders that no one should fight against an enemy out of his post. . . . Titus Manlius, the Consul's son, came with his troop to the back of the enemy's camp. . . . In that place were some Tusculan cavalry, commanded by Geminus Metius. . . . Geminus, advancing some distance from his own party, said to Manlius: 'Do you choose then . . . to enter the lists with me?' Forgetful of his father's command and the consul's edict, he is driven headlong to that contest. . . . Manlius pierces his enemy through the throat; and, with his troop, proceeds to the camp and thence to the general's tent to his father. . . . He says: 'Father, when challenged, I slew my enemy and have taken from him these equestrian spoils.' When the consul heard this, immediately turning away from his son, he ordered an assembly to be summoned by sound of trumpet. When these were assembled, in great numbers, he says: 'Since you, Titus Manlius, have fought against the enemy out of your post contrary to our orders, . . . and have brought me to this necessity that I must forget either the Republic or myself and my family. . . . Either the authority of consuls is to be established by your death, or is to be for ever annulled, if you are pardoned. Go, lictor, bind him to the stake.' All became motionless, more through fear than discipline, astounded by so cruel an order."

In Greek history, Timoleon did not allow fraternal love to override civic duty. His brother Timophanes made himself tyrant of Corinth. Timoleon tried to remonstrate with him, and once went with two friends to him Plutarch says: "The three men now stood around Timophanes, and besought him even now to listen to reason and repent of his ambition; but as Timophanes at first laughed at them, and then became angry and indignant, Timoleon stepped a little aside, and, covering his face, stood weeping, while the other two drew their swords and quickly despatched him. The Corinthians praised Timoleon for his abhorrence of wickedness and his greatness of soul."

The advent of the Christian Church showed that men and women could overcome family-egotism in the service of the larger community, which was called "the Church," "Our Holy Mother." Many zealous Christians who had wives and children courted and suffered martyrdom. The supreme example of such idealism was given by St. Perpetua, who left her little baby and died for the cause of justice and equality, which the early Christian Church represented. She was a well-educated married woman, twenty-two years old. Her parents were living; and she had two brothers, and a son, who was an infant at the breast. She was arrested, refused to recant, and was condemned to death about 5202 A.H. She was first tossed by an infuriated cow, and then killed. An ancient document describes her superhuman psychology in her own words: "While we were still with the persecutors, my father persisted in seeking to turn me away and cast me down from the faith. . . . After a few days, we were taken into the dungeon. I obtained leave for my infant to remain in the dungeon with me and suckled him. . . . Another day we were suddenly taken away to be heard and arrived at the town-hall. In my anxiety for my child,

I addressed my mother and comforted my brother, and commended my son to their care. We mounted the platform. The procurator said, 'Spare the grey hairs of your father, spare the infancy of your boy. Offer sacrifice for the well-being of the Emperors.' I replied, 'I will not do so.'"

Guru Gobind Singh, of India, willingly sacrificed his four sons in the War of Independence that he waged against the Moguls; he did not try to shield them from danger and death. Rousseau steeled his heart against parental affection, and condemned himself to life-long separation from his five children in order to be able to preach his fiery gospel. Pierre Leroux, father of a large family, lived in exile and penury, and served the cause of Democracy and Socialism. Karl Marx and his wife Jenny suffered severe hardship and privation in London, and their children often went hungry for want of bread: but they cheerfully sacrificed family interests for the good of Humanity. These children were brought up in poverty and simplicity; and they too, Jenny, Laura, and Eleanor, devoted themselves to Socialism, like their parents. Here is a glorious example of a whole family inspired by the highest moral Ideal, which freed them from all taint of family-egotism. Great men and women love Humanity more than their own family. You should go and do likewise. Family-life need not be an insuperable obstacle to moral development. Family-egotism can be destroyed, even when men and women have a family to love and cherish. If all couples live in this spirit, there will be no harm at all in allowing them to rear their own children. But it is very, very difficult.

Therefore, if you have children, do not regard them as your own private property, but look upon them as little citizens of the World-State, entrusted to your care. Do not train them to love you too much as their parents: their first duty will be to Society and not to you. Do not try to earn much money for them. Do not teach them that their mission in life is to make as much money as they can. Do not attempt to secure unfair and undeserved privileges for them at school or college, in business or politics. Be not guilty of treason to Society by putting them in lucrative posts, for which they are not fit. Do not imprison their minds in paltry family-affairs: strive to direct their attention to municipal, national and international questions. Develop the civic spirit in them when they are young, and they will fulfil their social duties satisfactorily in later life. Free their growing souls from the fetters of familyism, and they will easily avoid the snares and pitfalls of public life. If you bring up your children in this way, you will deserve well of mankind, and your children, like Cornelia's, will be bright jewels shedding lustre on your old age. You will then be the lucky individual, of whom Euripides wrote: "Greatly to be envied is that man who is fortunate in his children."

The Relatives.

You are united in blood-relationship to your father and mother, your brothers and sisters, your uncles, aunts, nephews, nieces, and cousins. You owe a duty to this group too. As they say, "Blood is thicker than water."

To your parents or foster-parents, you owe love and gratitude. Always treat them with respect, kindness, and courtesy. If they are poor, help them with money. If they are old and infirm, procure for them the necessary comfort and medical treatment. If you live near them, visit them often, and take small presents of fruits, flowers, and other things. Remember that your mere presence gives them the greatest pleasure. Be patient with them, and bear with their garrulity and other little foibles of old people. If you are separated from them by distance, don't fail to write to them frequently, even if it is only a few lines. Old parents only wish to know that you are happy, and also that you have not forgotten them. You should realize that your parents are the only people in the world who will always be proud of your success in life. Even your brothers and sisters may be envious, but your parents, never. Your parents, especially your Mother, are also the only persons who will never reject or disown you, even if you fall to the lowest depths of a misspent life. You may rise to be a prosperous and famous citizen, or you may sink to be a poor tramp, a despised outcast, or a condemned criminal: but for your Mother, you will always be the same dear Tom or Harry, whatever the cold cruel world may say or do. She will pray for you, weep for you, intercede for you, exhort and rebuke you, hope for better days for you; but she will never spurn you or turn you away from her door. In Christ's parable, the Prodigal Son should have said: "I will rise and go to my Mother." If you have failed in life or brought dishonour on yourself, there is one Sanctuary where you will always be safe against the slings and arrows of uncharitable Society, and that inviolate Sanctuary is your Mother. May you never need that refuge and shelter! But always remember that mother-love is the only kind of love that, like the velocity of light, invariably remains unchanged under all circumstances whatsoever. It never fails; it is not decreased by time and distance; it is not weakened even by your unworthiness or ingratitude. You may forget your Mother, but she will never forget you. Mother-love is the true type of that human love which should be your moral Ideal. Adapting Gautama Buddha's precept, you should say: "As my Mother loves me, so do I love all men, women and children, those now living and those yet unborn."

You should honour, help, and comfort your parents, and make them happy. But you should love them "according to your bond," neither more nor less, as Cordelia loved Lear. Beware of two fatal mistakes, which arise from loving them overmuch. It is not your duty to live with your parents in the same house, and you are not bound to obey them in religion and politics. You owe them love, but not obedience. When you are a full-grown man or woman, your home belongs to you, and not to your parents. Your conscience is also your own, and not your father's or mother's. Many young persons wreck their lives by disregarding these two great principles.

Young married people should have a new home of their own; they should not live in the old parental home. The fledged bird leaves the nest. The Oriental custom of the joint-family must be condemned altogether. It robs both the parents and the children of peace and happiness. Old and young do not mix well, like oil and water. As Shakespeare says: "Crabbed age and youth cannot live together."

Young married couples and their children must make all sorts of loud noises in the house, which becomes a veritable torture-chamber for the old parents. If the young people slam the doors, or come home late at night, or vociferously carry on debates and discussions with their friends, or sing and play, the old inmates are disturbed by day and by night. Their health must suffer under the strain. Old people need special food, regular rest and sleep, much quiet and silence. All such requisites of happy old age cannot be secured in a house which is occupied by old and young together. The joint family-system only results in discomfort, annoyance, and ill-health for the parents. It often leads to unseemly disputes and altercations between the parents and the children, and thus undermines mutual affection. It does not really unite the family in love and harmony; it has, as a rule, exactly the opposite effect.

In Europe and America, the Oriental joint-home is not known; but many young men and women, who are economically independent, continue to live with their old parents, simply because they are not married. There is no logic or common sense in this bad custom. The young people are often prevented from ordering their lives according to their own ideas. They yield to the subtle influences of authority, affection, and propinquity. In some cases, many years are wasted before they finally get married and have their "home." It is clearly absurd that the right to a personal domicile should be denied to the young men and women who are not married. Every self-supporting person, single or married, who is over twenty-one, should have his or her separate lodging, be it only a small room in a garret. That room is "home" for that individual: a "home" need not always be occupied by a married couple. Marriage has nothing to do with this question. Such a home is the external symbol of adult personality, like your trade or profession, your books, your dress, your friends, your hobbies, and your religious and political activities. Your Personality cannot be developed without your own little "home," whether you are single or married. Unmarried young people in Europe and America should begin to set up their own "homes," and thus achieve complete moral independence.

For reasons of hygiene and psychology, old and young should live apart. But there is even a graver evil inherent in the present custom of a common domicile for the old and the young people, married or unmarried. It prevents the young men and women from developing their Personalities. It compels them to pay excessive deference to the old parents in all moral questions. It installs the old folk on a pedestal of authority, as the unity of the family necessarily demands the acceptance of the same ideas, customs, tastes, standards, and ideals by all the members. Uniformity is expected and exacted. It is not possible to have two religions or three political parties in one home. Harmony can be preserved only by servile acquiescence in all the old practices and beliefs. The young people who never learn to think independently follow their parents like so many ducklings; or they must compromise and temporize, and lead a life of hypocrisy and subterfuge. In either case, the soul is crushed. The whole system is based on spiritual murder. Whether the young people are married or unmarried, they should not obey their parents, uncles, and aunts blindly and reverently. The theory of filial obedience (which was developed in its worst form in China) must be condemned and rejected as a relic of the dead unprogressive past. It presupposes a static view of history, as the children are expected to think and act exactly in the same way as their parents, who obeyed their parents, who obeyed their parents, and so on right back to the good old times of Moses, Confucius, and Manu. Such notions must convert Society into a stinking cesspool of stagnation. Changes and new experiments are rendered impossible, and rebels and iconoclasts can never arise. But we now hold the dynamic view of social progress. Each generation should think more wisely and act more nobly than the one that went before. We believe in perpetual progress. We are spiritual mountaineers: behind the lofty peaks that we can see, there are higher summits that are invisible. No ideal is final and ultimate. Mankind will never follow old Faust and say to the passing moment: "Verweile doch: du bist so schön" (Stay, thou art so fair). Humanity will always pursue new goals and preach new gospels, as the horizon recedes while we approach it. To our generation, a certain ideal may appear to represent the very acme of Wisdom, the *ne plus ultra* of Development. But when our descendants will have realized that ideal, they will be and should be as discontented with their lot as we are with ours. New possibilities and new perfections will dawn on their dazzled eyes. New stars will beckon them on. For this reason, parents and children should never be alike in all respects; some beneficent variation should appear in every family. Children should inherit only a few right time-tested ideas from their parents; they should exercise their minds independently and forge other new ideas for the future. If all the children obey and imitate their parents, Mankind is lost. The old people already possess sufficient power and authority, as they must control and direct the education of the young. They must not now be allowed to keep the grown-up citizens in leading-strings, or the human race will be crushed under the sheer weight of senility and tradition, like travellers under an avalanche.

I knew an old lady who was always lamenting that her grandchildren were not baptized, and she was continually urging her son to take them to the font. The son was a rationalist, and did not yield to her entreaties; but her piety was a daily nuisance for him.

A young German lady of my acquaintance sent away her sweetheart whom she loved with all her heart, simply because her mother advised her to marry a middle-aged merchant for money. Old people generally believe only in £ove.

A young undergraduate at Oxford resolved to devote his life to a social movement; but he broke his vow and deserted his comrades, because the father wrote that such a step would break his old heart!

Many great men have disobeyed and disappointed their commonplace parents. Gautama Buddha, St. Francis, Petrarch, and Karl Marx paid no heed to the entreaties and remonstrances of their fathers. Petrarch's father threw the son's copy of Virgil into the fire, and exhorted him to qualify himself for the lucrative profession of law; but Petrarch preferred poetry and initiated the great Renaissance. Karl Marx also neglected professional studies, much to the chagrin of his father, who knew that there was no money in Hegelianism and Socialism.

Youth is creative, adventurous, and critical; Age must be conservative, cautious, and quiescent. Youth looks forward and plans for the future; Age turns its eyes backward and sighs for the past. Youth takes risks and does not mind making mistakes; Age plays for safety and dreads suffering. Youth and Age must not be placed in the same home. Tie not the dead to the living.

The habit of consulting the old folk on all occasions and paying too much heed to their opinions must be deprecated, as it is detrimental to the best interests of Society. There is no special merit in being old; Time does not always make men better. The natural gifts of old age may be lumbago and rheumatism, but not necessarily Wisdom and Virtue. In primitive tribes, it may have been true that the old people were wiser than the young, as Odysseus boasted to Achilles: "I excel thee much in prudence, because I was born before thee, and know more." But the ascendancy of the old parents and the older grand-parents in our times is an unmitigated calamity. Old men and women are, as a rule, mere bundles of antiquated prejudices and reaction-patterns, living fossils fit only for a museum of Sociology. They represent the ideas of thirty, forty, or fifty years ago, when they learned certain principles and habits. William James says that it is practically impossible to change one's mental outlook after the twenty-fifth year! So early does the mind lose its elasticity and its power of growth and adaptation! Psychology thus discredits the claim of the old to superior wisdom. It is sometimes said that Age has the advantage of "experience." Well, what most people call their "experience" is just the record of their misdeeds, mistakes, and misfortunes. They lead one-sided, unenlightened lives, and their personal "experience" has no universal validity. The path of Youth is illumined and flooded with the sunshine of optimism, courage, and sincerity: it does not stand in need of such feeble and flickering candle-light as the musty, out-of-date "experience" of cynical and disillusioned pentagenarians and sexagenarians can provide. Bacon, in his wisdom, wrote: "Men of age object too much, consult too long, adventure too little, repent too soon, and seldom drive business to the full period." Some old men expressed a deep truth in this "Irish bull" when they said of young people: "Their future is all in front of them, while ours, alas! is behind us."

What does history teach us? It proves beyond a shadow of doubt that the old people have always been averse to reform and innovation. They are not to blame. They cannot help being obstructive reactionaries, as they can never appreciate new ways and customs. Arteriosclerosis inhibits adventure into unknown realms. How can they value what they have never tried? They are waiting for death, not for an active life. Let them depart in peace, but let not the young be buried alive in their graves. The great War has once for all exploded the dangerous fallacy that old men are always wiser than the young. Why did the old men not prevent that most horrible nightmare of human history? Why were they guilty of such incredible folly and wickedness? Why did they send the young people to be slaughtered in thousands and millions, all for shams and lies and outworn slogans? The blood of murdered youth cries out for vengeance against the senile statesmen, who are entrusted with power and authority in the State apparently because they are no longer fit for any other trade. Youth must now boldly issue its Declaration of Independence. Every thirty years or so, it must proclaim its advent in Schiller's words:

> "New times come on A race is springing up,
> That think not as their fathers thought before"

To all middle-aged or senile critics and censors, Youth should say firmly and respectfully: "Remember your horrid war, and please shut up. You have enjoyed your span of life; you have lived as best you could. Now it is our turn; we will live according to our lights. We have inherited from you much that is good, but also much that is evil. We will not tolerate all that evil, simply because you did not or could not do away with it. The world is now ours to rule and organize, not yours. We will shatter to bits the entire sorry scheme of things that you bequeath to us, and we will 'remould it nearer to our heart's desire.' You are old: take your well-earned repose, and rejoice in the love and respect of your children. But you should now be spectators, not active players in the great game of Life. *Our* future is at stake: allow us to win success and happiness in new ways unknown to you. Don't worry about us: we shall be all right. Elizabeth Barrett Browning has already voiced our claims:

'The young run on before, and see the thing
That's coming Reverence for the young, I cry
In that new Church, for which the world's near ripe,
You'll have the younger in the elder's chair,
Presiding with his ivory front of hope
O'er foreheads clawed by cruel carrion birds
Of life's experience ' "

To your brothers and sisters, you owe love and sympathy. You are linked to them by the sweet memories of childhood, when you all shared the home and the affection of your parents. It is your duty to visit them, write to them, send them gifts on special occasions like festivals and birthdays, and help them with money if they need it. Brother-love has often been regarded as the symbol of civic unity: "fraternity" was one of the three watchwords of the French Revolution. Members of various friendly Orders call one another "Brethren," and sign their letters, "Yours fraternally." You should therefore take especial care to cherish the fraternal relation, and hallow it with words and deeds of unfailing love and kindness.

Affectionate sisters, like St. Scholastica, Dorothy Wordsworth, Caroline Herschel, and Henriette Renan have also been associated with the work of some great men. A sister's love is indeed a precious gift. A distressed unemployed miner said: "My sisters make me feel I am not alone in the world. . . . Without them I don't know what I should have been. Often enough I have felt like stealing some fruit off a stall. If it had not been for my sisters, I should have become a thief."

Towards your uncles, aunts, cousins, nephews, and nieces, you should also behave with affectionate regard and cordiality. You should not neglect visits, letters, invitations, and financial assistance, which are due to them. If any of your nephews and nieces are orphaned, it is your duty to bring them up like your own children.

Thus you will diffuse love and good-will in the entire circle of your kinsmen by blood.

The Municipality.

Your family and relatives are bound to you by the ties of biological blood-relationship; but the next institution, to which you belong, is of an entirely different character. It is territorial and political in its nature and scope. You live in a village or town, and that village or town is a territorial unit. It is bounded on the north, east, south, and west by other villages or towns. It has a name, perhaps a very ancient name, and it has also a historical tradition. It is your "political home," as distinguished from your domestic home. In this political home, you are "a citizen," and not a father, mother, husband, or wife. You are united to the other inhabitants of the village or town by the civic bond of a common political organization. This sacred tie of citizenship really elevates you to the rank of a "civilized" person. Even barbarous tribes and nomadic hordes recognize the claims of consanguinity, but they have no ideal of citizenship. The very word "civilization" is derived from the Latin word "civis," meaning "citizen." As a member of a community living in a town, you may call yourself a "civilized" individual. In Ethics, too, a "good man" is only an abstract term: you should be a good "citizen." There is no true Ethics without citizenship. The town or village is your real sphere of political activity. You love that little portion of the Earth. You know all the streets, fields, meadows, hills, and streams that make up your political home. You are rooted in that soil. It is essential to the development of your Personality that you should have this special personal relation to the town in which you reside and work. Perhaps it is also the place of your birth. In that case, it should be doubly dear to you. The membership of the Municipality as a political body provides the requisite territorial basis for the personality of every man and woman. A tree must strike root somewhere in the ground: it cannot grow hanging in the air. Even so it is with human beings. We have now left the primitive fruitarian, hunting, and pastoral stages far behind us. With the advent of agriculture, mankind settled down in villages and towns on a permanent economic basis. The Greeks spoke of civilized nations as "people eating cereals." We are not wanderers like Abraham and Lot; we have organized ourselves in stable communities on the firm foundations of rice, wheat, barley, rye, maize, and oats. It is now very important for you to cultivate this municipal spirit, this keen sense of belonging to your town as an integral part of it. You should be able to say with Byron:

> "I live not in myself, but I become
> Portion of that around me"

Those unfortunate persons who must frequently change their abode and live in a new town every year or every other year are rootless creatures. It is very difficult for them to develop genuine public spirit. In new countries like the United States, the excessive mobility of the population is certainly a serious obstacle to the growth of a high ideal of citizenship. People who must often shift their territorial basis are in danger of acquiring a butterfly-mentality, devoid of stability, constancy, and serenity. The necessity of migrating to different places in search of work exposes the modern industrial worker in all countries to the same risk of becoming a rolling stone that cannot gather the moss of genuine citizenship. We must find a remedy for this increasing rootlessness of many men and women in contemporary society.

Do not deceive yourself. You may imagine that you are citizens of a " country " like Great Britain and belong to a " nation " like the French or the Germans. You may believe that England or France is your political home, and not your little town. This idea is a delusion and a snare. True public spirit can be developed only within the limit of your Municipality: there is the cradle of citizenship. You cannot feel at home in all England. " Nation " and " Country " are too vague, distant, and extensive to provide you with a suitable basis for your civic personality, which is only human and not Brobdingnagian. " Nation " and " Country " are rather artificial and abstract entities, which have been evolved for certain definite purposes; but they cannot train, inspire, and discipline you in the same way as your Municipality can. You cannot shake hands with your " nation." You cannot see and love all the streets and fields and meadows of your " country." No modern French statesman can speak of France with the affection and enthusiasm that mark every utterance of Pericles about his native city of Athens. This is not strange. Pericles knew Athens and almost all the Athenians quite well; Gambetta or Clemenceau could not possibly know France and her people in the same direct intimate fashion. When you speak of your " country " or " nation " and work yourself up into an unreal enthusiasm for it, you are trying hard to think of geography and history and pretending that they have breathed life into the dry bones of economic and political statistics. But do what you will, the imaginary John Bull, Uncle Sam, or Marianne can never be as real and interesting for you as your neighbours of the municipality of Lincoln, Kansas, or Caen. Therefore, learn the first principles of true citizenship in your Municipality; you will find many opportunities of applying them in the vaster political organizations of Nationality and Humanity.

As the Municipality is only the local organ of the World-State, the general political and economic institutions of the Municipality will be discussed in connexion with the World-State. Here I shall mention a few other important points.

Municipalities are of two kinds: the agricultural municipalities (also called " villages ") and the commercial-industrial municipalities (called "towns"). There is a suitable size for each type of municipality. At present, most villages are too small, and cannot provide the necessary amenities of civilized life on account of the scanty population. They are often without public sanitation, pure water, libraries, concert-halls, theatres, and high schools. Formerly a village had to be small, as the farmers walked to their work in the fields. The modern villages can be made three or four times larger than they are at present, as we have bicycles, motor-cycles, tramways, and omnibuses. Science enables us to increase the most convenient size of the agricultural unit and endow the villages with the educational facilities and other institutions that are now possessed only by the towns. There is also an optimum size for the towns, which subsist on trade and industry and exchange manufactured goods for the food and raw material produced in the villages. A town should be neither too large nor too small. A modern municipality should be so constituted that the average citizen who rides a bus can make himself or herself thoroughly acquainted with every nook and corner of it. Its population should be limited to such a figure that all the citizens can comprehend all the questions at issue, attend all the necessary meetings, know and hear all the leaders, and attain to a keen and vivid realisation of the unity of the town and their responsibility towards it. These conditions cannot be satisfied in enormous overgrown cities, which have sprung up during the last century on account of our defective industrial organization. Such cities are not municipalities, but monstrosities. In fact, the municipal spirit is kept alive by dividing them into several boroughs, which are the real municipalities for all practical purposes. Thus, if you are a Londoner, your political home is not that amorphous mass named "London," but Hampstead, Battersea, or Poplar. Democracy always requires the effective limitation of the size of municipalities. If the town is allowed to grow to excessive proportions, despotism and bureaucracy will soon enslave it. I may suggest that no modern municipality should have more than a hundred thousand inhabitants. Enormous cities, like an over-swollen neck or an obese stomach, are symptoms of disease and disorder.

True democracy cannot flourish in over-populous towns. But considerations of hygiene must also lead us to the opinion that our vast urban agglomerations are fatal to the welfare of the people. They are not cities, but cemeteries. Every town should be so planned that the citizens are within easy reach of the fields and meadows of the countryside. It is every child's birthright to see (but not to pluck) the snowdrops, the primroses, the lotuses, and the wild roses, to hear the song of the lark and the call of the cuckoo, to gather berries and mushrooms, and to feel the thrill of Mother Earth's magnetic touch in every nerve and fibre of its body. Every adult is also entitled to his or her share of the glories of spring and summer, autumn and winter in the woods. If the town is too extensive, Man is cut off from Nature, and is then doomed to dwindle and decay. A town that needs underground railways stands self-condemned. The feet of the people there never touch the life-giving soil, but are always separated from it by stone and asphalt. They must slowly lose health and vitality. Instead of the daily dose of the rural Nature-tonic, they have to be content with a weekly excursion costing much time and money. Many of them cannot get even a weekly outing, and must spend weeks and months in the dismal and dreary labyrinths of streets and walls without once seeing a wild flower or hearing a bird sing on the bough. All who cannot be in daily touch with Nature are the unfortunate victims of our over-urbanized civilization. If the modern cities were not continually replenished from the villages, they would die out, as the inhabitants somehow tend to become sterile nervous degenerates. Thus does a spurious " civilization " commit suicide!

Nature-study is also an essential part of education. But how can you study Nature, if you have no access to her? The people of our big cities study luminous advertisements of soap and beer instead of Nature's beauties and mysteries.

The limitation of the size of towns is also necessary for the maintenance of a proper standard of health and physical fitness, because a regular supply of fresh milk, fruits, and vegetables must be assured for every citizen. No town should ever be so large that it cannot receive the day's milk, fruits, and vegetables from the adjacent villages. All physicians now teach us that *fresh* milk, fruits, and vegetables are indispensable for good health; there is no substitute for them. They must be fresh for each day. They lose much of their flavour and hygienic value, if they are not consumed within twenty-four hours of leaving Nature's storehouse. At present, our population is so unwisely distributed that almost all the milk drunk at breakfast in London or New York is stale and devitalized. We desecrate the fields and meadows and convert them into streets, while we import fruits and vegetables from the ends of the earth. No wonder that disease takes such a heavy toll of the population.

You should try to cultivate the civic spirit of unselfishness and active service. The Athenians despised a citizen who did not take an active part in public affairs, as Pericles declared in his "Funeral Oration." In fact, they regarded him as an arrant fool. The English word "idiot," in its original Greek form, only means "an individual in a private station, as distinguished from one holding public office or taking part in public affairs." So if you do not wish to become an "idiot," you should take care to do your duty in all municipal matters. You should always vote at all elections; your vote not only confers a right, but also imposes a duty on you. If you are too lazy or indifferent to vote, you are guilty of a grave dereliction of duty. In the last century, the people agitated and rebelled for the right to vote: now that they have got the vote, many of them do not care to go to the polls. In some elections, as many as 50 per cent. of the citizens do not vote. This is criminal apathy, suicidal surrender of political power that has been won by the struggles and sacrifices of your ancestors. Why should you miss the chance of furthering your principles and defending your interests in civic administration? Why should you refuse to exercise the *Power* that has been placed in your hands? A citizen who neglects this duty on several occasions should be severely warned and admonished. In some of the ancient Greek cities, the timid or indifferent citizens, who remained neutral in civic disputes and disturbances, were despised. Plutarch, in his Life of Solon, says: "The strangest of his remaining laws is that which declared disfranchised a citizen who in a party conflict took neither side; apparently his object was to prevent anyone regarding home politics in a listless uninterested manner." It is indeed a grave peril for a municipality to have a large number of citizens who habitually do not vote. Such a town would be rent asunder by the extreme factions, while the sensible practical people sit at home and take no part in politics. There will always be certain groups of citizens who are ambitious, intolerant, or aggressive; they can be kept in check only by the sagacious and impartial majority. But if many wise citizens do not vote, civic life becomes only a battlefield for foolish and destructive minorities, and the State must ultimately perish. As Voltaire says, "The cowardice of the honest people ensures the success of the scoundrels." That is why Tammany ruled New York. A citizen who is too indolent or thoughtless to record his vote is like a soldier who deserts his post. Therefore, you should always vote, even if you have to vote once a week.

You should also discharge all the other duties of citizenship as an honest and trustworthy citizen. Do not revile or traduce your opponents: courtesy must sweeten the bitterness of political strife.

Do not borrow your opinions from the newspapers or the leaders: study each question thoroughly and independently. Do not be rowdy and disorderly at the meetings of other parties: respect the right of free speech and assembly for all citizens. Do not accept bribes for voting for a particular candidate or party: the vote, like your soul, must not be sold. Do not bribe other voters: corrupt not the conscience of your fellow-citizens. Do not try to exact a free car-ride as the price of your vote: walk to the polling-station on two honest legs, and despise the motor-cars of the wealthy snobs. Do not indulge in irrelevant or malicious personal attacks: discuss principles and policies first. Do not tell lies and half-truths: you will find that falsehood is a broken reed to lean upon. Do not exaggerate the merits of your own policy or the perils of your opponents' schemes: empty rhetoric will make mere windbags of all the citizens. Do not appeal to base instincts or vile passions: a victory is bought too dear, if it is won with such tarnished weapons. Act like a free, independent, intelligent, honourable, and courteous citizen at all times. If your friends wish to elect you to public office, do not behave like a vain and ambitious politician. Be modest and conscientious. If you believe that you have not the time or the capacity to discharge all the duties of that office, then decline the honour politely but firmly. Do not be over-persuaded by others, who do not know you well, or by your wife, who may wish to shine in reflected lustre. If you think that you are competent, you may accept the nomination; but you should never intrigue for such positions of public responsibility. Do not advertise your personal merits (which may be largely imaginary); do not form cliques and coteries in order to secure your election. Democracy is to-day infested with unprincipled, self-seeking adventurers, whose sole ambition in life is to get elected to some council, board, or committee. They covet the money, or the honour, or both. They are as a rule active, energetic, and eloquent men and women, who wish to rise to power on the bent backs of their simpler fellow-citizens. They are skilled in the specious arts of demagogy, and often foment strife in order to retain power and influence. If they are once elected, they leave no stone unturned to secure re-election as often as possible. They become professional politicians, detestable parasites and sycophants, who are as dangerous to the State as rats in a granary or cobras in a tropical garden. Do not join the ranks of these professional politicians: rather expose and combat them. If you have the greatness of public office thrust upon you by your fellow-citizens, then accept it in all humility, and do your duty with meticulous care and unremitting industry. Be just and incorruptible, like Aristides; be simple and sincere, like Lenin; be patient and magnanimous, like Pericles. Beware of family-egotism; do not take advantage of your position to procure jobs for your sons and nephews or to enrich yourself. You must leave office as poor as you were on the day of your election. Eschew personal rancour and domineering speech and manners. Democracy cannot succeed without tolerance and moderation. If you are a member of a Council or Committee, do not speak too much; do not lose your temper; do not press your point with unseemly obstinacy; do not talk as if all the other members were ignorant fools; do not try to impose your views on your colleagues by discharging the disconcerting hose of your oratory at them; trust rather to free discussion and persuasion. No one loves autocratic arrogance in an assembly. Democracy must be led, not driven.

You should also take a deep pride in your Municipality and its history. Your town is not a mere agglomeration of streets and houses: it is a community with a past, which should not be forgotten. Study the full and varied record of its development. Find out when it was founded; when the beautiful town-hall was built, who was the architect, and what it cost; when the citizens erected that statue and that fountain, purchased that picture for the museum, laid out that park, built that school and that hospital, instituted that festival and that musical contest. Take an active part in holding civic pageants and celebrations in commemoration of the great events and the noble citizens that are associated with the history of your town. Thus Besançon should celebrate the birthdays of Fourier, Victor Hugo, and Proudhon; Frankfurt a/M should invite the world to a Goethe festival; Vaucluse should commemorate Petrarch; and Newtown should offer a dramatic representation of Robert Owen's career. Statues and streets are not sufficient; joyous festivals and gorgeous pageants should be held in every town. Thus the civic spirit will be developed in peace and gladness. The citizens will eagerly render unselfish service to the World-State in the place where they live and work. To wear the perfect crown of citizenship is the highest reward of Virtue.

Love your Municipality with a deep and ever-deepening love, as Dante loved ungrateful Florence, as de Boigne loved Chambéry, as the six burghers of Calais loved their home, as the author of the 137th Psalm loved Jerusalem, and as Pericles loved Athens, of which he spoke thus:—

" In our democracy, all are equal before the law; each man is promoted to public office not by favour, but by merit. Our citizens can administer affairs both private and public. . . . Her glory was won by men who did their duty. . . . We are not angry with our neighbour, if he does anything to please himself. . . . We have provided for ourselves numerous means of recreation. . . . We throw our city open to all. . . . Athens is the school of Hellas."

Thus, both as a voter and as a public delegate, you should set before yourself a high ideal of citizenship and attempt to realise it day by day and year by year. The highest Citizenship is also the highest Ethics.

> "A time like this demands
> Strong minds, great hearts, true faith, and ready hands,
> Men whom the lust of office does not kill;
> Men whom the spoils of office cannot buy;
> Men who possess opinions and a will;
> Men who have honour, men who will not lie;
> Tall men, sun-crowned, who live above the fog,
> In public duty and in private thinking"

The Nation

The Municipality is your immediate sphere of daily work and service. But another group also claims your allegiance: that is your Nation. Nationality is a natural product of geography, language, religion, and other factors that establish propinquity and social homogeneity. Different peoples and tribes have been separated from one another by mountains, seas, deserts, and forests. This geographical severance has produced tribal feeling and tribal institutions. The diversity of languages has also cemented the bond of union among such groups, while it has rendered intercourse with other language-groups very difficult, if not practically impossible. Speech marks the limit of mutual intelligibility, and the nation is usually a definite language-group occupying a certain territory, which is idealized as the "Fatherland," "La Patrie," "Fosterlandet," "Al Vatan," etc. Walter Scott emphatically associates national sentiment with the land: "This is my own, my native land." B. Vico defined a nation as "a natural society of men, who, by unity of territory, of origin, of customs, and of languages are drawn into a community of life and of social conscience." Other writers like Mancini, Mamiani, and Pierantoni enumerate race, religion, language, geographical position, manners, history, and laws as the constituent elements of nationality. F. Lieber thus defines a nation: "The word nation, in the fullest adaptation of the term, means, in modern times, a numerous and homogeneous population (having long emerged from the hunting and nomadic state), permanently inhabiting and cultivating a coherent territory, with a well-defined geographic outline and a name of its own—the inhabitants speaking their own language, having their own literature and common institutions, being citizens or subjects of a unitary government, and having an organic unity with one another as well as being conscious of a common destiny."

In so far as Nationalism is a natural phenomenon based on local homogeneity, it should be cherished and preserved in due subordination to the central institution of the World-State. The value and vitality of Nationalism have been emphasized by Viscount Cecil, who says: "Nationalism is so strong and in many ways so admirable a quality of mankind, that, if it be really the antithesis of internationalism, the success of the latter becomes very improbable." I agree that Nationalism is a historic force that must be reckoned with. We cannot ostrich-like bury our heads in the sands of doctrinaire Cosmopolitanism and ignore the existence of Nationalism. It is unwise to dismiss "national consciousness" as "a hallucination," as J. M. Robertson does. It would be more consonant with the truth to admit sadly and sorrowfully the correctness of Aravinda Ghose's dictum: "At the present stage of human progress, the nation is the really living collective unit of humanity." But there are two forms of Nationalism: Social and Anti-social. Both forms may again be sub-divided into Political Nationalism and Cultural Nationalism. Social Nationalism is the sentiment of preferential attachment to your country and its landscape, food, literature, history, dress, customs, etc., when such a sentiment has been brought into harmony with the ideal of Humanity and Cosmopolitanism. Just as the individual is not suppressed by the family and the family need not be abolished by the municipality, even so nationality may also be one of the five concentric Circles within which our life unfolds itself. It is natural and permissible for you to take a special interest in the region and the people that are easily accessible to you on account of geographical situation and community of speech. In this sense, your "country" can be a local sphere of service for you in many ways. Thus an Englishman can often work for Humanity most effectively in England, where his compatriots can understand him; and a Turk can be employed to the best advantage as a servant of the World-State in Turkey, not in Chile or Japan. The natural feeling of love and devotion for your "Country" and "Nation," that must arise and develop under these circumstances, is not an evil at all; it is perfectly legitimate and laudable. Thus a Scotsman may sing "O Caledonia, stern and wild, meet nurse for a poetic child." A Swede may chant "Du gamla, du fria, du fjällhöga Nord" without violating the principle of human unity and solidarity. Æschylus voiced such praiseworthy patriotism, when he addressed Athens thus:—"Your City and Nation will shine to the world through all time, As the lovers and doers of Justice, the foes and avoiders of crime." Euripides cried: "Dear Land of my Fathers, would that all loved thee as I do." Dante was a universal genius, but even his great soul was responsive to the charm of the "sweet name of his native city"; and he was "constrained" by "the love of his native place." H. von Fallersleben sang: "I hear German words again; Land of Joy and Song, I greet thee, lovely, happy Fatherland." Schenkendorf wrote: "Mother-tongue, Mother-song! How dear, how full of charm thou art!" Blake spoke lovingly of "England's green and pleasant land"; and Browning exclaimed, "Oh to be in England, now that April's there." These poets thus gave utterance to natural patriotism, which is not antagonistic to the ideals of cosmopolitan citizenship.

This natural and harmless form of Nationalism may demand concrete expression in political and cultural institutions. Such a demand should be granted without demur. Thus we may effect what Professor H. J. Laski has called "the equation of Nationalism with right." Each nation may and should cultivate its literature It should love its poets, whom it can read in the original. It should sing its own songs and hymns. Poetry, like climate, is a peculiarly autochthonous product. Translated foreign poetry can never replace national poetry. Cultural Nationalism may temporarily establish such institutions as the Eisteddfod of the Welsh people and "Hindi-sahitya-sammelan" of the Hindi-speaking people of India. If a nation takes pride in its own literature (without neglecting the study of world-literature), it does not weaken or undermine the idea of Humanity. A nation may even be allowed to choose its local heroes and heroines for historical commemoration, if they are not important enough for universal homage; but they must have rendered estimable service to Humanity in constructive and praiseworthy achievement. Thus, the English people may celebrate Crabbe, Purcell, Hampden, and Wilkes, though we cannot institute a universal festival in their honour. Similarly, Labrador may keep alive the memory of Dr. Grenfell, Sweden may gratefully remember St. Anskar, and Ceylon may continue to revere Mahinda. Even the Catholic Church has its local Saints. Natural Nationalism may thus cherish its historical tradition within the framework of universal history. In the sphere of politics, the national territories may at first be recognized as the regional administrative divisions of the World-State, as Essex, Kent, and Sussex are now counties of England, and Bengal and Gujrat are provinces of India. We must build upon the foundations that have already been laid by those two architects, Time and Custom. Let Albania, Holland, and Peru be administrative divisions of the World-State for some time. Later on, it will be possible to ignore these national territories and re-distribute the Earth into new convenient sections for administrative purposes, as the provinces were abolished and the departments were established in France. The old names and organizations can flourish under the flag of Humanity for a time, but they will be stripped of sovereignty. Wales and Scotland retain their national identity for religious and cultural purposes, but they are not sovereign states now. The "Fatherlands" will not be altogether destroyed, when they are incorporated in the World-State. They will keep their names, forms, and outlines; but they will be strictly subordinated to the World-State and its policy. The nations may for a time enjoy what H J. Laski has called "non-sovereign statehood"; but they will be prepared for the complete abrogation of their "statehood." Then no one will be permitted to say, "I am a Frenchman," or, "I am an Englishman." He will be trained to think and speak like this: "I am a Man and a World-Citizen, and also a Frenchman, Burgundian, and Dijonian"; or, "I am a Man and a World-Citizen, and also a Briton, Scotsman, and Glasgowite." Thus the great Whole will not crush and demolish the small Parts, of which it is composed; it will only organize and harmonize them. The World-State comes, not to destroy, but to fulfil.

Such is natural and social Nationalism as it can manifest itself in literature, history, and politics It is not the enemy of the World-State, but its faithful and humble ally. But there is also unnatural and anti-social Nationalism, which is a destructive and diabolical force. It demoralizes and disintegrates Mankind. Natural Nationalism may be compared to a gentle breeze on a summer evening or a camp-fire on a cold night; but this unnatural Nationalism is like a Caribbean hurricane or a raging prairie conflagration. When ordinary men and women are possessed by this demon of anti-social Nationalism, they lose their reason and conscience, and act like mad dogs and howling wolves. It is in fact a kind of homicidal insanity, the malady of "xenophobia" (fear of the foreigner), which causes men to run amok. Such diseased, debased, demented, dehumanized nationalists may be known by the following characteristics:—

(1) They think and talk only of their own nation, and are indifferent or hostile to other nations. They are so short-sighted that they can see only their little country on the map of the wide earth. Their minds are thus cramped and deformed, like an old-fashioned Chinese lady's foot. Their intellect remains stunted and dwarfed, as it is always immured in the strait-jacket of unnatural Nationalism. A prominent Egyptian leader once said to me, "I am interested only in Egypt." Sometimes one reads such headlines in the newspapers: "Storm at sea. Vessel wrecked. All British passengers safe." The Editor evidently believes that the public are not concerned with the fate of the other travellers! Such narrow-minded collective egotism is the parent of distrust and hatred. Unnatural Nationalism speaks in literature with the bitter and raucous tones of contempt, hate, and envy. Tennyson described the French people's love of freedom as the "schoolboy heat, the blind hysterics of the Celt." H. Heine wrote: "Nature has denied to the English everything that is beautiful and lovely." Shakespeare praises England as "this earth of majesty, this seat of Mars," but hints at "the envy of less happier lands." Kipling speaks of "lesser breeds without the law." The Germans sang a war-song: "May God punish England!"

(2) Such nationalists study the history of their own nation, but neglect world-history. They are taught the history of their country at school, and they can cherish only that historical tradition. They are like a horse harnessed to a carriage: it can be prevented from seeing the entire landscape; the blinkers compel it to see only the road before it. A nationalist of this type knows all about the past rulers, warriors, poets, and statesmen of his own country, but is woefully ignorant of the history of other nations. If he is an Englishman, he can tell you the exact date of Aethelred the Unready and the names of Henry VIII's wives, but he has a very faint notion of the Huguenots or the Thirty Years' War or the French Revolution. A Japanese "patriot" is conversant with all the details of the wars of Gempei between the Taira and Minamoto clans and the battle of Sekigahara, but he knows nothing of the fall of Baghdad or the battle of Lepanto. Such nationalists are much to be pitied. They are like the foolish traveller, who should visit England and insist on eating only plums, and no strawberries, cherries, and apples at all

(3) Such nationalists also believe (or pretend to believe) that their

country and their nation are the best in the world in every respect. This is a peculiar and absurd article of the creed of Nationalism. Lowell wrote of the United States: "Among the nations bright beyond compare." A Swedish gentleman asked me: "Don't you think that the climate of Sweden is the best in the world?" I replied, "Yes; and in Sweden, I prefer the climate of the town of Gothenburg where I live at present; and in Gothenburg, I think the climate of my street is the best." An English lecturer made the same claim about the climate of England! Cecil Rhodes declared in his will: "I contend that the British race is the finest which history has yet produced." Körner sang: "German Nation! thou best and most glorious of all!" Daniel Webster cried: "Thank God, I—I also—am an American." W. E. Henley calls England "chosen daughter of the Lord, spouse-in-chief of the ancient sword," while Shakespeare describes his country as "this other Eden, demi-paradise." (Was Eden so damp and foggy?) Silvio Pellico sang: "O Italy, art thou not the gentlest of all the lands? Art thou not the mother of every fine art?"

A wise nationalist loves his country, as a dutiful son loves his mother: he is not expected to argue that his mother is superior to all other women in the world. But the unnatural nationalist loves his Fatherland like an infatuated lover, who sees no defect in his sweetheart and thinks (while the illusion lasts) that she is a peerless paragon. The fact is that every nation has its merits and its faults, just as the climate of each country has its advantages and disadvantages. But when did furious fools care for Fact and Truth? And how can self-flattery be content with mutual appreciation? Nationalism is organized hypocrisy.

(4) The anti-social nationalists claim that their nation has a special and unique mission in history, and is therefore superior to the others, which are called by opprobrious names. The Hebrews thought that they were the chosen people of the Lord; other nations were "Gentiles." The Greeks despised the "Barbarians." The Hindus look down upon the "mlecchas." Victor Hugo exclaimed: "O France! it is the need of the universe that thou shouldst live. I repeat it, France is necessary for the human race." Mazzini disseminated the wrong idea that each nation had its own "mission." He wrote: "We believe . . . in nationality, which is the conscience of the peoples, and which, by assigning to them their part in the work of association, their function in humanity, constitutes their mission upon earth, that is to say, their individuality." Mazzini regards a "nation" as a metaphysical

entity, which must remain separate and distinct from all other nations for all time. G. Ferrero also speaks of a "national mission." It cannot be proved that any nation has a special "mission." "Nationality" is only a geological and historical accident. The nations will be slowly merged in the unity of Humanity. Such megalomania betrays the curious psychology of the inmates of a lunatic asylum, each of whom believes that he is Cæsar, Napoleon, Jesus Christ, or Almighty God Himself! It is a mad mad world!

(5) The anti-social nationalists claim complete and unrestricted national sovereignty, embodied in the independent nation-state, which they adore and glorify. Thus Savigny defines the State as "the organic manifestation of a nation." J. S. Mill taught that "it is in general a necessary condition of free institutions that the boundaries of governments should coincide in the main with those of nationalities." Oliver Wendell Holmes sang rapturously: "One flag, one land, one heart, one hand, one Nation evermore." A true cosmopolitan wishes to vest sovereignty in the World-State and regards his country only as an administrative division of that State. He knows that there should be one, and only one, sovereign State, as there is one Earth, and one Human Race. He does not dote on any flag or any anthem. He does not believe that the nation-state is a necessary or beneficial institution. But the anti-social nationalist is enamoured of his petty nation-state and its symbols. He loves a coloured rag, called his "flag." He sings some boastful lying doggerel verse, called the "national anthem," with passionate sincerity. He is ready to die for the nation-state at a moment's notice; and he is quite willing to kill others for its sake. Homer sounded this note long ago: "The best omen for a man is to fight for his country." The nation-state is for the patriot what the fetish is for the primitive African and what Dagon was for the Philistines. H. Heine crooned: "It is sweet to live or to die for the Fatherland." (Horace had spoken only of dying.) Browning asked: "Here and here did England help me,—how can I help England,—say." Schiller inquired: "Say, what is holy, innocent, and good, if not to combat for our Fatherland." Metastasio cried: "Our country, to which we may sacrifice everything."

(6) The anti-social nationalists teach that Nationality is the highest principle of organization in human society. Thus Bernhardi wrote: "Any action in favour of collective humanity outside the limits of the state and nationality is impossible. Such conceptions belong to the wide domain of Utopias." Even Schiller,

who was not a narrow-minded nationalist, declared that the *Trieb zum Vaterlande* (the patriotic impulse or feeling) was the most precious of all ties (*das teuerste der Bande*)! Such theorists deprecate internationalism in all its aspects. They try to cast even religious and scientific institutions in a national mould. They even organize sport and art on purely national lines. They establish "national" Christian Churches, forgetting that Christianity is a universal gospel, in which there can be no Jew or Greek, Teuton or Celt. A "national" Church is really a contradiction in terms. Every universal movement is soon caught in the net of Nationalism, and then tied up securely in "national" bonds and fetters. The Flag has now supplanted the Cross. Similarly, Socialism has broken up into many "national" sections, which have been swallowed up by that all-devouring monster, the nation-state. Thus every institution in every country is at present slowly but surely assimilated to Nationalism, as all plants and animals are petrified in the rocks.

(7) Anti-social Nationalism glorifies and deifies the nation-state. As a corollary of this vulgar creed, it attaches infinitely greater importance to the nation's military triumphs, political supremacy, and economic success than to its achievements in religion, art, science, and literature. It is the open cult of brute-force and money-power, the obscene worship of Mars and Mammon, the two guardian deities of the nation-state. Such nationalists erect more magnificent monuments to Napoleon, Nelson, and Frederick than to Goethe, Victor Hugo or Shakespeare, St. Martin or St. Boniface, Pasteur or Lister. The ferocious Mongol and Assyrian conquerors were more honest than these modern patriots; they raised towers of skulls to commemorate their victories, but these "civilized" hypocrites build towers of metal and stone in Trafalgar Square and the Place Vendôme. The mind's eye, however, can easily see the stone and the metal suddenly transformed into the skulls and bones left on the battle-fields that are thus celebrated. Such Nationalism demoralizes and brutalizes all children, as it pays perpetual homage to ruthless mass-murderers like Alexander, Julius Cæsar, Mahmud of Ghazni, Cortes, Pizarro, Napoleon, Wellesley, and Kitchener, while many saints, sages, and scholars are hardly remembered with a modest shrine or statue. The British people celebrate Empire Day on the 24th of May; and a teacher who refused to join the disgusting orgy of flag-waving imperialism was dismissed. The real religion of England is now Empire, and not Christianity. An atheist or deist is not persecuted so cruelly as a conscientious

objector to war. The French celebrated the centenary of the conquest of Algeria with great pomp and splendour. Some of the most important monuments in London and Paris smell of blood. In the capitals of Europe, the streets and stations reek of militarism: Trafalgar Square, Avenue Wagram, Avenue Friedland, Siegesallee, etc. Poetry is also prostituted to the service of militarism. To Kipling, God is "Lord of our far-flung battle-line." Tennyson celebrated Wellington and Waterloo. Shakespeare glorified Henry V as a warrior. Valmiki honoured Rama for conquering Ceylon and its wicked ruler. Camões confessed his desire to immortalize his "warlike nation" and "the invincible warriors, who founded a new empire." Well may we re-echo Lamartine's cry: "Nations! that's a word that means barbarism."

We read with horror that human sacrifices were offered to the gods in Carthage and Mexico; but what were those paltry sacrifices to the enormous holocausts of victims that are immolated by the bloodthirsty priests of this modern religion of Nationalism? The nation-state may truly be compared to the dinosaurus and the tyrannosaurus of the Mesozoic Age. Like those gigantic reptiles, the sovereign nation-state has a very small brain with which to think and plan, but tremendously powerful teeth and claws to tear and rend, to destroy and dismember. Let us hope that, like them, it will soon be extinct.

Natural and cultural Nationalism, on the contrary, is sincerely ashamed of wars and victories. It wishes to raze the military monuments to the ground. It will erect beautiful memorials to the poets, scientists, artists, and other really great men and women, whose names shed lustre on the nation, as the Scotsmen have honoured Walter Scott at Edinburgh. When such praiseworthy Nationalism comes into power, it will cleanse history of all taint of blood.

The Nation-State breeds wars among the nations. War is indeed its main purpose and activity. The armies, navies, and air-fleets are the symbols of sovereignty. There may be States without schools and sanitation, without hospitals and clean water; but who ever heard of a State without an army? As each nation is taught to have no regard for the welfare of the others, the citizens of each State consider it their duty to compete with those of all other States not only in peaceful ways, but also in murderous warfare. Ethics is thus annulled and repudiated, for the very first and most universal ethical precept is: "Thou shalt not kill." When murder is thus approved and glorified, other minor sins are of course committed without compunction in war. The citizen is taught to steal and lie for the "honour" and profit of his nation.

War among the nations is an unmitigated evil, born of avarice and hatred. What they fight for is Money in some form or other. Instead of sharing the wealth of the world among themselves in a friendly and fraternal spirit, each nation attempts to grab more than the others, and also tries to exploit the labour of weaker nations. This greed, this gruesome and ghoulish greed, is the root-cause of war; and, in this epoch, its concentration and culmination are in Capitalism. The nations fight for land, slaves, tribute, trade-markets, fields for investment, supplies of raw materials, administrative jobs and posts, and other economic advantages. The real motive of all wars was laid bare long ago by Marcus Cato, when he threw down in the Roman senate-house the large figs that grew in the soil of Carthage. Plutarch says: "When the Senators admired their size and beauty, he remarked that 'the country which produced this fruit, is only three days' sail distant from Rome.'" The wars of the Teutons against Rome were waged for the acquisition of land. In modern times, the Spaniards fought the English to preserve their monopoly of the gold and silver of America; the English fought the Dutch and the French, and the Dutch fought the Portuguese, for the trade and tribute of the East; the Germans built a navy and entered on the great war in order to acquire colonies in Africa, which had been partitioned among England, France, and Portugal. The English were also anxious to end the commercial and industrial rivalry of Germany by war. Thus the collective egotism of each nation has led to bloody wars during the last four centuries.

War is thus a very ancient and chronic malady in the body politic of Humanity, a deep-seated gangrene that has been eating into its vitals since the dawn of history. Its terrible consequences are as follows:—

(1) It involves tremendous loss of life. Who can count the number of men killed in war since the days of Menes of Egypt? Many millions of men have been slain in battle, and many millions have died of famine and pestilence that follow in the wake of war. Life is a sacred and precious blessing; yet we find men fighting one another, as the tigers and wolves do not fight. We speak of war as something "bestial"; but no beast is so cruel and pugnacious as Man. If the wild animals could speak and write, they would express their horror of war, especially of war within the same species, by saying: "Such war is human: we animals should

eschew it." Plutarch says of Julius Cæsar: "In somewhat less than ten years during which he carried on his campaign in Gaul, he took by storm above 800 cities, and subdued 300 nations, and fought with three millions of men at different times, of whom he destroyed one million in battle and took as many prisoners." In the single battle of Gravelotte in the Franco-German War (18th August, 6870 A.H.) 609 French Officers, 809 German Officers, 11,705 French soldiers and 19,260 German soldiers were among the killed and wounded. In the world war of 6914–18 A.H., 8,538,315 men were killed and 21,219,452 were wounded, according to an official estimate. How many young poets, scientists, sages, artists, inventors, novelists, dramatists, musicians, physicians, teachers, and professors were lost to the world in those four years!

(2) War causes enormous loss of wealth. War devastates the fields and destroys the factories, leaving smoking ruins in its train. It diverts the energy of the people from work to murder, and thus hinders production. It wastes the economic resources of the nations on armaments and ammunition,—entirely unproductive and unconsumable commodities, whose economic value is negative and less than zero. The great War cost £55,486,000,000. At present, the nations of the world spend £900,000,000 each year on armaments. According to J. Novikow, "from 1648 to 1912, war has cost the European nations alone £16,000,000,000." The same author adds: "It would not be exaggerating to say that, in the entire historic period (up to 1912), war has cost at least ten times that amount. Thus, at the lowest estimate, war has cost in all £160,000,000,000." Professor E. Krehbiel has calculated that the cost of all the wars from 6793 A.H. to 6910 A.H. was 23,323,546,240 dollars. War has also destroyed many buildings, temples, churches, libraries, statues, pictures, and artistic treasures. The Parthenon stands as an awful warning of the vandalism of war.

(3) War intensifies and perpetuates cruelty. It is only a synonym for brutality and inhumanity. The Assyrian warrior thus boasted of his prowess in a royal inscription: "Their men, young and old, I took prisoners. Of some, I cut off the feet and hands; of others, I cut off the noses, ears, and lips; of the young men's ears I made a heap; of the old men's heads I built a tower. I exposed their heads as a trophy in front of their city. The male children and the female children I burned in the flames." The sculptured marbles of the Assyrian palaces exhibit the tortures inflicted upon the prisoners; some are flayed alive; the eyes of some are bored out with the point of a spear; and others are having their tongues torn

out. Cromwell thus described the massacre of the Irish soldiers and civilians at Drogheda: "I forbade our men to spare any that were in arms in the town, and I think that night they put to death about 2,000 men. I ordered the steeple of St. Peter's church to be fired, where one of them was heard to say in the midst of the flames, 'God damn me, I burn, I burn.' In the church itself, nearly 1,000 were put to the sword. I believe all their friars were knocked on the head promiscuously but two."

The massacres of Amboyna and Omdurman, the butcheries of Wexford and Herat, the slaughter of the Armenians and the Tasmanians, are typical scenes of war. The following instructions are issued to young European recruits at present: "In hand-to-hand combat, to jab two fingers in the enemy's eyes and force them back into his brain; to twist the bayonet after delivering the point, to prevent the wound closing; to slit open the stomach from top to bottom with a dagger; to finish off wounded men lying on the ground, placing one knee on the chest, and then jerking up the head with a short sharp movement to dislocate the spinal column."

(4) War leads to racial degeneration. As Professor David Starr Jordan has shown, War is anti-biological and dysgenic in its effects on the population. The strongest and bravest men are cut off in their prime, and the inferior stock is left for breeding. A warlike nation is like a man who is continually losing precious blood. It is believed that the average stature of the next generation of the French people was lowered by the drain of the Revolutionary and Napoleonic wars on men of more than average stature. War is slow suicide for every nation.

(5) War is inimical to Democracy and Liberty, and tends to establish despotism and bureaucracy in the State. War is waged with armies, and an army must be drilled and disciplined like the citizens of Sparta and old Prussia. An army is a mechanical device: it is not an association of free and intelligent men. The soldier's highest duty is obedience: "Theirs not to reason why, theirs but to do and die." Victory in war often requires the concentration of power in the hands of an autocrat or a small junta. The Romans appointed a dictator in time of peril. Their wars led to the downfall of republican government and the establishment of the autocracy of the Emperors. The Committee of Public Safety was supreme in Paris on account of the foreign war, which ended in the despotism of Napoleon. The French sacrificed their freedom for the sake of military success. During a war, the Press is censored; the rights of free speech and public meeting are

encroached upon. The Government is everything, and the individual is nothing. Even in "free" England, the General Election of January 6916 was not held and Parliament prolonged its own life. The Cabinet was too unwieldy for the conduct of the War: authority passed to a smaller body. A successful military leader often abolishes democratic assemblies and establishes a tyranny. Every citizen must fight even against his will. The unity of the nation is achieved by suppressing dissentient voices and punishing critics and opponents of the government. War is indeed the very negation of liberty. Personality can never develop freely in a militarist society, as a soldier ceases to be a free man and consents to act as a slaughtering automaton, a mere cog in an immense mass-murdering machine. Therefore, you must choose between war and freedom. You cannot have both.

(6) War lowers the position of women. The qualities that win success in war are brutality and courage. The gentler virtues that shine in peace are despised among warlike nations. The reckless, self-indulgent warrior, fond of meat and wine and women, is the hero of militarism. If he wins battles, his vices do not matter. In such a society, women are regarded only as the mothers or mistresses of soldiers; they cannot find any scope for noble activity. When the State is based and built up on War, the women must occupy an inferior position, as they cannot fight (except the unnatural legendary Amazons). This disability was indeed adduced as an argument against women's suffrage! Woman's love, self-denial, purity, temperance, intelligence, intuition, gentleness, æsthetic sensibility, and moral fervour are suppressed and smothered by War. What a loss to Humanity! All women should wage a relentless war against War. War has kept them down; it has humiliated and degraded them; it has crushed and enslaved them. Women can work and rule on equal terms with men only under the ægis of peace.

(7) War increases economic inequality within a State. It makes the rich richer and the poor poorer in the long run. At all times, it worsens the relative position of the common people. The Roman patricians took the land of their Italian enemies, and the plebeians were given only the booty. Both got something, but the privileged classes got much more than the labouring poor. Great Britain has waged many wars and established a vast Empire; but London is the city of palaces and slums. War has produced the extremes of wealth and poverty in English society. J. R. Green, the famous historian, says of the war between England and France (6793–6815 A.H.): "The war enriched the landowner, the farmer, the

merchant, the manufacturer; but it impoverished the poor. It is indeed from these fatal years, which lie between the peace of Luneville and Waterloo, that we must date that war of classes, which still forms the main difficulty of English politics." War always produces a debased proletariat class, whether in Rome or London, and ends in misery, degradation, and demoralization.

(8) War prevents and delays social and political reform. The money spent on armaments and the indolent military and naval services forms such a large percentage of the national Budget that little is left for schools, houses, old-age pensions, widows' pensions, medical aid, etc. For the cost of a modern battleship, how many schools could be built, how many orphans fed and clothed, how many sick men, women, and children treated to a holiday in the country? The nations to-day resemble a lunatic who should spend so much money on fireworks and crackers that he must go short of food and drink. Further, the agitation of the working-men for economic and political reform can be sidetracked and disorganized, if the Government declares war on a foreign nation and asks the patriots to fight for their country. The appeal to their patriotism rouses the wild tribal passion, and makes them forget and suspend the vital class-struggle that promised them a speedy success. Whenever the embattled socialist forces threaten to storm the citadel of Capitalism, they can always be diverted from their proper task, and employed to cut the throats of the working-men of some other country by sounding the blaring trumpet of Nationalism, as the Siberian sledge-travellers escape the fangs of the wolves by throwing out clothes for them to chew. The war between Revolutionary France and England delayed political reform in England for a whole generation: the ardent republicans of 6792 A.H. were converted into the loyal and patriotic subjects of 6800 A.H. J. H. Rose, the eminent historian, says: "In 1792, English public opinion seemed about to become scarcely less Jacobinical than that of France. . . . The end of the century saw the prospects of democracy gloomier even than amidst the torpor of 1780." The growing power of German Social Democracy in 6914 was first harnessed to the ghastly juggernaut car of carnage, and then destroyed by rabid "national" sentiment. Nationalism must be recognized as a very potent obstacle to the triumph of Socialism. It divides human society permanently into warring "nations," and tries to weaken and deaden the class-consciousness of the workers. Socialism, on the contrary, divides Humanity temporarily into two warring classes, and seeks to rouse and stimulate the class-feeling

of the proletariat. The wars of the nation-states will again and again sweep away the Socialist parties and organizations, as the ocean erodes the coast-line in England, and the earthquakes destroy the houses in Japan. The working-men must vow not to take part in any international wars, even though they may be implored to fight for "king and country," or "freedom," or "justice," or "honour," or "empire," or "religion," or "national liberty." With all such cries and slogans, the capitalists will try to lure them to their doom. If they do not understand this simple truth, they deserve to remain slaves for ever. Socialism is not for asses and owls: it is for intelligent men and women.

War is thus an immeasurable folly, an inexpiable crime, an irreparable disaster, an unpardonable sin, a homicidal madness, an outbreak of savage fury, and a recurrent catastrophe that maims and mars human civilization. It can be abolished only by abolishing the sovereign nation-state and establishing the sovereign World-State. No palliatives will cure this age-long, deep-seated malady. Pacts, treaties, and conventions among the nation-states will be found to be illusory and ineffective. As M. Valbert has said: "From the year 1500 B.C. to 1860 A.D., more than 8000 treaties of peace meant to remain in force for ever were concluded. The average time they remained in force is two years." The nation-state fosters the mentality of selfish Nationalism, which will always seek money and power by crushing and robbing other nations, as these are considered to be beyond the pale of morality and humanity. War cannot be prevented by proving that the victors will lose as much as the vanquished. This pretty paradox of J. Novikow and N. Angell may sound beautiful, but it is simply not true. Wealth can be acquired by conquest, spoliation, and colonization to-day, as it has been acquired in the past. Self-interest will never teach the nations to eschew war. The anti-war propaganda must be conducted along ethical, cultural, political, and economic lines. Ethically, war must be shunned individually by you and me as a sin, as we refuse to kill or steal in our daily lives. Collective murder is just as sinful as individual assassination. Culturally, the cosmopolitan mentality must be created by the study of world-history, world-literature, and a world-language. Politically, Nationalism must be undermined by developing and glorifying Municipalism and Cosmopolitanism. Economically, Capitalism must be transformed into democratic Socialism. The World-State can be reared on this solid foundation of Ethics, Culture, Politics, and Economics. Only the World-State can abolish War for ever. Let us now consider this Queen Irene, guardian-deity of Peace, the World-State one and indivisible.

The World-State

The City-State and the Nation-State will find their logical consummation in the World-State of the future. Humanity will not remain divided into fifty or more Nation-States for ever. It will be organized as one political community with the Earth as its territorial basis. One State, one Flag, one Language, one Ethics, one Ideal, one Love, and one Life: that is our goal.

This ideal will not be realized through arbitration-treaties among sovereign Nation-States or occasional peace pacts, or even the present League of Nations. We have resolved to abolish the sovereign Nation-States for ever: we will make a bonfire of all their flags, a big, blazing and beautiful bonfire that will cheer the souls of a war-weary world. The League of Nations is like a mechanical mixture of heterogeneous and discordant elements: the World-State will resemble a chemical compound, produced out of different constituents, but homogeneous and harmonious in structure. We do not wish to perpetuate the barbarous term "Nation" for all eternity; we shall finally relegate it to oblivion in our onward march towards world-unity, as an adult throws away the toys and trinkets of childhood. The League of Nations confers the same voting power on very small "nations" like Holland and Siam, and on big populous "nations" like Germany and China. This arrangement is absurd. Representation in a World-Parliament should be proportional to population. The "League of Nations" is a misnomer; it excludes conquered nations like Algeria and Annam. It has no internal unity, no common spirit, no unquenchable vitality. It has not even a common language for conducting its business. It is like a house of cards that threatens to fall asunder at the slightest breath of windy Nationalism. It may be compared to a Meccano building, which can be resolved into its component parts at a moment's notice; it does not impress the spectator as a solid, unified, enduring structure like the majestic Eiffel Tower. It aims at the mere juxtaposition of sovereign Nation-States: it does not unite the nations in the higher synthesis of a sovereign World-State. As the go-cart of the cosmopolitan ideal in its infancy, it has been valuable and indispensable; but it must be developed and reorganized until it fulfils all the needs and aspirations of advancing Humanity. We cherish it as the noble "War-memorial" of the millions who died, infinitely more precious and inspiring for us than those nationalistic cenotaphs and burning flames of some great cities. We love the League, but we love it as a father loves his child. We long to see it grow to maturity, not to remain stunted in dwarfish feebleness and deformity.

The World-State will be broad-based on six pillars, which will never be shaken by any storms of national or religious hatred.

1. WORLD-HISTORY. The perversion of World-history is the foundation of the present Nation-State. As this wretched national history produces the mentality of a nationalist, so will our World-history create what H. G. Wells has called the "international mind." As H. J. Laski says, "Nationality is a psychological phenomenon rather than a juridical principle." The historical tradition and the psychology of the people must be thoroughly and radically changed, or you will build the World-State on shifting sands. The history of world-civilization is the necessary intellectual pabulum for the world-citizens whom we shall educate. National history divides and disrupts mankind; World-history will unite and amalgamate all peoples and nations. History is the very life-blood circulating in the veins and arteries of a State. The commemoration of the great men and women, who have bequeathed to us the priceless legacy of civilization, will instil the spirit of cosmopolitanism into the children and the adults. The Nation-States celebrate the deeds of many ferocious brigands and cut-throats; but the heroes and heroines of the World-State will be the eminent scientists, artists, saints, and sages of all the countries of the world. The birthdays of Washington and Lincoln, the Shakespeare Festival, the fall of the Bastille, the Wesak festival of the Buddhists, the Christmas of the Christians, the 6th November of the Swedes, the 1st August of the Swiss: all these and other local festivals will be converted into universal festivals, while new world-festivals will be instituted in memory of other events and personalities that are at present neglected.

2. WORLD-METROPOLIS. The World-State will have its metropolis. The League of Nations has already chosen Geneva; it is a lovely, centrally-situated, free city. But perhaps it will be advisable to select Athens as the capital of the World-State. Modern civilization owes more to Athens than to any other single town. The historical tradition of culture points to Athens as one of the most sacred pilgrim-shrines for civilized Humanity. Athens is situated between East and West, and enjoys a mild climate.

3. WORLD-LITERATURE AND WORLD-LANGUAGE. Nationalism is founded on the inescapable fact of a common language and

literature. The World-State must have a universal language, into which the works of the great writers of all countries will be translated. The members of the World-Parliament must be able to understand one another, otherwise Babelism will make confusion worse confounded. The Roman Catholic Church employs Latin as its official medium of communication. All Moslem scholars at the University of El-Azhar can read and speak Arabic. Political unity is impossible without the use of a common language, at least among the leaders, who will assemble in congresses and conferences as representatives of their countries or regions. International conferences at present are tragi-comic, theatrical performances. No genuine feeling of comradeship can be engendered among delegates who cannot speak to one another. Nationalism is violently vociferous in a hundred tongues: but internationalism is a pitiful deaf-mute at such gatherings. The World-State will adopt Esperanto or coin another suitable language as its universal intellectual currency for the exchange of information and ideas.

National literature is one of the strongest props of Nationalism. World-literature will train the world-citizens in cosmopolitan ways of thought, as Goethe clearly foresaw. Then the great poets, philosophers, novelists, and other writers will become the common property of all mankind. A quotation from Victor Hugo will be appreciated as quickly at Peiping as at Paris. The plays of Shakespeare, Euripides, Molière, Corneille, Chikamatsu, Alfieri, Schiller, Chehov, Wedekind, and other dramatists will be acted in Esperanto (or whatever the universal language may be) at Baghdad and Bogota, Melbourne and Madrid, Toronto and Timbuctoo. The national languages have hitherto confined the minds and souls of men and women in narrow grooves, as prison-convicts are kept in separate cells; but the universal language will enable all to meet and greet one another like friends and fellow-citizens on an Italian piazza on a feast-day.

4. World-Travel. The World-State will encourage world-travel as an essential part of education. Every citizen will be given the opportunity of seeing the Earth and the glory thereof. World-history and World-language will make the trip a perpetual feast for the mind and a silent sermon for the soul. As Ariosto says:

> "Who travels into foreign climes shall find
> What ne'er before was imaged in his mind"

Cosmopolitanism will then become a potent spiritual force in every citizen's life. At present, Nationalism often robs travel of its educational value. A British nobleman perhaps carries his Nationalism, like his gout, over the whole world; and his much-travelled body still encases a stay-at-home mind. Of such Nationalists has Saadi remarked: "If Jesus Christ's donkey should go to Mecca on pilgrimage, it would still be a donkey when it came home."

5. World-Society. A State is the political organization of a community; it is not merely a joint-stock company for arresting thieves, repairing roads, and disposing of sewage. A human community cannot last without a certain degree of social homogeneity. Absolute uniformity in matters of food, dress, and recreation is not required; but excessive diversity of customs and manners is also a bar to friendly intercourse. The members of the World-Parliament at Geneva or Athens must have a common club-life, which is the symbol of social unity. Shylock said to Bassanio: "I will buy with you, sell with you, talk with you, walk with you; but I will not eat with you or drink with you," as he belonged to the exclusive Jewish community of Venice; but the world-citizens will abandon and abjure such social exclusiveness for ever. The World-State will not be only for buying, selling, talking, and walking, but also for eating and drinking together, which is indeed the universal sacrament of friendship. It is easy to provide a common social life for the Europeans, but it will be more difficult to bring the Europeans and the Asiatics together at the same club. The Europeans and the Asiatics should meet half-way and consent to compromise. The Europeans should eschew strong alcoholic beverages that taint the breath, and the Asiatics should emancipate and educate their women. The excessive alcoholism of the West and the seclusion of women in the East are the two chief obstacles to the establishment of a harmonious social life. Uniformity in dress need not be aimed at: variety makes social life picturesque. The costumes of mankind have also been changing in the past: there is no fixed permanent style or fashion. This process will continue in the future, and the World-State will not attempt to stereotype any particular costume in the interests of social unity. Let the hat, the turban, and the fez compete for popularity in the social arena; the best headgear will win. As regards recreation, most outdoor sports and indoor games have already become universal, *e.g.* tennis, golf, football, billiards, chess, cards, etc. Musical education should be standardized over the whole world. At present, it is at very different levels in Europe, India, China, and Persia. The consequence is that Western

music is not appreciated by most Orientals, and Oriental music appeals to very few Europeans. This is a real misfortune, as music is the sunshine of social life. A uniform system of musical education will train the world-citizens to enjoy the best music of all countries and epochs. The foundations of social unity will thus be laid broad and deep in emotional harmony and concord.

6. World-Philosophy. The State represents the essential elements of unity among mankind, and Philosophy is one of the cohesive forces that weld an aggregation of individuals into a well-ordered community. We should accept the wise old rule: " Unity in essentials, Liberty (*i.e.* variety) in non-essentials, Charity in everything." Some may believe that sound Philosophy and scientific Ethics are not to be regarded as very important factors in the World-State. They may approve of the " modern " doctrine that Philosophy and Ethics are non-political matters, like food and dress. Philosophy is the theory of the best life for individuals and communities, while Ethics is practical philosophy, which applies the theory and embodies it in social customs and institutions. Now the World-State cannot be created and maintained without a common Philosophy of Life and its practical counterpart, a common system of Ethics. The State must represent the highest ideal of physical, intellectual, æsthetic, and moral life for the citizen; otherwise it would not command the whole-hearted allegiance of the wisest and most virtuous men and women, who would prefer to devote themselves to the service of the organization that promotes their Ideals. The perfect State is unitary and harmonious; it will not separate Economics and Politics from Ethics. It will not follow Rudolf Steiner's precept: " In a healthy society, the spiritual life has a sphere of its own and must function alongside the spheres of politics and economics." If Morality is organized in many mutually exclusive militant Churches, then they will be troublesome thorns in the side of the World-State. The State will then be in chronic conflict with the Church or Churches, as often happened in the Middle Ages, when the cleverest and noblest men were in the service of the Church and not of the State. The World-State must draw unto itself all the brain and brawn, all the light and love, all the power and passion that are available at any moment in the whole world. It must be a jealous mistress and say to its citizens: " I brook no rivals in your affections. Love me and me alone. Serve me and me alone. I am the first and the last, the Alpha and Omega for you all. Ye shall have no other idols beside me." If the World-State is modelled after the police-

state of Bentham and Spencer, and discharges only the negative duty of protecting life and property, it will be overwhelmed in chaos or expire through inanition. It will evoke no enthusiasm and elicit no soul-response. It will be as dead as the dollars it guards, as wooden and lifeless as the policeman's baton that is its sceptre. It will not stand for the complete Ideal of Life, but only for the means of physical subsistence. It will protect our bodies, but it will not cater for our minds and hearts and souls. It will thus assume an inferior function, as its living symbols will not be Prophets and Philosophers, but policemen and prison-warders. Such a mean and mutilated State will be compelled to play *second* fiddle to the powerful Churches, which teach the citizens how to live nobly and die peacefully. The first and deepest concern of every human being is and must be just this question: "How can I make the best of this life?" The World-State must teach its Philosophy and Ethics to all its children; it must not leave them to the mercy of ignorant and stupid priests and charlatans. Upon this teaching, the life and death of the State will depend.

Further, social harmony and political unity are not possible without a common Philosophy that trains all citizens to strive for the same goal and work in the same spirit. John Dewey deplores the spiritual chaos of modern civilization in these words: "There is no such bond of social unity as once united Greeks, Romans, Hebrews, and the Catholics of medieval Europe. There are those who realize what is portended by the loss of religion as an integrating bond." Without the strong cement of a common Philosophy, the World-State would be like a tower of bricks without mortar. The different Churches would rend the State asunder, like wild horses pulling a chariot in different directions. The State possesses Power, and each sect would try to wield this Power for the good of the human race. If the brains of the citizens do not think alike, and if their hearts do not feel alike, then their hands will not work in unison and their feet will not march in step. The feuds of Catholic and Protestant, Moslem and Christian, Shiah and Sunni, Moslem and Jew, Hindu and Moslem, and other such sects now turn the politics of some States into a perpetual boxing-match, in which no rules of honour are observed. Some shallow thinkers are misled by the spectacle of modern England and America, and believe that peace and co-operation are possible without religious unity. But England is united on the basis of Protestantism, and the law lays down that a Roman Catholic cannot wear the crown. The Catholic Church is already making trouble in the United States, and the State in that country is worm-eaten with venality and corruption. If the population of Great Britain consisted of ten million Zoroastrians, ten million Catholics, ten million Protestants, ten million Bahais, ten million Moslems, and ten million Buddhists, it would be impossible to secure political harmony even in such a patriotic nation as the British. A State presupposes unity of purpose and principle. The World-State will be a home for the people, not an hotel or a caravanserai. Many Churches are very intolerant and aggressive against one another. Their members carry about in their pockets the explosive hand-grenades of the dogma of exclusive salvation, which is more fatal to the unity of a State than a hundred civil wars. If the citizens of the World-State hate and despise one another as "infidels," "heretics," "mlecchas," "kafirs," "heathen," etc., the State will be a sad mockery of the ideal of human unity. It would be better for such bigots and fanatics to stay in their respective Churches and States, as they are not fit for the World-State. Rousseau pointed out the peril of this theological pastime of mutual damnation, and said: "I think that those who distinguish between civil intolerance and theological intolerance make a mistake. These two forms of intolerance are inseparable. It is impossible to live in peace with people whom one regards as 'damned'; to love them would mean that one hates God who will punish them; it is absolutely necessary to convert them or persecute them. Wherever theological intolerance gains admittance, the sovereign no longer is in possession of sovereignty; the priests are thenceforward the real rulers." This warning must not fall on deaf ears. In the World-State, the citizens will not keep swords and pistols in their houses. How can they then harbour the deadly antisocial thoughts and feelings bred by religious intolerance, which are more destructive and disruptive than all the weapons and engines of war? The zealots of intolerant creeds will always

> "Build their faith upon
> The holy text of pike and gun,
> Decide all controversies by
> Infallible artillery,
> And prove their doctrine orthodox
> By apostolic blows and knocks."
>
> (Hudibras.)

The different Churches that now infest the world are not concerned merely with creed and ritual: they have their peculiar social and political doctrines. The Roman Catholic Church disapproves of democracy and divorce; the Calvinists champion popular government; the Moslems sanction polygamy and confer uncontrolled powers on an elected caliph, and so on. It is idle to argue as if the present religions of the world had no political function and significance. Every Church has its politics.

The World-State will have no Church or Churches within it: the State will also represent Ethics, as in Confucian China. Its Ministers will be sages and saints; its civil servants will be scholars and scientists. It will be responsible not only for administration, but also for education and edification. It will train the citizens in all Virtue and Wisdom. It will correspond to Aristotle's definition of the State: "The society, which is called a State, aims at the highest Good and is the most excellent. It embraces all other associations. . . . It contains in itself the perfection of independence. It is first founded that men may live, but is continued that they may live happily. It is a community of families and villages, formed for the sake of a perfect independent life. It is founded, not for the purpose of merely living together, but for living as men ought to live."

Such a many-sided and full-orbed State is our goal, not the police-state of the Liberals and not the bread-and-cinema State of the ordinary socialists and communists. It will hasten the advent of the time heralded by R. Browning,

> "When all mankind alike is perfected,
> Equal in full-blown powers"

The Philosophy and Ethics that will create and sustain such a State must be universal, scientific, and optimistic. The World-State will not educate its children in theology or pessimistic metaphysics. It will make no truce with superstition, inert quietism, or philosophical "defeatism" that teaches despair and renunciation. It will honour Science as the Athenians worshipped Athena. It will give all citizens the best possible education and then leave them full freedom of opinion and action. If they have been properly educated, they can never go astray. The World-State will encourage free scientific speculation on all problems, as its citizens enjoy immunity from superstition on account of their excellent education. "No theology and no metaphysics, but Science in abundance for all": this will be the simple general creed of the new polity.

SECTION IV.—ECONOMICS

THE World-State will be founded on the granite bedrock of Economics as the science of universal Production, Consumption, and Distribution.

I. *Production.* It will own and administer the entire Earth, its fields, orchards, meadows, mines, forests, fisheries, workshops, factories, and all the materials and instruments employed in Production. It will hold the title-deeds to all Property. It will give us our daily bread, for which millions now pray to "God" in vain. It will provide and guarantee Plenty for All. It will be the foreseeing and far-seeing Providence for every man, woman, and child, even for every useful beast and bird, over the whole earth. At present, Production is mismanaged and thwarted everywhere by the double competition among nations and among individuals. Each nation attempts to enrich itself without thinking of its neighbours; or it desires to exploit and impoverish them, if it thinks of them at all. Each nation imposes tariffs in order to "protect" the home-market, and thus impedes the free circulation of the life-blood of commerce. Each nation follows the comic and paradoxical policy of selling much to other countries and buying very little from them in order to defend its currency in the interests of the rentier class. No nation stops to think for a moment and ask, "If everyone wishes only to sell, who will there be to buy?" The leaders of the nations do not understand that buying and selling must go together. It is as impossible to sell without buying as it is to clap with one hand. But they have lost their wits, and they persevere in their efforts to secure one-sided commerce and economic self-sufficiency. This is the crazy economics of Bedlam. There is inconceivable confusion and competition among the producing nations. Competition is only a longer name for Confusion. Every country tries to manufacture many commodities for which it has no natural advantages and facilities. England and Japan establish the textile industry, though not a wisp of cotton grows within or near their territories. Scotland makes sacks out of jute, but the jute grows only in far-off Bengal. Switzerland offers us delicious chocolate, though cocoa has to be brought thousands of miles from Africa. Thus the bewildered nations defy Nature, forgetting that they are inevitably hurrying to their doom, like the lemming rats that are drowned in the sea. There is no plan or order in world-economy to-day. Each nation must grab at the raw materials produced in the tropics, find new markets and fields for investment, and therefore acquire colonies and dependencies. Sometimes there is over-production of certain commodities and price-cutting. At other periods, the people suffer from scarcity and high prices The numerous national currencies can never be stabilized and adjusted: they will always be jumping up and down and round and about, like the mad dervishes of Morocco. So ridiculous and so inefficient is this national Economics of to-day! Its organizers remind me of that frivolous young man Hippoclides, who, according to Herodotus, lost his bride, because he made a fool of himself by dancing on his head at a social gathering. Our industrial and political leaders are also dancing a devil's dance in this inverted position. What is worse, they are dancing and fiddling and orating and prating at futile long-drawn-out conferences held on the slopes of the volcano of Demos. They believe that the old volcano is burned out. They cannot hear its ominous rumblings and grumblings, because they are deafened by the din of their own vapid oratory and the shrill music at their Lucullean banquets. But the eruption is imminent. The schemers and scoundrels of nationalist Economics will soon be submerged under the burning lava of popular discontent and indignation. These things shall come to pass, and very soon.

Nationalism makes a rational and stable world-economy impossible. Within each nation again, the private ownership of land, capital, and all the means of production and distribution has landed all countries in a hopeless mess and muddle. Production is carried on solely for profit. If no profit can be made on some commodities, they will not be produced, however necessary they may be. Thus the houses required by the people could not be built in England by private enterprise during and after the Great War, and the State had to step in. The municipal houses can be let about two to three shillings a week cheaper than those built by private firms Luxuries are sometimes manufactured for wealthy customers living in distant lands, while the poor people cry for the necessaries of life. Capital does not always stay at home, when it is needed for production. It scents Profit from afar, as a vulture smells carrion. It flies quickly from its native country to another on the wings of greed, lured by the prospects of making more dividends out of cheap and unorganized labour. Speculation, mismanagement, and competition ruin thousands of industrial enterprises each year. "Never morning wore to evening, but some heart did break," and not a day passes without some failures and bankruptcies in the chaotic world of Capitalism. In 6932, there were in Great Britain 4645 Receiving Orders, the liabilities of the bankrupts being estimated at £10,131,126 and the assets at £2,075,388. The charge of fraudulent conversion was brought against ten bankrupts.

Speculation and swindling are immensely facilitated by the disorder inherent in this system, which gives birth to predatory, unscrupulous adventurers like Stavisky and Kreuger, as the dark tropical jungle shelters jaguars and cheetahs.

Capitalism is the acme of disorganization. Several firms and companies manufacture the same commodity; hence keen competition, unnecessary waste, excessive overhead charges, alternate periods of glut and unemployment, dishonest dealing, mendacious advertising, adulteration, crashes and crises, law-suits and suicides, lamentation and despair. The F— F— Co., Ltd., invited the public to subscribe £50,000 at a time when its issued capital was only £65. Small capitalists often set up as usurers, who give short-term loans to the poor. They are legally authorized in some countries to charge interest at the rate of 48 per cent. per annum. Many of them in practice demand and get a penny in the shilling per week, or 433 per cent. per annum! Half-a-dozen milkmen perambulate one small street; a score of manufacturers try to force their beer or ale or soda-water down the throats of the gullible public. This multiplicity of producers and sellers entails the daily and hourly misuse of energy and life. Each industrialist wishes to conceal a new invention from his rivals, and patents are taken out in order to secure a monopoly of the gift of Nature. Genius invents, and Capital prevents and circumvents. Useful production can be thwarted and hindered at each step. But Capital eagerly produces tons of drugs like heroin and cocaine, and abundance of arms and ammunition, if it can obtain high profits. It sells guns and rifles to compatriots and enemies impartially; its Fatherland is Money. It can sell milk or morphine, bread or brandy, honey or hashish with equal alacrity, if it can but make money. Capital does not ask, "Is a commodity useful or necessary?" Its only query is: "How much per cent. can I make off it?" It often tries to create an artificial demand for injurious commodities by mass-suggestion. It provides debasing entertainment and panders to the lowest passions. Our capitalists have neither intelligence nor morality. They are like a group of short-sighted, half-witted boys, let loose in a restaurant, rushing in all directions and colliding with one another and swearing and cursing in a mad scramble for the food that is there. Our civil service and post office are organized and socially managed; but our industry and agriculture are left to suffer and languish through the inadequacy, inefficiency, and immorality of private possession and unregulated competition. What folly is this?

II. *Consumption*. It is a curious fact that most economists of all schools, including the socialists, avoid a full discussion of the question of Consumption; and yet Consumption is surely the key to the problem of Production, for society produces what men and women wish to consume. Commodities are produced and distributed in order to be used and enjoyed. The wants, tastes, and needs of the people determine what shall be produced. The farmers do not produce much pork in Moslem countries. Snails are reared for the market in France, but not in England. Very few books are printed and published in Zanzibar and Liberia. A brisk trade in gramophones is done in Asia, as the secluded and indolent ladies are fond of hearing chamber-music at home. Thus Consumption sets the pace for Production.

Under the present system, Consumption is carried on under the influence of two vicious principles: Hedonism and Luxury. Hedonism is practised by all classes, rich and poor alike. Luxury is the besetting sin of the wealthy people, who have a large income. Luxury can be indulged in, when the necessaries and comforts of life have already been secured. It is thus confined to a very small minority of the population in each country. But Hedonism flourishes among all classes, as it can be cultivated even by very poor working-men who may lack the barest necessaries. Even a tramp may be a hedonist.

Hedonism may be defined as the principle that the maximum of temporary pleasant and stimulating sensations should be obtained, even if they are not conducive to a person's lasting welfare. The true principle of Consumption is Eudaimonism, which aims at the individual's development and permanent happiness and well-being. But Hedonism is the false guide that most people now follow, the will-o'-the-wisp that leads them into the bogs of misery and suffering. Thus Hedonism creates a craving for noxious narcotics and stimulants like alcohol, tobacco, hashish, hemp, tea, coffee, opium, betel-leaf, and other drugs, which are consumed in enormous quantities every day over the whole world. Production must satisfy this demand. Drug-addicts are the most degenerate victims of such Hedonism. Millions of acres of earth, vast capital, and a prodigious amount of labour are needed for the pernicious trade in such commodities. All such production *is* worse than waste; it is a minus quantity in the mathematics of rational Economics, as it impairs the health and ruins the character of the people. This tragic folly of unwise Consumption is not due to Capitalism or Nationalism, but solely to Hedonism. It may subsist even when both Capitalism and Nationalism have disappeared.

Men and women of all classes in all countries consume many deleterious and superfluous commodities, such as pastry, sweets, rouge, lip-stick, henna, spices, and ornaments. This is the seamy side of Consumption at present. Luxury is the ugly offspring of excessive Hedonism and inordinate wealth. Sometimes it is born of the union of vanity and wealth. When certain commodities that Hedonism appreciates are very expensive, they are consumed only by the wealthy class and regarded as "luxuries." Cost makes all the difference between a luxury and an article of popular consumption. Thus a mango is a common fruit in India, like an apple in England; but it is a luxury in London, where it may cost as much as eighteenpence apiece Fresh figs are sold very cheap in Italy and Greece, but they are luxuries in England. The rich sybarites take delight in purchasing such expensive commodities as game, grouse, duck, pheasant, partridge, candied fruits, pillau, fruits in liquor, sturgeon, caviar, lobster, turtle-soup, champagne, whisky, Blue Mountain Jamaica coffee, rose-water, "haleva," kofta, almond-balls, "pakvan," "biryani," Darjeeling and Lapsang-souchong tea, Balkan sobranje cigarettes, saffron, hot-house grapes and melons, pistachios and pistachio sweets, pâté de foie gras, bird's-nest soups, bamboo-shoots, "awabi," silk dresses, gold jewellery, jade necklaces, ornaments set with precious stones, fine shawls, delicate perfumes, high-priced motor cars, gold watches, furs, rare books and pictures, candelabra, Persian carpets, porcelain vases, diamond rings, and pearl necklaces. There is no end to this shameful, senseless, wanton waste of human labour and life for the glittering but ghoulish Vanity Fair of the moneyed drones. Here are a few authentic items:—

A store in London stocks some handkerchiefs that cost £3 13*s*. 6*d*. apiece.

A lady (Miss B. H.) spent £5,000 on her trousseau. Among other things, she purchased the following at an average cost of £50 each:

"a red shantung afternoon costume with a small white print design worn with a small organdie ruff; a black shantung skirt and jacket embroidered in white with a white pique waistcoat tied with a large bow at the neck; a blue shantung afternoon dress with a white design of stars."

A Russian landowner's life before the Great War has been thus described by his nephew: "Each of the six daily meals had the solemnity of a banquet. My uncle saw that the garden supplied the chef with materials worthy of his skill. Incomparable glass-houses harboured not only palm-trees a hundred or more years old, and flowers for decorative purposes, but also strawberries in mid-winter, peaches in June, and grapes equal to those of Fontainebleau. The eggs were numbered and dated each day, eggs from prize hens The calves were milk-fed only, so that their flesh was white. There were five lakes, fed by specially constructed streams, to provide carp and trout."

W. E. H. Lecky refers to the British aristocrats and their "lives of mischievous self-indulgence or scandalous vices," and says: "There are circles where luxury is carried to such a pitch that men almost come to resemble that strange species of ant, which is so dependent on the ministrations of its slave ants that it would starve to death, if these were not present to feed it. The enormous and elaborate waste of time, the colossal luxury of ostentation, the endless routine of dressing and gossip and frivolous amusements, that prevail in some great country-houses form an atmosphere which is well fitted to kill all earnestness of purpose and conviction. The pleasures of life are made its business. The slaughter of countless beasts and birds is treated as if it were a main object of existence. Life is looked down upon as from an opera-box, till all sense of its seriousness seems to vanish!"

The first-class passengers on some boats are served the following *menus* for lunch and dinner on the voyage from Europe to India and China: *Lunch* 1 p.m. Hors d'œuvre (8 kinds), consommé, 3 soups, 2 dishes of eggs, 4 ready dishes, 3 dishes to order, cold buffet (8 kinds), 6 kinds of sauces, 6 salads, 5 dishes of vegetables, 3 kinds of sweets, assorted cheese, fruits, compote, coffee. *Dinner* 7 p.m. Consommé, soup (3 kinds), fish (2 kinds), 2 dishes of meat with 3 kinds of vegetables, 2 dishes of roast meat, 5 kinds of vegetables, buffet (6 kinds), salad (5 kinds), 5 kinds of sauces, sweets (2 kinds), ice cream (3 kinds), fruit, cheese, coffee.

At some shops in London you can buy smoked Scotch salmon at 12*s*. per lb , pure foie gras at 24*s*. per lb., strawberries in sherry at 10*s.* 6*d.* per bottle, Jamaica sun-dried turtle at 15*s.* per lb., terrapin soup at 7*s.* 6*d.* per bottle, harlequin fruit in Brandijel at 16*s.* 6*d.* per bottle, cherry brandy sauce at 6*s.* 6*d.* per bottle, Chinese ginger at 10*s.* 6*d.* per jar, Benia rhum syrup pineapple at 21*s.* per bottle, Astrachan caviar at 22*s.* 6*d.* per jar, and Darjeeling tea at 18*s.* per lb.

Some ordinary stores in London stock shoes at 55*s.* and more, chemises at 3½ guineas, nightgowns at 10½ guineas, gloves at 30*s.*, hats at £2, ties at 15*s.* 6*d.*, caps at 49*s.* 6*d.*, shirts at 39*s.* 6*d.*, cuff links at £6 6*s.* and £8 15*s.*, and fur coats from £200 to £800. Precious stones and pearl necklaces, up to £20,000 and more, may be purchased in Hatton Garden. On October 7th, 6933, a London newspaper reported "a luncheon, when a white Burgundy—Bâtard-Montrachet, 1926—accompanied whitebait, and a red claret—Château Latour, 1920—was served with a partridge, while Cockburn's 1904 port introduced the Stilton, and the luncheon was concluded with Denis Mounie Cognac, 1863, which . . . had matured in the wood for nearly seventy years." Such is Luxury, self-centred, spendthrift, sensual, suicidal. It is a sign and symbol of Parasitism and Exploitation. It demands useless and wasteful Production for the titillation of a few million palates and the gratification of the vanity of the fops and fools of the world. It weakens the moral stamina of the community, as the idle rich flaunt their vices and their finery in the face of the whole society. They are not ashamed of themselves, not they. They strut about like peacocks in the crowded streets, feed like hogs in the restaurants, and waste their time at the beauty-parlours, cinemas, and theatres. They openly advertise and display their follies and frivolities, their hectic criminal festivities, and their brainless aimless "social" activities, their balls, cock-tail parties, whist-drives, dinners, courts, races, receptions, shooting-parties, petting-parties, nautch-parties, night clubs, and brothels. Capitalism is indeed twice accursed. It is a curse for the rich and a curse for the poor. It gives too much to one class and too little to another: thus it defaces the human lineaments of both, and makes them brutal and brutish. It pampers the rich and pinches the poor. It consumes the rich with the Nessus-shirt of ill-gotten wealth and self-loathing indolence, while it torments the poor with the strait-jacket of penury and excessive toil. It is the accursed dam of luxury, debauchery, snobbery, servility, starvation, ignorance, waste, idleness, falsehood, envy, violence, hatred, disease, prostitution, suicide, and premature death.

III. *Distribution.* Nationalism and Capitalism thus diminish and misdirect Production. They also flout Justice and Fraternity in Distribution. Among the nations, some countries like England, France, and Portugal have secured possession of vast colonies in Asia and Africa, while other industrial nations like Italy and Germany have no such outlets and markets for their manufactured goods. Such inequality must lead to many wars. Humanity must not be divided into wealthy nations and indigent nations. Some countries like Argentina and India are favoured with a fertile soil: they can easily produce enormous wealth, and amass it or squander it. Other countries like Arabia, Scotland, and Afghanistan are handicapped in the race by Nature, who is indeed a niggardly stepmother to them. Their poverty often brings about conflict, as Roderick Dhu cogently explained to James Fitzjames:

> "Where dwell we now? See, rudely swell
> Crag over crag, and fell o'er fell
> Ask we this savage hill we tread,
> For fattened steer or household bread?"

Some advanced nations like the Japanese and the Swedes can acquire a large amount of wealth through their superiority in scientific technique and equipment, while some ignorant peoples like the Chinese and the Persians have not yet mastered the magic power of machinery. Thus the average income per head of the population in different countries varies enormously. It amounts to less than £3 in the poorest countries and to about £40 among the wealthiest nations.

Such economic inequality prevails among the nations as a consequence of imperialism, geographical situation, or differences of education and culture. Inequality always breeds war.

Nationalism strives to perpetuate this inequality among the nations, which always try to defend their privileges and possessions by war. Within each nation, the private ownership of land and capital makes a mockery of Justice and Fraternity in the distribution of Wealth and Work. The landlords who are said to "own" the land in England, Bengal, Oudh, Germany, and other countries never plough, sow, or reap in the fields. They compel the working farmers to pay them "rent" out of the crop that is the product of the joint labour of the peasant, his family, and his hired labourers (if any). This system of crude and direct exploitation had its origin in conquest. The marauding warriors settled in the conquered land as barons and landowners, and have exacted tribute from the defeated people ever since. Thus a wealthy landlord class has arisen.

The manufacturers who own the factories appropriate the surplus-value produced by the working-men's labour. The wholesale merchants exploit the community by charging high prices for the commodities that they sell. The financiers and bankers lend money to the manufacturers, the merchants, and other persons, and earn "interest." The priests live on "tithes" and endowments. The higher Government officials get their enormous salaries out of the taxes paid by the citizens; and the interest on what is called the "national debt" is also paid out of the taxes. Thus all the members of the exploiting class live on the labour of the working class. Some of them have very large incomes. In England, in 6928, society was divided into several groups with unequal incomes. All families earning more than the average national income may be said to belong to the exploiting class.

139	persons had an income of over	£100,000
250	,, ,, ,, ,, ,,	£75,000
521	,, ,, ,, ,, ,,	£50,000
2,976	,, ,, ,, ,, ,,	£20,000
9,805	,, ,, ,, ,, ,,	£10,000
29,658	,, ,, ,, ,, ,,	£5,000
104,514	,, ,, ,, ,, ,,	£2,000
14,875,000	,, ,, income of about	£159
7,000,000	,, ,, ,, less than	£76

In 6931, about 6 per cent. of the population took £1138 millions in rent, profit, and interest, while 80 per cent. of the population (the working-class) got £1376 millions in wages!

Such statistics show that our civilization is founded and grounded on injustice and inequality, on robbery and roguery, on tyranny and moral turpitude. There are very wealthy individuals in all countries: they may be compared to the free-booters, buccaneers, dacoits, and pirates of the Middle Ages. Thus Lord N—— has an income of £150,000 a year; Sir R. H—— gets away with more than £100,000; the heiress of Sir D—— has in trust an annual income of about £1,000,000; Lady C—— left £25,000 to each of her ten grand-daughters. There are 494 persons in France with an annual income of more than 1,000,000 francs.

In contrast with such ill-gotten wealth, think of the farm-labourers with less than £2 a week, the unemployed with less than 30s. per week, the clerks and the artisans with less than £3 per week! Professor Henry Clay has asked this pertinent question: "How many working-class homes would have fetched more than £20, if sold up, before the War?" In the jute mills of India, the capitalists have been paid dividends of 200 per cent. and 400 per cent., while the labourers, in 6926, were given £12 10s in wages for the year. It has been calculated that about £100 surplus-value was extracted out of each of the 300,000 working-men that sweat and toil in the factories. In the rubber industry of Malaya, the average wages are £25 per annum, while about £109 surplus-value is wrung out of each wage-slave. Well may we cry with Crabbe:

> "When Plenty smiles—alas! she smiles for few—
> And those, who taste not, yet behold her store,
> Are as the slaves that dig the golden ore—
> The wealth around them makes them doubly poor."

The consequence of such exploitation is that the working-men live in abject poverty and squalor. They are underfed, and many drag on a miserable existence in overcrowded slums. Here are a few authentic cameos of working-class life under Capitalism among the most "advanced" nations:—

1. Dr. Borland (cited by Allen Hutt) says: "Only 22.5 per cent. of Bethnal Green children are well clothed and shod, compared with 60.8 per cent. throughout London. The irony of this situation is that the clothing and boot and shoe trades are two important local industries, in which there is much unemployment."

2. The Deptford Public Health Committee, reporting in February 6933 (cited by Allen Hutt), says: "It is impossible to escape the conclusion that there are to-day many homes in which, after the rent is paid, and allowance made for heating and clothing, there is an insufficient sum available for food of the character and quantity necessary to maintain physiological health."

3. "There are 30,000 cellar dwellings in London—dark, damp, beetle-infested basements—inhabited by 100,000 people. There are 250,000 people living in slum conditions, while 500,000—one-eighth of the population—live more than two to a room." (Statement by the Chairman of the London Trades Council on the 28th October, 6933.)

4. In many families in England, the sum of 4*s*. per head per week is available for food, while the medical estimate of quite plain food is 11*s*. 6*d*. per head per week.

5. In St. Pancras, a working-man, with a wife and six children, pays 15*s*. a week rent for one room; his wages are £3 a week.

6. "I am not a bit surprised to find that girls become dishonest, when they are given such low wages," said Mr. Hopkin Morgan,

presiding magistrate at Pontypool, recently, dealing with a girl of seventeen, accused of stealing a shilling from her employer. Ira Grace Hackleton, aged seventeen, of Church village, said she was paid 6*s*. 8*d*. a week, out of which she paid 3*s*. a week 'bus fares.

7. "There are farm-workers' cottages, built in swamps, or in such bad repair that rain drips on to the dinner table, or where families of six to nine people live in two rooms. There are others uncomfortably near manure yards and piggeries. Cattle on many farms are living in palaces compared with the hovels occupied by the men who tend them. Horse-boxes, costing thousands of pounds, have more light, air, and warmth than the nearby cottages, which cost only a few hundred pounds."

8. "Starving girls of Vancouver (Canada) are threatening to parade naked through the streets of that city to call attention to their plight, unless the Canadian Government comes to their rescue. . . . The women are starving, and are in want of decent clothes to wear. Three or four of them live in a room together, and one borrows clothes from the others, while she goes down to collect her relief. . . . There are 900 girls in Vancouver on unemployed relief, and hundreds more who cannot even get that." (6933.)

9. "'How people can be said to exist under these conditions is almost beyond comprehension. It is shocking to think of such hardship and misery.' This comment was made at a Lambeth inquest by the coroner, Mr. A. Douglas Cowburn, when told how a woman had £2 18*s*. a week to feed eleven persons. A verdict of suicide while of unsound mind was returned on Walter Harvey, aged fifty-six, who was found gassed. Harvey, who had been unemployed two years, wrote a letter to the coroner, in which he said, 'Do not put me down as mad. I am quite sane. I am only fed up with life.' The mother and daughter worked in a laundry. The two grown-up sons were out of work. There were six children under thirteen in the family, and, after £1 rent had been paid, they had 58*s*. to feed eleven persons."

10. "A common charwoman, aged sixty-four, a widow and mother of thirteen children, was bound over for six months for stealing £1 from a house where she worked. Her total earnings amount to 10*s*. 6*d*. a week, and she has to pay 8*s*. 6*d*. a week rent. Sometimes she gets a shilling or two from her married children, but not regularly."

11. "Colliery-owners in South Wales are seriously perturbed at the amount of coal-stealing that is going on in Glamorganshire and

Monmouthshire. In these two counties alone, no fewer than 5,000 persons were proceeded against last year either for coal-stealing or trespassing on colliery sidings in search of coal. An official estimate places the loss sustained by the coal-owners through coal-thefts at not less than £300,000. The Benyon Colliery sold five tons of coal to the unemployed every week, but 30 tons were stolen weekly." (Who were the thieves?)

12. A working-man says: "I live in a house in which there are six families, in seven rooms, thirty-one people in all. My family live in a damp basement. There are seven of us, all sleeping in one room. It is in such bad repair that we cannot leave the babies alone because of the rats. We hear them scratching at night. For the damp basement, we have to pay 14*s.* 8*d.* a week." (*The Daily Herald*, London.)

The terrible misery of the mass of the population is not the only evil that the private ownership of land and capital produces in all countries. Capitalism must also be indicted on the following counts:—

1. It demoralizes the rich by luxury and indolence, and brutalizes the poor by overwork and ignorance.

2. It establishes two classes, whose lives are so different that Disraeli rightly called them "two nations" One class receives higher education and does no manual work, while the other class is given only rudimentary instruction and labours with its hands. Humanity is thus artificially bisected.

3. Class-rule must rely on force for its maintenance. The privileged classes are always afraid of the revolts of the poor. Militarism is thus inseparably associated with Capitalism. The police and the army protect the property of the rich against the danger that threatens it from the exploited class. The working-class is not given the whole product of its labour: hence consumption in the home market does not keep pace with production. Foreign markets must be secured, and the different national gangs of capitalists compete for them, even by war and immense slaughter.

4. Class-rule corrupts religion, art, and literature. Everything and every person in a class-society must support and serve the owning class, or perish. All institutions are controlled and directed in order to ensure the permanence of class-rule, as all roads in the Roman Empire led to Rome. All churches, schools, studios, universities, academies, seminaries, publishers, and printers mus praise and justify class-rule, and teach the people that it is their duty and privilege to pay and submit. The so-called "freedom"

of individuals, associations, and institutions is an optical illusion, which is caused by certain temporary phenomena of prosperous and prudent Capitalism. But, in a crisis, when it is a question of life and death for the class-régime, the capitalists will always declare: "He that is not for us is against us." The preservation of property and privilege is the first and foremost concern of all owning classes. Their life is in their land and their money, which give them leisure and luxury; and they consider it their duty to transmit their possessions intact to their children. They love Property with a deep, passionate, unchanging love. For them, Property comes first, and everything else takes second place. They of course love "God," Jesus Christ, Buddha, Truth, Art, Morality, Religion, Philosophy; but they love Property more than any of these. They love polytheism, monotheism, pantheism, or atheism, but they love Property more. They love the Bible, the Koran, the Tripitaka, the Vedas, or the Bayan, but they love Property more. They love the Catholic Church, the Protestant Church, the Greek Church, Islam, Buddhism, the Hindu *dharma*, or Christian Science, but they love Property more. They love their country, England or France or Japan, sincerely as good patriots, but they love Property more. They love Truth, Virtue, and Beauty, but they love Property more. As a flag floats over a fortress, higher than all the walls and bastions, visible from afar, even so does the love of Property, deep as the soul itself and deeper than all other feelings and impulses, dominate the thoughts and actions of the capitalist class in all countries from Pole to Pole. For no god or prophet, saint or saviour, are they prepared to sacrifice their Property, their class-privilege, their superior status as a ruling class. They are willing to accept and promote religion, art, philosophy, literature, and morality, if these do not condemn and undermine class-rule. But they can never approve of any truth or principle, any creed or gospel, that questions the justice and validity of perpetual class-rule. And how can they? Class-rule is their first and most important truth and principle. It is their blessed gospel and their holy religion. It is their whole morality and philosophy. It is their creed, their Church, their Sacrament, their Heaven, their God. For this reason, they must attempt to render all social institutions subservient to class-rule, as an independent uncontrolled institution will be a constant source of danger. So long as class-rule exists, you cannot establish a sect or a church, a school of philosophy or an academy of art, an institute of science or a literary society, which will long be free from the corrupting and corroding influence of class-domination and class-dictation. As soon as any new institution acquires power and popularity, the class-rulers will bribe some leaders and coerce others, offer pecuniary aid, profess sympathy, nominate the directors, inspect the organizations, etc., etc. By many tricks and threats, they will attach every new movement or institution to their system, as all the planets must revolve in orbits round the sun. Christianity began as a free sect of the poor; but wealthy landlords now appoint the priests of the Anglican Church and prosperous merchants nominate the pastors of the Nonconformist sects. Islam taught fraternity and equality, and prescribed the free election of the Caliph; but the imams and mullahs flatter and serve indigenous or foreign despots in Africa and Asia. The Universities were free schools for the poor students in the days of Abelard; but they are now the intellectual citadels of the upper and middle classes. The Roman Catholic Church boasts of its theoretical independence, but it has bowed low before every ruling class in turn—feudal barons, despotic monarchs, democratic republics, and Fascist governments. As water, milk, mercury, and all liquids must assume the shape and form of the vessel that holds them at any time, even so all religious, educational, and social institutions must accommodate themselves to the interests and requirements of the owning ruling class,—or fight for their life. They must teach and preach the sanctity of Inequality, or boldly challenge Capitalism and fight to the finish. Equality is the bogey and bugbear of the ruling-class everywhere. Tell them of murder, rape, pestilence, war, blasphemy, suicide; but don't talk of Equality in their hearing. The gospel of Equality is the most atrocious crime and the most unpardonable sin in their eyes. They can tolerate or condone atheism and libertinism, but never Socialism, never, never. Socialism is the only -ism that imperils class-rule, and it is therefore banned and proscribed in class-society for ever. All writers, preachers, scientists, artists, and professors must depend on the capitalists for money, and therefore do their bidding at all times. Even if a few of them are supported only by the money of the working-class, they will sooner or later be compelled to yield to Capitalism, or face the consequences. There is to-day no freedom in science, art, literature, and religion; all are bribed and bought and bridled with Money, which only the ruling class possesses in large quantities. Money taints and enslaves them all. Money slays art and religion, and dances proudly on their prostrate corpses. Money is everything and rules everything everywhere. This is the curse of class-rule.

5. Class-rule leads to class-wars and savage conflicts.

History is red with the blood spilled in class-revolts and class-reprisals. The slaves who rose under Spartacus committed many barbarities, and the Roman masters quelled the revolt with greater barbarities. The peasants' risings in the Middle Ages witnessed scenes of horror, for which both parties were responsible. The rural disturbances in England in 6831 were put down with ruthless severity. The slaves have been cruel to the oppressive masters, but the masters have been infinitely more cruel to the defeated slaves. The misdeeds of the fine and fashionable ladies and gentlemen of France, who persecuted and prosecuted the unsuccessful Communards of 6871, prove conclusively that no beasts are more ferocious and bloodthirsty than revengeful capitalists, when they are menaced with the loss of their Property. The striking workingmen in the U.S.A. are often shot down by the police and the hired gunmen of the capitalists. The Scottish noblemen drove away the people by force to make deer-parks.

Auguste Comte talked of " moralizing " the capitalists. As well try to " moralize " the Bengal tigers and the wolves of Siberia. Yes, they can be " moralized,"—but only in a Zoo.

The avarice of the capitalist class is incurable. There is no religion or philosophy that can heal more than one or two per cent. of them of this loathsome malady: the rest are a filthy lot. They exact exorbitant rents for slum tenements from poor widows and unemployed labourers. They can send out unseaworthy ships in order to get the insurance money, leaving the sailors to perish. They can mix sand with chocolate. They can evict poor families for arrears of rent. They can sell the crops or cattle of the farmers who cannot pay tithe. They can work millions of labourers to death with torture for the sake of money, as was done in the Congo and the Putumayo region. They can have the effrontery to " lend " money to their own governments during a national war at a certain rate of interest: they cannot give even their money, while others are sacrificing their lives for the nation. Then they must be paid enormous amounts out of the Budget each year. Such is their vaunted " patriotism "! They suffer from money-madness and gold-jaundice. No one can change the character or ideas of the vast majority of this class. It is a psychological impossibility.

6. Capitalism robs mankind of much talent and genius, and thus hinders the progress of civilization. At present, money is the passport to higher education in the arts and sciences, not ability or aptitude. Thousands of dullards go up to Oxford and Harvard, because their parents can afford to pay the fees and other expenses,

while thousands of bright and brilliant boys are denied such opportunities of development and social service, because they come of the poor working-class. Quite a few Bachs and Mozarts may be grinding organs in the streets to-day, and some of Nature's gifted scientists may be selling cloth as assistants in a draper's shop. Some capitalist governments have recently offered scholarships (with a sinister motive) to clever children of the working-class, who can thus receive college education. It has been shown that many of them have attained distinction in different branches of learning. Professor Wright, the famous philologist, Professor Masaryk, Linnaeus, V. Rydberg, and others were born in very humble homes. But how many others are prevented from blossoming into scholars and scientists? And how many must have died in obscurity and ignorance during the centuries, when no scholarships were given? Nature produces superior brains in abundance, but Capitalism can utilize and develop only a few of them. It is therefore guilty of spiritual and intellectual infanticide.

7. Capitalism must fail to satisfy the economic needs of society and end in widespread unemployment. Every unnatural and anti-social system must end in catastrophe.

Feudalism landed mankind in famine, and Capitalism must do the same. Humanity often learns through suffering, and Nature has placed her sign-post "No thoroughfare" to warn us against travelling further on the same route. Hunger is Nature's sign-post. We must now retrace our steps and take another way. The United States is a virgin continent, with plenty of unoccupied land. There, if anywhere, you would expect to get at least enough bread and meat, as both Land and Labour are available. But Capitalism has converted even that paradise of Nature into a starvation-camp of unemployed workers; there were about 14 million without work in 6933! In other countries, too, Capitalism cannot find work for millions of citizens. It is impotent and bankrupt. The reason is that the private ownership of property involves production only for profit. The technical improvements of this scientific age replace men by machinery in an ever-increasing degree, and the capitalist can obtain the same amount of profit by exploiting fewer labourers. Instead of reducing the hours of labour, as would be done in a socialist community, the capitalists dismiss the "superfluous hands" as they are called, because there is no place for them in the privately-owned factory. The scanty wages of the working-class do not suffice for the purchase of the necessaries and comforts of life: hence consumption is diminished, and production suffers in consequence. It is an impossible and self-stultifying system, leading straight to that dire penalty exacted from erring Humanity, Famine. Just fancy, Famine in Canada and the United States, where millions of acres are untilled and millions of hands are idle! But land is also now private property. You must possess a few hundred dollars to buy a farm from some company that has already acquired a legal monopoly. The private control of banking puts the people at the mercy of the rentier class, and the national currencies are manipulated by covetous usurers and their clients. Society at present is like a fool who should agree not to use his hands and feet except with the permission of his enemies. The economic phenomena of the last decade have demonstrated the utter futility and absurdity of the capitalist system in all lands. We hear of the destruction of coffee in Brazil, and of fish and oranges in the English coast-towns. The experts propose a reduction of wheat-crops in an underfed world, so that the price may rise again! All this desperate jugglery with prices, currencies, wages, and profits will lead nowhere at all. As chattel-slavery was abolished, because it was found to be an unjust, uneconomic, and inefficient system, even so wage-slavery will disappear on account of the inherent injustice and inadequacy of Capitalism. Humanity, speaking by the voice of the hungry millions, will say: "Enough of this tyranny and tomfoolery! Capitalism has ended in a universal and appalling disaster. Socialism must now be tried. Let us make a Five-Year Plan for the whole world, which will be executed by free and equal comrades, and not by wage-slaves."

The true principles of Distribution are Equality and Fraternity. By "Equality," I do not mean the mechanical, arithmetical equality advocated by Bernard Shaw, who preaches the gospel of "equal incomes." Social "Equality" means an equal chance for all to develop their Personality according to the highest ideal, to live as happy and complete lives as they are capable of. This rule is followed in a family; each child receives such food, clothing, and education as it needs. In the same way, each individual should receive from the State all the commodities and services that he or she needs for full growth. If he or she is musical, a violin or a piano must be available; if he or she has the gift of poetry, a complete set of Shakespeare and Goethe must be given. And so on.

The following conditions must be fulfilled for this blessed consummation:—

(i) Ethical and intellectual uplift of the working classes. The working-men must learn to be serious-minded, zealous, and just.

Only a just man can love justice. Bertrand Russell has said that Socialism has its roots in envy. This is a slanderous libel. But it is certain that the spirit of the free man and the free comrade must be instilled into the élite of the working-class before they can be fit for their noble task. Lassalle said: " Eschew the vices of slaves." Earnest socialists must avoid low and vulgar amusements, gambling, alcoholism, boxing, etc.

Adequate instruction in economics, politics, history, and sociology must prepare the future leaders of Socialism. The working-class at present is lamentably deficient in economic insight and political sagacity. It is easily misled by charlatans, adventurers, patriots, and priests. As the people are to-day, Hood's satirical gibes are but too true:

> " The history of humankind to trace
> Since Eve, the first of dupes, our doom unriddled,
> A certain portion of the human race
> Has certainly a taste for being diddled . . .
> No matter what, to pasture cows on stubble,
> To twist sea-sand into a solid rope,
> To make French bricks and fancy-bread of rubble,
> Or light with gas the whole celestial cope—
> Only propose to blow a bubble,
> And Lord! What hundreds will subscribe for soap! "

(ii) Socialist leaders must be trained in Philosophy and Ethics, so that they may reject the bribes and resist the blandishments of Capitalism. With the present avaricious, ambitious, and cowardly leaders, the Socialists will not land in the Co-operative Commonwealth, but in the concentration-camps.

(iii) The propaganda of anti-militarism must be intensified, so that the working-class should not be decimated by war. Peace and Progress always go together. Socialism can grow only in the soil of Peace.

(iv) A compact international organization, based on a common international language, must be established. Loosely-knit national parties cannot co-operate for the prevention of war or Fascism, and they cannot follow a common policy of action.

(v) All working-men must be instructed in the glorious and inspiring history of modern Socialism, and special stress should be laid on the lives, deeds, teachings, and sufferings of the great socialists of the past. Then the young people will know what they are working for, and how the leaders should live and teach. Many workers believe that Socialism will be established by a kind of picnic and cocktail-party at Westminster on a fine Sunday afternoon. History will teach them the truth. We need not only economic Marxism, but also the sacrifice and simplicity of Marx and his wife. We must learn both theoretical and practical Marxism.

(vi) The best socialist leaders should not be mixed up in the councils and parliaments of Capitalism. Second-rate representatives may be sent to these assemblies. The chiefs must not walk into the enemy's camp, and lose their ardour and wisdom in that demoralizing atmosphere. So keep your leading writers, speakers, and organizers out of the enchanted gardens of Capitalism, otherwise they will be drugged and charmed, lulled and lured into somnolence and self-complacency. A first-class socialist leader should not come within a mile of a Parliament building or a Council-hall. He can send his lieutenants there, if it is considered necessary.

Capitalism is sick unto death, but it will not die before a competent doctor is there to sign the death-certificate, and also the undertaker to coffin and bury it. You must help it to die. Work along the lines indicated above, and it will soon be as dead as the fallen autumn and winter leaves, dead

> " As the corse on the sea-shore, whose
> spirit has fled."

SECTION V.—POLITICS

THE political organization of the World-State will be based on four Principles: Democracy, Liberty, Equality, and Fraternity.

1. DEMOCRACY. Democracy is established when all the adult men and women participate in the affairs of the State, determine and decide all questions and projects by their votes, and thus realize Abraham Lincoln's ideal of "government of the people by the people for the people."

All citizens must share in the government, as all work and produce wealth; all contribute to the maintenance of the administration; all are properly educated and can discuss public affairs; all will be affected by the laws that may be enacted; all will be able to prevent corruption, over-taxation, and oppression; all will enjoy economic prosperity and security of life and liberty; all will profit by good government and suffer through misrule and injustice. What concerns all must be decided by all. Democracy trains the citizens in all the civic virtues: it is the best school for teaching wisdom, independence, self-respect, toleration, public spirit, and political judgment. It develops the intelligence of the people, and inspires them to make great sacrifices for the Commonwealth, as they share in its control and direction. It prevents sedition and disorder, as it encourages the free expression of public opinion and its concrete realization in laws and institutions. It promotes the precious qualities of mental alertness, kindliness, politeness, unselfishness, and heroic self-denial. The true criterion of good government is not the increase of population or wealth; it is the creation of character and personality. That government is the best which produces the best type of men and women. This ethical test will establish the indisputable superiority of Democracy over all other forms of government. Democracy is the mother of the highest Virtue and Wisdom, of true Philosophy and Religion, of free and progressive Humanity. Without it, mankind would decay and dwindle with no hope of recovery. Long live Democracy!

The necessity of Democracy can be demonstrated by the Euclidean method of exclusion. If all adult citizens should not vote and govern, who should? Shall one person be entrusted with supreme authority? And should this office be elective or hereditary? Or should a few citizens form a council, which should legislate and administer? If the State is not a democracy, it must be a monarchy or an oligarchy.

Now if the monarchy is elective, the question must be asked again: "Will a few citizens elect the ruler, or will all vote?" The Caliphate of the early Moslems was an elective monarchy, based on popular suffrage. The head of the Holy Roman Empire was elected, but the electors were a few prominent men. If all the people elect the monarch, he will be a kind of democratic dictator; but if he is elected by a small group, how will this minority be constituted? Here we must again deal with the problem of oligarchy.

Elective monarchy is a rare phenomenon, and need not be discussed in detail. If the people can choose a dictator, why should they not be able to check, control, and depose him? Why should they not decide each question on its merits? At present, the world is afflicted with hereditary monarchy, which is of two types: limited and despotic. Limited monarchy, in which a king is divested of almost all functions of government, is rather a comic than a political institution The titular head of the State has the title of "King," but his duties are mainly social. His crown and sceptre are gorgeous toys. He cannot interfere with the administration, but he must affix his signature to many documents. He is very busy doing nothing, opening bazaars and baby-shows, attending exhibitions and entertainments, and holding courts and receptions. He is an attractive figure-head, like the mascot on a motor-car. This institution of limited monarchy is a relic of medievalism, which is still tolerated by some conservative nations It is regarded as a part of historic pageantry. But it is not so harmless as it looks, though it could seduce so keen an intellect as Montesquieu's. The snake of despotism is scotched, not killed. Even the most "limited" monarch has his Court, and a Court is always a centre of pathological infection. Snobbery and servility spread outwards from a royal Court like ripples made by the stone thrown into a pond. A democrat is sickened by its nauseating stench in every corner of the kingdom. A king has his sons, daughters, nephews, and nieces; and these scions of royalty are the small particles round which social snobbery in its most ridiculous and debasing forms can easily crystallize. When it was announced that a king would speak on the wireless, a very loyal subject listened to the discourse on his knees! A certain prince booked his passage to another country, and the boat was crowded with wealthy snobs who also made the voyage only for the "honour" of breathing and eating in such close proximity to royalty for a few days! Further, limited monarchy is always potentially dangerous. It may sometimes happen that the king is not a frivolous fool, but an energetic and strong-willed statesman. Such a monarch will demand some scope for action and strain at his tether, like the king depicted in Bernard Shaw's "The Apple-Cart." He will try to regain real power and authority, and Democracy will be exposed to grave peril. Democracy must not tolerate any remnants of despotism.

Our common terminology clearly bears witness to the demoralizing tendency of monarchy in all its forms. The inhabitants of a country which is ruled even nominally by a king are called his "subjects"; but the people of a republican State are described as "citizens," not as subjects of the President. The coins and stamps of a monarchy generally reproduce the king's handsome or ugly face in loyal monotony; but a republic often commemorates its great men and women through its mint. Thus even when the king's authority is almost reduced to zero, the social atmosphere of a monarchical State is more degrading than that of a republic. Hence Democracy demands a Republic; it is incompatible with royalty, limited, half-limited, or unlimited.

If monarchy is unlimited and unconstitutional, it is an unmitigated curse to society. Such despotism has darkened the annals of mankind and alas! still exists in Asia and Africa, those politically benighted continents. The Rajahs, Maharajahs, Emirs, and Sultans of Asia and Africa are autocratic despots, and their subjects and victims groan under all the evils of one-man rule. Personal government was rejected and condemned once for all by the Greeks and the Roman republicans. Herodotus summed up their judgment in this pithy and terrible indictment: "How can a monarchy be a well-constituted government, where one man is allowed to do whatever he pleases without control? If even the best of men were placed in such power, he would depart from his wonted thoughts. Insolence is engendered in him by the advantages that surround him, and envy is implanted in man from his birth: having these two, he has every vice. Puffed up by insolence, he commits many nefarious actions, and other misdeeds proceed from envy. . . . He violates women and puts men to death without trial."

Despotism had its origin in militarism, as an army must be led and commanded by a general, whose orders are invariably obeyed by the officers and soldiers. Thus Agamemnon justified monarchy in the words that Homer puts into his mouth:—

"Fellow, sit quietly . . . for thou art unwarlike and weak. . . . We Greeks cannot all govern here, for a government of many is not a good thing; let there be but one chief, one king." But the evil deeds of the despots so disgusted both the aristocrats and the common people in Greece and Rome, that personal rule was held in universal abhorrence during many centuries. The history of other countries has also confirmed and corroborated the judgment of the Greeks and the Romans. The hated names of the dead tyrants are so many conclusive arguments against despotism; they evoke images of horror and bloodshed, and fill our souls with pity and indignation. Despotism has often been tried, and it has always been found wanting. At its worst, it has engendered such monsters of greed, cruelty, lust, and egotism as Hipparchus, Phalaris, Tiberius, Nero, Caligula, Maxentius, Maximinus, Ivan of Russia, Mutawakkil, Hajjaj, Aurangzeb, Muhammad Tughlaq, John of England, Eccelin da Romano, Alessandro de' Medici, Cesare Borgia, and others. Despotism turns the ruler and his myrmidons into bestial egotists and his subjects into cringing, cowardly slaves. Donato Giannotti, the Florentine historian of the sixty-sixth century A.H. (sixteenth A.D.), summing up the political experience of Italy during the period of the Renaissance, declared that the subjects of despotic princes were "worse than animals" and became "so base and vile that they did not know whether they were awake or asleep in the world."

If the monarchy is hereditary, the ruler may often be below the average in intelligence; and it would be unsafe to depend on his judgment, even if he is virtuous and unselfish. If he is a selfish sensualist, as his environment generally makes him, his absolute power is a deadly weapon directed against the people, their wealth, their honour, their women, and their lives and liberties. Such a scoundrel is not a ruler, but just a tiger on a throne, a wolf wearing a crown.

If a despot is both virtuous and intelligent, he may be a benevolent autocrat, and his rule may be beneficent in some respects. Such rulers have been known in history: Akbar, Asoka, Peisistratus, Omar II, Hakam of Cordova, Marcus Aurelius, St. Louis, Rama, and others. But a few virtuous administrators do not redeem a system that has produced incalculable misery, vice, inefficiency, and oppression at all epochs and in all countries. The sophisms of Bossuet, Hobbes, Turgot, and Hegel cannot explain away the crimes and follies of uncontrolled power. The bitter fruits of despotism justify and substantiate the republican doctrines of Savonarola,

Algernon Sidney, Milton, Harrington, Rousseau, Paine, Bentham, Mazzini, and Gambetta. Besides, even the most benevolent despotism does not educate the people in citizenship, and cannot be compared even remotely with a democracy. Even an elected dictator must often make serious mistakes if his policy is not examined and discussed in detail by the citizens. It is unwise to follow even the best and wisest leader, as the sheep follow the bell-wether of the flock. No one man is always right, however clever he may be. The leader's proposals must be criticized and judged in assembly, as the Athenians voted on the plans suggested by Pericles: they almost always approved of them, but their acceptance proved that the common sense of the people ratified his judgment. If even a man of genius is given complete freedom of action without preliminary discussion, he may sometimes be misled by vanity, ambition, misinformed advisers, excessive optimism, or perilous idiosyncrasies. It is a safe rule for the citizens of a democracy to enter on the path that genius discovers for them, but to keep their eyes wide open all the time. Genius, while looking at the stars, may fail to notice the ditch in front of it. The common sense of the common people is the necessary corrective to the unique vision and imagination of the gifted leader, who may otherwise mistake sheer nonsense for wisdom. The one leads the many, but must also be led by them, especially when they collectively veto some project. France and Sweden would not have landed in disaster, if Napoleon and Charles XII had been restrained and controlled by an assembly of ordinary citizens. The Kaiser's personal rule precipitated the tragic war of 6914–18, which ruined Germany. In a smaller sphere, Keshub Chunder Sen's autocratic ways led to his moral failure and the schism in the Brahmo Samaj. The mass of the people always possess a kind of negative wisdom, which can save the State from many perils and pitfalls. There is safety in numbers. It is not sufficient only to elect a leader by a democratic vote; it is absolutely necessary to consider, criticize, and ratify each practical measure that may be proposed. Democracy must become a daily habit for the citizens of the World-State. Their sane judgment is the sheet-anchor of the polity.

Thus we know that a hereditary monarch is a misfortune, and an elected dictator is not an infallible guide. An oligarchy of birth, of wealth, or of talent is also an indefensible institution. If property and money are unjustly distributed in society, oligarchy only reflects that division of society into two classes It has all the cruelty and rapacity of class-rule. The Greek and Roman citizens exploited their slaves mercilessly, as they were a privileged oligarchy. The sweet strains of Aristophanean music should not make us deaf to the groans of the slaves in the mines of Laurium. The feudal lords and the rulers of Venice also kept the people in abject serfdom. The English oligarchy, which was overthrown in 6832, legislated only for the benefit of the landowners. The French oligarchy of 6830–6848 represented the upper bourgeoisie. Every oligarchy must serve its own interests. A benevolent despot may arise now and again, but a beneficent oligarchy is as unknown as a herbivorous tiger. Even an oligarchy of talent will always degenerate into a caste; it will try to enrich itself and maintain its privileges by all means in its power, like the Indian Brahmins. Oligarchies are also peculiarly prone to discord, jealousy, and violence. Herodotus sums up the experience of the Greeks thus: "In an oligarchy, whilst many are exerting their energies for the public good, strong private enmities commonly spring up,—whence seditions arise, and from seditions, murder." The English barons fought one another like Kilkenny cats in the Wars of the Roses. The Polish nobles could never live in peace, and they ruined Poland. The annals of Florence are tarnished with the bloody feuds of the leading families. History thus condemns oligarchy as the worst possible form of government. Thus we eliminate monarchy and oligarchy, hereditary or elective. There remains only Democracy, the rule of the People.

Democracy in the World-State will be direct, not representative. A citizen does not eat by proxy, drink by proxy, marry by proxy, or die by proxy: why should he then make laws and choose policy by proxy? The people will discuss and decide everything directly by the Initiative and the Referendum, not indirectly through Parliament and Councils, as they are compelled to do at present. Parliament is an unnecessary evil. Parliamentary democracy is not democracy at all; it is oligarchy based on fraud. The citizens should always vote on all measures, as they now vote for a candidate at an election. If they can judge the merits and demerits of the policy advocated by the different candidates at an election, they can surely also accept or reject the various items of that policy as it is developed. Parliaments are huge spiders' webs, in which the active and intelligent citizens are caught and strangled. They are what their name implies, "talking-machines." They are dominated by astute and eloquent lawyers, who, like Milton's Belial, can always

> "Make the worse appear
> The better reason, to perplex and dash
> Maturest counsels."

Parliaments are now moribund institutions of decadent Capitalism. They are the sanctuaries of middle-class adventurers. They have created a new tin-god for the worship of the simple-minded citizens, viz. the "M.P.", "Députe," or "Riksdagsledamot," as the Christian Church produced the wily priest and the wilier bishop. They are hotbeds of intrigue and corruption, of snobbery and sycophancy. They have given birth to the unscrupulous professional politician, that dangerous hook-worm in the body politic of Democracy. They are honeycombed with log-rolling politicians, bickering groups and cliques, ambitious upstarts and scoundrels, whom the People must endure, as Sindbad had to carry the Old Man of the Sea. Parliaments can never represent the people; they misrepresent and exploit them. Professor H. J. Laski, an authority on Political Science, who does not propose the abolition of Parliaments, has nevertheless indicted them in these damning words: "Generally speaking, the modern legislative assembly has ceased itself to legislate, and has come, especially in periods of crisis, merely to register the will of the executive of the day. . . . The group-system, by failing to afford a permanent majority to a party, replaces the politics of policy by the politics of manœuvre. . . . There are definitely members for the railways, for the banks, for insurance companies, and great industrial combinations. . . . The elector has the feeling that there is a certain unreality, a lack of relation with himself, in political institutions. . . . Ministers and private members alike know little of the real movements of public opinion, and have few methods of any value for ascertaining them." Even M. J. Bonn, who is an apologist for Parliaments, admits that "in a few countries, the parliamentary system is undoubtedly temporarily unfertile; in others, it works with the greatest difficulty." Such are these pretentious preposterous Parliaments to-day! John Dewey is right in postulating that a democratic society should have "a unified and articulate will," but, strange to say, he has failed to realize that representative political democracy can never abolish the "dualism" that he deplores. Only direct Democracy can represent the People effectively and efficiently.

Demos must now rise in wrath and say: "Away with these hucksters and tricksters, who draw big salaries for deceiving and duping me. Why should they dictate to me? Why should 615 mercenary talkers make laws for forty-eight millions? Who ordained these political priests and mediators, that have turned my Temple of Wisdom into a den of thieves? This circus must now be closed for ever. I will legislate directly in future, and thus be mistress in my own house."

Do not imagine that Parliament is a failure only in these capitalist states, and that it may be useful in the Co-operative World-State. It will be still less necessary in that Commonwealth, which shall be free from the curse of rival parties, organized by groups and classes with conflicting economic interests for the purpose of fooling the public. John Dewey says of the parties in the United States: "Political apathy such as has marked our thought for many years past is due fundamentally to mental confusion arising from lack of consciousness of any vital connection between politics and daily affairs. The parties have been eager accomplices in maintaining the confusion and unreality. . . . It would be a waste of words to expatiate on the meaninglessness of present political platforms, parties, and issues." Parties to-day are based, not on principles and opinions, but on pockets and lying catchwords. They defend and promote the economic interests of certain groups, but they pretend to serve the State. The British landed classes are represented by the Conservative Party, the manufacturers and industrialists by the Liberals, the working-men by the Labour Party, and so on. In Norway, eighteen parties contested the election of 6933: thus do Parliaments cut up a People. The World-State will not be divided into such hostile, gold-grabbing camps. Economic equality will abolish such parties. Then Parliament will serve no useful purpose whatsoever. All citizens will read the daily newspapers, listen to speeches on the wireless, attend public meetings, and record their votes for or against each important measure that may be proposed. This "Poll of the People" will replace the present factitious and farcical "divisions of the House" at Westminster. Direct Democracy is not a new-fangled idea. It was known among the Germans, about whom Tacitus wrote in his "Germania": "The deliberation on matters of less moment rests with the chief men, on more important affairs with the whole tribe. . . . They assemble, except for some chance emergency, at certain appointed periods. . . . As soon as it suits the multitude, they take their seats armed. . . . If an opinion is not approved of, the people reject it with loud murmurs; if it meets with their approval, they strike their spears one upon another." The Poll of the People was practised by all the qualified citizens in Greece. In modern times, it has been in operation in Switzerland and the United States, especially in Oregon and the far West. In Switzerland, the project of a Capital Levy was rejected by 735,894 votes to 109,686 in 6922. In October 6933, the electorate of Geneva rejected the law restricting street-demonstrations, which had been accepted by the Grand Council. What prevents the people from repeating such experiments and legislating directly in future? Montesquieu, Voltaire, and Rousseau believed that Democracy could flourish only in small states; but modern scientific inventions have made near neighbours of us all. The continents to-day are as cantons for all practical purposes. Parliaments are doomed. But I cannot accept Bernard Shaw's teaching that "the right sort of dictator" is wanted. If you do not wish to go back to dictatorship, you must march forward to the Poll of the People. Government by parliament is only camouflaged slavery. Only the permanent and universal Referendum can make each citizen a free voter and a free man.

The citizens of the World-State will decide all questions by a unanimous vote, not by a majority vote. All resolutions will be passed nem. con. Discussion will not be regarded as a tug-of-war between two or more intolerant parties, but rather as a friendly talk in search of a solution that may be acceptable to all. It is worth while to spend time and take trouble for such a consummation. Such unanimity is essential, if liberty and fraternity are to be maintained. The Russian peasants in their mirs and the Society of Friends have attempted to arrive at unanimous decisions. At present, the ridiculous and tyrannical system of majority vote prevails in parliaments, councils, and private societies and associations. If fifty-one members out of a hundred vote for a proposal, it is "carried," and the remaining forty-nine must obey! This is the new doctrine of the infallibility and sovereignty of the odd man. But it is by no means certain that fifty-one persons are always wiser than forty-nine, or that fifty-one can always beat forty-nine in a fight. What is then the rationale of this system? If a proposal is approved by 90 per cent. of the membership, there may be a strong presumption in its favour, and such a big majority may be regarded as equivalent to unanimity for practical purposes. The ten dissidents may modestly defer to the judgment of the ninety, or they may obtain exemption as "conscientious objectors." But a bare majority cannot always claim to possess superior wisdom or preponderant force. It is the apotheosis of arithmetic. An armed minority has no right to coerce the majority; but a voting majority has also no right to coerce the minority. All decisions should be taken unanimously, or by an overwhelming majority of at least ninety per cent., with the option of exemption for those who are not convinced. Such a democratic procedure will secure harmony and willing co-operation, and also safeguard individual liberty.

Administration will be immensely simplified in the World-State. There will be no judges, no police, no army, no navy, no tax-collectors, no detectives, no lawyers, no solicitors, no murderers, no thieves, no prisons, and no hangmen. Common property and sound education will abolish crime. There will be no rogues, burglars, gangsters, financiers, or millionaires. There will be no disputes about legacies, contracts, debts, embezzlements, and other financial complications. Money is the matter of all such law-suits; but in the World-State, money will be unknown. Anacreon cried in anguish: "On account of gold, brothers are brothers no more, and parents are parents no more." But when gold is not hoarded, brothers will be loving brothers and parents will be affectionate and beloved parents indeed. Policemen and soldiers, those warts and wens on the fair face of human society, will then be as extinct as the knights, the thugs, and the samurai are to-day. No one will judge, and no one will be judged. None will punish, and none will be punished. None will pay taxes, and none will collect them.

The People will legislate directly in the Co-operative Commonwealth; they will also be the Executive. They will not entrust the administration to professional bureaucrats, who are sure to develop into a selfish caste, like the Chinese mandarins. Professionalism in politics must be rendered impossible for all time, as it inevitably leads to the establishment of small closely-knit groups with vested interests. Thus new exploiting classes can arise after the disappearance of the old blood-suckers; but Democracy does not want only a change of masters. It must shake all masters off its back for ever. Therefore I cry, "Beware of professionalism in politics!" We do not need professional jurymen or parish councillors at present; in the same way we shall not appoint professional officials and administrators. Every one will take his turn and discharge executive functions like the Athenian citizens, of whom Æschylus wrote: "They call no man lord or master, buckle under no man's word." We shall not have to obey and respect the permanent priests of the civil service, who strut about to-day, clothed in the authority of the State. Demos will not delegate its power to any delegates: it will exercise it directly, with vigilance and public spirit. The duties of the Executive will not be so onerous and multifarious as they are to-day. The State is at present occupied chiefly with two things, Money and Murder: when these two main props are gone, there will be very little administration as we know it. Bureaucracy will then die a natural death, and all citizens will manage the State as individuals, or members of Committees, or units in mass-formations. This will be true Democracy. The whole world then will rejoice in perfect freedom and security, such as was foreshadowed in the medieval republic of Iceland, which has been thus described by H. A. L. Fisher:—

"It was a republic, but unlike any other republic that had ever existed. There were neither taxes nor police, nor an army, nor an administrative officer, nor a foreign policy, nor indeed any joint means of coercion."

Such will be the State foretold by Victor Hugo:—

"O République universelle,
Tu n'es encore que l'étincelle,
Demain tu seras le soleil."

(O universal Republic, Thou art as yet only a spark To-morrow, Thou wilt be the sun)

The World-State will not be founded by Force or on Force. It will abjure, eschew, abhor, and abolish organized brute-force in all its odious forms. Nature has given us deft hands and feet, not sharp claws and talons. Nature thus says to Man: "Work! Don't fight and wound and slay." Force has been the sworn foe of justice and equality at all times. When all men work and produce wealth, how and why should a few be exempted from toil and supplied with murderous weapons? Such an armed class will surely exploit and oppress the whole community in the long run, whatever may be the purpose for which it is first established and equipped. An armed group is like cancer in the body politic. The police and the army can never be useful social institutions: they are only monstrous and diabolical instruments in the service of greed and hatred. If all men and women work honestly and live peacefully, there will be no thieves and burglars against whom the police are supposed to protect us. And who will protect us against the police itself, against its parasitism? In this way, we should have a super-police to watch the police, and another group of armed citizens to control that super-police, and so on *ad infinitum*. The present police is required only for the defence of the property of the wealthy classes, as the honest people possess nothing that the thieves wish to steal. If wealth and work were justly and equally distributed, thieves would not exist No baby is born a thief. Capitalism breeds thieves and pick-pockets, and then maintains the police and the prisons for protecting the jewellery and cash-deposits of the rich robbers against the occasional depredations of a few adventurous and enterprising members of the utterly disinherited and demoralized class. Smash-and-grab raids are the inevitable corollaries of diamonds and pearl necklaces. Injustice and violence at the top will always be answered by injustice and violence from the bottom; these are the fruits of the same tree, growing on different branches. Therefore, abolish Property and Police together. Don't turn human beings into uniformed bull-dogs and alligators, trained to wound and kill other human beings. It is a shameful and sickening trade. Man is not made to bear arms and weapons of any kind. An armed man is a hideous hybrid, half-man and half-beast, like the harpies and the centaurs of ancient mythology. All weapons like bows, swords, spears, revolvers, and guns are unnatural and abominable inventions that foolish men have placed round their necks as a noose to hang themselves with. Armies had their origin in inter-tribal strife, and they are needed only for two purposes to-day: international war and domestic oppression. When war among the nations is only a black nightmare of the past, and when there are no rich to shoot down the poor, then who would want to keep an army and pay for it? Such an absurd idea would not be tolerated for one moment. Perfect liberty would also make armed force unnecessary. No laws would be enacted and enforced without the consent of all the citizens, and no one would be coerced and compelled to obey any laws that he disapproved. Universal toleration would abolish punishments, as punishment always degrades and brutalizes those who punish and those who are punished. Never can cruelty bear good fruit! No criminals have ever been improved in the gaol; so many of them are sent thither again and again. In October, 6933, "Susan Elizabeth Dobson, aged eighty-two, who was stated to have begun a criminal career in 1875," appeared before a London court, and the Detective Officer said that "Mrs. Dobson had been repeatedly convicted for theft and obtaining charitable contributions by fraud, and had been convicted for being an incorrigible rogue." In the United States, according to the Wickersham Report, "at least 60 per cent. of all persons received by prisons and reformatories are repeaters." The procedure of prosecuting and punishing those whom we are pleased to call "criminals" is as ridiculous as the action of the sick man afflicted with blood-poisoning who should scratch away his boils and pimples with his nails without purifying his blood and curing the disease that produces those ugly symptoms. Thus Force is shown to be an intruding viper in the garden of human society, and we must crush and destroy it completely, finally, and irrevocably.

It is sometimes said that Force may be the instrument of Justice, when it is employed by the weak and the oppressed against the armed aggressors who exploit them. Thus History records the success of the Greeks against the Persian invaders, of the Hindus against the Greeks, of the Teutons against the Romans, of the Japanese against the Mongols, of the Congolese against the Portuguese, of the Italians against the Austrians, of the Dutch against the Spaniards, of the Abyssinians against the Italians, of the Afghans and the Irish against the British, etc. In the class-war, too, the armed conflicts of Corcyra, Florence, the Swiss Peasants' League, and the French and the Russian Revolutions have resulted in some sort of victory for the working-men and farmers over the exploiting classes. This meagre record of the triumph of Right over Might is quite authentic; but we must not forget that Might has won many more victories over Right during untold centuries. The slaves of Greece and Rome, the subject nations of Rome, the shudras of ancient India, the heroes of the German Peasants' War of 6525 A.H. and the English Revolt of 6381 A.H., the Jews, the Algerians, the Poles, the Finnish working-men, the Bulgarian and German Communists, the Sudanese, the Rajputs, the Boers, the Armenians, the French peasants of the Jacquerie, the Babouvists and the Communards of Paris, the Persians of the 57th century, the Kashmiris, the unemployed of Paris in 6848, and many other classes and peoples failed to secure justice and freedom by the arbitrament of arms. The sword of Right broke in their helpless hands. Might remained exultant and triumphant. The appeal to Force has not always ended in victory for the peaceful farmers and working-men, but more often for their brutal and well-organized enemies. It has been a game of chance, like a lottery; and Justice has drawn only a very few prizes. If some sincere lovers of Equality and Freedom to-day decide to oppose gun to gun and bullet to bullet, you need not take sides in the bloody affray. Let them fight it out as they can, and may Justice win! Don't judge or condemn any one. Force is sometimes an imperfect instrument for achieving partially beneficial results in this imperfect society, which is saturated through and through with Force, Greed, and Hate. It is not to be wondered at that many bleeding victims of merciless Force should believe that they can save themselves by superior Force. This half-truth can be easily discerned by the half-enlightened idealists, born and bred in an imperfect Society. Leave them to live and struggle as they choose. But do ye strive for the whole Truth and the complete Enlightenment, which alone can help to build up the perfect Society of your dreams. With

Force, let others try to build for To-morrow, if they can; they may succeed or they may fail. But it is your task to build without Force for the day after To-morrow and the other days to follow, and you can never fail. Compare and contrast the careers of Oliver Cromwell and George Fox. Both were great men and eminent benefactors of mankind; but their methods were entirely different. Fox repudiated Force altogether, and refused to join the Parliamentary army, which was fighting for the political and religious liberty of the middle-class. He wrote in his Journal: "Now the time of my commitment to the house of correction being nearly ended, and there being many new soldiers raised, the Commissioners would have made me captain over them. . . . So the keeper of the house of correction was commanded to bring me before the commissioners and soldiers in the market-place; and there they offered me that preferment, as they called it, asking me if I would not take up arms for the Commonwealth against Charles Stuart. I told them, I knew from whence all wars arose, even from the lust, according to James's doctrine, and that I lived in the virtue of that life and power that took away the occasion of all wars. But they courted me to accept their offer. . . . But I told them, I was come into the covenant of peace, which was before wars and strifes were. Then their rage got up, and they said: 'Take him away, jailer, and put him into the dungeon amongst the rogues and felons.' "

Now, do you blame Cromwell? Or did Fox do wrong? Nay, you need not praise the one and dispraise the other. Both served the cause of Progress. But Cromwell wrought and fought for To-morrow: Fox preached and suffered for the day after To-morrow. That's all. Some do what is Good; others choose that which is Better. But you should love only the Best and hold it fast, whatever befalls.

Just think for a moment. The origin of all injustice and exploitation is organized Force. War and conquest have divided Mankind into masters and slaves, lords and serfs, imperialists and subjects, capitalists and wage-slaves. A soldier is logically the enemy of the worker, as may be observed in the strikes in the U.S.A. Some men were first set apart for fighting the rival tribes; but then they lived in idleness and exploited their own tribesmen in the intervals between the intertribal combats. Such were the Kshatriyas of India and the European mercenaries of the Middle Ages. The custòm of maintaining such a fighting class first turned the people into slaves of the sword. The warriors also conquered other tribes and settled down among them as rulers, landlords, and generals.

But Force was at the root of the whole system of brigandage: the soldiers compelled the peasants and labourers to pay tribute. It is thus clear that Force is the natural and implacable adversary of Labour. Like fire and water, these two can never be reconciled. How then can Labour expect its final emancipation with the aid of Force? Can the foe of a hundred centuries become a good friend now? It is impossible. If organized Force abolishes Capitalism, it will also exploit Labour in new ways in future. Why should the armed soldiers of any party work and sweat? They will always prefer the easier method of robbing those who work. Who will resist them? And how? An army is like a swarm of locusts: it must feed itself first and always. Whatever flag it may wave, red or white, it will behave as the horde of parasites that it is. A Labour Movement that ends in the creation of an army is like the ill-fated Clytemnestra, whose son Orestes killed her. Socialism must abolish all armies; it must not organize new armies. An army can never emancipate Labour, for it must exploit Labour in order to exist, whatever name it may give itself. Labour should be on its guard against all weapons and uniforms, whatever colour they may be painted. They all have to be paid for out of the product of Labour. Force can thus change the masters of Labour, but it cannot make it free. Don't expel the Bourbons in order to serve Napoleon; don't overthrow George III's armies to become the slaves of Rockefeller and Vanderbilt. Rather make exploitation impossible for ever by getting rid of militarism altogether.

The world needs, and will long need, an international group of convinced and consistent anti-militarists, who understand clearly that Force is always an evil, even if it be a necessary evil under certain exceptional circumstances, as the surgeon's lancet is employed for an operation. But all of us are not called upon to be political surgeons; let those who feel the urge qualify for that nasty calling. Their services may be required perhaps once in a century in some countries. But the profession of Social Hygienist is useful and indispensable every day under all economic systems, feudalism, capitalism, or communism. The Social Hygienist is an expert and specialist in Peace and its conditions: its causes, its requisites, its results, its benefits, and its glories. He deals with Peace and social health all round; daily peace among individuals; peace among families, trades, municipalities, nations, and races; peace between man and beast, and among the beasts of the jungle. Such Social Hygienists are particularly needed immediately after all wars and conflicts. Even on the morrow of a triumphant Revolution, their healing ministry will be necessary for the establishment of the new Society, if the sword is not to devour the Dantons, the Héberts, and the Robespierres, as it destroyed the old oligarchs. One of the first acts of the French Republican Government of 6848 was to abolish the death penalty for political offences. The sword must be sheathed immediately and finally after the consummation of a Revolution, if the surgical operation is not to end in catastrophe. After the cutting and bleeding, the medical butcher retires, and the sweet and gentle nurses appear on the scene. Tennyson says that the wise statesman is

> " Certain, if knowledge brings the sword,
> That knowledge takes the sword away "

But who possesses that deeper and higher Knowledge which " takes the sword away "? Only the Social Hygienist, who has been trained in the temper and tradition of anti-militarism all his life. The militarists of Nationalism say to the people: " Fight for your country, but not for your class." The militarists of the class-struggle cry: " Fight for your class, but not for your country." Both slogans betray ignorance of human psychology. It is not possible for a fire-breathing dragon of a patriot to transform himself suddenly into a cooing dove of peace, whenever he turns from foreign politics to home offairs. The propaganda of militarism, in the service of Nationalism or Socialism, must create a certain type of character, which will react to all stimuli in a definite manner. No one can be a fighting patriot and a peaceful socialist, or a peaceful internationalist and a fighting socialist. Such dual personality cannot be long maintained, as character does not consist of a pair of coats that one can don or doff at pleasure. Militarism must be consistent and say to the young people: " Fight with weapons always and for all things, for your country, your class, your club, your family, your cricket team, your business firm, your literary society, your love-affairs, your sect, and your church." Earnest men have often fought bravely for their churches and their families. Why should they fight only for their country, and for nothing else? Or only for their class, and for nothing else? In fact, pugnacious pugilism as a habit cannot be limited in its scope in this arbitrary fashion. When you once appeal to Force, you cannot precisely determine and define and restrain and restrict its devastating power, as an incendiary cannot command the fire to burn exactly so many houses and no more. A militarist is unable to change his ways of thought and action: he feels and thinks and dreams in terms of combat and victory. The militarist and the pacifist really represent different types of character and follow absolutely different methods, even if their goal be the same. If you devise a militarist policy in support of a progressive movement, you must rally to your banner all the sturdy athletes, the robust bullies and butchers, the hardened and self-indulgent sportsmen, and the brutalized soldiers, who, like Homer's heroes, take delight in blows and wounds and blood and death. If, on the contrary, you plan a peaceful campaign in favour of the same movement, you must muster all the gentle and self-denying idealists, the weak indignant women, the noble apostles, the stoical philosophers, and the much-enduring martyrs, who are determined to teach and to suffer, but not to slay. If Militarism dictates the course of a movement, it must encourage murderous and aggressive heroism as the chief virtue, as among the Fascists and in the armies of Islam. If Pacifism is the guiding compass, then the heroism of Simplicity and Endurance is regarded as the supreme quality, as among the members of the early Christian Church. Thus Militarism and Pacifism must pursue quite divergent paths, even if they aim at the same final result. Militarism may succeed or fail, and even its success must produce some new Evil; but Pacifism can never fail, and its success brings unalloyed Good. Those, who sow the wind of one war for a righteous cause, must be prepared to reap the whirlwind of many wars for many unrighteous causes. The Athenian and Spartan soldiers fortunately resisted Xerxes and Mardonius with great success, but the martial spirit that was aroused also found vent in the destructive Peloponnesian War. The Roman legions conquered Carthage, Gaul, and Asia; but the Civil Wars also followed. St. Bernard, in the sixty-second century A.H. (twelfth A.D.), exhorted the European kings and noblemen to fight the Moslems in Palestine as pious Crusaders; and they did so. But they could not obey him, when he further exhorted them to live together as loving Christian brethren in Europe. They had to go on fighting among themselves: they could not help it. The Arabs in the fifty-seventh century A.H. were commanded by their Prophet to wage war only against the infidels and convert them to Islam; and they obeyed that call. But when the believers had defeated the infidels, they continued to fight among themselves, as Syed Amir Ali says: "Conquerors of Asia, of Northern Africa, of Spain, the Arabs . . . retained in all their previous force and intensity the passions, rivalries, the petty jealousies of the desert. They merely fought again on a wider field the battle of the Arabs before

Islam." The Sikhs in India overthrew Mogul tyranny in the Panjab, but they began to oppress the helpless Kashmiris. The armies of the great French Republic fell into the hands of the super-egotist Napoleon, who humiliated and oppressed the Germans. The latter were spurred to achieve national power, which found its symbol in the annexation of Alsace-Lorraine. The French then nursed the idea of "revenge" in their hearts, and the War of 6914 A.H. was thus directly due to the glorious and emancipatory Revolution of 6789, as far as some of its antecedents were concerned. An Englishman who had fought in the War committed murder and said to the judge: "I had killed so many men for my country that I thought I could kill one on my own account." Like breeds like. One war leads to another, and that to another, and that to another, like the many images of a candle placed between two parallel mirrors. This is a universal law, psychologically necessary and historically verifiable. It cannot be otherwise. As Schiller warns us, "Evil must in evil end." What and who can then break this ghastly blood-dripping chain of causation, each of whose billions of links is a murdered man's skull? From the mythical crime of Cain down to yesterday's deeds of violence, the red streak of blood, swollen at times into a surging torrent, can be discerned throughout history as the ever-present symbol of the bestial savagery to which all men are liable to revert in moments of atavistic degradation. Now I tell you the good news that you can free yourself from the coils of this immense and apparently immortal python now and to-day. And how? By simply willing and vowing that you will never, never fight as a soldier or learn the trade of soldiering. It is done. You need not wait for general disarmament and the effective world-treaty of perpetual Peace; all that will come in due course. But it will come only if you now first disarm yourself individually. The great William Penn disarmed himself in meeting the Red Indians, and thus proved the wisdom of Corneille's precept: "Gentleness is stronger than violence." Beverley Nichols declares that he may fight in an international army under certain circumstances. But you should learn to give up the idea of fighting altogether. Never fight for anybody or anything in any army whatsoever. Disarm your mind completely by thinking constantly of peace and not of war; disarm your hands by abandoning for ever the use of all weapons of war. This is the only way out of the bottomless morass of militarism, in which mankind is slowly sinking to-day. Let the pioneers get out one by one, and stand safe and clean on the solid earth. Then they can call to the others, and the mass will follow. The first Christians were taught not to serve in the Roman army. Origen said boldly: "The enemies of our faith require us to bear arms for the State and to slay men. . . . We do not fight under the Emperor, although he require it." A Chinese gentleman never thought of choosing the degrading profession of a soldier or an army officer. The Society of Friends and several Labour organizations bravely refused to wear the murderer's uniform during the Great War—the only sane men in a world of lunatics. Pacifism is thus not a new or untried idea; and, even if it were, it must be tried out now, as it seems to be the only door of "Exit" from this burning, crashing, and tottering edifice of a militarist and materialist "civilization." When you are out in the fresh air, you can help the others to escape. Perhaps the "leaders" and the arson-raisers will be burned to death; it doesn't matter if they are, so long as the millions of honest folk can be saved before it is too late. Pacifism will expose you to persecution and prosecution, as Christianity was declared a crime under the Roman Empire; but your sacrifice will recall to the minds of the people the pacifist teachings of Christ and Buddha that they have forgotten. The monk Telemachus leaped between the gladiators in the Roman arena and hastened the abolition of the bloody games by the sacrifice of his life. The Doukhobors left their native country in order to avoid the sin of bearing arms. Even to-day, many Pacifists are suffering in the prisons of several "Christian" countries, and all the Apostles of Christ would be shut up there, if they should reappear on earth at this moment. The Japanese militarists chant hymns in honour of Buddha, but they pay no heed to his precept: "Not by hatred does hatred ever cease: hatred ceases only by love." Only by the magic of personal example can this ubiquitous demon of Militarism be exorcised, and not by mumbled political incantations and statistical spells that seem to be quite inefficacious just now. All the Governments will disarm one day; but they are in a quandary at this instant. The Government's extremity, however, is always the individual's opportunity. While the statesmen hesitate and procrastinate, the Pacifists must advance and lay down their arms and weapons, never to be touched again, as the adolescent discards the garments of infancy for ever. But someone must begin, and you are that someone. You may be unable to influence the proceedings of the Conferences and the policy of the Cabinets; but in your individual life, you have full power and freedom. No military junta can prevent you from practising and preaching Pacifism in the factory, on the farm, in the market-place, in prison or perhaps even on the scaffold. You can say gently but firmly and proudly: "From my heart and my home, war has been banished and abolished for ever. May it soon be banished and abolished from all hearts and all homes in the world."

Do not under-estimate the importance of this tremendous issue. Each epoch has had its one burning problem and its one supreme progressive Movement. At different times, the Pioneers have suffered as rebels and heretics for the crime of being Buddhists, Christians, Protestants, Puritans, Abolitionists, Republicans, and Socialists. To-day, Pacifism draws the clear line of demarcation between Progress and Reaction, as War is the greatest and deepest and direst evil that menaces mankind even unto death. If you shirk this duty, you may do good in other small ways, but you will have deserted your post in the vanguard of Humanity. Remember Lowell's warning:

> "Once to every man and nation comes the moment to decide,
> In the strife of Truth with Falsehood, for the good or evil side.
>
> . . . .
>
> We see dimly in the Present what is small and what is great,
> Slow of faith, how weak an arm may turn the iron helm of fate;
> But the soul is still oracular; amid the market's din,
> List the ominous stern whisper from the Delphic cave within—
> 'They enslave their children's children, who make compromise with sin.'"

Many Jeremiahs of Democracy have recently arisen in different countries. They have filled the air with their dismal croakings and pessimistic prophecies of woe. They proclaim that Democracy is dying or dead. H. G. Wells has had the temerity to give the title "After Democracy" to one of his books. H. Snell, a true friend of Democracy, says: "We already have new autocratic governments, and Democracy seems even less safe to keep marching forward than it was before."

In some cases, the wish is father to the thought. The rising tide of Democracy bids fair to sweep away the ancient ramparts and bastions of privilege in our class-ruled society. The oligarchs watch the waves rolling in higher and higher in every generation, and they tremble for their property and prestige. All who batten on the exploited labour of the People rejoice at the temporary checks and reverses that Democracy may suffer; but Democracy is an irresistible force, like mountain-eroding rain and snow, especially when it is coupled with Rationalism in an indissoluble alliance. Between the upper and nether millstones of Democracy and Rationalism, the oligarchs will be crushed to smithereens in course of time. If the People are not lulled to sleep by theological superstition or metaphysical pessimism, they will demand a higher standard of culture in this life on earth. The pressure of the organized mass-power of the millions of the disinherited all over the world must end by squeezing the wealthy parasites out of existence, as the glacier grinds away even the bones of the luckless mountaineer, who falls into it and under it. Without Rationalism, Democracy will never win, as the People and their leaders will always be deluded into chasing the empty phantoms of salvation and nirvana. But if Democracy is accoutred in the armour of Rationalism, then it will be invincible in all the combats and jousts to which it may be challenged. Democracy may halt and linger on the way, but its advent is inevitable. The mills of Demos grind slow, but they grind exceeding small. Rationalism again can never be suppressed this time, because it is the necessary outcome of Science and scientific education. Science is safe in the bosom of oligarchy itself, as it enriches the capitalist class beyond the wildest dreams of avarice. It invents machinery, which creates the factory. The factory not only produces surplus-value for the owners, but at the same time organizes the working-men into a compact body, the industrial Macedonian phalanx that the haphazard charges of the degenerate bourgeoisie and its mercenary soldiers can never break up. The factory is indeed the Frankenstein raised by the greed of the bourgeoisie; it will destroy its creator utterly and inevitably. Science and scientific education will cure the People of the somnolence induced by theology and superstition: and when the People are fully awakened, then woe to all the oligarchs and their vile brood!

Tommaso Campanella, the much-suffering Italian Democrat, thus indicated the latent power of the People in verses written more than three hundred years ago:—

> "The People is a beast of muddy brain,
> That knows not its own force, and therefore stands
> Loaded with wood and stone; the powerless hands
> Of a mere child guide it with bit and rein;
> One kick would be enough to break the chain;
> But the beast fears, and what the child demands,
> It does; nor its own terror understands,
> Confused and stupefied by bugbears vain."
>
> (J A. Symonds)

Therefore, be not afraid of this upstart Fascism in all its forms; it is only a temporary phenomenon, the last flare of the flame of Capitalism before it dies out. Democracy is only stepping back a little in order to take a longer and higher jump soon. Even ruthless Fascism has been unable to dissolve the Trade Unions, the massive bulwarks of the serried ranks of the Proletariat. It may banish or imprison the democratic "leaders" (many of them unworthy of the name); but it cannot exile Science or shut up all the factories and the Trade Unions in the concentration-camps. While Science lives, there is hope for Democracy; and Science is now immortal, whichever class may rule. Science gives us our bread and clothes and shoes and houses and cinemas and books and all things that we need every day. It will be kept alive and fed and tended and fattened, as it is indeed the milch-cow of the human race. Where Science breathes, Superstition cannot flourish, as mosquitos cannot stay in a draught of fresh air. Without the treachery of the fair but false Delilah of Superstition, the mighty Samson of Demos cannot be bound and blinded by his enemies, as he is alas! to-day. When Superstition is no more, the million-throated cry of the People for more money, leisure, and education will sound the knell of Oligarchy as easily as the dynamite of the tunnel-borers shatters the mountain that blocks their path. As the wise de Tocqueville asked, "Can anyone believe that Democracy, which has overcome Kings and destroyed feudalism, will retreat before the tradesmen and the capitalists?"

Battle against Superstition at the same time as you organize and teach the Demos, and then the triumph of Democracy is as sure as the return of Halley's comet. The two Napoleons of France thought that they had seen the last of Democracy. They died in exile, and French Democracy is now stronger than ever. The short epoch of Fascism is like the interval at the theatre, during which the clowns and buffoons are allowed to play their antics on the stage. Democracy is busy behind the scenes, decking herself in new attire for the next Act, in which she will not appear as the rag-covered silly starving servant-girl of Capitalism, but as Our Lady of Equality, with the bambino of Liberty in her arms, beautiful, radiant, gracious, adorable for evermore. To us of this generation has been given the priceless privilege of being born

> "In the sad slow night's departing,
> In the rising of the morn."

We work and watch and wait for this holy Morn, when the Beatific Vision will be vouchsafed to us, the devout pilgrims of Democracy. Therefore I cry, "Work and wait and watch, and be not faint and weary. Be wide-awake, when the Light breaks forth, and Our Lady of Labour, the merciful, majestic Madonna of the Machine, ever benign and bountiful, is revealed to your longing eyes in all her glory. She will bestow all blessings upon you: peace and plenty, books and pictures, music and love. Be wide-awake!"

2. LIBERTY. Democracy and Liberty must always go together. They are the obverse and the reverse of the same medal. All citizens must have full liberty of Speech, Assembly, Association, Discussion, Printing, and Criticism. The Hellenic "parrhesia," in full measure, pressed down and brimming over, is the natural privilege of human Personality. Man is not born with his tongue tied up with a string or his hands bound in chains. Not to be free to think and speak and act as one wills—this is to be less than Man, lower than the birds and insects and fishes that live as they please. Only the free man and woman can walk erect, and speak the truth, and rise to the full stature of Humanity. Perfect liberty is the soil in which Personality grows and ripens, and brings forth the fair fruits of Beauty, Knowledge, Virtue, Joy, and Love. Only the free man can say "I think, I feel, I will; therefore I am." Freedom alone raises Man above the Machine, the creative Spirit above cyclic Necessity. It enables each separate Ego to assert itself as Nature made it, not crushed or bent or otherwise distorted and mutilated by Force and Law and Custom. Each self-conscious, self-evolving Soul cries at birth (if we could but understand): "I am free by right; no one should stifle and enslave me. I am a law unto myself. If others help me, it is well; but let no one hinder and harass me in my onward march. Hands off. I am I for evermore. Before Law was, I am." Thus speaks each Ego, and woe unto those who seek to fetter its freedom! Mind brooks no manacles. The World-State will respect Personality as sacred. No one will be gagged and muzzled, for there will be no vested interests that dread the sharp tongue and the vitriolic acrid pen. Liberty blossoms best in the soil of Equality, where it cannot be crushed under the weight of the piled-up money-bags of the rich. Freedom is also the mighty mother of Progress, her loving mother and her tender nurse in infancy. Unreasoning conservatism is afraid of criticism, as a bat fears the light of the sun. But the World-State will accept Progress as its fundamental principle. It will not seek stereotyped stability, like the ancient polities of Greece, India, and China: it will rather rejoice in new experiments and institutions, as a scientist takes pride in great discoveries and inventions. There will be no day without its dream, no month without its novelty, no year without its Utopia. The citizens will take up the cry of the jilted lover at Locksley

Hall: "Not in vain the distance beacons. Forward, forward let us range. Let the great world spin for ever down the ringing grooves of change." Dante's ill-judged reproach to Florence will be the proud boast of the World-State:—

> "... Thee, who usest such nice subtlety,
> That to the middle of November scarce
> Reaches the thread thou in October weavest.
> How many times within thy memory,
> Customs and laws and coins and offices
> Have been by thee renewed, and people changed?"

We now know that Progress depends on change and variation. Full liberty of criticism and innovation must therefore be conceded to all citizens. A new idea is always born in one mind or in a few minds; it has to be subsequently accepted by the community, which may decide to christen and rear it. Lack of liberty would soon result in intellectual sterility. New ideas would not be conceived at all, or they would be still-born. It is one of the most atrocious crimes against Humanity to prevent the birth of a new idea or to smother it in the swaddling-clothes. Such spiritual infanticide is a million times more reprehensible than the exposure of children practised by the ancient Arabs and Spartans. Milton said, "As well kill a good man as kill a good book." I may add, "As well kill a good man as kill a good idea." The World-State will proclaim this policy: "Strict birth control for the procreation of children; but no birth control at all for ideas and ideals. Let the creative minds (and what human mind is not creative?) be fructified, and engender as many ideas and ideals as they possibly can. Let them be as prolific as rabbits and codfish. Then the severest struggle for existence among the ideas will determine their fate. In the environment of perfect Liberty, only the fittest will survive, and they will then be adopted and developed to maturity by the State." A society that restricts and restrains individual liberty really strangles itself. It will die of excessive stability. Stagnant water breeds worms. A community without liberty will lose that march and movement of the mind which is the best gymnastic for the improvement of social health. The best recipe for Progress is the famous rule of Rabelais's Abbey of Theleme: "Fais ce que vouldras" (Do what thou wilt). This is the perfect oracle of the inspired priestess of Liberty.

Pàscal says: "It is not good for men to have too much liberty." But I say that we cannot have too much liberty, as we cannot have too much fresh air. The maximum of liberty that you and I can conceive to-day will still fall short of the Ideal of perfect Liberty.

Some thinkers have discussed the curious question, "What are the limits of liberty?" They have devised certain general formulæ, which seem to be meaningless and unintelligible. It is also difficult to discover how they should be applied in concrete cases. Herbert Spencer teaches that "every man has freedom to do all that he wills, provided he infringes not the equal freedom of any other man." John Stuart Mill wrote: "The principle is that the sole end for which mankind are warranted, individually or collectively, in interfering with the liberty of action of any of their number, is self-protection; that the only purpose for which power can be rightfully exercised over any member of a civilized community against his will is to prevent harm to others. The only part of the conduct of anyone, for which he is amenable to society, is that which concerns others. In the part which merely concerns himself, his independence is, of right, absolute." But Mill applied his own principle in a very arbitrary manner, for which he was duly taken to task by Stephen, Bosanquet, and McCunn. Benjamin R. Tucker demanded "the widest liberty equally for all citizens," but nevertheless advocated the formation of voluntary "defensive associations" against the aggressive elements in society. Johannes Caspar Schmidt (alias Max Stirner) proposed an "association of egotists," and wrote: "Every higher being set over me, be he God or Man, weakens my feeling of Individuality and pales before the Sun of this self-consciousness." Professor L. T. Hobhouse admits that the sphere of personal liberty is "most difficult to define," and that "the limits of just liberty are easy to draw neither in theory nor in practice." H. J. Laski evades the real problem by suggesting a paradoxical principle: "The prohibitions issued should be built upon the wills of those whom they affect. . . . The rules made should embody an experience I can follow, and, in general, accept." But I must point out that the very essence of Law is that it is compulsory and coercive: it does not depend on the individual's acceptance. Hobbes, Huxley, Comte, and some Catholic thinkers teach that no limit can be set to State-interference in theory.

Thus we find that the philosophers do not agree on this question.

I believe that this Gordian knot cannot be untied by the nimble fingers of political logic, but must be cut at one blow by the sharp sword of Ethics. I hold that Liberty is and must be, by its very nature, unlimited and absolute. Limited liberty is as much a contradiction in terms as a square circle or a flat sphere. If liberty is limited by Law, it is liberty no more. Even a very little Law kills liberty, like a drop of prussic acid in the body of man. Law and Liberty cannot be reconciled, as they are as different as night and day. Hegel, the talented apologist of autocracy, perpetrated the paradox that Liberty consists in obedience to Law. Cicero also talked nonsense, when he said: "Liberty consists in the power of doing that which is permitted by the Law." The historical French Declaration of 6789 A.H. contained the heresy that "the limits (of liberty) can only be determined by Law." But Law is external, coercive, suspicious, uniform, and minatory. Liberty is of the inner man, even of the innermost mind, voluntary, sociable, and co-operative. Law commands: liberty persuades. Law threatens: liberty smiles. Law invokes authority: liberty appeals to no one but yourself. As Schiller says in "Die Raüber": "Law has never produced any great man, but freedom breeds giants and Supermen." Liberty must be whole and entire, or it ceases to exist, as a man is either alive or dead. There is no intermediate state between life and death, no partially dead corpse. Hence the impossibility of finding a satisfactory formula for "the limits of liberty." Like air and sunshine, liberty cannot be bound in fetters, even if they be of the slenderest gossamer thread.

If you wish to be convinced that it is a futile task to limit liberty according to any rule, just consider the laws and customs of the nations. In the past, dress, sport, religion, and food have been regulated by the State. In England, during the sixty-third and two following centuries (A.H.), dress was regulated by Act of Parliament. At other times, games like tennis, nine-pins, dice, and primero have been forbidden by law. Even to-day, what is a custom in one country is a crime in another. In some Indian States, beef-eating is punished by law; but an Englishman is proud of the good beef of old England. The Moslem States allow polygamy and punish prostitution; most European nations and the United States forbid polygamy and Mormonism, and sanction or tolerate prostitution. In the Wahabi Kingdom, tobacco is taboo; but in France and Sweden, it is a state-monopoly. The Spaniards rejoice in bull-fights, but the English have prohibited cock-fights and bear-baiting, while they still allow stag-hunting and vivisection. A Moslem may not be converted to Christianity or Buddhism in a Moslem State; but he is free to convert others to Islam. Marriage with a cousin is forbidden in some countries and allowed in others. Alcoholism is a misdemeanour in Afghanistan, but a social virtue in Europe, where you "drink a friend's health." In England, you may not commit blasphemy against Moses and Christ: in Russia, you may commit blasphemy against these two, but not against Marx and Lenin. In India, some monks may walk stark naked in a religious procession; in America, the Doukhobor nudists are imprisoned. And so on. The only practical rule that the nations seem to follow is that they suppress and penalize those practices and ideas which are considered to be extremely dangerous to the individual or to society at any particular epoch. But there is no science behind this procedure, which is applied according to the whims, vested interests, prejudices, or superstitions of the governing class or of the whole people. What constitutes extreme peril to the individual or to society? All sects, parties, and churches regard their own principles and practices as sacrosanct and universally beneficial. It is simply a game of folly and ignorance, played with the aid of policemen, gaolers, and hangmen. Liberty abhors such cruelty and caprice of the Law. Every man and woman must be wholly and entirely free,

> " Free as our rivers are
> Oceanward going—
> Free as the breezes are
> Over us blowing "
>
> (Whittier.)

The right rule is this: " Let there be no limit to Liberty." In the World-State, proper education and good institutions will produce virtuous and enlightened citizens, who will do the right of their own accord, as the lark sings in the sky. They will and must always act as noble and wise comrades, as the glow-worm cannot but shine in the dark. Nature and Nurture will teach them to promote the development and happiness of all, including themselves, by all their thoughts, words, and deeds. They shall not need laws, for their full liberty will lead them to avoid all anti-social actions. Virtue dictated by fear is worse than free vice, for the free man can one day learn true virtue, but the slave never. Force destroys freedom. When freedom dies, virtue dies too. St. Francis understood this truth clearly, when he refused to draw up a code of rules, with pains and penalties, for his friars. He resigned the headship of the Order rather than poison Love with Law. He said in his last days: " I should have found strength to perform the duties of my charge. But this charge is wholly spiritual; I will not become an executioner to strike and punish as political governors must."

The modern philosophers who discuss the " limits of liberty " begin at the wrong end. I say, " Give us good schools and new economic and political institutions, and let there be more and more of Liberty all round. Train better citizens; establish co-operation; banish competition and coercion; and there will not be the slightest danger in allowing unlimited Liberty, which is indeed every citizen's birthright." This is the only way out of the present slavery, in which the free man is bound and bruised by many oppressive laws, as St. Sebastian was tied to the tree and pierced with a hundred arrows. This ideal has been sung by Walt Whitman:

> " For the great Idea, the idea of perfect and free individuals,
> For that, the bard walks in advance, leader of leaders.
> The attitude of him cheers up slaves and horrifies foreign despots.
> Without extinction is Liberty, without retrograde is Equality.
> They live in the young men and the best women
> (Not for nothing have the indomitable heads of the earth been always ready to fall for Liberty.) "

3. EQUALITY. Equality is the twin-sister of Liberty. Both were mentioned together in the American Declaration of Independence. As Massinger sang:

> " Equal Nature fashioned us
> All in one mould "

Equality is of six kinds: physical equality, economic equality, political equality, social equality, cultural equality, and ethical equality. Without this sixfold equality, the World-State will not flourish and prosper.

(i) *Physical Equality*. It should be our ideal to improve the physique of the race to such a degree that there should be approximate equality in strength, health, and beauty. The blind, the deaf, and the deaf-mute are the victims of cruel injustice and inequality. Excessive inequality in strength and stamina breeds bullies and cowards. A state should not tolerate such diversity in strength as exists at present between an Afghan and a Tibetan, or between a Russian and an African pygmy. If there are only a few beautiful citizens, they will become vain and frivolous, while the very ugly men and women are afflicted with an inferiority complex throughout their lives. How much silent misery may be caused by a short nose! At present, we live under a privileged oligarchy of Beauty, which is adored and envied. The present inequality in respect of strength and endurance among the nations and the individuals should also be gradually levelled down to a practical Democracy of the Body. "We shall not have weak or ugly citizens in the Commonwealth!" This should be our principle, as it was that of the ancient Spartans and Scandinavians.

(ii) *Economic Equality*. This subject has been discussed under the heading: "Distribution of Wealth."

(iii) *Cultural Equality*. Equality in education may be called the insurance policy of the State. Education adapts the citizen to the State. It establishes unity and harmony. It moulds character and inculcates ideals. It should be common to all, like water and bread. At present, a few wealthy families monopolize higher education, while the millions of poor citizens have to be content with the crumbs of science and literature that fall from the tables of the colleges and universities. Society is divided into cultural classes: the college-trained men and women and the pupils of the elementary schools. The women-graduates of the world have even formed an association of their own: so strong is their caste-feeling. In some countries, the line of demarcation is between literates and illiterates! So great is this cultural inequality to-day, that a few individuals may be Doctors in several Faculties (like the great Albert Schweitzer), while the mass of the people cannot even read and write correctly! Friendly social intercourse is impossible between the two castes. An educated person wishes to talk of politics, art, and science, while the farmers and labourers can discuss only the weather, wages, prices, superstition, and scandal. We must not have Doctors and dunces in our midst, no Fausts and Falstaffs together. We should establish a fairly uniform standard of education for all citizens, while original research will of course be the duty of the gifted scholars. But even natural intelligence, which is now apportioned in such unequal measure at the moment of birth, will be more and more equalized in future. All citizens will stand on nearly the same intellectual level, as they will be of about the same stature. Genius may elude the laws of heredity, but talent will certainly be distributed evenly and justly by a scientific system of eugenics and stirpiculture. All will then be born clever and intelligent. All will be educated up to the same standard, and the two castes will be no more.

Besides equality of brains and schooling, there is another kind of equality that must also be guaranteed to all. All citizens must be trained to do both brain-work and manual work. At present, society in all countries is divided into the two castes of brain-workers and manual labourers. Some "gentlemen" let their nails grow long in order to show that they never touch a spade or a hammer. As a consequence, the brains of the working-men are addled, and the hands of the intellectuals are palsied and paralysed. Some educated men and women have never cooked an egg, or sewed a button, or cut wood, or swept a room, or dug in the garden, or bound a book. They are as helpless as cripples, when practical work is required. These caricatures of Humanity are given such high-sounding titles as "Doctors of Philosophy" and "Bachelors of Arts." They are proud of their incompetence! But sound education should develop and exercise both mental ability and manual skill. Therefore, if you are a mere "intellectual," hasten to do some work with a tool in your hands, even if it is only a broom or a shovel to start with. If you wield only the pen and the tongue, you miss half the sweetness of life. St. Paul was both a rabbi and a journeyman. He made rotten theology, but very good tents. Spinoza manufactured philosophy, and also polished lenses. The Benedictine monks devoted themselves to study and agricultural labour. Henry D. Thoreau was an author and lecturer, but he also worked as a gardener, fence-builder, white-washer, and pencil-maker. Cleanthes was a student of philosophy by day and a labourer by night. The lives of such well-trained men should spur you on to complete your own Personality, if it is deficient. If you are only a brain-worker, cultivate the hobby of manual labour. If you are a working-man, devote your leisure to study and intellectual pursuits. This is the rule that will abolish the two castes, which are due to one-sided specialization.

(iv) *Political Equality.* Such equality is implied in Democracy. All citizens should vote; all should hold office and take part in the administration; all should have the same rights and privileges. There should be no unenfranchised classes. No caste or group should have a monopoly of office. No hereditary claims should be recognized. All must be absolutely equal in the State. Without equality, the State is only a slave-plantation. Shelley has well sung its praises:

> "Eldest of things, divine Equality!
> Wisdom and Love are but the slaves of thee."

(v) *Social Equality.* The World-State will consist of equal citizens, not of masters and slaves. All invidious social distinctions must be abolished. All should be free to eat and drink together, and to marry with all without any social ban or bar of any kind. No titles should be awarded. All will be "comrades" in the World-State, and there will be no knights, lords, earls, viscounts, chevaliers, pashas, sirdars, hon'bles, grafs, dewans, etc. No citizen will like to adorn himself or herself with such peacock's feathers. If you are not content with the noble title of "Comrade," you are a vainglorious fool, and should learn better. Go and learn from Robert Burns:—

> "You see yon birkie ca'd a lord,
> Wha struts an' stares, an' a' that;
> Tho' hundreds worship at his word,
> He's but a coof for a' that.
> For a' that, an' a' that,
> Their dignities an' a' that,
> The pith o' sense an' pride o' worth,
> Are higher rank than a' that."

(vi) *Ethical Equality.* Virtue should be equally disseminated among the citizens, or the State will perish. All must be unselfish, temperate, and industrious. A uniform standard of Ethics must be maintained. A society of saints and scoundrels cannot flourish. At present, there are vast differences in the moral calibre and capacity of the citizens, as there are plains, hills, and mountains on the surface of the earth. Some persons are very virtuous and admirable, while others are rakes and rogues. History introduces us to such contemporaries as Plato and Critias, Nero and St. Paul, Alaric and St. Jerome, Ajatasatru and Buddha, Landru and Irigoyen. Such ethical inequality is fatal to the State, which needs a safe and level base. It also creates unreal utopianism on the one hand and sordid corruption on the other. Comradeship and Citizenship must be ennobled and safeguarded by ethical equality, which will be established by a sound system of education.

When the sixfold Equality has been secured and realized, we shall pass on to Fraternity.

These are the principles of Democracy, Liberty, and Equality, on which the Co-operative Commonwealth will be founded. But you may ask, "What can I do for the furtherance of these principles to-day?" You can do much. If you live in a country where the government is not democratic, begin to agitate for the establishment of universal suffrage and responsible government, which should guarantee all the rights of the individuals and free associations. Form a political society, hold meetings, deliver lectures, pass resolutions, and educate public opinion in other ways, until the king and the oligarchs yield and a Constitution is granted. Remember also that slavery still exists in some parts of the world; join and support the movement for its complete abolition. Help all democratic organizations and parties in other countries. Study the history of the great Revolutions that have changed the political and social institutions of Holland, England, America, France, and Spain during the last four hundred years. Pay special attention to the glorious record of the French Republican Party that finally triumphed in 6870, and the Russian movement that produced so many ardent apostles and martyrs of Freedom. If your country has achieved parliamentary Democracy, commence the agitation for the Referendum. At all times, remain watchful and vigilant in defence of Liberty against the tyranny of officials or popular majorities. If you have to sacrifice much in the service of such movements, think of Campanella, who spent twenty-six years in prison, of Blanqui, who was incarcerated for different periods totalling thirty-seven years altogether, and of Vera Figner, who was immured for twenty years in Schluesselburg. Read also the biographies of Rousseau, Diderot, Marat, Buonarroti, Victor Hugo, Garrison, Ernest Jones, Leroux, Paine, Herzen, Kropotkin, Marx, Mazzini, Bakunin, Plekhanov, Sun Yatsen, Lenin, Lavroff, De Leon, Debs, Louise Michel, Owen, St. Simon, Fourier, Blanc, Gandhi, and other famous democrats and socialists. The lives of such benefactors of Humanity will teach you that the champions of Democracy and Liberty have lived and died in poverty, exile, and suffering, but have overthrown powerful oligarchies and tyrannies by the might of their Sacrifice All the armies and navies of Empires and Capitalists are in the end quite helpless against the magic power of Sacrifice. Sacrifice can end the cruelty of the rich and the apathy of the poor: sacrifice of wealth, sacrifice of health, sacrifice of love, sacrifice of Life itself. Give yourself and win the world! Further, look around you wherever you live, and begin to organize and educate the exploited poor groups in your country. They will be found among the farmers, agricultural labourers, apprentices, factory workers, domestic servants, shop assistants, clerks, and other overworked and underpaid men and women, who are sweated by the well-to-do class. Organize trade unions among them in order to improve their condition. Trade Unionism is the first step towards Equality. Form also a political Labour Party out of the oppressed class. Establish Co-operative societies for production and consumption. Open schools and evening classes for their instruction in politics, economics, and other subjects. Promote the fourfold Labour Movement, which consists of Trade Unionism, Political Agitation, Co-operation, and Independent Education. These are the four wings of the world-wide Labour Movement.

Above all, practise Democracy, Liberty, and Equality in your daily life. Governments will change slowly, but your daily life is a noble institution that you can establish forthwith. Treat all alike as comrades. Don't fawn on the rich, and don't frown on the poor. Be simple in your habits and tastes. Scorn snobbery; despise all titles and tinsel trappings of capitalist society. Shun luxury like poison. Be tolerant towards all. Don't try to force your opinions on others by aggressive methods. Respect the rights of those who differ from you in religion and politics. Be jealous not only of your own liberty, but of the liberty of all. In team-work, don't play the autocrat. Cultivate simplicity, independence and tolerance, and thus be a worthy herald of the World-State, like Henry David Thoreau, who could say with pride:

> " My life more civil is and free
> Than any civil polity "

4. Fraternity. Liberty and Equality prescribe the minimum that all citizens shall be entitled to claim in the World-State. But Fraternity will indicate the maximum that they will get. Fraternity is only a long Latin word for "Love," that Pole Star of society around which all the laws and institutions must revolve for ever. Nay, even the axis of the earth shall not always point to the same star; but the soul of Man will at all times remain true to the eternal ideal of Love. Liberty and Equality clamour for just rights; but Love thinks of giving more than is due. The rule of Fraternity in Distribution is: "Every one should work according to his ability, and receive everything according to his need." The children do not grow and thrive on Rights, but on free and full love. The sick do not produce wealth and cannot claim anything according to the strict law of justice; but love is far stronger than justice and gives to the sick more than it offers to them that are well. In Cabet's Icarian community, the earliest grapes were reserved for the sick adults and the smallest infants. Love indeed is the Infinite, where the parallel lines of Law and Liberty meet at last. Love thinks, not of self, but of all. It cares not for the pleasures of sense, but tastes the joys of the spirit. It is pained with others' pain, and rejoices in others' happiness. It talks not over-much, but sees everything in silence and serves quickly. It is always full of smiles and gentle words. It feels and knows another's need before that other himself. It waits not to be asked, but hastens with help betimes. It judges not, and forgives everything, as it understands everything. It does not call a fool a fool nor a liar a liar. It boasts not, nor does it remind a debtor of

his debt. It gives and forgets, gives more and forgets again. It takes its equal wages for work, but shares them with all. It does not speak often of "mine" and "thine," but rather of "ours" It accuses no one, but finds excuses for all. It never lacks time for service; it is never too busy or too tired. It draws all unto itself, as the magnet moves the iron. It observes the virtues of others very quickly, but is slow to discern their faults. It is always pleased to praise, but is not willing to blame. It repeats the good words said by others, but it buries the evil that is spoken into its ears. It comes like a ray of sunshine into every circle. It brightens up every face and cheers every heart. It makes all feel that men and women are not Many, but One, the One that remains when the Many change and pass. That One is Humanity, the World-State, in which all shall live and move and have their being Thus is Love twice blessed It is blessed to-day as the harbinger of joy and peace, and it will be blessed to-morrow as the corner-stone of the State, whose citizens will live according to this creed: "Each for All and All for Each."

Now I have spoken of the World-State. But you may ask, "What can I do personally for the establishment of such a State?" You can do much for it. Remember that a world-fellowship of virtuous and well-educated Rationalists must blaze the trail for the World-State. The small Christian communities of Antioch and Corinth paved the way for the consolidated Byzantine Kingdom. The World-State needs its pioneers now. You can be such a pioneer. Do your duty within the nation-state to-day, but do it in the spirit of a world-citizen of the future. Eschew all hatred and contempt for other nations and races. Study world-history, travel as often as you can, learn a world-language, read world-literature, cultivate the society of foreigners and strangers, and thus make yourself and your friends worthy of world-citizenship. Establish a Cosmopolitan Club in your town. Join an international correspondence society. Preach peace, when others howl in hate or rage for revenge. Welcome all to your home and your heart, whites and blacks, browns and yellows, creoles and mulattoes, gypsies and Hottentots—all men and women and children without distinction of race or colour. Eat and drink with all. Love and serve all. Do good to all. Don't support the cruel and corrupt institutions of Capitalism and Nationalism. Keep aloof from them as much as you can. They shall perish. Build up your world-fellowship. Don't participate in the parliaments, councils, armies, navies, law-courts, parties, and churches, that uphold the present system. The early Christian community spurned and shunned the institutions of the Roman Empire. Work thus, and wait for the World-State. It shall come, not to-day and not to-morrow, but in its own good time. But if you live in the light of its Ideal now and here, you are already a citizen of that State. You belong to it. You may be born in the present nation-state, but you are not of it. Your heart is elsewhere. Waking and sleeping, you think of the World-State and long for its advent. When the Sun is still below the horizon in the early morning, he cannot be seen; but he sends before him sister Dawn, holy Ushas, radiant Aurora, who has also been deemed worthy of adoration. Such a slow-brightening Dawn are ye privileged to witness in this age, though your eyes cannot behold the Sun. Your children and grand-children will rejoice in the light and warmth of the Sun that shall illumine the Earth in the days to come, the serene and spacious World-State, one and indivisible.

> "There amidst the world new-builded shall our earthly deeds abide,
> Though our names be all forgotten and the tale of how we died"

. . . . . .

> "Where lies the land to which the ship would go?
> Far, far ahead, is all her seamen know
> And where the land she travels from? Away,
> Far, far behind, is all that they can say"

INDEX